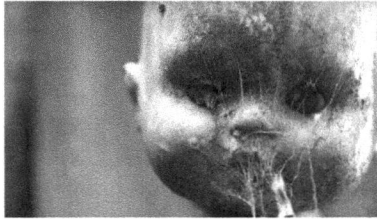

MANY YEARS AGO, IN MEXICO, I VISITED A PLACE THAT HAS HAUNTED ME EVER SINCE. IT WAS AN ISLAND, AMONG THE XOCHIMILCO CANALS OUTSIDE OF MEXICO CITY, THAT WAS FILLED WITH HUNDREDS OF DOLLS. THEY HUNG FROM THE TREES. SOME WERE MISSING LIMBS, WHILE OTHERS HAD SPIDER WEBS OVER THEIR EYES. THEIR FACES HAD BEEN BLEACHED AND DISCOLORED BY THE SUN. THEIR CLOTHING WAS ROTTING AWAY. WHY DID SUCH A PLACE EXIST?

THE DOLLS BEGAN TO APPEAR ON THE ISLAND IN THE 1950S, AFTER A RECLUSE NAMED DON JULIAN SANTANA BARRERA DISCOVERED THE BODY OF A GIRL WHO DROWNED IN THE SURROUNDING LAKE. HE BECAME FIXATED ON THE GIRL AND BELIEVED HER SPIRIT HAUNTED THE ISLAND. TO APPEASE HER, HE BEGAN COLLECTING DOLLS AND ARRANGING THEM ON THE TINY PIECE OF LAND.

OVER THE NEXT 50 YEARS, HE COLLECTED HUNDREDS OF PLASTIC CHILDREN AND CAREFULLY SUSPENDED THEM FROM TREES AND WIRES ON THE ISLAND. HE CONTINUED TO BE HAUNTED BY THE SPIRIT OF THE DROWNED GIRL — AND EVENTUALLY JOINED HER IN DEATH.

IN 2001, BARRERA'S BODY WAS FOUND IN THE WATER IN THE SAME SPOT WHERE THE GIRL HAD BEEN DROWNED.

ALTHOUGH THE TROUBLED MAN WHO CREATED THE SHRINE TO A DEAD GIRL IS GONE, HIS UNSETTLING CREATION LIVES ON AS A REMINDER THAT SOMETIMES THE SPIRITS OF CHILDREN CAN BE THE MOST DISTURBING HAUNTINGS OF ALL.

Dead Men Do Tell Tales

SUFFER THE CHILDREN

AMERICAN HORRORS, HOMICIDES & HAUNTINGS

TROY TAYLOR

TABLE OF CONTENTS

INTRODUCTION

If you're a parent, what's your greatest fear?

Just about every person that I know with a child will answer this question almost immediately – it's that some sort a tragedy might befall their children. Accidents, calamities, automobile crashes, natural disasters, fires – the list goes on. All these things terrify parents. These are the things that keep them awake at night, staring at the ceiling of their bedrooms and wondering how they would handle the nightmare if something terrible happened to their child.

Of course, accidents and calamities are cruel twists of fate. Bad luck – if you believe in luck, or perhaps providence if you don't – plays no favorites. The idea that a terrible accident might occur that claims the life of your child may keep you from sleeping at night but, in the end, there's nothing you can do about it. Accidents happen, right?

But what about that terrible thing that's not an accident at all? What about when the horrible death of a child comes at the hands of another? There are, without a doubt, killers who walk among us. Is there a more loathsome killer lurking in the darkest corners of America than one that would prey on children?

Such monsters have been with us since the first settlers arrived on American shores. We often fool ourselves into believing that the "good old days" were actually good, but this is far from the truth. Monsters have always been with us. They stalked the innocent in the days when children stayed close to the rugged settlements of the colonies, afraid to wander into the dark forest. They were among us before the Civil War claimed the lives of thousands of men and boys. These monsters claimed the lives of the young and naïve during the Gilded Age, at the dawn of the twentieth century, through the Depression, and beyond.

These monsters are not the stuff of fiction. They are bloodcurdlingly real. They have been among us since the nation began – and they are with us still, always looking for their next victim.

We know this, as did our parents, and their parents before them. The fear of "strangers" and their terrible deeds has been rooted in the minds of multiple generations of Americans.

We created myths and legends of monstrous shapes, hoping to scare children so that they never strayed too far from the welcoming light of home. And yet blood was spilled. Children vanished, never to be seen again. They became faces on milk cartons and cautionary tales of what happened when children were left alone. We must keep our children safe, parents told themselves, but even the most watchful eyes weren't always enough.

Our cautionary tales created one of the most popular – and most terrifying – urban legends of all time. It involved just two things: a babysitter and a telephone.

It tells the story of a babysitter who has been left in charge of young children for the night. The parents, hoping for a much-needed night out of dinner and a movie, left this trusted neighbor girl with their children. She was experienced, she was reliable, and the parents had nothing to fear. The night is quiet and after finishing some homework, the babysitter turns on the television. And then the telephone rings. When the girl answers, she hears a man's harsh voice. "Have you checked the children?" he asks her.

Startled, but assuming it to be a prank call, she hangs up the phone. The telephone rings again and once more, the same man's voice repeats the question. The babysitter slams down the receiver, but it keeps ringing and the same man keeps asking her about the children. Now terrified, she phones the police who assure her that they will have the calls traced and find out who has been harassing her. A few minutes later, the police operator calls back with horrifying news: "The calls are coming from inside of the house!"

When officers arrive on the scene, they find a distraught babysitter and two murdered children in the upstairs nursery. The killer had somehow gotten into the house. He had made the calls to terrorize the babysitter and lure her upstairs to her death. Of course, this morality play ends in tragedy for the young woman who did not watch the children closely enough – she loses her mind and has to be locked away in a mental institution for the rest of her life.

Of course, this is only a story, right?

We all know that it's just an urban myth that illustrates the perils of being a babysitter and the fact that children are never really safe, even in the most innocent circumstances. Stories like this – and a lot of others like it – have been told and re-told thousands of times over the years. It's only a story – or is it?

When you were growing up, how many times did you hear stories like that one? Or were told never to talk to a sketchy-looking man that your mother pointed out on the street? Or to never accept a ride in a car with someone you didn't know? Or to never accept candy from strangers – especially at Halloween. It was at Halloween when every horror story that your mother could ever imagine came to life. Never knock on a door of a house without a porch light on. Never accept treats that were not professionally packaged. Never bite into an apple that your parents hadn't carefully checked – they were filled with needles and razor blades, don't you know?

It all boiled down to never take candy from strangers.

But that was crazy, wasn't it? It was Halloween, for pete's sake. Who's evil enough to stick razor blades into apples or put poison into candy bars? Those are just stories, aren't they? Those kinds of things never really happen.

Well, as it turns out, stories like this often get started for a reason. And sometimes the monster is not a stranger after all.

On Halloween night, 1974, Timothy O'Bryan and his sister, Elizabeth, had anxiously waited for their father, Ronald, to get home from work so that they could go trick or treating. The family, which included their mother, Daynene, lived in the suburb of Deer Park, Texas. Ronald was an optician at Texas State Optical in Houston, was a deacon at the Second Baptist Church, where he also sang in the choir and was in charge of the local bus program, and was, as far as everyone who knew him was concerned, a wonderful, loving father.

When he finally walked through the door of the family home, the children rushed to him, hurrying him back out to the street. Still wearing his white optician's lab coat, Ronald took Timothy and Elizabeth out to celebrate Halloween. They met some friends and went to the first house of the night.

Timothy rang the doorbell. There was no answer. If anyone was home, they were taking far too long to answer the door. The children impatiently ran to the next house on the block, leaving Ronald to catch up. When he did, he had five Giant Pixy Sticks in his hand – tubes of pure sugary goodness that the kids couldn't wait to consume. But Ronald promised he would distribute the candy among the children when they got back to the house.

It was late when they returned home. Ronald got the children ready for bed, but before he fell asleep, Timothy asked for just one treat from the night's bounty of sweets. He chose a 22-inch Giant Pixie Stix. The sugar had hardened in the tube, so his father helpfully rolled the candy between his hands to loosen the contents. Timothy poured the confection into his mouth, but his face wrinkled in disgust. It tasted terrible. Ronald quickly ran to get some Kool-Aid for his son to wash the bad taste away.

Timothy never had the chance to drink it. Within moments, he began to choke, vomit, and then convulse. Something was terribly wrong. When paramedics arrived, they found Ronald cradling Timothy in his arms as the little boy gagged and foamed at the mouth. He was pronounced dead at the hospital less than an hour later.

An autopsy later revealed that the eight-year-old had died from a fatal dose of cyanide. Where had it come from? The top two inches of the Giant Pixy Stix that Timothy had been so excited about contained enough poison to kill two grown adults. The little boy never had a chance.

Word spread about Timothy's death, naturally starting a panic in the community. Numerous parents in Deer Park and the surrounding area took the candy their children had collected from trick or treating to the police, terrified that it was laced with poison. None of it was, but the authorities could understand the fear that Timothy's death had caused. They had already started their investigation into the boy's murder.

Thankfully, the other four laced Pixy Stix – which Ronald O'Bryan claimed that he received from the first house on the trick-or-treating route after the kids had run ahead -- had not been eaten. When questioned by detectives, Ronald sobbed as he suggested that an unidentified monster must have handed out poisoned candy to trick-or-treaters. He told police that he vaguely remembered where the candy had come from – but he never got a good look at the owner. All he saw was a shadowy hand, clutching the Pixy Stix from behind a door.

The police went to the address and questioned the owner of the house, Courtney Melvin, who worked as an air traffic controller at Hobby Airport. But the police were confounded when they learned that he had not left work until 10:30 p.m. on Halloween night. His wife had stopped answering the door when she ran out of candy, around 6:45. That was before Ronald O'Bryan claimed that he was there. In addition, Mrs. Melvin had not given out any Pixy Stix that night. Detectives interrogated the entire neighborhood and still couldn't find the source of the deadly candy.

Ronald O'Bryan was grief-stricken by his son's death. He was already having a terrible year and Timothy's death seemed to have pushed him over the edge with grief. Ronald was eight months behind in car payments and was being threatened with repossession. He had defaulted on several bank loans and was suspected of theft at Texas State Optical and was close to being fired. He had held 21 different jobs over the last decade and was more than $100,000 in debt. He further strained his family's finances by taking out a $10,000 life insurance policy on his children earlier in the year, to which his wife protested as an unnecessary expense. She also probably would have objected to the additional pair of $20,000 life insurance policies Ronald took out on Timothy and Elizabeth on October 3, if she had known about them.

And she definitely would've been horrified to find out that, mere hours after Timothy's death, her husband called to collect on the policies.

The police didn't know about the life insurance policies – not yet, anyway – but they did discover that Ronald had visited a chemical supply store in Houston to buy cyanide just a week before Halloween. He left without purchasing anything after the smallest amount available to purchase was five pounds. When they found out about the life insurance policies, they were convinced they had their man. Detectives theorized that he had laced the candy with poison so that he could kill his own children for the life insurance money. Poisoning their friends with the extra Pixy Stix would help cover up his crime. Luckily, none of the other candy was ever eaten.

Investigators repeatedly questioned Ronald, but he maintained his innocence. He blamed the whole thing on some "mad poisoner," just like in the stories, who handed out Halloween candy laced with poison or needles and candy apples with razor blades inside. Surely the police had heard those stories, hadn't they?

O'Bryan was arrested and brought to trial. On June 3, 1975, a jury took just 46 minutes to find the dedicated father and devout member of the Second Baptist Church guilty of capital murder and four counts of attempted murder.

Ronald was sent to Death Row in Huntsville, Texas. He was so hated by the other inmates that they reportedly petitioned to hold an organized demonstration on his execution date. They had to wait a while for that date. His first execution date was set for August 8, 1980, but his attorneys managed to drag things out until March 31, 1984. Shortly before midnight, he was executed by lethal injection. Outside of the prison, a crowd of about 300 demonstrators cheered, while others yelled "Trick or treat!"

Ronald O'Bryan didn't just kill his son – and try to kill four other children – on October 31, 1974, he also killed the idea of "Halloween" for several generations of kids that hadn't even been born yet. Ronald, who was known as the "Candyman" by his fellow death row inmates, successfully perpetuated the legend that there are strangers out there, intent on killing children with poisoned Halloween candy. The truth was, there had never been a case of a stranger handing out poisoned candy to kids on Halloween. That really had been just an urban legend. In 1974, there finally was such a case – but he was no stranger. Ronald O'Bryan was a monster in human form and a nightmare brought to life.

This is your last chance to turn back.

If you are reading this book, it's very possible that you have read other books that I have written in the past. If you have, then you know that I write about some pretty disturbing things. The "good old days" weren't always good. In fact, they were terrifying. I have liberally splashed the pages of a lot of my past books with blood. I have recounted some brutal, agonizing, and terrifying scenes of horror.

But trust me when I tell you, this one is the worst so far. It is not for the faint of heart and it is not for those who are easily disturbed. If you are bothered by the subject of this book, I urge you not to go any further than this.

Seriously, do not read this book. Close it. Give it away. Do not read beyond this introduction.

And don't say I didn't warn you.

Troy Taylor
Summer 2018

1865:

"THE MOST MONSTROUS AND INHUMAN CRIMINAL OF MODERN TIMES"

John Joyce strolled down the street toward his grandmother's house in Roxbury, an independent community that would soon become a neighborhood in Boston's South End. John was a handsome, active boy, small for the age of 12, but mostly happy and eager to make his mother proud. He did all that he could for her these days. His father had died a few years before and her work as a seamstress barely allowed her to earn enough money for both of them to live. John's older sister, Isabella, had gone to live with an aunt in Lynn, but John had stayed with his mother. He sometimes heard her weeping at night and the boy often felt his heart break for her.

Today, June 12, was a special day. Isabella was in Roxbury, visiting their grandmother, and John was excited to see her. His friends would probably tease him if they knew how much he wanted to see Isabella – and how badly he missed her – but John gave that little thought. He had spent the morning attending class at the Dwight School, eagerly watching the clock, and as soon as the class bell tolled, he hurried for the door.

His grandmother's house was at the corner of Newland and Concord Streets, a brick home that was divided into several flats. John and Isabella's grandmother lived on the first floor. She was an older woman and was glad to not have to navigate the stairs when it was time for bed each night. Her children were grown, her husband had passed away years earlier, and she doted on her grandchildren. She was happy to have Isabella in the city for a visit and quickly prepared a small dinner so that John could eat before he returned to school for the afternoon session.

Isabella was restless all morning. The weather was fine, and she wanted to get out of the house. She was nearly as excited to see her younger brother as John was to see her and she decided that they could take their dinner as a picnic. There were plenty of places in the neighborhood where they could spread a blanket and eat. When John arrived, she told him of her idea and he excitedly agreed to the plan.

Their grandmother was not so excited at the prospect. She asked the children to stay and eat lunch with her. She missed Isabella and John barely had time to visit her with his studies at school and his chores at home.

But Isabella wanted to go out into the fresh air. John agreed and told his sister, "I'll show you some first-rate woods."

Their grandmother still had concerns. "I don't want you to wander too far," she said. "Johnny has classes again this afternoon."

Isabella patted her on the back. "Don't be afraid, Grandma. We'll be back in time for Johnny to go to school."

The siblings had decided to go to nearby May's Woods for their picnic. It was a recreation area – this was in the days before there were many public parks – located right there in Roxbury. It was about a mile and a half from their grandmother's house and a walk of less than a half hour.

Their grandmother watched them as they walked down the front stoop and start off down the street toward May's Woods. For some reason, she had a feeling of dread in her chest. She started to call out to them and forbid them to leave. But why? She didn't know. She only knew that she felt something was wrong.

As it turned out, she was right. Something was terribly wrong, and she never saw her two grandchildren alive again.

Six days later, on June 18, the bodies of Isabella and John Joyce were found in the woods – not in May's Woods, but in Bussey Woods, four miles away. Isabella had been raped and mutilated. John was found a short distance away, beaten and stabbed more than a dozen times. The murders would have gone unsolved if the killer did not eventually confess to the savage crime.

That killer -- called the "most monstrous criminal of modern times – or indeed of any time" – preyed on children, the most innocent of victims. His crimes were horrific, and the monster was unrepentant, but he has largely been forgotten over the years.

At least two of his victims have not, though. Local lore claims that Isabella and John Joyce do not rest in peace.

The Joyce children were not the killer's first victims. He began his savage career as a "repeat killer" – as creatures such as he were known at the time – on October 30, 1850. According to his later confession, this was the first time that he tasted human blood. It would not be the last.

As he passed by the house of a man named Stephen Mills in Derry, New Hampshire, he looked in a window and saw a little girl, about five-years-old, playing with dolls on the floor. There were no adults nearby. Possessed by what he later called the urge to "procure a body for surgical purposes," he entered the house, snatched the girl, and took her off into the woods, where he strangled her. When he stripped off her clothing, though, he discovered that "one hip and part of her spine were deformed." Filled with revulsion, he abandoned his plans to "examine her" – the name he gave to postmortem rape and sexual mutilation – and buried the corpse under a rotten tree stump. Her remains would not be found until many years later, after her killer finally confessed to his crime.

Twelve years later, the killer struck again in the town of Strong, Maine, a few miles from Augusta. On Sunday morning, September 14, 1862, nine-year-old Lura Ville Libby left her family's farm on her way to service at the Methodist Church. She made the mile and a half walk each Sunday, weather permitting. Her parents, Isaac and Susan, never feared for her safety. Sunday School began each week at 10:00 a.m., followed by services until around 3:00 p.m. For her lunch, Lura carried two apples and a piece of gingerbread. She always walked straight home once the afternoon service came to an end.

Until the Sunday when she didn't.

The Libbys became concerned by 4:00 p.m. when Lura had still not arrived home. They rode into town looking for her. They checked with the minister, but he said that Lura had not come to church at all that day. They spoke to Lura's friends, but no one had seen her. With help, they searched late into the night. There was no trace of the little girl.

The next day, townspeople gathered to help with the search. They combed the fields, pastures, and woods between the Libby farm and the village. Late in the afternoon, searchers stumbled across a shallow grave about a half mile from the farm. When they removed the earth, they found the body of Lura Libby. Her dress had been removed and she had been raped. Her head was cut and bruised, and her throat was cut so deep that her head was nearly severed from her body.

The entire community was stunned by the murder. A committee promptly offered a $1,000 reward for the capture of the killer. Suspicion fell on the Libby's farmhand, Lawrence Doyle, who lived and worked on the property. He had behaved strangely on Sunday morning, some said, explicitly asked Isaac Libby if he planned to accompany his daughter to church. Doyle denied any involvement in the murder. He said that he had been taking care of sheep in a pasture far from the Libby house on Sunday morning. With no one to vouch for his location – and largely because he was a stranger with no real ties to the village – he was arrested and held for trial.

The evidence against him was incredibly circumstantial. The trial lasted just 25 hours and ended with a deadlocked jury. At his second trial, he was convicted and sentenced to hang. Doyle's attorney, E.F. Pillsbury, was thoroughly convinced of his client's innocence, and convinced the governor to commute his sentence to life in prison. When Doyle died in prison six years later, Pillsbury continued the fight to exonerate him and find the real killer. He would end up playing an important role in the case against the monster who he believed actually killed Lura Libby more than a decade later.

The child killer would not be stopped. Less than three years later, on June 12, 1865, he struck in Roxbury and murdered Isabella and John Joyce.

The siblings had grown up in Lynn, Massachusetts, where Isabella still lived with her aunt. Their widowed mother had taken work as a seamstress after their father had died and moved to Boston, taking John with her. They lived a short distance from John's school and from the children's grandmother. Isabella was 14-years-old but described by the newspapers as "having an appearance scarcely less than 18." She was visiting her grandmother on the warm, late spring day of June 12. After John arrived from his morning session at school, they made plans to visit May's Woods, just a mile and a half from their grandmother's home. They promised to be back in time for John to return to school for the afternoon.

But they never returned.

How the pair ended up at Bussey's Woods – where their bodies were later discovered – remains a mystery to this day. Bussey's Woods was about four miles away. The police later theorized that they had missed their streetcar stop and ended up at the end of the line. But what street car? The siblings had told their grandmother that they planned to walk. Had they changed their mind and decided to take a street car to ensure that John was back on time? Perhaps – but if so, how did they "miss their stop"? They were both well-acquainted with the area and it seems unlikely they would make this kind of mistake. Getting to Bussey's Woods was not simply a matter of "missing a stop." They had to take the Forest Hill car, the Dedham Turnpike route, all the way to the terminus. After that, they had to walk across the railroad, across the Jamaica Plain Road, over several hills, and out the road to the woods. It would have had to be their intention to go there in the first place, but why? Why pick such a distant spot when they had to be back so that John could return to school at 2:00 p.m.? We will never know – but we do know they ended up there somehow and the decision to travel to Bussey's Woods turned out to be a fatal one.

When the children did not return, their grandmother became frantic. She had trouble contacting their mother – she was out of town making dresses – and so she turned to the police. The following morning, they began a search of May's Woods, where the children had said they were going. The next day, Wednesday, Mrs. Joyce returned home and learned of her children's disappearance. She collapsed with worry and grief and likely from despair since the search had

A NEWSPAPER ILLUSTRATION OF THE BODY OF ISABELLA JOYCE

offered no clues. Search parties scoured the forest but there was no sign of Isabella and John.

Then on June 18, after nearly a week, two men – John Sawtelle and J.F. Jameson – who were hiking in Bussey's Woods, stumbled across the savaged remains of the two children.

From the scene, it appeared that Isabella and her brother had been playing contentedly in the woods, creating little hillocks of moss and fashioning wreaths out of oak leaves and twigs, when they were unexpectedly attacked. The assailant – which the newspapers called a "fiend in human shape" – went after the girl first, cutting her savagely with a knife, tearing off her undergarments, and raping her. The coroner found 27 stab wounds in her torso and another 16 in her neck. The ground around her body was saturated with blood. She had apparently put up a desperate fight, grabbing the long blade of the knife and trying to wrest it from the attacker's hands. The index finger of her right hand was completely severed, and the rest of her fingers were mangled, bloody, and hanging loosely by bits of skin. Her clothing was soaked in her blood and clumps of grass and dirt had been roughly shoved in her mouth to try and stifle her cries.

Apparently, poor John had stood paralyzed for a few moments in terror, watching the attack on his sister. When he finally turned to run, it was too late. He was found lying face down in the dirt, possibly having tripped over a tree root when he was attempting to escape. The killer had pounced on the boy's back and stabbed him several times. The wounds were so deep that, in several instances, the blade had gone all the way through the young boy's body and pierced the earth beneath him. The police believed that, "the boy was for a time amazed or paralyzed by the attack on his sister, and that when he turned to run it was too late."

There were two houses within a few hundred yards of the murder scene, but the occupants were so used to hearing shouts, laughter, and yells from the nearby picnic area that, as the newspapers noted, "They would not have paid any attention even if they heard screams on this occasion."

Even hardened detectives were so shaken by the gruesome scene in the woods that they failed to inform Mrs. Joyce of the murders until the following day. The newspapers reported that "upon hearing the fate of her children she swooned and has since reported to be a maniac." After a wake and funeral, the children were both interred at Pine Grove Cemetery in Lynn.

But their murders were not forgotten. The horrific savagery of the case provoked a tremendous response throughout the state. From church pulpits, ministers pointed to the murders as a sign that the country was descending into a deplorable state of vice, immorality, and crime. Rewards totaling more than $4,500 (more than $60,000 in today's money) were offered by local residents, while an enormous manhunt was started for the "inhuman wretch" that was responsible for the outrage. Newspapers issued confident predictions that the perpetrator would be "speedily arrested" and "subjected to summary vengeance."

In the days, weeks, months, and years to follow, there were arrests, suspicion, and even confessions but it would eventually go cold. The search parties and well-meaning volunteers had destroyed whatever clues were present at the crime scene, even if the knowledge had existed at the time to collect them. There were no witnesses to the murders, of course, but one woman remembered seeing a frightening stranger with long, black hair near Bussey's Woods that day. The sighting led nowhere.

On June 21, the police arrested their first suspect. He was a painter named Thomas Ainsley and he lived in the same rooming house where Mrs. Joyce and John lived at 6 Cottage Place. Ainsley had quarreled often with Mrs. Joyce and threatened her and the two children on several occasions. Ainsley had an alibi, however, and was soon released.

On July 9, a second man was arrested. He was a "bounty jumper" from West Roxbury named John Stewart. During the Civil War, he had joined up with various army units, collected the incentive bounty that was offered, deserted, and then did it again. He joined nine different military units during the war. Stewart was alleged to have "confessed his guilt to certain parties," and he was said to have returned home on the night of June 12 with cuts on his hands and his clothing covered with blood. This got the attention of the police. When he was finally tracked down – he had enlisted in the army again at Fort Independence –

he denied all knowledge of the crime. He was able to prove that he was nowhere near Bussey's Woods on June 12 and he was released.

It wasn't until March of the following year that the police had another viable suspect. A prisoner at the Charlestown State Prison named Charles Aaron Dodge – who went by the nickname of "Scratch Gravel" – came to the attention of Warden Gideon Haynes. He had been arrested for burglary but was boasting in prison that he was much more than a housebreaker. He suggested that he had committed other crimes, notably the murders of the Joyce children. He liked young girls, he said, "and when he wanted anything of them, he generally took it, employing force if necessary." He told another inmate that he had "stabbed the Joyce boy in the back several times, and that after having his way with the girl, put her out of the way."

Warden Haynes notified detectives. This seemed like the man the police had been looking for. They planted a detective in his cell who listened to enough bragging from Scratch Gravel that they were able to try and charge him with the murder of the Joyce siblings. The District Attorney, B.W. Harris, wasn't interested, however. All the information that Scratch Gravel spewed to the undercover detective could have come straight from newspaper accounts. It turned out that he was not even in Massachusetts at the time of the murders and that he had embellished the news reports to make himself look more important in prison.

Another lead that had looked promising had failed to pan out. The police were all out of options, so when the skeleton of a man was discovered in Needham Woods, just outside of Boston, in December 1866, they seized on the opportunity that it offered. Lying next to the skull that was found in the woods was a mass of long, black hair – just like the hair reported on the head of the "frightening stranger" that was seen near Bussey's Woods on the day of the murder. From this, the police suggested that the skeleton belonged to the man who killed the Joyce children. He had hidden in the woods to elude capture and had died there. While not everyone was satisfied with this conclusion, the case was essentially closed.

Closed, perhaps, but not solved. The details of the murders – which newspapers called "one of the most horrible and revolting crimes which has ever occurred in New England" – faded with time but were not entirely forgotten. They were recalled with the same sense of terror that the murder of the Mills girl would have been, if widely reported, and with the same dread as that of the killing of Lura Libby. But nothing would have connected these three heinous New England crimes if not for the disappearance of 13-year-old Georgiannia Lovering on October 25, 1872.

The disappearance of Georgiannia Lovering was no great mystery. There seemed to be little doubt as to who was responsible for her rape and murder – her 64-year-old great-uncle, Franklin Evans.

The events of the young girl's death were set in motion when Evans came to board with his elderly sister, Mrs. Deborah Day, at her farmhouse in Northwood, New Hampshire.

Evans was a gaunt, grizzled old man with gray hair, a long gray beard, and dark, piercing eyes that gave him a sinister expression. He had led a shiftless existence for most of his life, traveling about New England and Canada. A contemporary writer later said of him, "He belonged to that numerous class of deadbeats that are always broke." Wandering the New England countryside, he survived by sponging off his adult children, "borrowing" small amounts of money from relatives and acquaintances, and blatantly seeking handouts from strangers.

GEORGIANNIA LOVERING,

Aged Twelve Years.

GEORGIANNIA LOVERING

He had married three times and had a son in Derry, New Hampshire, and a daughter in Lawrence, Massachusetts.

What little honest money he made came from supplying a Manchester physician, Dr. F.W. Hanson, with healing roots and herbs that he scrounged up in the forest. His vagabond life had given the old man a deep knowledge of the land and "his reputation for obtaining medicinal products of the woods and fields was unsurpassed." Even in this line of work, though, Evans could not keep from betraying his lazy and dishonest nature. Claiming that he himself was a "botanical physician," he peddled worthless cures to rural families.

He also passed himself off as an itinerant preacher. Taking advantage of the religious fervor of the era, he joined the Second Advent Society, declared that he was a minister of the Gospel and managed to raise a little money from his brethren to support himself while on his sacred mission. The religious society naturally took offense, however, when he was arrested for consorting with prostitutes. And this incident wasn't his only brush with the law. At various times, he was charged with petty theft, attempting to pass crudely forged $10 bills, and – most seriously – scheming to defraud the Traveler's Insurance Company of Boston of $1,500.

If these crimes were the worst of his transgressions, Evans would have been nothing more than a small-time scoundrel, a snake oil salesman, and a con artist. But as the country would eventually learn –much to its horror --- he was something far worse: a creature so depraved that, to the people of his time, his crimes seemed the work of a supernatural evil – "too horrible," as one newspaper stated, "for anything in human form to have perpetrated."

There were four people living at the Day farm when Evans showed up there in June 1872: Mrs. Day and her husband, Sylvester; their widowed daughter, Susan Lovering, and Susan's daughter, Georgiannia. This poor young woman – Evans' grand-niece – immediately became the object of the depraved old man's lust. Within days of his arrival, he began trying to seduce the girl. When she repulsed his advances, he concocted a diabolical scheme. It was, as one account stated, "A deeply laid plan designed for no other purpose than to lure his victim into his lecherous grasp."

Near the Day farmhouse was a deep forest, the largest tract of woodland in the county, covering an area of more than 2,000 acres. Late on Monday, October 21, after being away from the farm for most of the day, Evans returned to his sister's home, explaining that he had been off in the forest setting snares for partridges. The following morning, he invited his niece to accompany him into the woods to see if he had caught anything. For reasons unknown, she agreed. The traps turned out to be empty, but he showed Georgiannia how they worked – little hoops concealed inside the hedges, designed to snag birds by the throat as they scrambled through the foliage. Georgiannia was intrigued by the snares, never suspecting that their purpose was actually to trap her.

Early Friday morning, October 25, Evans asked the young woman for a favor. He had agreed to take care of some chores for a neighbor, a farmer named Daniel Hill, and would be gone all day. He asked Georgiannia if she would mind going into the woods and check the partridge traps for him. Surely, he told her, they must have caught something by now. She was reluctant at first but allowed herself to be persuaded. Evans left soon afterward, presumably for Hill farm several miles away. A short time later, Georgiannia stuck a comb into her thick brown hair to hold it in place, threw on a shawl, and walked into the forest.

It was the last time she was seen alive.

When Georgiannia failed to return by lunchtime, her grandfather went to look for her. Unable to find any sign of her, Sylvester came back home and told her mother, Susan, that the girl was missing. She immediately became alarmed. The two of them hurried back into the woods. As they frantically made their way along the forest paths, shouting the girl's name, they spotted her shawl on a tree branch. A short distance away, they discovered her comb, broken in half, with strands of her hair still tangled in its teeth. The earth all around had been trampled with footprints – one made by a man's boots, the other by a girl's shoes – evidence, Sylvester Day would later testify, of a "squabble." Terrified now, Day and his daughter pushed deeper into the trees, but found no other signs of the missing girl.

The two of them ran home, alerting the neighbors as they went. Throughout the weekend, all day on Saturday and

FRANKLIN EVANS

Sunday, hundreds of people scoured the woods, but found nothing. By then, however, suspicion had fallen on Franklin Evans. The authorities checked with Daniel Hill and found that Evans' story didn't hold up. He had not asked him to help with chores that day. In fact, Hill hadn't seen him for more than a week. Another witness, a young man named James Pender, testified that he had seen Evans cross into the forest at around 8:30 on Friday morning, just a half hour before Georgiannia had disappeared into the same woods.

County Sheriff Henry Drew grilled Evans but the old man could offer no convincing account of his whereabouts on the day that his grand-niece went missing. He was promptly taken into custody. Inside Evans' pockets, Drew later stated, he found "a wallet, money, obscene books, a bottle of liquor, and a common bone-handled knife with two blades, blood-stained and keen as a razor."

Even after he was arrested, Evans initially denied knowing anything about what had happened to Georgiannia. But when Drew assured him that "no harm would come to him if he confessed," Evans changed his story. Georgiannia, he insisted, was alive and well. He had arranged to have her "carried away by a man from Kingston," a farmer named Webster who wanted her for his bride and was willing to pay for her. Although Sheriff Drew was skeptical, he immediately started for Kingston, where he quickly confirmed the story was a "base falsehood."

Back at the jailhouse, he continued to badger Evans, plying him with liquor and even telling him that he would help him escape to Canada if he told him the truth. Finally, on October 31, six days after the girl's disappearance, the old man gave in.

Drew leaned in close to him as he spoke, "In the hearing of no persons but us two and the Great Being above, I ask you this question: Is the body of the girl cold in death?"

Evans hesitated for several seconds before he choked out his reply. He said, "It is, Mr. Drew. I have done wrong."

Evans told the sheriff he would accompany him to the place where the body had been left. Even though it was close to midnight – on All Hallows Eve – they left for the woods. Through the dark forest they silently made their way along, over rocks and logs and along narrow trails. Then, in a clearing at one of the deepest points of the woods, Evans took the sheriff and an assembled group of deputies to a spot underneath the roots of an upturned tree. He pointed a shaking finger at a pile of dried leaves and quietly murmured, "There she is." The sheriff gently brushed away the leaves and by the dim light of his lantern, he saw the pale face and mangled remains of Georgiannia Lovering.

Two townsmen who were at the scene -- Eben J. Parsley and Alonzo Tuttle -- had brought the local physician, Dr. Caleb Hanson, with them. Gaping in shock at the body of the naked, savaged girl, Parsley couldn't help but speak. He demanded of Evans, "How did you come to do such a bloody deed?"

The old man shrugged as he replied, "I suppose the evil one got the upper hand of me."

Dr. Hanson bent down to examine the dead girl. A glance at her face, with its bulging eyes, swollen and protruding tongue, and dark bruises at her throat, told him that she had been strangled. Her body had been hideously mutilated. Evans later confessed that he had raped her corpse and then had torn open her belly with his bone-handled knife to get to her uterus. He had also excised her vulva, which he carried away with him and hid under a rock. When a stunned Sheriff Drew asked him why he had committed such butchery, the old man calmly replied that he did it "to gain some knowledge of the human system that might be of use to me as a doctor."

As he was dragging the man back to jail, Drew had one more question for him: "What did you set those snares for, Frank?"

Evans answered with a self-satisfied smirk: "I set them to catch the girl – and I catched her."

☠

Franklin Evans' trial opened in the town of Exeter, New Hampshire, on February 3, 1873, but it was a perfunctory affair. The outcome was a foregone conclusion to everyone involved, including the defendant. Only one dramatic moment occurred during its three-day duration. Early on the morning of Tuesday, February 5, while his guard was off fetching him a glass of water, Evans took one of his suspenders, tied it around his neck, attached the other end to a clothes hook on the wall of his cell and tried to hang himself. Just then, the newspapers reported, the guard returned, "seized Evans and disengaged him from the hook."

Most observers believed that the man's half-hearted suicide attempt was nothing more than a ploy to set up an insanity defense. If that was the case, the effort failed. The jury was out only 45 minutes. He was convicted of murder in the first degree and sentenced to hang on February 17, 1874. For "his unnamable and incredible crimes, he will be swung like a dog," celebrated one local newspaper, which went on to recommend that those wishing to attend the hanging should make "early application in order to secure 'reserved seats,' which will be scarce."

Accompanied by the high sheriff of Rockingham County, J.W. Odlin, Evans was transported by train to the state prison at Concord. A crowd of more than 800 people gathered at the station to get a glimpse of him. One newspaper stated that they were "excited to a remarkable pitch of feeling." This frenzied fascination was not entirely based on Evans' notoriety as the killer of Georgiannia Lovering. By then, he had confessed to other crimes as well – atrocities that marked him as one of the most appalling killers of the era.

He was known to have been in Derry at the time the Mills girl was kidnapped, and reportedly had been a suspect. Through his connection to the Adventists, it was determined that he had been in Boston when the Joyce murders took place. E.F. Pillsbury, attorney of Lawrence Doyle – who had been convicted of the Lura Libby murder – believed that he had evidence that proved Evans was her killer.

A newspaper from Boston sent out a "commissioner" to get to the bottom of the allegations – and Evans's confessions – and reported on what he learned. Sheriff Drew had pressed Evans on his whereabouts during the years before Georgiannia's murder. Evans said that he had spent quite a lot of time in Derry, and when questioned about the Mills kidnapping, he admitted that he had taken the child, but her body would never be found. People in Derry believed that Evans was telling the truth. They remembered him, and they had disliked him. He was a man of "low character" and was familiar with the Mills house. There was a rumor that went around that claimed that he sold the skeleton of a child to a physician in Lawrence, Massachusetts, two years after the kidnapping.

Sheriff Drew traced Evans's movements to Rhode Island, then to Roxbury, Massachusetts, linking him to the Joyce murders. Evans admitted to being in Roxbury and knew more about the case than Drew did. Evans, while plant collecting for herbalists, was constantly walking in the woods around Boston. He argued back and forth with Drew about the details of the case, eventually admitting to information about stab wounds and locations of the bodies that were unknown to anyone except for the police – and the killer, of course.

The reporter who investigated Evans's confessions managed to find a young Boston woman who had been visiting friends in Roxbury in June 1865. She was surprised in the woods by the appearance of a wild, haggard-looking man of "horrible aspect." When the man came near her, she "screamed at the very top of her voice." The reporter showed her a picture of Evans – along with several others – and even though it had been seven years since the incident had occurred, "she immediately, unhesitatingly identified it as the portrait of the man who had so frightened her."

This was enough for investigators. Evans's pieces of information and a witness who placed him at the scene was enough for officials to accept that he had killed the Joyce siblings. Headlines were soon appearing around the country with the news that the murders had finally been solved.

The Libby murder was harder to pin on Evans, though. At one point, Evans asked Drew if there had been anyone from Maine after him. Drew asked what part of Maine and Evans replied somewhere near Augusta. He said that he knew of a little girl there in 1861, or 1862, whose throat had been cut. When he was told that no one from Maine was investigating him, he replied, "I won't say another word about it then."

Beyond the hints he offered Sheriff Drew, he would not admit to killing Lura Libby. But attorney F.F. Pillsbury was convinced that Evans had done it. He claimed that Evans had preached in Augusta, and that the Libbys were Adventists who had entertained Evans in their home. This was verified by a witness who knew the Libby family. Pillsbury also said that there were aspects of the crime not reported by newspapers that implicated Evans.

We will never know for sure if Evans committed the Libby murder, but the method and circumstances certainly fit his pattern of crime. Could Pillsbury have been using Evans as a scapegoat to clear his client of the crime? It's possible, but for what reason? An obsession with the case? Lawrence Doyle had been dead for several years by the time Evans was arrested. Pillsbury simply wanted justice for him. He believed that Doyle had been innocent of the crime – just as strongly as he believed that Evans was guilty.

Franklin Evans spent the last night of his life quietly, falling asleep around midnight with the Reverence Church of Providence, Rhode Island, at his side. Around 5:30 a.m., he ate a hearty breakfast and drank a cup of tea. When Church asked him if he had any last-minute statements to make, he replied, "I have confessed everything. If the people don't believe it, I can't help it."

A large, excited crowd gathered outside the prison walls as the hour of execution drew near. At 10:50 a.m., they were admitted into the building, where the gallows had been set up in the corridor between the guardroom and the cells.

Within minutes, every available space was packed with spectators, some of them standing on the stairways leading up to the cells, others crowding around the scaffold.

At 11:00 a.m., Evans, dressed in a black suit, was led through the crowd by the prison warden. He climbed the scaffold on his own and muttered something under his breath as his arms and legs were tied. He appeared "quite calm and possessed," although the people who were standing closest to the gallows later reported that his knees were trembling. The noose was adjusted around his neck and a black hood was pulled over his head. After reading the death warrant, Sheriff Odlin placed his foot on the spring that controlled the drop and – at exactly 11:06 a.m. on Tuesday, February 17, 1874 – the elderly serial killer was "launched into eternity."

His neck didn't break. He dangled in the air, slowly strangling, for nearly 20 minutes before his heart stopped beating and the attending physician declared him dead.

After the execution, Evans's official written confession was released to the press. In it, he detailed the murder of Georgiannia Lovering, but attempted to mitigate the crime by describing the members of the household as intemperate and immoral -- his sister's husband, Sylvester, was drunk and abusive; his niece, Susan, was a woman of loose morals, and even 13-year-old Georgiannia was sometimes drunk and lewd, talking of her "shameful intercourse" with three young men. Evans claimed that he, himself, had consensual sex with Georgiannia, and she threatened to expose him. He stated that he was completely under the young girl's power and that was why he decided to kill her.

Evans also confessed to murdering the Mills child. He heard moaning from inside of the house, he said, climbed in the window, and found her sitting on the floor, apparently very sick. He concluded that she would not live until morning and he wanted a body to examine for "surgical purposes" so he took her to the woods and strangled her. He stopped the examination when he found that she had a deformed hip and spine and buried the body in the woods under a tree stump, in a spot that he was never able to find again.

These were the only murders to which he confessed in print. He admitted to theft, counterfeiting, and attempted insurance fraud, but despite what he told Sheriff Drew, other investigators, and reporters, he did not commit the other murders – the Libby and Joyce killings – that he had earlier taken credit for.

Was he telling the truth? Or rather, which version of his story was the truth? Evans's confession had been dictated to the warden and the chaplain of the prison. They wrote it down and read it back to him and he accepted it as correct and signed it. Later, though, the two officials admitted to some creative editing. They explained that much of what Evans said was "too gross and indelicate to be written or read" and cut it out. Thanks to this, we will likely never know the extent of Franklin Evans's crimes.

Whether he committed only the two murders that he confessed in his final statement or was the killer of several others – as so many believed then and now – he was a monster. Ironically, since he claimed that his murders were committed so that he could gain anatomical knowledge to "aid him as a doctor," his corpse was donated to the Dartmouth Medical College so that it could be dissected by the students there. His skeleton still resides in the college's anatomical museum after all these years.

☠

The execution of Franklin Evans was not quite the end of our story. Evans had confessed to two murders, even though he was suspected of others. The Libby murder case had been officially solved with the conviction of Lawrence Doyle – whether he actually did it or not – but the Joyce murders remained a mystery and a source of ongoing speculation in Boston.

A few years after Franklin Evans went to the gallows, a ghost story came to be connected to the murders of the children in Bussey's Woods. The slayings had a tremendous effect on the local community. As one local resident wrote in 1878, "Of the many dark deeds of blood which have disgraced this age few have been fraught with more harrowing details than the one enacted right here."

The newspapers repeatedly recalled the details of the crime for their readers. Isabella and John Joyce vanished on June 12, 1865, but were not found until the following Sunday, when their bodies were accidentally discovered by hikers in Bussey's Woods. Isabella had been raped and stabbed repeatedly and her brother was found a quarter-mile away by Bussey Brook in a condition that sickened the war-hardened Civil War veterans who saw the body.

The children were brought back to Lynn for burial. The funerals became the scene of public sorrow, especially since they occurred just two months after the assassination of President Lincoln. Rewards were offered by the authorities and seven suspects were interrogated and released. Visitors to the girl's murder site raised a memorial cairn. For the protection of the public, a police beat was established in the Bussey Woods.

Then, 13 years later, the story took another bizarre turn.

"The details of our area's terrible atrocity and barbarity fueled a feeling of unprecedented horror," wrote an author of a book about the murders, published in Boston in 1878. The book asked how a crime so terrible could ever have happened, "in a section as civilized, a community so guarded, a population so abundant, in the marginal outline of a great city."

The book's author was Henry Johnson Brent, founder and editor of the New York City magazine, *Knickerbocker*, which was widely enjoyed from 1833 through the Civil War. In June 1865, he happened to be staying with friends who lived within a few hundred yards of the murders. He wrote his book, *Was It A Ghost?* to focus attention again on the murders, which by then had gone unsolved for more than a decade.

Brent himself had immediately become a suspect in the case when a boy told police that he had often seen a man of Brent's description in Bussey's Woods with a knife and gun. Fortunately for Brent, he was an artist, whose palette knife and target-shooting practice was known in the neighborhood. He was also acquainted with members of the police force. The police quickly dismissed him as a suspect.

By the end of June 1865, the search for the killer had grown cold. A week or so later, in a bizarre personal twist, Brent saw the ghost of a man on the far side of his host's property between Bussey and Motley Woods. Brent truly felt that the event was something beyond his ability to reconcile by the usual rules of explanation and that it deserved publication.

He had gone down to meet his host – who was supposed to be returning from Boston via Forest Hills -- only to learn later that his friend had returned home via Centre Street at 10:00 p.m. Brent revisited the site where he spotted the apparition at 9:00 p.m., within half an hour of the event, but nothing more was seen nor found. Initially, Brent connected the apparition with his host, whom he feared might have met with some kind of misfortune, but during this second visit -- which included a walk to where Isabella Joyce had been murdered -- Brent suddenly connected it with the murders. Could it have been the ghost of the children's deceased father?

He took his story to a perplexed police chief, who urged him to publish it. H.J. Brent detailed his encounter with the spirit in chapter 10 of his book. An abridged version of it appears below. Since we already established that he was out that night waiting for his host, we will jump ahead to the ghostly event:

Knowing that my host was irregular as to his hours of return home at night, I was not surprised when I saw a figure lean over the wall for an instant within about 20 feet of me, pause a moment, and then cross over to the side on which I was. Seeing that he stopped, I spoke aloud these words, "Hello, Dan, is that you?"

Though I could discover the figure and recognize its movements, there was too great a shade thrown over the wall to enable me to distinguish a face so familiar to me. To my appeal there was no reply, and then in an instant the impression came upon me that if it really was my friend, he was testing my nerves. Up to this moment I never had a thought apart from him.

While I stood perfectly motionless, waiting for some recognition of my appeal, the figure advanced slowly in a direct line from the wall, leaving the shadow, and stopped before me and not

20 feet away from me. I saw at once that it was somebody I had never seen before. When in the light without even a weed to obstruct my vision, as soon as he stopped, I called, "Speak or I will fire!"

It was at this period that I observed especially the behavior of the dogs. Up to this time they had been quiet, lying on the grass, but now they both got up, and I felt on each side of me the pressure of their bodies. They were evidently frightened, and I saw that they were looking with every symptom of terror at the figure that stood so near us without a motion.

The figure never once turned its head directly toward me but seemed to fix its look eastward over where the pine-trees broke the clear horizon on the murder-hill. This inert pose was preserved but for a moment, for as quick as the flash of gunpowder it wheeled as upon a pivot and, making one movement as of a man commencing to step out toward the wall, was gone!

To my vision it never crossed the space between where it had stood and the outline of the shade thrown by the trees upon the ground. One step after turning was all I saw, and then it vanished. What I saw I relate exactly as it happened. Can I describe this figure you will ask?

It looked like painted air. There was no elaborate appearance, indeed I could not make out the fashion of the garment. I was more occupied in the effort to recognize a human being in the figure that was before me. He looked dark grey from head to foot. Body he had, legs, arms, and a head, but the face I could not distinctly see, as he turned it from me.

Brent published his book long after interest had died in the case and it is believed that many local residents never accepted Franklin Evans claims that he had killed the Joyce children, despite the similarities to his other crimes. Brent hoped that his book would stir up a renewed investigation and would goad the murderer -- if still alive -- into remorse and confession. The ghost story is the centerpiece of his book, and rightly so, given the title.

Many locals must have had theories about the murders. Brent, believing the murderer was still alive, did not state his complete details. The change of the picnic from May's Woods – where the children told their grandmother they were going -- to the more secluded Bussey's Woods prompted a suspicion that the children were accompanied by someone they knew. The coins their grandmother had given the children to ride the streetcar were found lying near the girl's body. Someone else had apparently paid their fare.

Brent's book alternates between a detailed description of the double murder and an argument for the existence of ghosts. He even noted the results of séances that had recently occurred in which letters were read that were alleged to be written by the murdered girl and her father. A communication purportedly from the boy also was circulated. Though unacquainted with Spiritualism, Brent felt that he had to include these reports with his ghostly account. Brent maintained a terrible feeling of guilt over the fact that he had been in Bussey's Woods painting and target shooting on the day that the murders took place and yet had seen nothing.

Unfortunately, his unorthodox look at the murders – weaving together the crime and the ghost stories – drew scorn from many contemporary reviewers. One of them wrote, "We are disposed to consider this a very unsubstantial pretext for making a book. What good it accomplishes, what end it serves, it is impossible to discover. It does not help the identification of the murderer. It throws no light on the supernatural speculations so prevalent these days. The curious public will probably hang with fresh interest on the horrible details of the crime. But no one, as far as we can see, will be benefited by its perusal."

1879:

THE POCASSET HORROR

Charles F. Freeman was a man obsessed with God. Freeman's God was a cruel and jealous being, demanding much of his followers, who were expected to follow him blindly and without question. And when God demanded a sacrifice --as he did from Freeman in the spring of 1879 -- his servant was expected to provide it. Charles Freeman was expected to murder his daughter. He knew it was the right thing to do because God had told him to do so.

Freeman had been content to offer himself as sacrifice, but after two weeks of prayer, he heard the voice of God telling him what he must do. He awoke with a start on the morning of April 30 and shared his revelation with his wife, Harriet. She was horrified and did all she could to dissuade him, but it was no use. God had told him what to do. Freeman had no choice but to do what he had been instructed.

That night, after attending a church gathering at the home of another fervent worshipper, he returned home and tucked his daughters, Bessie and Edith, into the bed they shared and kissed them goodnight. He went to his own bed and began drifting off to sleep. He thought of his daughters as he did so, and later recalled, "They never seemed so dear to me as then."

At the darkest hour of the night, he jerked awake and began to shake his wife's arm. He told her that the time had come. "The Lord has appeared to me," he whispered feverishly. "I know who the victim must be – my pet, my idol, my baby, Edith."

"No!" Harriet wailed, bursting into tears. She never believed that her husband would go through with it. She believed that God spoke to Charles, but she never believed that he would tell him to kill their daughter. She shook with horror as she made one last plea to spare the little girl's life.

But Charles would not be deterred. "The Lord has said it is necessary."

And now Harriet also believed. It was not her place to disagree with her husband, and certainly not with God. If God had willed it, then who was she to stand in the way of his wisdom. She told her husband, "If it is the Lord's will, I am ready for it."

But Charles had not needed his wife's blessing – he was doing God's work. He praised the Lord through song as he dressed and as he walked out of the house to the shed in the back yard, he mumbled prayers under his breath, murmuring the words over and over again. Charles opened the door to the shed and stumbled inside. It was dark, but he knew what he was looking for. A large sheath knife was hanging on the wall. He pulled the blade from the leather sheath and carried the knife back into the house.

His prayers increased in volume. He was now praying, singing, and laughing at the same time. His mouth was stretched in a mad, rictus grin as he lighted and oil lamp, and carried into his daughters' bedroom. Bessie, the older girl, woke when he entered the room.

"Papa, what's wrong?" she asked, rubbing sleepily at her eyes.

"Nothing is wrong. All is right," Charles replied. "Leave this room and go get into bed with your mother."

Confused and still only partially awake, the six-year-old pushed aside the blanket on the bed and put her bare feet onto the floor. As she padded out of the room, she looked back at her father and saw the reflection of light on the knife that he held behind his back. A jolt of panic went through her heart and she rushed out of the room and hurried to her mother.

Something was terribly wrong with her father.

Alone with a sleeping Edith, Charles placed the lamp on the chair next to the bed and he silently got down on his knees. He pulled aside the blankets on the bed, uncovering the sleeping little girl. He prayed that she would not wake up and he prayed that God might stay his hand at the last moment, as Abraham's hand had been stayed when he was told to sacrifice his son.

But God did not stop Charles Freeman.

Charles lifted the hand holding the knife high above his head, and, at that instant, Edith opened her eyes and looked up at her father. But this did not stop him. He drove the knife deep into the little girl's side.

"Oh Papa," she gasped – and then she died.

Charles climbed into bed next to his daughter and took the corpse into his arms. He remained there until the sun came up later that morning. He later said that a great feeling of peace – even joy – came over him. He had been tested and found worthy. He had done God's will and he would be rewarded.

In three days, God promised, his little girl would return from the dead.

In the early decades of the nineteenth century, a great fervor of religious revivalism ignited America. It was a time of great change in the country, particularly among religious movements.

Christianity had long taught that the way to betterment was through God. America's religious teachings had always raised mistrust about the extent to which people could make personal improvements but only if they did so through the intervention of the Holy Spirit. The revivalists offered the opportunity to be "born again" through fundamentalist Christianity, maintaining that people could "take responsibility" for seeking their own deliverance from sin and damnation. This is a common religious teaching today, but at the time, it was groundbreaking.

An area that saw some of the greatest religious revival was Western New York, which had been opened to settlement by the Erie Canal in 1825. As the people moved west to build the new towns, religious men and women followed. Traveling preachers found fertile territory in which to convert many to evangelical Christianity in the newly-settled communities. There were ministers who preached fire and brimstone, hell and damnation, and the end of days. The era became known as the country's "Second Great Religious Awakening." Eventually, so many fiery preachers flocked to Western New York that it seemed there was no one left to convert. It became known as the "Burned-Over District." It became home to the Shakers, the Mormons, utopian communities, abolitionists, suffragists, and even the founders of the Spiritualist movement.

It was also home to a clergyman named William Miller who preached that the end of the world was coming very soon. He was so convincing that his church numbered into the thousands by the 1840s.

Born in Pittsfield, Massachusetts, Miller grew up estranged from his Baptist upbringing, largely indifferent to religion. After serving in the army during the War of 1812, though, he began to embrace a view that was common among returning soldiers – that his survival had been divinely ordained. The man who had largely ignored religion came home with a deep interest in questions of faith and immortality.

Convinced that the Bible was a literal record of truth, Miller undertook an obsessive study of every word, line, and letter to determine the exact date of Christ's return – a date that he believed would usher in a millennium of peace. Although only moderately educated, Miller spent the next 14 years poring over the scriptures, organizing and cross-referencing all that he found, to build an orderly blueprint of what he believed was God's plan. After all his grueling efforts, his research pointed to the end falling somewhere between March 21, 1843, and March 21, 1844. But he wasn't finished. Wanting to narrow the date even further, he went back to work and finally decided on October 22, 1844. In the end, he based his prediction on a single line in the book of Daniel: "And he said unto me, in two thousand and three hundred days; then shall the sanctuary be cleansed." By counting "days" as years, be calculated the second coming of Christ.

He had no desire to start a cult or seek converts and kept his insight to himself for more than a decade. But Miller eventually thought people might be interested and wrote a document about his findings in 1833. He soon began to gain a serious audience as one of the Burned-Over District's wandering religious speakers.

He seemed an unlikely preacher, though. He had terrible stage fright in the early days, but soon gained both confidence and zeal. Within a few years, he was speaking to packed audiences and began to gain attention in the larger cities. After he got the blessing of Boston clergyman and publisher Joshua Vaughan Himes, he became a national phenomenon. Miller captivated people as few other preachers had done before or since.

As Miller's portentous date neared, hundreds and then thousands of his followers gathered at tent revival meetings across Central New York. They filled, and often overflowed, the largest tent in the country, one that could seat as many as 3,000 people. Once, near Rochester, a strong wind snapped 15 of its chains and several inch-thick ropes, violently ripping the tent into the air. Amazingly, no one was hurt – which just deepened the belief in the region that Miller was somehow blessed by God.

A financial depression that hit in the late 1830s and early 1840s, followed by several astronomical events – like a huge meteorite shower and Halley's Comet – served to only heighten the need for deliverance. To many, Miller's radical predictions made it all clear – the end of the world was coming.

By 1844, his followers – known as Millerites – numbered more than 100,000, while another million had attended million Miller's lectures and kept a watchful eye toward the predicted date with general fear. Millerites took joy in the impending doomsday and considered those who scoffed to be damned to hell – they alone would be saved.

Many sold their possessions and gave away their money to church officials, as it was recommended to meet Judgement Day debt-free. In cities and small towns across the country, droves of followers donned white robes and gathered on hilltops with their arms outstretched. Stories spread that the Millerites ran amok, engaging in "free love," and throwing all their money into the wind, anticipating a world without wants or demands. Others were said to take the words from the scriptures that claimed none will enter the kingdom of God unless child-like so literally that adults began to regress, skipping and hopping around while others sucked their thumbs or stayed in bed in a fetal position.

Whether or not such stories were true remains unknown. The most embarrassing seem to have been concocted by critics and neighbors who laughed at the Millerites and their controversial beliefs. But even the less religious responded to the possibility of the apocalypse. They built bunkers and one safe company saw brisk sales after modifying their "fireproof chest" to accommodate food, water, and a small fan so that the owners could use it as a safe haven to ride out the impending doomsday.

When October 23 passed uneventfully, Miller tried again to recalculate the date. However, most of his followers were so stunned when nothing happened that they abandoned his sect. The event became known across the nation as "the

Great Disappointment." Millerites were beaten, tarred and feathered, and spat upon for causing a panic.

But the failure of Jesus to appear at the predicted time did not, as we might imagine, mean the end of Miller's cult. Miller believed, until the day he died five years later, that it was all a math error and the Second Coming was still going to take place on some imminent – but undetermined – date. The "Great Disappointment," he told his followers, was a divine test of their faith. His adherents remained devoted to his prophetic vision long after his death in 1849 and became known as the Second Adventists.

After Miller's death, one faction of the church split off under the leadership of Ellen Haron, who believed so fervently in Miller's dogma that she began to announce her own visions and prophecies of impending doom. She claimed that angels took her on an arduous journey to heaven and was sent back to start a new branch of Miller's church in Battle Creek, Michigan. She established many creeds regarding worship and health, hydrotherapy, and simple food. John Kellogg was the doctor in charge of the Adventists' health food division and invented corn flakes. Sylvester Graham, interested in Ellen's visions about flour, promoted whole wheat products and invented the graham cracker.

Ellen's branch of the church exists today as the Seventh-Day Adventists. The seven-day part of their name means they rest on Saturday instead of Sunday, like most Christian groups. Adventists still believe the world faces an imminent end, but, wisely, no longer offers an exact date.

Around the end of the Civil War, another small group of Second Adventists set up a church in Cataumet, Massachusetts, a small village at the extreme western end of the Cape Cod peninsula, on the shores of Buzzards Bay. Among the members of the church was Charles Freeman, a local farmer who lived in the nearby town of Pocasset with his wife, Harriet, and his two daughters – six-year-old Bessie and four-year-old Edith, who was her father's favorite.

Charles was later described by the newspapers as a man of "upright life and conduct," and he was admired – perhaps even revered – by his fellow Adventists for the strength of his religious convictions. He spoke often of the need to prove his faith through sacrifice and declared that "he had given his whole family to God." None of his friends or fellow church-goers doubted his sincerity, but they had no idea that his dreadful fixation on blood sacrifice was growing stronger in him with each passing day.

It would finally erupt into madness with the murder of his daughter.

On the morning of May 1 – the day when Charles Freeman stabbed his daughter to death on orders from God – several dozen of his neighbors were summoned to his home. They all received a message that they would be given a great revelation when they arrived. The sun had been up for just a few hours when 25 people – nearly all of them Adventists – crowded into the Freemans' parlor.

They fell silent when Charles began to speak. He rambled on for nearly an hour, pausing often to fall into eerie silence or, even stranger, into bouts of weeping. He spoke about the imminent coming of Christ, as foretold in the Book of Matthew, and the overwhelming feeling that had taken control of his soul during the two weeks that had preceded this glorious morning. Then – with his sobbing wife next to him – he led the gathering into the adjoining bedroom, where a little form lay beneath a bloodstained sheet. He reached down, drew back the covering, and revealed to his neighbors the sacrifice that he had made at God's behest.

As his fellow Adventists looked on in confusion, Charles assured them that they need have no concern for Edith. In three days, the child would return from the dead. Her resurrection would be a sign that Christ had returned.

The crowd was shaken by the sight of the butchered child, but instead of immediately summoning the authorities or taking Charles into custody on their own, they praised him for his astounding act of faith. Charles had been right in what he had done, they agreed, and expressed a belief that God would raise Edith up on the third day as a sign for those who did not believe.

They soon dispersed to their homes and, without mentioning the awful scene they had just witnessed to anyone outside of the sect, returned to their daily affairs. The *Boston Journal* would later report, "It is almost impossible to conceive of an assembly of people in such a state of mind as to attempt to conceal such an atrocious deed, but they told no one and went about their usual vocations."

What followed was a bizarre wake at the Freeman house as Charles and his fellow sect members waited for Edith to be resurrected. In an interview with a local newspaper, Edith's grandmother asked the reporter not to say anything to the surviving child about her sister's death – Edith would soon return with no harm done. When nothing happened after the third day, the local Adventists were genuinely astonished. Some of them even went as far as to accuse God of breaking his promise with Charles by not resurrecting Edith.

By this time, despite the silence of the sect members, word of the murder had reached the ears of the local constable. Charles and Harriet were soon under arrest and lodged at the Barnstable jail.

Meanwhile, Edith's funeral was taking place. It was widely attended. According to newspaper accounts, the Methodist Church where the services were held was packed to capacity. Hundreds were left standing outside. The Adventists were all in attendance, keeping an eye on Edith's coffin and hoping for a last-minute miracle. Tension was high between the sect and the rest of the community. After the pastor lectured the Adventists on their false beliefs, Alden P. Davis -- who was leading the sect with Charles in jail – was prevented from making a speech under threat of arrest.

Undeterred, Davis managed to speak in the churchyard after the service had concluded. His speech was a ringing endorsement of Charles Freeman and his sacrifice, which stirred up the angry crowd even more. Many in the crowd threatened to kill Davis, the Freemans, and any other Adventists they could get their hands on. The sect members fled the churchyard before violence broke out.

The horrific nature of the murder – combined with the complicity of the Adventists – set off a firestorm of outrage throughout New England. Ministers gave sermons about the danger of religious fanaticism, a phenomenon that was seen as a growing social threat. The New England Adventist Association, on the defensive after the murder, quickly distanced itself from the sect members in Cataumet and Pocasset, denounced Charles'

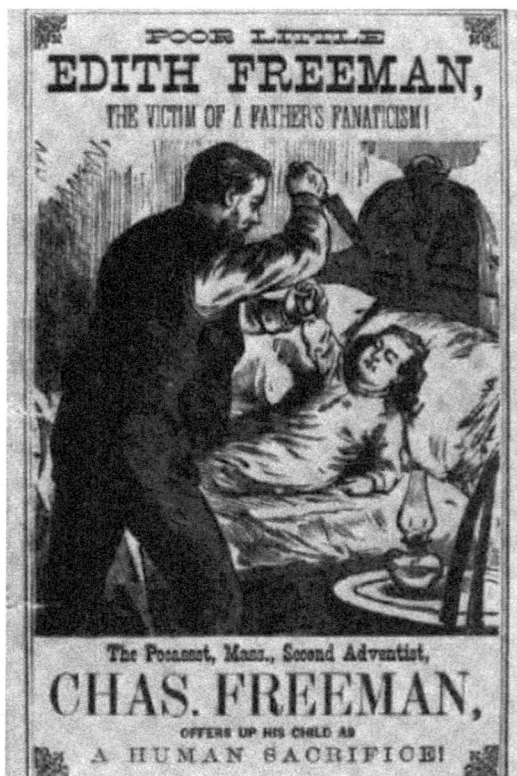

POOR LITTLE
EDITH FREEMAN,
THE VICTIM OF A FATHER'S FANATICISM!

The Pocasset, Mass., Second Adventist,
CHAS. FREEMAN,
OFFERS UP HIS CHILD AS
A HUMAN SACRIFICE!

THE STORY OF EDITH'S MURDER – AND HER "HUMAN SACRIFICE" – BECAME WIDELY REPORTED

act as "red-handed wickedness, diabolical bigotry, and inexcusable religious frenzy." The newspapers spread the story with lurid headlines, ghastly illustrations, and wild editorials about the dangerous behavior of religious cults.

An editorial writer for the religious newspaper, the *New York Evangelist*, wrote, "We hope that this murderer would be treated as all murderers should be, and that it will not be admitted that religious fanaticism is to justify human sacrifices. The law expressly holds that crime committed while a man is intoxicated is the same as if the man was sober; and so Mormons, Adventists, and Spiritualists should be held responsible for offences against the law, notwithstanding their pretended revelations of a higher law. There is no safety in society if any other principle prevails."

In the hours after his arrest, Charles had calmly and cheerfully greeted visitors to his cell with the assurance that he would soon be vindicated. His daughter was dead, but she'd soon be back. He told one reporter, "I can't conceive of such a thing as God failing to justify me. His power is about to be revealed in an astonishing manner to the world, and all disbelievers will be humbled in the dust at His feet." Edith, he insisted with confidence, would shortly be "restored to earth life."

But, of course, Edith did not awaken. Three days after she was slaughtered – on the very morning when she was supposed to be resurrected – the dead girl was buried in the Pocasset cemetery.

☠

On the day after Edith's funeral, Charles and Harriet – displaying "not the slightest regret at the commission of their sacrificial act"—were brought before Justice Hopkins at Barnstable and charged with murder. They were then returned to their cells to await the action of the grand jury, which, indicted Charles during its October session. Although Harriet was regarded as a willing participant in Edith's death, she was released.

At a special session of the Supreme Court in January 1880, a sanity hearing was held and, after listening to several alienists and medical specialists, the justices ruled that Charles was insane and unable to stand trial. Charles, of course, scoffed at the ruling, insisting that he was not insane. He was simply embodied with the "spirit of Truth."

He told reporters, "I represent Christ in all his parts, prophet, priest, and king. All good is represented in one person, and that person is me. I feel sure that my name will be honored above any other name except Jesus." When asked how he felt about the death of his daughter, he calmly replied, "I feel perfectly justified. I feel that I have done my duty. I would not have her back."

Nope, nothing wrong with Charles Freeman – obviously sane.

As readers will not be surprised to learn, he was promptly committed to the State Lunatic Asylum at Danvers. It took a few years, but by 1883, Charles' perspective on things had changed. Interviewed by some of Boston's leading alienists, he acknowledged that he had been an "insane man" when he murdered his daughter and regretted it as "the most dreadful act that was ever perpetrated." Having seemingly recovered from his violently delusional state, he was ordered to stand trial.

The proceedings were held in Barnstable on December 3, 1883, and only lasted one day. During his testimony, Charles wept openly on the witness stand. He claimed to have recovered his senses while in the asylum. He was finished with religion, he said, and vowed never to return to the Second Adventists.

Harriet Freeman testified that her husband had always been kind to their children and was a good provider for the family. After his religious conversion, though, everything changed. Not only did he neglect his business and devoted himself to the cult, but he began experiencing religious visions that told him to send a message to the world. His newfound religious mania became so problematic within the family that Harriet's brother had threatened to shoot him on one occasion.

She explained that Charles' visions in which he had been told to sacrifice Edith had come after going several days without food and water. Though she admitted to agreeing with her husband that he needed to kill their daughter, she defended herself by saying that she could not believe he would ever hurt Edith. She regarded it as a test of faith – like Abraham and Isaac – and God would stop him before he went too far by causing Charles to come to his senses. His faith had been tested in the past, she said, but he had never gone so far as to endanger her or the children – until this time.

On the night Edith died, however, she was told by her husband that God has asked him to make a great sacrifice. She then saw him "leave the room, and when he came back he had the child in his arms; it was dead; he walked the room with it and prayed and wept; he took it to bed with him and kept it with him all night; the whole scene is like a terrible dream, which one remembers, but can't distinctly connect, and which, when I try and think of it, seems like an awful recollection."

Several expert witnesses followed Charles and Harriet on the stand – all of whom testified to the defendant's derangement at the time of the murder – and the jury took only 10 minutes to find him not guilty by reason of insanity. He was sent back to the Danvers Lunatic Asylum, presumably for the rest of his life.

Charles' "life sentence" turned out to be just four years. By order of the governor, he was pronounced "cured of his delusion and harmless" and was set free in 1887. Little is known about what happened to him after his release from the asylum, but he died in Lawrence, Michigan, in 1928. Apparently, he left Massachusetts and headed west to Chicago, where he owned a restaurant for a time. He later returned to farming in Michigan. The last public records of Charles Freeman are an application for his military pension from the Civil War in 1908 and his obituary on November 4, 1928.

We'll never know what happened in his life during the years after he left Danvers State, or what happened to his wife, and surviving daughter. Was Charles really "cured" of his religious delusions by his stay in the asylum? I'd like to think so and perhaps if he was, he finally released that Edith's death was not a "sacrifice to God" but the result of his own madness.

I'd like to think that he grieved, not for himself, but for a life that was snuffed out before it was ever truly lived.

1889:

THE GIRL IN THE CELLAR

The sun was shining brightly in Cleveland on the morning of May 9, 1889. The air was cool and crisp. It had been an unusually chilly spring in the city, but warmer days were ahead. The leaves had come to life on the trees and flowers were finally starting to bloom.

All these things delighted little Maggie Thompson, a vivacious seven-year-old who lived with her parents, Jacob and Clara, on Merchant Avenue in Tremont, which was then still known as the "Heights." The pretty little girl was the light of her parents' lives. She was one of four children but there was something special about Maggie. She was happy, affectionate, and always seemed able to put a smile on the face of her parents, siblings, teachers, and neighbors. Grown men were known to giggle when they saw her passing on the street with her "windmill" walk – she vigorously swung her arms when she walked – and always gave her a friendly wave.

Maggie walked to the Tremont Street School every day. It was only four blocks from home – a short distance for the enthusiastic young girl – and her parents always told relatives that Maggie would be all right even if it was a greater distance. The Thompsons had lived in several large cities and Maggie knew that she should never talk to strangers.

But on Thursday, May 9, she did talk to a stranger – and it became the last day of her life.

The morning began like usual. Out of bed, fed, and dressed for school, Maggie left home shortly before 8:00 a.m. Before she went out the front door, she was showered with hugs and kisses from Clara and from Jacob, who had just returned home from his job as a night brakeman with the Valley Railroad. Just as Maggie reached the gate, though, she turned around and ran back to her mother, begging for one more kiss. Clara embraced her, sent her off again, and returned to her household chores.

It was the last time that she ever saw her daughter alive.

The story of Maggie Thompson is one of true American horror and one that will chill any reader to the bone. Even in the era that we think of as the "good old days" children were never truly safe. Monsters walked among us, even then. In this case, though, the monster in question was not an adult that preyed on a child, it was what the newspapers would soon call the "Murderer in Short Breeches."

Maggie Thompson fell victim to the depravity of another child.

Many of the details of Maggie's last day are part of the record. She arrived at the Tremont Street School and began her day promptly at 8:30 a.m. She left the school at 11:15 a.m., dismissed by her teacher, Miss Cottrell, so that she could have lunch at home. After that, things become murky. It seems that Maggie walked north down Pelton Avenue to Fairfield with a classmate named Mary Hull, who wanted Maggie to see some flowers behind her family's home at 17 Fairfield. Maggie was next seen several houses away at 5 Fairfield, where she played briefly with three-year-old Gracie Larsen. She had wanted to show Maggie her new tricycle. Maggie left the Larsen home about 11:30, turned the corner to walk the last block home to 24 Merchant Avenue – and disappeared.

A newspaper reporter later wrote that she disappeared so suddenly and silently that, "the sidewalk might have opened and swallowed the girl."

Maggie was missed almost immediately. When she didn't come home for lunch, Clara woke Jacob just after noon and sent him to look for Maggie at school and at the homes of neighbors and Thompson relatives who lived nearby. It was a close-knit neighborhood. Everyone knew Maggie and each other – but no one had seen her.

When the quick search turned up no trace of her, the police were notified. Detectives – aided by family and friends – began a thorough search of every street, sewer, outbuilding, and waterway in the area. The frantic search continued for more than 24 hours. Notices were posted all over the city, instructing citizens to be on the lookout for the little girl. Her detailed description was given to the newspapers and handed out to passersby. All of Cleveland seemed to be in an uproar over the missing girl.

By Friday, the search had become bogged down in the all-too-familiar chaos of false leads and people looking for attention. Cranks and curiosity-seekers – always a part of every investigation – hindered the police and plagued the Thompsons with wild tales of clairvoyant visions and mysterious men who lurked on street corners. A number of "eyewitnesses" proved to be no more helpful. Several people claimed to see Maggie dragged into a bakery on Fairfield by an unknown man, but the bakery in question was located at Gracie Larsen's home and the baker – her father, Peter – was not at home on May 9.

One of Maggie's classmates, Helen Pasternack, told police that she saw Maggie with a woman on the Centralway Bridge – several blocks from Maggie's home – around 12:30 on the day she vanished. Helen said that the woman was dressed in black and carried a red parasol. She was dragging a weeping Maggie with her across the bridge.

Some of the people who lived in the area used the disappearance to display the prejudices they had against Jacob Thompson, who was Irish Catholic who was married to a woman who was not a Catholic. Rumors claimed that he had spirited away Maggie himself and sent her away to be educated in Catholic school. The Cleveland police were not much better. They stoked the rumor mill themselves, using dark and repeated hints – both on and off the record – that Jacob knew more than he was telling about Maggie's whereabouts and fate.

But Jacob knew no more than the police did. The search for his daughter continued for days, then weeks. May gradually turned into June and the case of Maggie Thompson grew cold.

The month of May 1889 had been cool and rainy in Cleveland, so the warmth of June was welcomed by all the people who lived on Merchant Avenue – well, almost all of them. There was one resident -- Mrs. Clarissa Shevel of 42 Merchant, a two-family house that was just seven doors away from the Thompson home -- who was bothered by something that was caused by the warm weather. There was a terrible smell in her home that had just started after the weather changed. She had no idea what was causing the foul stench, but it was driving her mad.

Clarissa and her husband, Joseph, lived in the back part of the house, which they rented from owner Henry Lueth, who lived in the front section of the home with his wife, Lena, and 16-year-old son, Otto. Henry had been out of town for most of the previous six months. He was a cabinet-maker and had been working in Fremont. During that same time, Lena had been residing part-time in a private insane asylum, where she had gone for treatment for her "nerves." With her landlords away, Clarissa had been unable to find someone to deal with the odor. It had become so bad that even neighbors were starting to smell it.

Finally, in early June, she saw Otto and asked him to do something about it. He took a nickel from her, bought three boxes of chloride of lime, and put them down a ventilation hole in the Shevel parlor. He told Clarissa that the smell was probably caused by dead rats in the cellar, or even a pet cat that had not been seen for several weeks. If it had gotten into the cellar and died, well, that would certainly explain the stench.

The following day, Otto also purchased some sulfur from a store in the neighborhood and asked the clerk for direction on the best ways to burn it as an antidote for odors. The clerk showed him how to do it, and even offered to help him, but Otto refused his assistance. Several days later, Otto was seen carrying some badly stained, maggot-infested bedding into a smokehouse at the back of the Lueth yard. He offered the information to a neighbor that he had vomited on the bedding after drinking too much a few weeks before. He'd forgotten about the mess and needed to clean it up.

More days passed and the smell coming from 42 Merchant Avenue got worse.

By the evening of June 9, Lena Lueth had reached her limit with the stench. Something had to be done about it. She had endured it since she had returned home from Dr. C. B. Humiston's asylum the previous week and she could stand it no more. Her husband, Henry, was also home and that evening, she confronted him and demanded that he go down to the cellar, search until he found what was rotting down there, and get rid of it.

Henry was no fool. His wife's anger could be legendary. He dutifully went down into the dank cellar, which was little more than a circular, brick-lined chamber that was only about nine-feet in diameter. Henry descended the ladder-like staircase into the dark room and raised his lantern high above his head. He peered into the shadows – and let out a choked cry. Henry turned and ran back up the stairs to where his wife was waiting. His face was ashen.

"There's a corpse down there!" he shrieked.

Henry hurried out of the house and went up the street. In those days, policemen still walked the neighborhood beat and it didn't take him long to find one. They ran back to the house together and Henry volunteered to go back into the cellar through a small window that was accessed by a dirt crawlspace under the house. As the police officer held the light, Henry wriggled through the window and disappeared into the shadows. He soon returned with a pungent bundle of clothing in his arms. He pushed it out into the yard and the officer pulled aside the cloth to see what had been concealed in what turned out to be one of Lena Lueth's old housedresses.

It was the nude, badly decomposed body of Maggie Thompson.

The little girl had been wrapped in the housedress with her own clothing underneath her. Her skin had rotted completely off her skull. Her brain was missing. Her lower limbs had detached when she was pulled out of the dark hiding place. She was a horrific sight – and one like nothing Henry or the police officer had ever seen. The young officer vomited in some bushes along the side of the yard.

Within minutes, the house and lot were full of policemen and neighbors. A hysterical Jacob and Clara soon identified Maggie by the scars on her hips, the result of a childhood accident.

Henry and Lena Lueth – along with Clarissa and Joseph Shevel – were placed under arrest, as was Otto Lueth, who returned home from a nearby ice cream parlor at 9:30 p.m.

"Do you know anything about this?" his mother demanded.

But Otto swore to his mother and to detectives that he knew nothing. It was the first lie that he told – it would not be the last.

The five occupants of the house were taken to the 9th Precinct Station on Barber Street for questioning. The coroner determined that Maggie had been beaten to death with a hammer-like object. There were three holes in her skull, her nose and jaw were broken, and she had been hit so hard that her teeth had been driven into her palate. Her right arm had been torn off at the elbow – probably before she died.

This news did not sit well with friends and relatives of the Thompsons. A crowd gathered outside the police station, calling out for justice. Someone that had been brought into the station from 42 Merchant Avenue was guilty of murder. If the police didn't find out who it was soon, there were Cleveland residents willing to lynch all five to make sure that the guilty one was punished.

The interrogations – "sweating sessions," as they called them then – went on for more than five hours, but almost from the start, detectives settled on their prime suspect – Otto Lueth. From 10:30 p.m. until the early morning hours of June 10, Captain E. K. Hutchinson, Captain A.S. Gates, and detectives Jake Lohrer, A.A. Lawrence, and Francis Douglass questioned the 16-year-old boy in isolation, constantly moving him from room-to-room around the station. They knew that both his parents had been largely absent from the home for the past month and they were also aware of his reputation in the neighborhood for mischief and bullying younger children. Even before Otto returned home on the night the body was discovered in the cellar, Clara Thompson asked one of the police officers at the scene if they had arrested Otto yet.

Once in an interrogation room, Otto was cooperative with the police at first, probably until he realized they suspected him. However, he grew more sullen and nervous as the hours passed. The inconsistencies in his story multiplied and he told several different versions of what he had been doing on May 9, the day Maggie disappeared.

Otto finally snapped around 3:30 a.m., when a woman's scream was heard echoing through the station house. The boy demanded to know who was screaming.

"It's your mother, I believe," Detective Douglass said.

"She had nothing to do with it!" Otto cried.

"Who did?"

"I did it! I did it!" Otto blurted out.

"Did what, Otto?" the detective asked him.

"The boy screamed, "I killed her! I killed her! Please give me your revolver so I can kill myself!"

CONTEMPORARY NEWSPAPER ILLUSTRATIONS OF OTTO LUETH AND HIS
VICTIM, LITTLE MAGGIE THOMPSON

A moment later, officials came into the interrogation room, wrote out Otto's confession, and had him swear to it and sign it. He was led away in manacles to a cell at the Cleveland Central Police Station on Champlain Street.

Otto's confession had been brief and to the point – and as twisted as the reader might expect. He told the police that he had been standing at the gate of his home at 42 Merchant Avenue at about 11:30 on the morning of May 9, when Maggie walked by. She stopped and asked him if he had any buttons for the "button string" that she was collecting. He replied that he would give her some if she came into the house to get them. He took her upstairs to his bedroom and as soon as they walked in, he tried to assault her. Maggie screamed, and he hit her with a small tinsmith's hammer that was lying nearby. He may have killed her with the first blow – we'll never know, but we can hope so – but he kept on hitting her until the bed was covered with blood. Otto pulled off the little girl's clothing and tried again to rape her. Unable to do so, though, he fled from the house. He returned briefly again that night, when he savaged her body, but then spent the next week at his brother John's house.

Six days later – the following Wednesday – Otto returned to the murder room. He knew that his mother might be released from the institution at any time, so he needed to get the body out of the house. Not knowing what else to do, he took it down to the cellar. He told no one what he had done, coldly returning to his daily activities, and even helping with the neighborhood search for Maggie.

Almost every day, he spoke to Clara Thompson and asked whether there had been any word about the lost little girl.

Otto Lueth was a psychopath before the word even existed.

At the same time that Otto was being arrested and questioned by the police, Maggie's parents were faced with the sad business of burying their slain daughter. Two days after she was found, a service was held for the little girl at nearby St. Augustine Catholic Church. The original plan had been to hold the service at the Thompson home but on the night of the wake, more than 2,000 ghoulish curiosity-seekers turned up at the house to file past her coffin, which was on display in the parlor. The family did not want a repeat of that hellish experience.

After the service, Maggie was buried in St. Joseph Cemetery.

Meanwhile, Otto's arrest and trial – while largely unremembered today – became the most sensational criminal proceedings in Cleveland up until that time. He spent his days in his cell, closely monitored by the newspapers, weeping, smoking cigars, reading the newspapers, and participating in the religious services offered to prisoners by the ladies of the Women's Christian Temperance Union.

On June 14, 1889, he was indicted on four counts of murder and his trial was set for later that same month, although eventually, it was delayed until December. The main cause of the delay was Otto's difficulty in finding an attorney to represent him. There were very few reputable lawyers in the city who wanted to represent a figure already known to newspaper readers as the "boy murderer-rapist." Finally, W.S. Kerruish agreed to take the case, but tragedy delayed the trial once more.

Jacob Thompson had fallen between two railroad cars several nights after Maggie's body was found and was badly hurt. At first, it seemed as though he would recover quickly but then he suffered a paralytic stroke and was gravely ill for some time. The death of Mr. Kerruish's son, and then Clara Thompson's serious illness, further delayed the trial. It did not begin until December 2 with prosecutors Alexander Hadden and C.W. Collister presenting the case for the state. The proceedings were presided over by Judge George B. Solders.

The prosecution's case was compelling and sufficiently gory to keep the attention of the audience – mostly female -- that packed the courtroom on each day of the three-week trial. The jurors were presented with a narrative of Maggie's last hours before she vanished, the discovery of the body in the cellar, and Otto's anguished confession. The evidence that was brought into the courtroom was even more exciting. Maggie's bloody dress, her felt hat, the blood-soaked headboard from Otto's bed, and her abandoned "button string" were all held up by Prosecutor Hadden for everyone to see. Several jurors were even wiping away tears during Clara Thompson's heartbreaking testimony.

But things took a turn on December 10 when prosecutors attempted to introduce the details in Otto's confession. Kerruish objected. He was revolted by his client. He even made a statement that included the line, "This boy, who is a disgrace to humanity, for whom I have little respect and no feeling..." But he had to do his job and that meant providing him with the best defense possible. He was willing to concede the facts of Maggie's murder in return for saving the boy from the hangman. To do that, though, he had to keep Otto's written confession out of the record. That document, signed and sworn to by Otto – although never read back to him – included both the admission that he'd killed her because he wanted to rape her and that he tried to rape her again after she was dead. If the jury heard that, they would hang him for sure.

Judge Solders sent the jury out of the courtroom and listened carefully to Kerruish, as well as Hadden's arguments. His subsequent ruling that the confession was admissible sealed Otto's fate.

But Kerruish didn't give up without a fight. He mercilessly grilled the prosecutors and detectives who had interrogated Otto on the night that Maggie's body was found. He argued that Otto's confession had not been voluntary, as they all claimed, stating that he was a young boy who had been terrorized by bullying adults into confessing. The problem was that Kerruish could make a case for Otto being pushed into a confession, but he couldn't deny the fact that Otto confessed to something that he had actually done.

Kerruish's other defense for his client was to paint Otto as a victim of tainted genetics. Otto, he claimed, was an epileptic, which was a condition linked to insanity in those days. In addition, his family line was filled with other epileptics and insane relatives. Otto's relatives claimed that the boy's maternal grandmother, aunt, uncle, mother, and brother all suffered from epileptic "fits." Otto himself, Lena Lueth testified, had suffered "spasms" and "night terrors" as an infant, suffered from debilitating headaches as an adolescent, and had a poor memory. Kerruish's argument was that, on May 9, Otto had experienced a sudden epileptic "fit" and acted without knowing what he was doing.

Kerruish didn't get far with his medical hypothesis, but he did manage to find several eminent physicians who supported his diagnosis of "masked epilepsy," although none could say that Otto really suffered from it. He did get Dr. Rueben Vance to testify and say that he had examined Otto and found a depression in his skull, an injury that might have caused brain damage. But the attempt to portray the boy as a "brain-damaged idiot" with a poor testimony collapsed after testimony from some of Otto's teachers at the Tremont Street School. He had dropped out at the age of 13, but all of them remembered his above average scores, his ability with numbers, and his skill at playing the violin.

Interestingly, Kerruish didn't pursue a line of argument that modern-day lawyers would have seized upon with ferocity – that he was an abused child. In the testimony about mental illness in his family history, it was well-established that his mother, Lena, suffered from maniacal fits of rage that were so fierce that she frequently spent time in an asylum. As her husband, Henry, her older son, John, and she herself swore under oath, Lena sometimes went into a demonic rage, during which she abused her children, especially Otto. From an early age, she admitted without expressing any guilt about it, she had pulled his hair, kicked him, beaten him, stomped on him, and hit him with any object she could reach. Once, when he was eight, she had beaten him with a chair leg and when Henry tried to intervene, she had stabbed her husband twice with a butcher knife. Just a few months before Maggie Thompson's murder, Lena had repeatedly slammed Otto's head with a wooden door.

It is a strange statement about parental discipline of the era that Lena's brutality was dismissed – and even excused -- because she was poor, and her methods were in "the German style." The courts certainly didn't feel that such treatment provided a reason for Otto to have committed rape and murder.

Lena's behavior in the courtroom also did nothing to help Otto's case. She constantly muttered to herself and experienced a number of "spasms" at climatic moments of the trial. Several times, she had to be removed from the courtroom until she returned to "normal."

After all the evidence was presented and testimony was heard, Kerruish and Hadden made their closing arguments. Holding up Maggie's bloody garments, hair, and "button string" one more time, Hadden reminded the jury that the law assumed everyone was sane until proven otherwise – and the defense had not produced a single witness who could certify Otto insane. He once again pointed to Otto's voluntary confession and to the four buttons found in Maggie's dress as the evidentiary link that proved Otto's primary motive was rape. Over Kerruish's objections, Hadden recalled the trial testimony that indicated Maggie had not had those four buttons in her possession when she left home on May 9. The suggestion to the jury about those buttons was unavoidable – that Otto had lured Maggie into his home with those buttons. He deserved to die for doing it, Hadden reminded them. The penalty was death for anyone found guilty of murder committed while attempting to rape a girl under the age of 14.

Kerruish followed Hadden's emotional closing with one of his own. He painted Otto as a "bad seed" of a genetically cursed family and the victim of an uncontrollable spasm. He railed against public attitudes toward insanity and stated that the atmosphere in the courtroom was nothing short of a "witch hunt." Otto, he told the jury, was "crippled in intellect; crippled in every way, crippled by his inheritance from his ancestors and crippled by the beatings he received from his mother. The maniacal outburst was bound to come!"

He explained that Otto left Maggie's body to rot in the cellar because that was just another symptom of his abnormality. He told the jury, "Why, a dog knows enough to bury a bone, yet this boy leaves this body in the cellar to fester and smell and tell its story to the community."

Otto had not tried to rape Maggie before or after he beat her with the hammer, he claimed. It was Detective Douglass, not naïve Otto, who had added this to the story, trying to provide a motive for what was a motiveless crime.

Kerruish reserved his greatest scorn for the press. He blamed the reporters and editors for the unfavorable public opinion that had been heaped upon his poor client. "It isn't the papers that make the opinions," he proclaimed, "but the boys here who write these articles. I don't want to refer much to these papers and reporters but if I ever got on the judge's bench I know I would find a way to prevent a common, scurrilous newspaper from interfering in the trial of a case. I think that there should have been power enough in the law of the state of Ohio to have that paper [the *Cleveland Leader*] from trying this case in their columns."

Kerruish paused for a moment, shook his head, and then glared back at the reporters in the gallery. "If you send this boy to the gallows," he said to them, "you will live to decide in calm and passionless reflection that you probably did wrong."

The jury deliberated for only four hours and 27 minutes before finding Otto Lueth guilty of murder. Otto took the news with white-faced calm, swaying only slightly when the verdict was read. But Lena refused to leave the courtroom after Judge Solders excused the jury. She began a sing-song chant: "No, I will not go. I might as well die here as outside. If they kill him, they kill me. If he is guilty, so am I. They are murderers. They will hang my poor boy though everybody says he is wrong in the head. I have no more use to live."

And then she started it all over again. Henry Lueth had to forcibly drag her from the courthouse.

Four days later, on New Year's Eve, Judge Solders sentenced Otto to hang on April 26, 1890, at the Ohio State Penitentiary in Columbus. Otto sank into his chair, but Lena let out another impassioned outburst: "Damn! Damn! Damn! The jury be damned! All 13 men be damned! They are fools! It is a damned shame to hang a child of 16 years. They all be damned, their children and grandchildren! I damn them, the mother of the murdered boy!"

When bailiffs Harry Lancefield and Peter Hill tried to restrain the crazed woman, she flew into a rage and screamed at them, "Don't touch me! I'll kill you! I'll kill you!"

Over the next few months, Kerruish's motion for a new trial made its way through the Ohio appeals system. The verdict was upheld but Otto's death date, which had already been delayed to allow time for an appeal, was moved back to August 29 so that the Board of Pardons and Governor Campbell could consider Otto's merits for clemency.

The decision to delay the execution came just three days after the death of Jacob Thompson, who succumbed to his physical ailments – and some say, a broken heart – exactly a year and a day after his daughter's body was discovered in that dark cellar.

Otto's time began running out. On August 22, the Board of Pardons turned him down, despite the pleas of former president Rutherford B. Hayes and four members of the original trial jury. Lena Lueth took the news badly. She threatened to kill herself -- but didn't.

Four days later, the governor refused to grant clemency and final preparations for Otto's execution began. Otto didn't take this news any better than his mother did. He cursed everyone that he could think of, aside from his mother, and told a reporter, "I just want to see the governor and tell him what I think of him! If he came down to see that nigger Blythe [an African-American who was also on death row] he might come to see me."

Meanwhile, Lena had confronted the penitentiary's Deputy Warden, screaming at him that she was going to shoot and poison Governor Campbell.

Considering the way that he had lived his life, Otto Lueth died with dignity. After a few tears, he pulled himself together, requesting only that newspaper reporters not "give it too hard to me" in their accounts and that the hangman do his business quickly and well. Wearing a black suit and white tie – and with a black hood over his face – Otto took his position on the gallows. At 12:05 a.m. on August 29, he spoke his last words: "All right, let her go."

The trap was sprung, and he died a second later from a broken neck. After 17 minutes, he was cut down in front of 29 witnesses and placed on a stretcher. A reporter later described the ghastly sight. Otto's eyes were bulging out, blood oozed from his mouth, his face was a dark purple, and the noose had left a vivid red mark around his neck.

Otto's short life had been an ugly one, leaving horror and chaos behind. Even his death was messy. When his family showed up at the church for his funeral, they found the doors were locked. There had been a misunderstanding about the time. His body was then shipped off to Fremont, Ohio, for a service and burial.

It should come as no surprise that Lena Lueth had the last word about the whole sorry situation. A week after the execution, she sent a letter to the Cuyahoga County sheriff in which she again cursed everyone who had participated in her son's arrest, incarceration, trial, and death. She claimed the jury was bribed, so there could have been no other outcome than one that led the boy to the gallows. She added:

I tell you, I, the mother of the murdered boy, cursed be you all. May his shadow pursue you by day and by night and in the hour of your death may you suffer the pangs that I now suffer. He was a murderer against his will. You murdered him with premeditation. Therefore, once more, all will be cursed that lent their hands, you murderers.

Lena Lueth

1911:

"TAKEN BY GYPSIES"

The lights were turned down low in the parlor of the house on Chicago's South Troy Street. The drapes had been pulled tight, cutting off the drab spring sunlight, which was shrouded by clouds. Bits of dust hung in the air above the table in the center of the parlor, which had been draped in a dark cloth. But no one assembled in the room had come to inspect how clean the house was. They were there for answers – seeking help from the spirit world. They wanted those in the afterlife to reveal secrets that the Chicago police had been unable to find.

The scratchy sound of music, played on a Victrola, could be heard coming from the next room. There was the rustle of a dress and then the medium entered the parlor. She was shrouded in mourning black and there was a veil across her face. They could see the glitter of her eyes through the thin fabric and she looked at each of them. She pulled back the veil and sat down in a heavy wooden chair on one side of the round table. The guests – Frank Paroubek, a painter who lived nearby; Charles Vopicka, a politician and brewery owner; and two other friends – watched expectantly as the medium arranged herself in her chair. She placed her hands on the fabric, inches away from the tools of her trade – a deck of cards, a clear crystal ball, a tambourine, a trumpet through which the spirits might speak – but she would use none of these today. She sought direct contact with the hereafter. She knew these men had come seeking information and she would do everything in her power to obtain it for them.

The medium's sister closed all the doors and covered the final window. The room was plunged into murky darkness. Only the light from a few candles now illuminated the scene. The sister then took a chair in the corner of the room and began to wait – just like the guests – for whatever would happen next.

There was no sound at first, except for the breathing of the medium, the faint chords of music from the record player, and the subtle shifting of the guests in their chairs. And then another quiet sound began to emerge from the shadows of the room. It was best described, one later said, like laundry blowing on the line on a windy day. It was a fluttering sound, shifting back and forth, and then it was gone.

The medium let out a deep breath and she began to speak. She said that her spirit guide was present and promised to lead her to where what they were seeking could be found.

He would, the spirit told her, show her where little Elsie Paroubek had been taken.

Suddenly, the medium's hand slammed down on the table, startling everyone in the room, including her sister, who was more used to dramatic scenes than the men in the room were. The medium's head flew back, and she let out a loud groan.

"I see a roadway through the forest," the medium spoke, now deep in a trance. "In the distance, the vague shapes of the outlying houses of a village. Traveling toward the village are several wagons, some of them covered with a white material and the others sheltered by wooden tops."

She paused, her brow wrinkled in concentration. Then, she continued. "The wagons are owned by a band of wandering gypsies, who are seeking a place to camp for the night. In one of them, I see a little girl, who is crying and sobbing. The father of the little girl is hunting for her and I can feel his presence beside me now."

Frank Paroubek sighed with relief. Could he and his wife's long nightmare finally be over? Could the spirit world have provided the information that the police could not? A tear of joy slipped from his eye and creased his cheek, making a single stain on the table.

"Where are they?" he blurted out, unable to contain himself any longer.

Charles Vopicka placed a restraining hand on his arm, although he was just as eager to hear. Vopicka was ready to send detectives to wherever the medium told them. He had already contributed a large sum to the reward for finding the missing girl.

The medium finally spoke: "The name of the village to where they are going begins with an A." She paused, hesitated, concentrated and then cried out, "Now I have it! It is Argo, and it is in Wisconsin!"

The medium then slumped forward onto the table. Her trance was over, and the séance was at an end.

The guests sprang from their seats. This information needed to go to the police right away. But Vopicka didn't plan to wait. He needed a telephone. He had officers to dispatch for Wisconsin. The savvy politician knew that he'd guarantee the votes of his Bohemian constituency if he could bring home the little girl that everyone had been looking for. He also knew – he realized as he looked at the weary man beside him – that he could help to keep a father's heart from breaking.

The men left the house, more excited than they had been in weeks. As Vopicka hurried to the nearest telephone, the other men spread the news that the missing girl's location had been discovered. Frank ran home to his wife so that he could share the wonderful revelations from the spirit world. It seemed Elsie's rescue was finally at hand!

But it was, of course, not meant to be.

If the spirit medium truly saw a little girl weeping and sobbing in a wagon that day, it was not Elsie Paroubek. By that time, she had been murdered and her body left in the drainage canal at Lockport. The tiny corpse remained there for nearly two more weeks before it was found.

The story of the kidnapping and murder of a young girl named Elsie Paroubek in the spring of 1911 is almost a forgotten tale in the annals of Chicago crime. Few but the most dedicated historians remember much about the case today, but at the time, her disappearance and the subsequent search for her involved law enforcement officials from three states and galvanized the people of Chicago. Nearly everyone was transfixed by the newspaper articles dedicated to the story – a story that did not have a happy ending.

To this day, the murder of Elsie Paroubek has never been solved.

Elsie – born Eliška Paroubek – was just five-years-old when she vanished. She was born late in life to her parents, Karolína and František. Her mother, Karolína Vojáček, was born in November 1869, in Míčov, East Bohemia, in what is now the Czech Republic. František – known as Frank – was born in Bohemia two years earlier. At the age of 15, Frank came to the United States, but returned to Bohemia for a decade between 1882 and 1892. He and Karolína were married in Bohemia just before he returned to America. In Chicago, Frank worked as a painter while Karolína took care of their home and raised a large brood of children. Eliška – who spoke only English and was known to her friends as Elsie – was their seventh child. She was a happy, friendly, little girl with light, golden hair, blue eyes, and a lovely smile.

On the morning of April 8, 1911, Elsie left the Paroubek home at 2320 South Albany Avenue in the Little Village neighborhood on Chicago's West Side. She told her mother that she was going to visit "Auntie," Mrs. Frank Trampota. She lived around the corner at 2325 South Troy Street. Elsie turned left on 22nd Street, then left again on Troy, and met her nine-year-old cousin, Josie Trampota, who, along with a number of other children, were listening to an Italian organ grinder, playing music on the street. When the musician moved on to the corner of 23rd Street, the children followed him past Mrs. Trampota's gate – except for Elsie, who stayed behind.

She had just gone missing, but no one knew it yet.

Several hours later, Karolína followed her daughter to the Trampota house. When she arrived at her sister's, she discovered that Elsie had never arrived. She

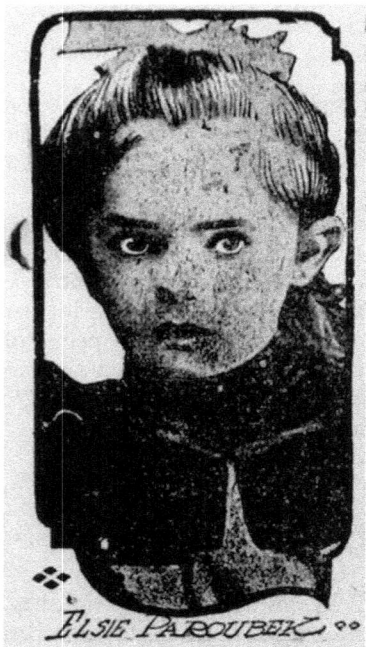

ELSIE PAROUBEK

wasn't surprised, or even worried. It was a close-knit immigrant neighborhood of friends and family members. Both women assumed that Elsie must be at another home, perhaps even spending the night there and returning home the next morning.

Around 9:00 p.m., Frank Paroubek arrived at home after a long day of work. When he learned of Elsie's absence, he was not as unconcerned as his wife and sister-in-law where. He immediately went to the Hinman Street police station and reported her missing. Officers on duty dismissed his worry, agreeing with the two women that Elsie must be staying with friends. They sent Frank home with a promise that all would be well.

He spent a nearly sleepless night, sure that something was wrong. By breakfast time, he was in a panic. Elsie had not come home. When he returned to the police station, Captain John Mahoney took personal charge of the search for the missing girl.

Detectives were called in from several stations. They canvassed the neighborhood and suspects soon emerged. A neighborhood boy named Joseph Jirowski told detectives from the Maxwell Street Station – led by Inspector Stephen K. Healey – that he had seen a "gypsy" wagon on Kedzie Avenue, a block away from Troy Street, around the time Elsie was last seen. He said that he saw two women in the wagon and heard a child crying. One of the women was holding the child down on the bottom of the wagon.

The police knew of several gypsy camps along the Des Plaines River, near Kedzie Avenue, so this seemed a viable lead. There was a great distrust by the police – and by the public – of the *Romani* people, an itinerant ethnic group who began migrating to America in the late nineteenth century. Perhaps because they traveled from place to place, they earned a reputation for lawlessness and theft. These prejudices led to them being widely-known by the term "gypsies," connected to the word "gyp," which meant to steal or cheat. This was a common term in 1911, used by the public, police, and newspapers. It was no surprise that Elsie being "stolen by gypsies" seemed plausible – especially because Elsie's disappearance was almost identical to that of a girl named Lillian Wulff, who had been taken by Romani people four years earlier.

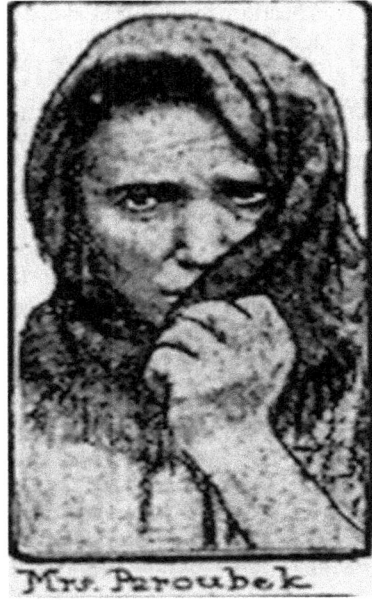

NEWSPAPER PHOTOGRAPHS OF THE PAROUBEK FAMILY – ELSIE'S
FATHER, FRANK, AND HER MOTHER, KAROLINA

When police officers went down to the camp along the river, they spoke with the residents and learned that one wagon had departed on the morning of April 9. If the eyewitness testimony was accurate, then these could be the people who had taken the little girl. Detectives had no description of the wagon, so they began rounding up all the "gypsies" they could find and following rumors and leads about the locations of camps in the area.

Meanwhile, Frank Paroubek had offered his life savings of $50 – more than $1,000 today – as a reward for Elsie's return. A lot of people came forward with information but none of their stories led to her discovery. Detectives from Maxwell Street followed their own leads. They searched the Italian neighborhoods around Halsted Street, where it was reported that a girl fitting Elsie's description had been seen with an organ grinder. Inspector Healey ordered the drainage canals be dragged for the child's body on April 12, and again on April 15, and Illinois Governor Dan S. Deneen asked the public to assist with the search. Soon, there were thousands of people on the lookout for the little girl – but she was nowhere to be found.

Everyone else was still chasing the "gypsies." Frank, accompanied by detectives Komorous and Sheehan, went in search of the wagon that had left the Des Plaines River camp. Others in the encampment told the police they believed it was heading for Round Lake, a small Illinois town about 50 miles northwest of Chicago. Before leaving, the detectives contacted the authorities in Round Lake, who confirmed there were seven wagons camped nearby. The authorities in Round Lake asked some local farmers to keep an eye on the wagons and to watch for a girl matching Elsie's description – but do not approach them. The farmers ignored the warning and took it upon themselves to question the people in the camp and attempted to search their wagons. In the middle of the night, the "gypsies" broke camp and left for Volo, Illinois. Volo residents reported seeing a child matching Elsie's description in the camp, adding that she appeared to be "stupefied" or "drugged" and partly covered with a blanket. They also attempted to search their wagons. The Romani refused to allow it, turned their wagons around, and left for McHenry, Illinois. It was in McHenry that detectives finally caught up to them. When they did, they discovered the little girl was part of a Romani family and didn't look like Elsie at all.

The *Chicago Daily News* consistently reported that Elsie was small, had "long curly golden hair, blue eyes, and pink, chubby cheeks with a prominent dimple in each." But the locals had seen what they wanted to see. It also didn't help matters that the newspapers and police were telling people that "gypsies" often kidnapped small children because of the "natural love of the wandering people for blue-eyed, yellow-haired children." At this point in the case, the authorities were convinced that "gypsies" had Elsie – but which "gypsies?"

It seemed the entire city of Chicago – if not the entire region – was on the lookout for Elsie Paroubek. On April 17, Captain Mahoney received an anonymous telephone call saying that a child of Elsie's description had been seen with a man in a hotel in Western Springs, Illinois. Detectives were dispatched to the hotel but, again, found nothing. In Sycamore, Illinois, the local police chief accompanied Frank Paroubek and two Chicago detectives – Thomas McAuliff and Frank Alex -- when they visited a Romani encampment near Cherry Valley. They were allowed to look around the camp and found a number of children present, but none of them were Elsie.

Meanwhile, Hinman Street police officers looked into a "Black Hand note" – a ransom letter – that was received by Karolína. It claimed that Elsie was alive and would be returned unharmed if $500 was left in a certain place. Nothing ever came of this ransom note. Sadly, it was one of many sent to the family in the weeks following Elsie's vanishing.

In the second week after Elsie's disappearance, Lillian Wulff, now age 11, came to the police to offer her assistance. She had been the subject of an identical manhunt four years earlier when she had been stolen by "gypsies" and forced to work for six days as a beggar. She was recovered after being spotted by a farmer as she was walking behind a wagon outside Momence, Illinois. Lillian provided what details she could about the typical behavior of the gypsies and offered to lead a "rescue party" if Elsie was found. She suggested that country people should ask every little girl that they saw on the road if she was Elsie. "When she begins to cry for her mamma, they'll know for sure it's her," she told newspaper reporters. She also advised the police to send circulars all around Chicago – that was what saved her, she said – and to send her description to farm houses, country stores, and post offices.

"You see, these people only take us little girls to beg for them," she added. "And they never like to have more than one little girl at a time, because two little girls eat more than one, you

LILLIAN WULFF, WHO ADVISED POLICE ON HOW TO PROCEED IN CASE ELSIE PAROUBEK HAD BEEN STOLEN BY "GYPSIES."

see. Therefore, they should look for one of these closed canvas wagons that only has one little girl in it. She'll be afraid and crying, you can bet. If she doesn't get enough bacon and eggs for them at farm houses, they'll whip her. I know. They whipped me with a horse whip."

Although the newspapers referred to Lillian as a "sleuth," the police didn't take her advice very seriously. Instead, Inspector Healey again ordered the drainage canal dragged, along with a search of wells, cisterns and other places into which Elsie might have fallen.

By late April, Elsie had been missing for almost three weeks and the city was in an uproar. Mrs. Ella Flagg Young, the Chicago superintendent of schools, sent an appeal throughout the school system and requested that all 200,000 children in the school system organize neighborhood searches during spring break. "I believe they can greatly assist the police in this search," she said.

Meanwhile, Frank Paroubek – more from desperation than an ardent belief in Spiritualism – consulted the spirit medium who told him that Elsie was in Argo, Wisconsin. Charles Vopicka sent officers to the area that she indicated during the séance, but there was no sign of the girl. Further messages from the "other side" sent searchers from Illinois to Wisconsin, from Wisconsin to Minnesota and then back again to Illinois – but with no luck.

The Czech community in Chicago rallied to support the family. All Czech-speaking policemen were put into plainclothes and assigned to the investigation. The women's auxiliary of the Club Bohemia also helped with the search, creating what they called an "endless chain letter," which was mailed to every party of the city, asking that recipients mail copies to everyone they knew. Various Czech-

American politicians became involved and the Bohemian Charitable Association offered a $500 reward. Other reward offers poured in. Governor Deneen asked the legislature to revise the statutes so that a reward could be offered by the state of Illinois. At that time, state laws did not allow the offering of a reward for the apprehension of kidnappers, as it did for murderers. Mayor Carter Harrison, Jr. contributed $25 ($600 in today's money) to a personal reward fund that was set up. Anton Cermak, then a Chicago alderman, stated that if Elsie was not found by the next city council meeting on May 1, he would call upon the city council to offer an even larger reward. Mayor Harrison instructed acting Chief of Police Herman Schuettler to assign a detachment of special policeman to the case.

But still, Elsie was nowhere to be found.

While all of this was going on, something sinister was becoming entwined in the case. A few days after Elsie had vanished, Frank Paroubek began receiving anonymous letters from an unknown source. The letters -- described as "insulting" -- were all written in English, which he could not read. He asked neighbors to translate. The letters claimed that Elsie had been taken by someone who "hated" the Paroubeks and accused the family of mistreating her. Frank was so angry about the accusations that he burned the letters. Regardless, detectives attempted to follow up on the lead. Unlike the "ransom" letters that the Paroubeks received, these letters seemed to come from someone with genuine animosity toward the family.

The police were overwhelmed by calls from helpful citizens. Every time a girl in a red dress was sighted in a gypsy camp, the tip was called into the police. In late April, a band of "gypsies" were reported as having a child with them who was light-skinned with blue eyes. They were moving north, toward Wisconsin, when they were encountered by a farm woman, referred to in the papers as Mrs. Goodall. She gave the child some cookies and then said to an older Romani woman, "That child does not belong to you, does it?" The woman hastily replied that it was her sister's child and the party soon left the place.

When locals saw the newspaper stories about the missing child, they reported the encounter to the police. According to their story, there was something mysterious about the movement of the "gypsy" wagons through the area. One wagon appeared to be traveling separate from the others during the day, joining them only during their night camps. When spotted south of Capron, there were only six wagons. The fair-skinned child, it was said, was traveling in a seventh.

The Boone County sheriff, a man named Gorman, contacted Captain Woods of the Chicago detectives, who told him that Frank Paroubek and some of his detectives had already searched the same wagons near Sycamore. But Sheriff Gorman explained that one wagon had not been searched and that if other officers were sent after the outfit, they should be certain to locate all seven of the wagons. Gorman refused to follow the "gypsies" into Wisconsin but he did trace their route, contacting Janesville authorities to let them know of their whereabouts. His call was followed by calls from officials in Chicago, who asked the Janesville police to search the camp.

Officers were sent to keep an eye on the camp that night and at daybreak on April 23, officers descended on the camp, routed the occupants, and searched the wagons. There were plenty of children found, but none of them were Elsie.

And there was no mysterious seventh wagon.

One of the Janesville officers suggested that the seventh wagon had somehow skirted the city and was on its way north. An alert was put out for officers to keep an eye on the roads, but that wasn't good enough for friends and neighbors of the Paroubek family. Four of Frank's neighbors – Frank Silhanek, Joe Bollis, James Geiger, and Joe Czelurnski – decided to form a posse and head for Wisconsin, where they had already applied for permits to carry firearms. Unfortunately, as had been the case for police searches, the four men turned up no new leads. By the time it was over, more than 25 Romani camps had been searched and their occupants harassed. Neither Elsie, nor any clue as to her whereabouts, were discovered.

Even though the search of the "gypsy" camps continued, by May 1, investigators had largely abandoned the idea that Elsie had been stolen by the Romani. They returned to their efforts of searching wells and cisterns and dragging the rivers and canals. The new Chief of Police John McSweeny took personal supervision of the case and announced that he would place every available officer at the disposal of Elsie's frantic parents. He expressed the belief that the girl had been murdered. It was no longer a rescue, he believed, it was a search for her missing body.

Judge Joseph Sabath was very unhappy about McSweeeny's surrender – he believed the girl was alive and with "gypsies" somewhere. The judge had devoted much of his time to an attempt to solve the case. He had been receiving letters from across

POLICE CHIEF JOHN MCSWEENY

the country, offering donations to the reward fund, as well as possible sightings of Elsie. He stated that he believed the Chicago police search had been "lackluster" and "listless" because the Paroubeks were poor. He increased his personal contribution to the reward fund from $50 to $100.

In the midst of this uproar, Detectives Zahour and Zalasky were still searching for the writer of the letters that had been sent to the Paroubeks. They believed that the man who wrote them lived near Madison and Robey Streets and that he knew more about the disappearance than he was saying. Lieutenant Costello, supported by Inspector Healey, flatly declared: "Elsie Paroubek fell into the drainage canal from the Kedzie Avenue Bridge or near it. She was not murdered." They believed the author of the letters witnessed her fall. But they never found him – and their belief that Elsie's death had been an accident soon turned out not to be true.

Five weeks after Elsie vanished, Captain John Mahoney – who had personally taken command of the investigation on the morning after her disappearance – sadly announced his belief that Elsie would not be found alive. He told reporters, "I am convinced she is dead, that her body is in the river, or in the drainage canal, or hidden somewhere. I intend to devote all further efforts to a search for her body."

That search didn't last much longer.

On May 8, an electrical engineer named George T. Scully, along with other employees of the Lockport power plant near Joliet, discovered a body floating in the drainage canal. At first, they thought it was an animal from one of the nearby farms, but three hours later, realizing that it looked like a child, they sent out a boat to bring it to shore. Undertaker William Goodale, who was called to examine the body, said that it appeared to fit the description of Elsie Paroubek: "The description tallied to the shade of the hair, the texture of the stockings, and the stuff and tint of the dress of little Elsie." He stated that he believed the body had been in the water for several weeks. It was badly decomposed, as might be expected.

Original reports said there were "no marks of violence" on the body – that would prove to be wrong.

Lieutenant Costello from the Hinman Street station called at the Paroubek home with the news. When she saw the grim-faced policeman on her doorstep, hat in hand, Karolína Paroubek cried out, "Mé drahé dítě!" (My dear child!) and she begged to be told Elsie was alive.

Lieutenant Costello couldn't tell her that. "Drowned," he said in a sad, quiet voice.

Frank Paroubek was taken to the Goodale Undertaking Parlor at midnight to identify the body. When he looked at the still, corrupted form, he couldn't be sure. He said, "The clothes look like Elsie's. But the face -- I can't recognize it. Her mother alone can tell."

THE DRAINAGE CANAL NEAR LOCKPORT IN 1911

The next morning, Karolína was brought to the Lockport undertaker's parlor by trolley car and she positively identified the dead girl as her daughter. She was quoted, "It's you, my darling. Thank God we've found you and you're not in the hands of the gypsies." For the next hour, she paced back and forth or sat nervously with her husband in an adjoining room. Frank held her hands and they wept and prayed together. Goodale, who had followed the investigation into the girl's disappearance in the newspapers, made a statement to reporters: "The body appears to have been in the water for about a month, which would tally with the date of Elsie Paroubek's disappearance. The child, when she left home, was without hat, and her clothing tallies in every respect with that found on the dead body. There was no ring or other ornament, and in that respect the descriptions correspond. Excepting only as to the color of the eyes, which cannot be clearly observed as to color, the descriptions are identical."

Later that night, Karolína spoke with reporters at the Paroubek home. She told them that she had experienced a psychic vision about her daughter's fate – days before Elsie's body was found. "I knew she had been murdered," she told the press. "A picture of the crime has been in my mind since the second week of her disappearance, and I am convinced that when the truth is known, as it surely will be, it will be shown that she was choked to death a week from April 8, when she was kidnapped while on her way to visit her auntie."

Arrangements were made for an inquest, with Coroner William Wunderlich of Will County presiding. Frank Paroubek was called as the first witness. Disregarding questions asked of him by the coroner, Paroubek insisted that his daughter had been murdered. Through a translator, he told the jury, "I am sure the gypsies stole my girl and then when they knew we were after them they killed her and threw her body into the canal."

At this assertion, chaos broke out in the jury room. Karolína began screaming and ran from the funeral parlor where the inquest was being held, shouting, "My Elsie is dead! She was murdered, murdered!" Her husband and Detective Zalasky tried to calm her down but, in her extreme distress, she started running up and down the street, drawing a crowd of curious onlookers. She insisted that she had known for three weeks that "gypsies" had killed Elsie and that the police had done nothing about it. Frank eventually was able to calm her down and assisted her in boarding a trolley car for home.

The results of the inquest were inconclusive. Coroner Wunderlich stated, "This case has attracted such attention that a minute examination will be made. We will be content with no perfunctory inquest such as this. The jury will refuse to state its convictions -- for it has none -- until after the autopsy has been held. We want the stomach of the little girl examined, and the lungs, as well. The father charges murder. It is certainly possible that he is right."

During the autopsy, two physicians, E.A. Kingston and W.R. Paddock, confirmed that Elsie had not drowned – there was no water in her lungs. Kingston said that she had been "attacked" (a euphemism of the era for rape) and murdered before her body was placed in the water. Paddock said that there was evidence that she had been "wounded" before she was killed. Lieutenant Costello later told the press that she had been "mistreated," which seemed to indicate that her death had not been the work of "gypsies." They also found "deep cuts" on the left side of her face. Although these doctors reported "blue marks on the throat as though the victim had been choked," another examination by Dr. E.R. LeCount and Dr. Warren H. Hunter of the Coroner's Office revealed that Elsie had been suffocated, not strangled. The official cause of death was listed as "unknown." Coroner Peter Hoffman agreed with Frank Paroubek as to the probable circumstances of Elsie's death – the little girl had been murdered, he believed.

Coroner Hoffman announced, "It is our belief that the abductor of the child suffocated her to death -- possibly by putting a hand over her mouth. It may have been that the kidnappers found the police were on their trail and murdered the child and cast her into the canal."

The coroner's report recommended that officials continue to investigate. Inspector Healey immediately detailed detectives on a case that had changed from that of a missing girl to a murdered one. He told reporters, "We have one or two theories, but nothing specific enough to talk about. I intend to place more men on the case tomorrow."

Meanwhile, Lieutenant Costello returned to investigating the anonymous letters that were sent to the Paroubeks, believing them to be the key to solving the case. The police were investigating the theory that Elsie was murdered after having been kept prisoner for more than a week – somewhere in the neighborhood where the Paroubeks lived. As he told the press, "I have forty detectives at work today on the theory that the criminals lived in the neighborhood of the Paroubek home. We are investigating every incident in the lives of the Paroubeks since they came to Chicago in order to trace a possible enemy. It will surprise me if the criminals are not arrested within a week."

We can only imagine how surprised the detective must have been when the case was never solved.

While the newspapers were hounding the police to catch the little girl's killer, the Paroubek family had other matters to deal with – namely Elsie's funeral, which they could not afford. Karolína told Judge Sabath that the search had exhausted all the money the family had and there was nothing left to pay for a burial. The judge gave her a check for $25 and promised to raise more funds. Friends and family members pitched in for the service and they also raised more money for the reward fund. Mrs. Sophie Johanes raised over $50 by giving a benefit party and soliciting donations from Bohemians on the West Coast.

On May 12, Elsie's funeral was held on the Paroubeks' front lawn. Hours before it was scheduled to begin, mourners and onlookers began to gather, numbering almost 3,000. They crowded into the yard, around the house, along balconies, and on porches of nearby homes. There was no hall in the neighborhood large enough to hold them all. The Paroubeks had been offered the use of a union hall, but Frank knew there were just too many people and he didn't want to turn anyone away. He said, "They have come to say goodbye to my Elsie. Don't let them be disappointed." Reserve police officers from the Hinman Street station were tasked with keeping order and preventing the crowd from breaking down the fence.

Elsie's tiny white coffin was placed on two brass stands, surrounded by lilies of the valley, roses, and carnations sent by Mayor Harrison, Judge Sabath, and numerous city officials. Eight little girls dressed all in white brought out huge sprays of lilies and roses and encircled the stand. Someone brought out two chairs from the Paroubek home, set them near the casket, placed a board across them and used it as a platform to hold the hundreds of floral offerings. Karolína was seated at the head of the coffin, while Frank and the other children stood nearby. The Paroubeks were not religious, so a simple service was read by Rudolph Jaromir Psenka, editor of the *Bohemian Chicago Daily Svornost*. He spoke of the need to cooperate with the police to find Elsie's killers. As the undertaker went to lift the coffin into the hearse, Karolína begged him to open it so she could see Elsie's face one last time, but her relatives persuaded her to let him go about his duties. Most of the attendees followed Elsie's casket to Bohemian National Cemetery, where Psenka gave another address.

Elsie Paroubek was laid to rest. Gone, but far from forgotten – at least for a little while.

With the funeral over, the police investigation was reinvigorated, despite the time that had passed. Police Chief John McSweeny vowed to devote the entire Chicago police force to finding the killer. Alderman Cermak asked Governor Deneen to increase the reward by another $200 and he announced that he would, "Ask the governor to issue a proclamation calling upon all the people of the state to interest themselves in this case, in order that her murderer be apprehended." Coroner Peter Hoffman also started a public reward fund, contributing $25 out of his own pocket.

Investigators soon had a suspect – a man named Joseph Konesti. Described as a "bearded Bohemian" and a "hermit peddler," he was said to have "frequently enticed little girls to his hut by the drainage canal" – the same canal where Elsie's body was discovered. He lived in a shack about a mile and a half from the Paroubek home and had "frequently been seen" nearby. The owner of the shack that he lived in, Mrs. David Shaughnessy, told police that she had complained to Konesti about "bringing children around the house," and had evicted him on May 9. The police searched the abandoned shack and found a long, green ribbon near the bed. Suspecting that it had belonged to Elsie, they took it to Karolína to see if she could identify it – she couldn't. But this didn't stop the search. In one corner of the house, they uncovered a spot where the floor planks had been removed. It looked as though a small hole had been dug in the ground – just large enough to hide Elsie's body.

The hunt was on for Konesti, who soon learned that the police suspected him of murder. On May 14, he threw himself in front of a train and committed suicide. Had he been Elsie's killer? It certainly seemed that way – until witnesses came forward and placed Konesti outside of the city when Elsie was taken. He was cleared of all wrongdoing.

More suspects emerged. Investigators learned of a man named Kinsella, a "religious enthusiast, supposed to be demented," who lived in a rundown house along the canal. Four detectives traveled to Stickney to speak with him but when the officers approached, Kinsella ran. They called out that they only wanted to ask him some questions, but he continued to run. Several shots were fired into the air to scare him – and it worked. Kinsella ran even faster, leading the detectives on a three-mile chase through gullies and underbrush. He vanished into the forest and was not seen again.

On May 15, Frank Paroubek contacted the investigators with information. He told detectives that he had spoken to a man he did not know, who told him that he had seen Elsie later in the afternoon on April 8 on Kedzie Avenue, south of 28th Street, long after she was supposed to have been taken by "gypsies." Lieutenant Costello tasked detectives with finding the man. A previous sighting of Elsie had her walking toward the canal on South Troy Street, a half block south of her aunt's house. If the unknown man was telling the truth, Elsie had been only three blocks away from the bridge. The man was supposed to live near the corner of Madison and Robey Streets but when the police searched for him, he was nowhere to be found. Like the mysterious letter writer who had plagued the Paroubeks during the search for their daughter, the anonymous witness was never heard from again.

The sighting of Elsie on the bridge fit into Lieutenant Costello's personal theory about the case. He didn't believe that Elsie had been murdered. He thought her death was an accident – that she had fallen into the canal and drowned. If he could prove that she had been seen closer to the canal than was previously thought, it would give more weight to his theory. The problem remained that the coroner's report didn't find any water in Elsie's lungs. There was also the issue that Inspector Healey had repeatedly dragged the ditches and canals during the search and her body was not found. And what about the signs of rape and abuse? Costello was convinced that the initial examination by Dr. Kingston – who said the girl drowned and was not attacked – was accurate, even though Kingston changed his report the following day. Costello followed his own leads in the case and – not surprisingly – they led nowhere.

But even the investigators who believed the autopsy report were running out of ideas. They spent their days on wild-goose chases, conducting a house-to-house search on the southwest side for a former boarder in the Paroubek home. They also kept looking for the unknown witness who passed on information to Frank and for the anonymous letter writer who seemed to know more than he should. Unfortunately, none of these men – like Elsie's killer himself – were ever found.

After more than a century, we still don't know what really happened to little Elsie Paroubek.

The same cannot be said for her parents, who were destroyed by their daughter's death. Two years later, on the anniversary of Elsie's funeral in 1913, Frank Paroubek died. He was only 45 years old. Karolína lived until December 9, 1927.

In death, they have been reunited. All three of them are buried together in Chicago's Bohemian National Cemetery, leaving a haunting mystery in their wake.

1921:

MURDER AT

KLUXEN'S WOODS

The sun had just dipped below the skyline in the town of Madison, New Jersey. Along Fairview Avenue, the street was already soaked in deep shadows by 5:30 in the evening. It was the woods that made the street so dark. The tall trees and the thick underbrush of what everyone called Kluxen's Woods loomed over the roadway. It would have made the journey of the young girl who was walking next to them an eerie one if she had not made the same trip so many times before.

Janette Lawrence, who lived with her parents at 142 Ridgedale Avenue, a house directly across the street from Kluxen's Woods, was on her way home. She had been babysitting for a couple of hours at the home of the James A.G. Sandt family at 19 Fairview Avenue. It was a regular job for her and she adored four-year-old Madeline Sandt, with whom she'd spent many afternoons. Each day, Janette had walked along this same stretch of road, past this same patch of woods – but this day would be different.

Janette, a seventh-grade student at the Green Avenue School, was a pretty girl, tall for the age of 11, with light-brown hair and a luminous smile. She was caring, smart, and very responsible, which was why she was so in demand by neighbor families to watch after their children when they were away.

On this particular day – October 6, 1921 – she had just left the Sandt house and was on her way home. Mrs. Mary Friedlander, a neighbor, saw her waving goodbye to little Madeline at 5:35 p.m. Janette passed Mary's house with a short wave and then continued on down the street. This was another ordinary occurrence. Janette was a friendly, polite girl and always had a smile for friends and neighbors.

It was a chilly afternoon and Janette buttoned up her coat as she walked. She carried her school books with her. She had hurried to Mrs. Sandt's house to watch Madeline after school and she had some homework that still needed to be finished.

As she was walking, she heard the clear ring of a bicycle bell behind her. She looked back and saw her friend, Bertha Crane, riding in her direction. Bertha grinned as she got close and slowed down. "I've got something to tell you!" she called out to Janette. "Can you stop by?"

"I can't," Janette replied, "I've got to hurry home."

"I'll see you tomorrow at school then," Bertha said and rode off in the direction of her house.

Janette waved and continued walking. She was almost home – but she never got there.

Bertha turned out to be the last person – except for her killer – to ever see Janette Lawrence alive.

☠

Anyone who grew up in Northern New Jersey in the first half of the twentieth century was probably familiar with the Kluxen Winery. The winery, founded by a German immigrant named Francis Kluxen, began operations in 1865. It survived Prohibition by producing sacramental wines for Catholic and Episcopal churches across the country. But by the early 1970s, its glory days were over. When the winery at 28 Fairview Avenue in Madison was torn down to make way for new homes, the demolition became a major event in the area.

The winery had been standing for nearly a century. The large, vine-covered structure had been located near Francis Kluxen's Fairview Avenue home. For many decades, there was a section of woods on the grounds of Kluxen's estate that was bordered on the south by Fairview Avenue and on the west by Ridgedale Avenue. The locals called it "Kluxen's Woods" and children from the neighborhood often played there, including his son, Francis, Jr., and his grandson, Francis III.

NEWSPAPER IMAGE OF JANETTE LAWRENCE FROM 1921

When Kluxen died in May 1914, the area newspapers published long, glowing obituaries, praising his many civic and political contributions to the community. By that time, one of his two sons, Herman, was running the winery, and his other son, Francis, Jr., his wife, Kate, and his son, Francis III, were living in the house at 28 Fairview Avenue. They were the most influential family in the area.

The success of the winery had spread the Kluxen name throughout the United States, but it was Kluxen's Woods – and not their fine wines – that made newspaper headlines in the fall of 1921. What happened in the woods remains one of the most chilling unsolved cases in the history of New Jersey murder.

It was on October 6, 1921, that Janette Lawrence vanished while walking home past Kluxen's Woods. The last person to see her was her friend, Bertha Crane, but it's possible that her mother heard the last sounds that Janette ever made. The young girl had been nearly home when Bertha left her and just moments later, Janette's mother, Rosetta, reported later that she'd heard an unusual cry – a kind of "gurgle" – in the fading light of the day. She said that it sounded "like a child in convulsed laughter." But was it the sound of Rosetta's daughter, or her killer?

A few minutes later, Janette's 15-year-old brother, Edson, came into the house and asked where his sister was. It was getting late and he offered to walk her home if she was still babysitting. Rosetta told him to go to the Sandts' house and see if Janetta was still there. After Edson left, Rosetta became worried. It was unlike Janette to be so late getting home. After pacing the kitchen for a few minutes, she finally went out and stood on the sidewalk and called Janette's name.

There was no reply.

When Edson returned and told her that Janette had left for home nearly an hour before, panic set in and the search began in earnest. Neighbors joined in and the police were contacted. Madison Police Chief Fred R. Johnson, along with Lieutenant William J. Ryan, arrived around 7:00 p.m. By then, it was dark.

At 7:30, two teenaged neighbors of the Lawrences – Walter Schulz and Chauncey Griswold, both Boy Scouts with experience in the forest – found Janette's lifeless body in Kluxen's Woods. She was lying near the stump of a large tree. A number of trees had recently been cleared for a new street through the woods and the stump was along a rough trail that the contractors had cleared.

Janette was lying on blood-soaked grass. She had been stabbed 23 times. A large handkerchief was tied around her neck and her hands were tightly tied behind her back with cord. Her dress was gathered around her waist and her underclothes had been pulled down to her ankles. Some of the stab wounds had torn through her clothing, but others had not, suggesting that some of the stabbing followed – or accompanied – the rape. The deepest wound penetrated her stomach and perforated her kidney. She had also been knifed in the throat and, according to the Newark pathologist, her death had been caused by the severing of the blood vessels in her neck.

When word spread about the murder, the residents of Madison were outraged. This was an unspeakable crime against a young girl and could not be tolerated in the upscale, industrious community that the people believed their city was. The sordid rape and murder of Janette Lawrence shattered the illusion that Madison was safe from the kind of crime that occurred in places like New York City.

The police promised that the case would soon be solved. Janette's killer, they said, would be brought to justice. But, as it turned out, that was a promise they were unable to keep.

On Friday, the day after the murder, Madison's acting mayor Frank F. Gibney, and the borough council directed Police Chief Johnson to arrest 14-year-old Francis Kluxen III on suspicion of the murder of Janette Lawrence. Lieutenant Ryan made the arrest, escorting the boy to police headquarters. After four hours of questioning, he was taken to the county jail in Morristown.

There was no explanation for the arrest and no information released about what was said in the interrogation room. Chief Johnson wasn't talking to reporters and neither was the mayor.

When Supreme Court Justice Charles W. Parker asked Mayor Gibney, "What facts have come into your possession creating evident proof where presumption of guilt warrants this boy being held?" the mayor seemed puzzled. "We have hardly had time to come to a conclusion," he replied, and yet they had ordered the boy to be arrested. What was going on?

After questioning Chief Johnson and the Morris County Sheriff Ethelbert Byram, Judge Parker reached his own conclusion. "He seemed to have been arrested without the slightest justification," he declared and added, as he granted bail, "The boy's people are substantial citizens."

COURT PHOTOGRAPH OF
FRANCIS KLUXEN III – JUST
ONE OF THE PEOPLE
ACCUSED OF MURDERING
JANETTE

From the start, investigators pursued what they regarded as the most significant clue – the cord that had been used to tie Janette's hands behind her back was the kind used by greenhouses to bind roses for shipment. Since the turn of the century, Madison had been known as the "rose capital of America." There were a number of greenhouses in the community that specialized in roses and shipped them throughout the country. Now detectives from Morris County and Newark began to question local greenhouse employees, including those at Barton's Greenhouse on Fairview Avenue – near the scene of the crime – and at Ruzicka's in Florham Park.

But there were also problems with the investigation from the beginning. No one from Madison had informed the Morris County prosecutor, John M. Mills, that Francis Kluxen was going to be arrested. After the borough council hastily demanded the arrest – with no evidence to support it – the prosecutor made his displeasure with the situation known. The resentment between officials in Morristown and Madison, caused by the council's actions, affected the entire investigation that followed.

One result of this disagreement was a stubborn refusal by Mills to consider the idea that Francis could have been involved in the murder. He was fixated on finding a greenhouse employee who was near the scene of the crime – and he soon found one. Frank Jancarek was 29-years-old and the brother-in-law of Arthur Ruzicka, owner of the greenhouse in Florham Park. Frank had been working there for several years.

Frank had come to the attention of detectives from the Morris County prosecutor's office – which highlights another problematic issue in that there were several different jurisdictions working the case, none of them cooperating with the others – because he had been near Kluxen's Woods around the time that Janette was murdered. That was the sole reason that he fell under suspicion. His explanation for being there seemed peculiar, but harmless. He said that he had made an appointment to meet his brother, Jerry – who worked at the nearby Barton's greenhouses -- at 5:00 p.m. at the corner of Ridgedale and Fairview Avenues. They were getting together so that Frank could tell him that day's score in the second game of the World Series between the New York Giants and New York Yankees.

On his trip to meet his brother, Frank brought with him a New York newspaper containing an account of the game, for which he'd had to wait at the

United Cigar Store in Madison until 5:20 p.m. That was when the latest edition of the paper was delivered. Now running late, he hurried down Central Avenue and arrived at the corner at 5:30 p.m.

This was what put him at – or at least near – the scene of the murder.

But it took a disgruntled, recently fired employee of Ruzicka's to get Frank into real trouble. The former worker, Frank McGrory, was a mentally unstable ex-convict who claimed he met Jancarek on the night of the murder and that Jancarek had confessed to killing Janette. McGrory told this story to the police about three weeks after the murder. Frank admitted that he had seen McGrory that night but denied making any such confession.

When the Morris County investigators found a "dagger" – it was actually a letter opener – in the bedroom of Frank's rooming house in Florham Park, he became the prime suspect. Later, two investigators from Newark found another knife, badly rusted, that McGrory claimed to have lent Frank on the morning of the murder and which he tossed off the Columbia Bridge that night.

Now, the prosecutor had two knives and a case built entirely on the testimony of an ex-convict with mental problems and a grudge against the family of the man he was accusing of murder.

What could go wrong?

Meanwhile, the case against Francis Kluxen III had not gone away. Even though evidence against the 14-year-old boy was just as flimsy as that against Frank Jancarek, the Madison borough council and the local police were just as convinced that he was involved in the murder. He had been in trouble numerous times and while that in itself did not make him a killer, they felt that it did make him a plausible suspect.

The single-minded pursuit of separate suspects by the town and the county prevented any possible cooperation between the two authorities. Each was determined to make a case against their own suspect – and damn the consequences.

On October 25, Prosecutor John M. Mills ordered the arrest of Frank Jancarek. Despite the protests of the Madison borough council, the scant evidence against him was presented to a grand jury in Morristown, starting on November 3. Justice Charles W. Parker supported the authority of the prosecutor, advising the grand jury "that in a case of unlawful interference in the exercise of your functions, a prompt indictment of the offender or offenders would be full justified." Judge Parker's warning quieted the protests from the borough council for the time being.

All the members of the Madison borough council were summoned before the grand jury, as well as Janette's neighbors, including Bertha Crane, the Friedlanders, and Mrs. Sandt, whose child she had often cared for in the afternoons. Some of the evidence presented seemed to implicate Francis Kluxen rather than Frank Jancarek, but Mills was not interested in seeking an indictment against the boy. His focus was on Frank, who allegedly had all but convicted himself of murder in the conversation with McGrory on the night of the murder – or so the ex-convict continued to claim. And the grand jury believed him. They indicted Frank Jancarek on November 29.

Frank's trial was originally supposed to start on January 9, but a series of delays moved it to April 3. Andrew Van Blarcom, a well-known Newark attorney, was hired to represent him. He was assisted by Joshua R. Salmon, a former Morris County judge. Van Blarcom promised to not only prove that his client was innocent, he would also expose the identity of the true killer.

Although John Mills had planned to oversee the prosecution, he announced soon after Jancarek's indictment that he would ask New Jersey Attorney General Thomas F. McCran to come to Morristown and present the state's case. McCran agreed to do so. Soon after, the Madison borough council decided to hire its own attorney, Robert H. McCarter, a former state attorney general, to counter the criticism that was being leveled against the council by both Mills and McCran.

Much of that criticism had to do with a letter that Dr. G.A. Smith, superintendent of the New York State Hospital at Central Islip, Long Island, had sent to Madison's Chief Johnson. Dr. Smith stated that a patient in his hospital, Reuben Weiss, had talked "in a raving manner about having murdered a young woman in Madison." Chief Johnson had filed the letter away and had forgotten about it. It was common to get such "confessions" in murder cases, he said. He didn't give this one any credence. It turned out that Johnson was right – Weiss knew nothing about the case other than what he'd read in the newspaper – but the fact that Johnson withheld the letter because he didn't want to muddy the waters with another suspect drew the wrong kind of attention to the borough council's investigation.

It was becoming obvious that, somewhere along the way, authorities on both sides lost sight of the fact that a young girl had been murdered. The investigation had been deteriorated into two feuding camps, each trying to convict an improbable suspect while Janette's actual killer remained unpunished.

Newspaper reporters covering Jancarek's case clearly believed that he was being railroaded. They also took a dim view of the upscale treatment that was being given to witness Frank McGrory, who they noted was "a star boarder at the country jail. The man is paid $1 a day for his meals. McGrory has developed into a 'man about town' at the county seat and is frequently seen at the moving pictures, wrestling matches, and other diversions."

In contrast, Frank Jancarek, "does not have things so easy. He is spending time in a cell that is said to be ill-ventilated. The place is dirty. Rats run over his bed during the night; the food is poor; paper and trash are allowed to accumulate. The matter was taken up with Sheriff Byram, who said it was up to the keeper to see the man got the right treatment."

Finally, six months after the murder – and more than four months after he was indicted – Frank's trial got underway. A large crowd gathered at the courthouse at its start on April 3 and grew larger with each of the eight days that followed.

One of the most important early witnesses was H.G.A. Nilsson, who lived at 150 Ridgedale Avenue, a few houses away from the Lawrence family. He said that on the night of the murders, he had arrived in Madison at 5:15 p.m., having taken a trolley home from Chatham, where he worked. He had walked from the trolley stop on Central Avenue toward his home, reaching the Lawrence home at 142 Ridgedale at about 5:40 p.m. There he saw Mrs. Lawrence and Janette standing in the yard talking. Nilsson also claimed that he saw Frank Jancarek lurking nearby, trying to hide behind a bush.

He'd never seen Frank before, but he knew it was him because Sheriff Byram had sent him into a room where several men were lined up and asked him to pick out the one that he had seen on October 6. Before making his choice, Nilsson left the room and discussed the man's appearance with the sheriff. When the defense attorney asked him why he did this, he replied. "I wanted to be sure." When Nilsson went back into the room, he pointed out Frank Jancarek.

Van Blarcom was obviously uncomfortable with the way that the identification was made. He asked Nilsson, "Didn't you pick out the man in your mind, and then change your mind after talking to the sheriff?"

"No, never," Nilsson said.

The issue is that Frank's presence on Ridgedale Avenue that night was never in question. He admitted to being there, planning to meet his brother to deliver the news about the World Series game. But why was he hiding behind a bush? It's unlikely that he was. Nilsson also claimed that he saw Janette talking to her mother in front of the Lawrence house – but Janette never made it home that night. Nilsson likely mixed at least two different nights together in his mind and then recalled them as happening the same evening.

Or he was lying, which is another very strong possibility. Whichever it was, no one called him on it and the testimony was allowed to stand.

On the sixth day of the trial, Frank Jancarek took the witness stand. He offered a chronology for himself – in great detail – about the day of the murder. Yes, he was near the Kluxen's Woods around the presumed time of the murder, but he was never in the woods. Yes, he had seen Frank McGrory as he was walking home. He knew him from working at Ruzicka's. According to Jancarek, he ran into him on South Orange Avenue. When McGrory told him that he'd had nothing to eat all day, Jancarek invited him to come home and have supper with him and his mother, which McGrory did. Afterwards, the two of them had walked toward the Columbia Bridge to see if work was being done on it. If it was, a construction job might be available for McGrory, who had recently been fired.

On the way back, they saw a car that had gone into a ditch. They helped the owner get it back on the road. Returning to the Jancarek house, McGrory retrieved a coat that he'd left there. Jancarek then accompanied McGrory to a nearby shed where the ex-convict had been sleeping. He left him at the shed and went home. Frank insisted that they'd had no discussion about any rape or murder.

The prosecution then went after the small amount of physical evidence that had been recovered. The letter opener from Frank's bedroom as turned over to Dr. Albert Edel, a chemist in Newark, to test for bloodstains. Edel was a German immigrant and graduate of the University of Berlin. He testified that he had performed such tests 12 times in the 22 years that he had been in the United States. He found no bloodstains on the blade, but when he pried off the handle, he found human bloodstains on the metal and wooden parts of the letter opener.

But whose blood? There was no way to know. Those kinds of tests wouldn't be available for many decades to come.

Dr. Edel was also given hair from both Janette and Frank Jancarek. Detectives also gave him the sweater that Janette had been wearing when she was killed. He found 12 hairs on it and one of them was not hers. He testified that the one hair "closely resembled" Jancarek's in color and texture, but, of course, he could not say absolutely that it was his. In any event, Dr. Edel had thrown the hairs away. He did have a slide that illustrated his comparison, but the actual evidence, was gone.

When defense attorney Joshua Salmon later summarized the case, he was particularly brutal with Dr. Edel and his evidence. He urged the jury that they should disregard anything the German doctor had to say simply because he was German. The trial took place in 1922, just four years after the end of World War I, and it was considered "patriotic" at the time to ridicule anything – or anyone – who was German, since they had been America's enemy such a short time before.

In addition to casting suspicion on Francis Kluxen because his ancestors came from Germany, they also introduced theories and evidence that looked bad for Kluxen. When Van Blarcom was cross-examining Chief Johnson, he was asked about the footprint measurements that were taken at the scene of the crime. They were found all around the tree stump near where Janette's body had been found and a trail led away from there to a water hydrant. Detectives surmised that the killer might have washed off blood from the murder there. Johnson had compared them with shoes taken from both prime suspects in the murder – and had found a match.

"Where did you get the shoes?" Van Blarcom asked, referring to the ones that matched the size of the tracks found in the woods.

"At the Kluxen house," Johnson replied.

Later in the trial, Kate Kluxen was called to the stand by the prosecution, perhaps to bolster her son's testimony, which had been mercilessly shredded by the defense. During his cross-examination, Van Blarcom noted that on the night of the murder, Mrs. Kluxen had placed her son's trousers in a pail of water to soak. She said this was because his pants often got stained when he worked on the wine press.

"Did you ever find it necessary to put Francis's trousers in to soak before?" Van Blarcom questioned her.

Mrs. Kluxen paused before she answered. "No, they were never before stained to the extent they were that night."

A long line of defense witnesses testified as to the good character of Frank Jancarek. Even Sheriff Byram – a prosecution witness – acknowledged that Frank had good qualities. Awhile back, in a rape case in Somerville, Frank had assisted the police in their investigation of the crime and had testified for the state. He was a solid citizen, a hard-worker from a good family who owned a local business, and he'd never been in trouble with the law. He was, some surmised, simply in the wrong place at the wrong time and fell under suspicion.

Frank McGrory – Jancarek's chief accuser – was another story. While a few regarded the former inmate as rational and believable, a greater number described him as mentally unhinged. Witnesses described a lot of bizarre behavior – throwing chairs, offering apples to imaginary people, speaking to imaginary people in the greenhouse before he was fired, and even wailing "fits" that stretched out for minutes at a time. When questioned, McGrory denied that he had been promised a reward or a job for helping to convict Jancarek, although he admitted that he knew a reward had been offered.

It took the jury less than an hour to find Frank Jancarek not guilty of the murder of Janette Lawrence.

The newspapers widely reported the story – most reporters didn't believe him guilty anyway – but asked the question that everyone wanted an answer for: If not Jancarek, then who killed Janette?

It was widely believed that Prosecutor Mills, aided by Attorney General McCran, had gone after the wrong man. Locals wanted the real killer brought to justice -- Francis Kluxen III. And they didn't want John Mills or Thomas McCran to be involved in the case.

Mills was happy to excuse himself from further participation but McCran, argued that he "was then, as I am now, in complete charge of the matter for the state." This announcement came in response to a letter from Robert H. McCarter, the attorney for the Madison borough council, who called on McCran to recuse himself because of his zealous prosecution of Frank Jancarek. As McCarter noted, "necessarily deprives you of the influence you should have in laying any further evidence that may be presented before the grand jury."

McCran wasn't swayed by the valid argument against him and in May, appeared before a grand jury in Morristown to present evidence in the case. This move caught McCarter and the borough council by surprise. McCarter had not yet prepared a response to McCran's last statement and yet the attorney general was trying for a new indictment. Several witnesses appeared before the grand jury, including Chief Johnson. As far as anyone knew, there was no remaining suspect in the murder except for Francis Kluxen.

On Friday, June 2, the teenager was indicted for murder and he was immediately taken back into custody. He was placed in the same cell that Frank Jancarek had occupied for five months. Kluxen's attorney, Elmer King, moved to quash the indictment on the grounds that his client had been a witness at Jancarek's trial, but Judge Charles Parker denied the motion. Francis entered a not guilty plea.

At this point, McCran decided that he didn't want to act as prosecutor in the new trial, so Judge Parker picked J. Henry Harrison of Newark, a former Essex County prosecutor to conduct the state's case.

The Madison borough council had gotten what it wanted – a trial with a new special prosecutor – but did any more evidence exist against Kluxen than there had been against Frank Jancarek? On the surface, the evidence looked just as weak and circumstantial. Kluxen was in the vicinity at the time of the murder and he owned a Boy Scout knife that could have been used as the murder weapon. He also had access to the same kind of cord that had been used to bind Janette, since the Kluxen Winery also used the same kind of cord that the local greenhouses did. So, what then was new in this case, other than the fact that Jancarek had a good reputation in the community while Francis was considered a troublemaker by those who knew him?

Rumors claimed that the evidence that Attorney General McCran had presented to the grand jury was much more detailed and persuasive than what Mills had presented against Jancarek the previous autumn. Many people in Madison believed Janette's murder was just about to be solved.

Unfortunately, they couldn't have been more wrong.

Convicting Francis Kluxen III was not going to be easy. Legal maneuvering by Elmer King started before the trial date was even set. He convinced the justices on the New Jersey Surpreme Court that a change of venue was needed. An impartial jury could not be drawn from Morris County, he stated. Public opinion was so strong in the Madison area that his client would not be able to get a fair trial. For that reason, it was moved to Morristown and the jury would be selected from Essex County.

The trial began in July and King – just as Jancarek's attorneys had done with Kluxen – tried hard to implicate Jancarek in Janette's murder. Many of the same witnesses appeared, telling the same stories they had already told.

One major difference in this trial was that was no purported "confession." Kluxen, now 15 and large for his age – six-feet, two inches tall and 170 pounds – denied that he had seen Janette on the day of the murder. On the morning of October 6, he told the jury that he had worked in the winery until 12:30 p.m. and had badly stained his trousers with grape juice. Ordinarily, he would have been in school that day, but he had recently been expelled from St. Vincent's parochial school in Madison. The principal noted that his behavior was "abnormal" and his behavior was too troubling for the nuns to handle. During the previous summer, he had been sent home from Boy Scout summer camp for repeatedly breaking the rules. At the time of his trial, he was still waiting to be enrolled in a boarding school in Baltimore.

Kluxen testified that he knew Janette "only slightly," having skated with her on a nearby pond during the winter, but he had never played with her. However, several people who knew both children disputed this claim. One of them, Mrs. Sadie Miller, a neighbor to both, recalled that she once heard Janette screaming, and going out of her home to see what was wrong, found Francis with one arm raised, apparently throwing something away. Janette complained to Sadie that the boy was always bothering her. She testified that Francis yelled at Sadie, "Damn you! I'll get you yet!"

Joseph Luciano, another neighbor, reported that he had once seen Janette and Francis near a shed on Ridgedale Avenue. They were yelling at each other. When Luciano walked over to see what was going on, he heard Janette cry, "Let me go!" When he reached the scene, Kluxen quickly left.

Whatever the relationship had been between the two of them, the newspapers reported that Kluxen "accounted for nearly every minute of his time on the day of the murder. He explained that, in the afternoon, he had gone to the train station and back in his uncle's truck, how he had gone for a ride in a pony cart with his cousins, and how he had walked in Kluxen Woods with 14-year-old Anna Nilsson, showing her where he had fired a .22-caliber bullet into a tree while trying to shoot a squirrel.

After Anna left, he went home, carrying two bottles of milk he had bought. When he got there, he discovered that his pet rabbit had escaped. He sent his dog, Brownie, in search of the rabbit, but Brownie, instead of chasing the rabbit, went off after a neighbor's cat. Francis then had to chase the rabbit and the dog through the woods, which was how he accounted for his footprints being found at the tree stump and the fire hydrant. He claimed that, sweaty from the pursuit, he opened the water hydrant to get a drink of water and rinse his hands and face.

Prosecutor Harrison pointed out that if Kluxen spent this much time walking and running around in the woods so close to the time of the murder, then he must have seen something. How could he have no idea about what had happened there? But the defendant insisted that he had seen nothing.

During his testimony, Francis did admit that he regularly carried a Boy Scout knife on his belt. He also agreed that his mother had placed his badly stained trousers in a bucket of water to soak. But he insisted they were stained with grape juice, not blood.

The most damaging testimony concerned two handkerchiefs that were found at the crime scene. One of them was wrapped around Janette's neck. The other – bearing the initial "F" – was stuffed into the tam-o'-shanter (traditional, beret-like Scottish hat) that she'd been wearing. Both handkerchiefs had been mended in a similar manner.

More than a month after the murder, investigators removed five handkerchiefs from a cabinet in a hallway outside of Francis's bedroom. These five handkerchiefs had all been mended in the same way as the ones from the crime scene. All seven were put into evidence and the prosecution called Mrs. Mary C. Brower, a teacher of sewing and dressmaking, to testify about the mending that had been done to them. Mrs. Bower testified that the mending was all the work of one person, using the same technique. In addition, they'd used the same thread in all seven, which was noteworthy because it was too coarse for the job.

This was damaging testimony but didn't actually prove anything. It was circumstantial, just like the rest of the evidence against Kluxen. No one had seen the murder committed. No one could even say that he was nearby when Janette was killed. Francis Kluxen may have been disliked by neighbors, but did that make him a murderer?

The jury didn't think so – or at least they didn't think that anyone had proved it. They deliberated for three hours before returning with a the second not guilty verdict in the same murder case. Kluxen appeared calm when the verdict was read, although his parents had fidgeted nervously. They took their son home to the house on Fairview Avenue. The Kluxen name had been sullied but it was not damaged beyond repair.

Two acquittals in two different Janette Lawrence murder trials raised serious questions about the way the case had been investigated in the first place. The crime hardly seemed beyond solution – the Madison borough council thought the killer was easily identified – but the case had not been solved to the satisfaction of two trial juries.

And it would never be solved.

Frank Jancarek left Madison soon after his trial. He moved to Johnson City, Tennessee, married a girl named Blen Duke Bryant, and had two sons and four daughters with her. He worked for many years at the Johnson City Foundry, attended the Methodist Church, and lived a quiet, peaceful life. He passed away in 1979.

Francis Kluxen III, however, made plenty of newspaper headlines in the 1920s and 1930s. His next appearance in the papers involved his bizarre adoption in Orphan's Court. A wealthy and highly respected 48-year-old bachelor, Monell Sayre, who lived in a grand mansion in Convent, had taken a liking to the boy during his murder trial. Sayre found Francis to have "such winning and upright qualities" that he proposed taking him under his wing and making him his legal heir.

Yes, this is all as strange as it sounds.

Sayre was an esteemed resident of the region. His ancestors had settled in Morris County in 1665 and Sayre himself had been born two centuries later in 1875. He graduated from Harvard in 1898 and taught history at Columbia University. He left Columbia to become a staff member of the Carnegie Foundation, specializing in pensions, and worked closely with Andrew Carnegie in several ventures. Sayre was a lifelong Episcopalian and held many high positions in the church, most notably as the founder and administrator of the Church Pension Fund for the national church organization. He was considered the father of the church pension system and helped establish the pension fund for the clergy of the Church of England, at the invitation of the Archbishop of Canterbury. Sayre was also active in Democratic politics. He ran unsuccessfully for the House of Representatives from New Jersey in 1922, 1924, and 1932.

To put it simply, Monell Sayre was an imposing presence in New Jersey. His plan to adopt Francis and make him his "ward" might have seemed very odd to people, but no one was going to say much about it – publicly, at least. The whole thing was peculiar. Francis had just been acquitted of murder and his parents had stood solidly behind him throughout his entire ordeal. His mother had wept unrestrainedly when the verdict was announced. And yes, five months later, the respected and well-to-do parents were ready to turn their son over to a middle-aged bachelor who had become acquainted with the boy only because he was on trial for murder. The upside was that Francis would soon become the sole heir to an enormous fortune. Was this the reason his parents went along with this weird and rather unsettling scheme? Or had they finally had their fill of the trouble that Francis was repeatedly getting himself into?

More importantly, did they believe that their son had committed murder? Perhaps – and perhaps they believed that Sayre's wealth would keep him from falling under suspicion the next time that a young girl was found dead in the woods.

In Orphan's Court, Kluxen's father testified that the expenses of the murder trial had drained his resources and made him amenable to the idea of the boy's adoption by a man of wealth and position. His mother agreed but wanted to make it clear to the court that her son's adopted name would be Francis Kluxen Sayre, a last vestige of the family from which he had sprung.

Whoever it was on the Madison borough council that was quick to suspect Francis of murder would likely have predicted that the relationship between the boy and Monell Sayre would be an uneasy one. They could have pointed to an incident in 1923 as proof of this. Just before Christmas, Sayre brought Francis, now 16, to a service at the Grace Episcopal Church in Madison. The rector, Reverend Victor W. Mori, along with most of the congregation – who believed the boy had not only gotten away with murder but was now living in a situation that was questionable at best – were outraged by the appearance of Sayre and his companion. He left the church and even moved out of the area to Princeton. This move indicated the seriousness of Sayre's problem, for his family had been the leading citizens of Morris County for 250 years. But the locals were angry over the situation he had created in ways that he had not expected. Sayre's life and career were permanently and adversely affected by his association with the boy whose "winning and upright qualities" had so impressed him during the trial.

Francis took advantage of the older man and disregarded any feelings that Sayre had for him. In 1926, he left Sayre's house and a year or so later, enlisted in the U.S. Marine Corps in Portland, Oregon. Although he rose to the rank of first lieutenant and reenlisted in 1931, he won no awards for distinguished service. On Christmas Day 1932, he attacked two men in San Diego with a meat cleaver during a robbery. Both men were badly hurt but survived. Francis was given a suspended sentenced and fined $50.

In June 1933, he shot and killed an African-American man named Joe Hollman in San Diego. According to the story Francis told the police, Hollman, who lived next door, had been drinking with him, another man, and a woman earlier in the evening. When Hollman became drunk and abusive, he was asked to leave. He did, but soon returned with a gun, which he pointed at Francis's friend, Douglas Mathewson, and Mrs. Ruth Foster, who owned the boarding house where he lived. Francis, who was out of the room at the time, slipped upstairs, grabbed a shotgun, came back down, and shot Hollman dead. A coroner's jury found that Francis had killed Hollman in self-defense.

In April 1934, he was arrested again in San Diego. He was accused of committing nine burglaries in the city and county. Also charged with him was Ruth Foster, the woman that he'd saved from Hollman the previous year. The two of them were living together in a "fashionable section of San Diego" at the time of their arrest. Police found dozens of rifles, shotguns, and pistols in the house, "plus a stock of ammunition and more than $1,000 in loot."

This time, Francis's rap sheet and the physical evidence caught up with him. He was convicted and sentenced to serve up to 14 years at San Quentin. During the trial, he married his accomplice, who only ended up with probation. Not surprisingly, the marriage didn't work out and sometime later, he married again. When he died on April 15, 1971, his obituary noted that he was survived by his wife, Thelma, and his daughter, Evelyn.

Four decades before his death, Francis had become estranged from Monel Sayre. The reason for the split is unknown, but Francis did continue to use the surname "Sayre" for the rest of his life. It probably didn't matter much to Monel

Sayre, though. He died unexpectedly at the Lafayette Hotel in Washington, D.C. on June 15, 1936. Whatever became of his estate seems to be a mystery. It's apparent from his lifestyle that Francis didn't inherit the wealth that he likely expected when Sayre adopted him. I have been unable to discover what might have happened to all the money.

The Kluxen Winery, freed from its connection to the boy that everyone in town believed was a murderer, continued to prosper. It finally came to an end in 1973 and the buildings were torn down. There is nothing that remains of the winery today. Kluxen's Woods have been replaced by homes and there are no reminders today of what occurred along these quiet streets.

But there are the stories.

After the crumbling ruins of the winery were torn down in the 1970s, houses were built on the land that it once occupied. The site where Janette was murdered – and her body was found – is now someone's backyard. Rumors spread that the area was haunted. Were they merely stories created because of a murder that had occurred more than 50 years earlier? Believe it or not, that seems unlikely. One of the families that moved into a new home was from outside the area. They knew nothing of Janette's murder and yet one of the children began reporting the ghost of a young girl who appeared in his room. She was thin, he said, and tall, with light brown hair – a description that certainly matches that of Janette Lawrence.

But more common were the stories that have continued for years – that motorists were spotting Janette's apparition on Fairfield or Ridgedale Avenues, walking down the street, trying to make her way home from her babysitting job, just as she did on that cool night in October in 1921. Of course, Janette never made it and, the stories say, neither does her ghost.

Some of those who have seen her say that she vanishes when the headlights of their car illuminate her figure. She is recognizable. They say she is thin, has brown hair, and is wearing an old-fashioned skirt, coat, and a hat that looks like a beret. It's not the usual clothing that children in the neighborhood wear, which is usually what gets their attention. As the car approaches, she disappears.

Could this be the ghost of Janette Lawrence, still walking the streets of the place where she once lived and unable to rest after a murder that has never been solved? It just might be. But until the day when she decides to speak to those passing motorists who see the girl by the side of the road, we'll never know for sure.

1924:

THE "PERFECT MURDER" OF

BOBBY FRANKS

The killers arrived at the culvert just as the sun was going down. Nathan parked the automobile near the Pennsylvania Railroad tracks. As he climbed out from behind the wheel of the car, he glanced off in the distance and saw the way that the sun glinted off the twin rails as they vanished on the horizon. He pressed his lips together in a twisted grimace and opened the trunk of the car. He pulled out a pair of rubber hip boots and sat down on the back bumper to slide them on over his shoes. As he did so, the passenger door of the car creaked open and his partner, Richard, climbed out. The other young man stretched casually and let out a sigh. They had been riding around the Indiana countryside for hours, waiting for it to get dark. It felt good to get out of the car.

Wordlessly, Nathan opened the rear driver's door and Richard walked around the back of the car to help him. Together, they reached for the bundle that had been shoved onto the floorboard behind the front seat.

As Nathan tugged on the bundle, wrapped in a gray blanket, he saw a crimson stain that was starting to seep through the heavy material. They needed to get this over with, get rid of it, and get on with the plan.

The bundle landed heavily on the muddy ground. Richard leaned down, grabbed one end of it, and unrolled it to reveal the still, bloody body of a young boy. Dressed in his school uniform, the thin, dark-haired boy was twisted in a tangle of limbs. His face was mottled and blackened, smeared with dried blood from the gaping wound in his head.

Nathan wondered for a moment if the boy might still be alive, but the corpse lay stiff and rigid on the ground. Its glassy eyes stared up at them, unblinking.

With no hesitation, Richard quickly began undoing the buttons on his jacket. Nathan started with his shoes, pulled off the boy's socks, and they stripped him naked. If the body was found, this would make him much harder to identify.

It was a warm night and Nathan was already sweating. His jacket felt tight and uncomfortable.

The dead boy, his arms by his sides and his legs slightly apart, now lay naked on the ground. Richard reached into his coat and pulled out a bottle of liquid. He handed it to Nathan. The other young man pulled out the glass stopper and held the bottle of hydrochloric acid above the corpse. He tipped it and some of the liquid fell on the dead boy's face. The acid would burn away the skin. If someone discovered the body, the police would never be able to identify it. Nathan had been told by someone that it was possible to identify a person by the shape of their genitals, so he poured the remainder of the acid on the dead boy's penis and testicles.

With this completed, they picked up the blanket like a stretcher and carried the corpse down a short slope toward the murky water that drained from the culvert and flowed into a swamp along Wolf Lake. Soon, they were standing knee-deep in the pool.

Nathan leaned down and picked up the boy's body beneath the shoulders. He lifted him as high as he could and shoved the top of the corpse into the culvert pipe. He pushed as hard as he could, struggling to get the torso up over the lip of the pipe. It was a cool evening, but Nathan was drenched with sweat. He needed to get his coat off. He shrugged out of it, one shoulder at a time, and then handed it to Richard. As he did so, neither of them heard the quiet splash from the water at their feet. A pair of eyeglasses were in the pocket of Leopold's coat and they fell into the water as he removed it.

This would be the undoing of their "perfect crime."

Richard took the coat and climbed up out of the water and mud as Nathan shoved the body into the pipe as far as he could. Satisfied that the corpse would not be seen, he sloshed out of the mud toward the car.

Both young men were convinced that the body would not be found until long after the ransom money had been paid. With darkness falling, though, Nathan failed to notice that one of the boy's feet was dangling from the end of the culvert pipe.

The murder of Bobby Franks was about to become front page news.

On May 21, 1924, Jacob and Flora Franks were waiting anxiously for their son, Bobby, 14, to return home from school. It was past 6:00 p.m. and dinner was on the table. It was unlike the boy to be late. Bobby's older brother, Jack, 16, could usually be counted on to watch out for Bobby, but Jack had been out of school all

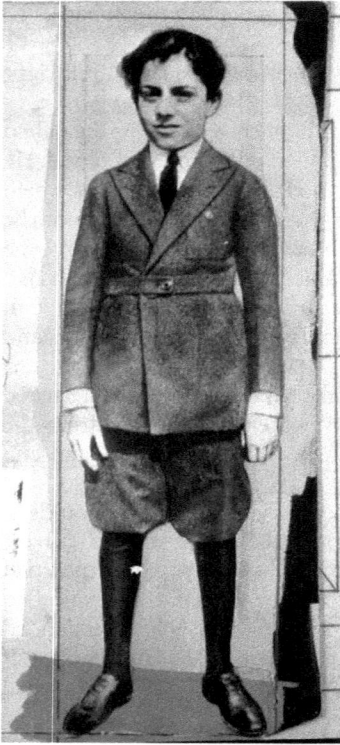
BOBBY FRANKS

week, in bed with the chicken pox. Josephine, 17, Bobby's sister, tried to ease her mother's fears. Bobby always played baseball after school. Perhaps he had lost track of time or had gone to a friend's house for supper.

Jacob Franks agreed with his daughter. He admitted that it was unlike Bobby to be late for supper, but he couldn't believe that anything bad could have happened to him. Their home was only three blocks from Harvard School, which Bobby attended, and the boy was old enough to know not to talk to strangers. Still, he was annoyed that his son could be so thoughtless and forgetful and was unhappy with him for causing his mother to worry.

Jacob and Flora were proud of their four children. Josephine had been accepted at Wellesley College in the fall. Jack, a junior at Harvard School was planning to attend Dartmouth College. Jacob, Jr. was the youngest child, still in elementary school, but showed signs of academic promise.

Bobby, the favorite of the entire family, was precocious and a bit of a troublemaker, but no one could stay angry with him for long. He was an independent boy, who got good grades, and already announced that he also planned to attend Dartmouth, where he planned to study law. The principal of Harvard School, Charles Pence, spoke glowingly of Bobby. Only a freshman, he was already a member of the debate team. He was a popular boy, a skilled tennis player, and an avid golfer. He had joined with some other boys at school and started a reading group. Only a few days before, he had won a debate on capital punishment, arguing for a link between criminality and mental illness. He protested the right of the state "to take a man, weak and mentally depraved, and coldly deprive him of his life."

Jacob loved his children so much because he had lost his own father as a young boy. Family was everything to him. His mother had run a clothing store and then a pawnshop in Chicago, and in 1884, Jacob started his own pawnshop on Clark Street, just south of Madison. It was a good location and a good time to be in the business – gambling was then unregulated in the city and there were at least a dozen gaming houses within a block of Jacob's pawnshop.

He soon built a loyal clientele. Gamblers soon found they could rely on Jacob to lend them as much as 90 percent of the value on their watches, diamonds, and rings and once their luck turned, they could easily redeem their property.

Jacob never ran for political office, but he was well-connected. Michael "Hinky Dink" Kenna, powerful and notorious Democratic alderman of the First Ward, spoke highly of Jacob as an honest businessman and so did many others. He became an integral player in the Democratic party and used his connections to make his fortune. An opportunity to buy stock in the Ogden Gas Company was a lucky break for Jacob and his business partner, Patrick Ryan, and they sold the stock to People's Gas Light and Coke Company for an enormous profit – some said as much as $1 million. Jacob bought land in the downtown district and watched its value soar when the city moved the taverns, gambling parlors, and brothels farther south to the Levee. By 1924, Jacob was wealthy beyond his wildest dreams. He had a wonderful home in an upscale neighborhood, a beautiful family, and a contented life.

But all of that was about to change.

By 7:00 p.m., Jacob and Flora were beyond annoyed and were becoming worried. Bobby was still not home. Jacob telephoned his attorney and friend, Samuel Ettelson. Jacob had known the lawyer for many years and Ettelson was one of the most influential men in the city. He had served as the corporation counsel during the mayoral term of William Hale Thompson from 1915 to 1923 and was now a state senator for Cook County in the Illinois legislature. A respected Republican, Ettelson still had considerable influence with the police department and with the state's attorney, Robert Crowe. If anything had happened to Bobby, Jacob could rely on his old friend to help launch a massive police investigation.

Ettelson arrived at the Franks house on Ellis Avenue by 9:00 p.m. The three adults spoke briefly in the living room and the attorney could see how upset Jacob and Flora were. He immediately got to work making telephone calls. He called teachers and staff members at the Harvard School but only Richard Williams, the athletic director, was able to offer much help. He said that Bobby had been the umpire at a pickup baseball game in a vacant lot at 57th Street and Ellis Avenue. Williams had seen Bobby leave the game to walk home around 5:15 p.m.

Ettelson suggested that perhaps Bobby had returned to the school for something on his way home. If he had, he could have been accidentally locked inside by the janitor. He and Jacob grabbed their coats and hats and hurried to the school. When they reached the building, they found it dark and quiet. The door was locked and there was no sign of the janitor. A window was open on the first floor so Ettelson boosted Jacob inside. He unlocked the door and the two men searched the building and then the school grounds. There was no sign of Bobby.

ATTORNEY SAMUEL ETTELSON (LEFT) WITH JACOB AND FLORA FRANKS

At home, Flora was waiting anxiously for her husband. It was now almost 10:30 and Jacob had been gone for nearly an hour. The children were asleep and the servants, except for one maid, had all retired to their quarters. The house seemed deathly quiet.

In the hallway, the clanging of the telephone caused Flora to jump in her chair. She heard the maid pick up the receiver and answer the caller. She brought the telephone into the living room and handed the receiver to Flora – had Bobby been found? She breathlessly answered and then heard a man's voice in reply. She remembered it later as "more of a cultured voice than a gruff voice."

The caller spoke quickly and clearly. Flora did not miss a word. "This is Mr. Johnson... your boy has been kidnapped. We have him and you need not worry. He is safe. But don't try to trace this call... We must have money. We will let you know tomorrow what we want. We are kidnappers and we mean business. If you refuse what we want or try to report us to the police, we will kill the boy."

The line went dead – the caller had hung up. Flora was motionless for a moment, still clutching the receiver, and then she fainted and fell onto the floor.

Just minutes later, Jacob and Ettelson returned. The maid was still holding Flora in her arms – she had tried to revive her with spirits of ammonia – and Flora regained consciousness just as her husband walked in the door.

At least they knew what had happened to their son – and that he was alive. Perhaps the kidnapper would call again that night, so Ettelson called the telephone company to put a trace on incoming calls. It was a risk – the kidnapper had specifically warned against it – but Ettelson was in a difficult position. He wanted to bring his friend's son home, but he was also a public official and refused to give in to blackmailers. From his years as Chicago's corporation counsel, Ettelson had vast experience with city affairs and with negotiating contracts with labor unions, utility companies, building contractors, and every kind of underworld boss that Chicago could send his way. However, nothing had prepared him for this. He was uncertain how to proceed. Should they inform the police? Or should they wait for another call? If they obeyed the kidnappers demands, were they still putting Bobby's life at risk?

Ettelson paced the floor, trying to decide how best to advise Jacob and Flora. Of course, there was no way that he could know that the threat they faced was much less sophisticated than they could have imagined.

Or that the kidnapping had already become a murder.

At 2:00 a.m., Ettelson finally decided that they should go to the police. Jacob was relieved. He could stand the inaction no longer – anything was better than waiting for the telephone to ring. Ettelson was not only connected in the police department, he was personal friends with Chief of Detectives Michael Hughes, and with Deputy Captain of Police William Shoemaker. Why not use his influence to get them to rescue Bobby?

The two men rushed to the central police station and explained the situation to the young lieutenant in charge, Robert Welling. He listened carefully but was reluctant to mobilize the entire department in the middle of the night. What if, in the morning, the whole thing turned out to be a juvenile prank? Ettelson agreed, perhaps fearing for his own reputation, if it didn't turn out to be a kidnapping at all. Besides, hadn't the kidnappers threatened to kill the boy if they contacted the police? "Perhaps," he decided finally, "we better wait until morning before doing anything about it."

Before Ettelson could return to the police station the next morning, a special delivery letter arrived at the Franks home. The envelope had six two-cent stamps on it and was postmarked in Chicago. It had been mailed either the previous evening or early that morning. The letter – written by "George Johnson"— promised that Bobby was alive, and it provided instructions for his return. It also warned again about the involvement of the police. The details of the typewritten letter were as follows:

Secure before noon today $10,000. The money must be composed entirely of old bills of the following denominations: $2,000 in $20 bills, $8,000 in $50 bills. The money must be old. Any attempt to include new or marked bills will render the entire venture futile. The money should be placed in a large cigar box and wrapped in white paper. The wrapping should be sealed with sealing wax.

Have the money prepared as directed above and remain home after one o'clock PM. See that the telephone is not in use. You will receive a future communication instructing you as to your future course.

As a final word of warning, this is a strictly commercial proposition, and we are prepared to put our threats into execution should we have reasonable ground to believe that you have committed an infraction of the above instructions. However, should you carefully follow out our instructions to the letter, we can assure you that your son will be safely returned to you within six hours of our receipt of the money.

The Franks were almost overwhelmingly relieved after the arrival of the letter. This was proof, they believed, that Bobby was alive. For a trivial sum, they would have their son back, safely home with them. Samuel Ettelson was also relieved – this was a professional kidnapping gang and the boy was now, as he'd feared, in the hands of some deviant.

His greatest fear had been alleviated – Bobby would be returned to them alive.

Around the same time that the letter arrived at the Franks house, a Polish immigrant named Tony Minke was walking along a path that ran parallel to the Pennsylvania Railroad tracks near Wolf Lake. Tony was a pump man for the American Maize Company and was coming off the night shift at the nearby factory. He was on his way to Hegewisch to pick up his watch from a repair shop before going home to sleep.

He usually enjoyed the walk along the wooded path – a scenic spot with a wide variety of trees, wild prairie rose, raspberry bushes, and scores of migratory water birds – but the morning of Thursday, May 22, would change his feelings about the area forever. As Tony passed a large ditch on his left, he looked down momentarily. Something caught his eye and he looked closer – was that a foot poking out of the drain pipe? He stopped and climbed down to take a closer look. He peered into the pipe and saw a child's body, naked, and lying facedown in the muddy water.

In the distance, Tony could see four railroad workers on a handcar traveling slowly along the tracks in his direction. He climbed up the embankment and waved frantically at them to stop. As the men climbed down, Tony walked toward them, pointing back at the ditch. "Look, there is something in the pipe!" he cried. "There is a pair of feet sticking out!"

As the men pulled the body from the pipe and turned it over, Tony could see immediately that the boy had been murdered. There were three large wounds on his forehead and toward the back of his head, he could see large bruises and swelling. There were also marks on his back, running all the way from his shoulders to his buttocks. But perhaps the strangest thing was the appearance of the boy's face – there were distinctive copper stains around the mouth and chin. The same stains were all over his genitals, too.

As the railroad workers carried the body to a second handcar on the tracks, Paul Korff, a signal repairman for the railroad, looked over the scene. He wondered if the boys clothing was lying nearby. If so, he should gather them up and bring them along. But Korff could see nothing – no shirt or trousers, not even shoes or socks. But he did see something. It was a pair of eyeglasses with tortoiseshell frames. They were lying on the embankment. The men must have dragged them out of the water as they were pulling the corpse from the pipe. Perhaps they belonged to the boy? Korff put them in his pocket and joined the other men at the handcars.

POLICE INVESTIGATORS AT THE CULVERT WHERE BOBBY'S BODY WAS DISCOVERED BY TONY MINKE AND THE RAILROAD WORKERS

Around 10:00 a.m., Sergeant Anton Shapino took charge of the body at the Hegewisch Police Station. Paul Korff handed him the tortoiseshell eyeglasses and Shapino, assuming they belonged to the boy, placed them on the child's forehead.

Later that morning, at the morgue at 1330 South Houston Avenue, undertaker Stanley Olejniczak laid the body out. He also noticed the unusual discoloration on the boy's face and genitals and the damage that had been done to his head.

Whoever this child was, he thought, someone had beaten him violently.

Meanwhile, at the Franks house on Ellis Avenue, the family was waiting anxiously for word from the kidnappers. Jacob had already obtained the $10,000 in old bills and was ready to deliver it to whatever location the kidnappers demanded. They expected the ransom instructions by 1:00 p.m. but the hour passed. Another hour passed. The telephone didn't ring. Jacob sat in an armchair and stared out the window at the street outside. His wife sat by his side, silently weeping.

Samuel Ettelson stayed in the library answering calls and talking with visitors. Ettelson was annoyed that the press had learned of the kidnapping. He assumed that someone at the telephone company had alerted a reporter after he requested a trace on all the incoming calls to the house. Even as the Franks waited in the living room for a call, he was being badgered by James Mulroy, a reporter for the *Chicago Daily News*, about the body of a boy that had been found early that morning near the Indiana state line. Of course, this was not Bobby. Mulroy had said the boy was found wearing eyeglasses and Bobby had never worn eyeglasses in his life.

But Ettelson had to be sure. He contacted Edwin Gresham -- the brother of Flora Franks and Bobby's uncle – and asked him to go down to the morgue with the reporter and take a look at the body. And if, by some chance, it really was Bobby at the morgue, he should telephone the house and say only one word – "Yes" – over the line; nothing more. There was a telephone extension in the living room and Ettelson did not want Flora to overhear the news of her son's death.

The telephone rang 30 minutes later. Ettelson picked up the receiver and he recognized Gresham's voice. "Yes," the man choked out. The line went dead and Ettelson placed the receiver back in its cradle with shaking hands. He walked into the living room. Flora had left the room, but Jacob was still sitting in the armchair, staring at the street outside. He looked exhausted.

Ettelson leaned over and whispered in his friend's ear that Bobby was dead.

Jacob looked up into Samuel's eyes. "What do you mean?" he gasped.

"That your boy is dead."

At that moment, the telephone rang. Ettelson picked up the receiver.

"Hello, is Mr. Franks in?" asked the voice at the other end of the line.

"Who wants him?"

"Mr. Johnson wants him."

"Who is that?"

"George Johnson."

"Just a minute," Ettelson replied and as he passed the telephone to Jacob, he whispered that it was the kidnapper. Jacob was still in a daze. He was still stunned by the news that his beloved Bobby was dead. "Yes?" he mumbled into the receiver.

"This is George Johnson speaking. There will be a Yellow cab at your door in 10 minutes. Get into it and proceed immediately to the drug store at 1463 East 63rd Street."

"Couldn't I have a little more time?"

"No sir, you can't have any more time. You must go immediately."

Ettelson didn't know what to do. Edwin Gresham said that Bobby was dead. Why was the kidnapper still looking for the ransom money? Could Bobby still be alive? The Yellow Cab soon arrived, waiting in the street with its engine running. Jacob was exhausted – he hadn't slept in more than 36 hours -- and couldn't remember the address of the drug store, only that it was on 63rd Street. Ettelson pleaded with him to recall the location of the drugstore but it was no use. Jacob was confused, shocked, and sad – it was simply gone from his mind. He sat back down in the armchair. He wasn't going to be delivering any ransom money today.

Ettelson paid off the cab driver and stood on the sidewalk and watched it drive away. Had they missed their only chance to rescue Bobby? No, it was too late, he knew. Bobby was already dead.

Word of the kidnapping and murder quickly spread. The newspapers began putting "extra" editions on the street, alerting the public to the gruesome crime. Morgan Collins, the chief of the Chicago Police Department, promised that he would commit all his resources to tracking down the killers. Collins undoubtedly exaggerated when he described the killing as "one of the most brutal murders with which we have had to deal. Never before have we come in contact with such cold-blooded and willful taking of life," but people were genuinely outraged. It shocked the entire city.

In the early morning hours of Friday, May 23, the police began rounding up the first suspects – teachers at Bobby's school. Walter Wilson, math teacher; Mott Kirk Mitchell, English teacher; and Richard Williams, athletics coach, were dragged out of bed and taken to the Wabash Avenue Station. Over the next two days, the police also brought in chemistry teacher Fred Alwood; George Vaubel, the physical education instructor; Charles Pence, school principal; and Edna Plata, the French teacher.

The reasoning behind the rounding up of teachers was simple – they had access to the boy, they knew Jacob Franks was wealthy, and, most tellingly, because the ransom note had been so well-written and without mistakes. Only an educated person could have written it, detectives reasoned. Hugh Sutton, an expert with the Royal Typewriter Company, thought the kidnappers had used an Underwood Portable Typewriter, less than three years old, and the typist had used two fingers to compose the letter. "The person who wrote this letter," he stated, "never learned the touch system. The touch system strikes the keys pretty evenly, with an even pressure on the keys. The man who wrote this was a novice at typing. Some of the letters were punched so hard they were almost driven through the paper, while others were struck lightly or uncertainly." Jacob's name had been printed by hand on the envelope in block letters. Handwriting experts determined the letters displayed a uniform slant and regular spacing character. It was obviously the penmanship of a capable writer.

In other words, the police surmised, it must be a teacher.

It wasn't, but it took detectives some time to figure that out. Some of the faculty were grilled harder than others. For instance, Walter Wilson was unmarried and had no girlfriend. He'd also shown an unusual interest in the Franks children. Several months earlier, he had taken Bobby and his younger brother, Jacob, Jr., on an excursion to Riverside Park and had not returned with the boys until almost 1:00 a.m. Could he be a pedophile?

Both Richard Williams and Mott Kirk Mitchell were held in police cells for five hours that Friday. Officers beat both men with rubber hoses, trying to get them to confess. Detectives had searched Williams's apartment and found four bottles of brown liquid. Could it be what had stained Bobby's face and genitals? Williams protested his innocence. The liquid was nothing more than a liniment that he used on the boys' muscles when they became sore after strenuous exercise. But it did him no good to explain – he remained a suspect.

It was learned that Mott Kirk Mitchell had a semiannual mortgage payment due on the day of the kidnapping and when it was discovered the amount of the payment was exactly $10,000, the police were sure they had their man. The police searched the sewers around Mitchell's house for Bobby's clothing but found nothing. Mitchell insisted that he was innocent.

Fortunately for the teachers, they all had solid alibis for the night of Bobby's disappearance. Mitchell's neighbors had seen him working in his garden at the time of the kidnapping. Richard Williams had had dinner at the Delphi Restaurant and Walter Williams's landlady stated that he had been home all evening. Friends, acquaintances, and neighbors said that it was impossible that any of them could have killed Bobby – there were kind, considerate, and upstanding gentlemen.

ROBERT CROWE, COOK COUNTY STATE'S ATTORNEY, WHO LED THE INVESTIGATION INTO BOBBY'S MURDER

But Robert Crowe, the Cook County State's Attorney, was still suspicious. Even though there was no evidence linking any of the teachers to the crime, he refused to order their release. The police held the suspects for four days, beating them regularly, and yet had been unable to force a confession. Finally, the men's lawyers had filed a petition for a writ of habeas corpus on Monday, May 26, alleging police brutality. There was no justification, they said, for their clients' continued detention. Against the pleadings – and even sly suggestions – of Robert Crowe, Judge Frederic Robert DeYoung ordered their release.

Samuel Ettelson was furious about the teachers' release, believing that the killer was among them. In a rare display of anger, he was quoted by Chicago newspapers as condemning the release – he asserted that at least two of the teachers had plotted to kidnap Bobby. "One instructor at the Harvard School killed Robert Franks," he claimed. "Another wrote the polished letter demanding

$10,000 from the family. The instructor who wrote the letter was a cultured man – a man with perverted tendencies – the man who committed the actual crime is a man who needed money and had mercenary motives."

Ettelson's anger was also being felt by police officials. One week after the murder, they had several clues, plenty of theories, dozens of leads, but no arrests. Then, they discovered they had a witness to the kidnapping – just after 5:00 p.m. on Wednesday afternoon, Irving Hartman, 10, a student at the Harvard School, had been walking behind Bobby on Ellis Avenue. Irving had looked away at some flowers in a yard and when he glanced back up, Bobby was gone. At that moment, Irving told detectives, a gray Winton automobile was pulling away from the curb where he had last seen Bobby.

Phillip van Devoorde, a driver for the Fay family, had also seen a gray Winton, spattered with mud, outside Harvard School on May 20, the day before the kidnapping. The driver provided a more detailed description of the car – it was a 1919 model with a gray-black top; the driver was 25-30-years old; a second man was in the passenger seat with a red face, pointed nose, and tan cap. He had also seen the same car standing near the front entrance to the school on Wednesday, around 5:00 p.m. – almost exactly at the time of the kidnapping.

When word got out, sightings of gray Wintons began pouring into police headquarters. One witness spotted a gray Winton near Wolf Lake on Wednesday evening around 8:00 p.m. A man had been behind the steering wheel and a woman had been in the passenger seat. In the back? They swore there was a large bundle that might have been a human form. A tax assessor named William Lucht said that he had seen a Winton with two bundles in the back seat near Cottage Grove Avenue and 67th Street on Wednesday evening. Stanley Milner had seen a gray Winton on Lake Park Avenue and 48th Street. Frederick Eckstein, a watchman, had noticed a gray touring car – "old and decrepit looking" – near Wolf Lake.

State's Attorney Crowe took each sighting seriously. Irving Hartman had no reason to lie about what he'd seen. Besides, the Winton was not a popular model and it wouldn't be difficult to track down every Winton owner in the city. It was a distinctive car with a boxy appearance and an elongated hood that made it instantly recognizable.

Anyone with a Winton found himself liable to be arrested on sight. Two days after learning of Irving's account, the police picked up Adolph Papritz, a draftsman for Armour and Company, because he owned a gray Winton. He was eventually cleared, but not before the newspapers had concluded that he was probably the killer. Papritz was understanding, though. When he was released, he told reporters, "I expected it. Everybody with a gray car is being taken in."

Joe Klon was unlucky enough to not only drive a gray Winton – he wore tortoiseshell glasses, too. After a dozen or so people turned him into the police, he started leaving his car in the garage and walking to work. Klon told newspapers, "This has got to stop somewhere. I'm going to have my car painted black. I've got to wear glasses to see, but I'm going to do away with these tortoiseshell rims. This is the third time that I've been arrested for murder in as many days."

The strategy of advertising the clues in the case brought in hundreds of leads – all of which led nowhere. Detectives searched out gray Wintons in every part of the city, hauling in their owners for questioning, and interviewing countless mechanics at car repair shops. Not a single gray Winton could be linked to the murder.

Irving Hartman's eyewitness account, Crowe eventually realized, had been mistaken.

The investigation shifted to try and understand the killer's motive. Chief Collins was convinced that this might lead detectives to the murderer. But why had Bobby been killed? No one seemed to be able to agree on a reason.

Could it have been for revenge against his father for a business deal that went bad? Jacob Franks had a reputation as an honest businessman, but it was difficult to believe that in his long career as a pawnbroker that he might not have crossed some vengeful gambler, thief, or pimp. In fact, Bobby's death had sparked a flood of hateful letters to the Franks household. One anonymous writer promised to "strangle you to death. You shall suffer minute by minute, you lowdown skunk." The letter concluded with a threat to kill Jacob's daughter, Josephine. The threats might have been the work of cranks, but they could not be taken lightly. Could his other children be at risk? No one was prepared to ignore the possibility that someone was planning a second kidnapping or attack against the family. Because of this, a police guard, made up of eight rotating officers, was set up around the Franks house.

Had Bobby been taken by a child molester? Publicly, coroner's physician Joseph Springer claimed that "young Franks had not been the victim of a pervert." However, in his final report, Springer hinted that someone may have raped the boy, based on damage to his rectum. Chicago had no shortage of pedophiles. Perhaps the abductor had molested Bobby and, fearing identification by the boy, decided to kill him.

But why the elaborate kidnapping hoax? Would a kidnapper interested in sexually abusing a young boy also telephone the boy's parents, arrange for a cab to arrive at the Franks house, and mail a letter asking for ransom? That was possible, of course, but in the opinion of state's attorney Robert Crowe, it was very unlikely.

Crowe believed the murder was a consequence of a ransom demand gone awry. The kidnappers had lured Bobby into an automobile – did he know his abductors? – perhaps with one of them hiding the boy in a remote location while the second kidnapper stayed in the city to telephone the parents and mail the letter. Bobby probably recognized the first captor, who had killed him not long after the kidnapping. The second man, unaware that their victim was dead, had proceeded with their plan.

Crowe suggested that cocaine addicts, in the employ of a criminal mastermind, had abducted Bobby Franks. It should be noted that there was absolutely no evidence to support this wild conjecture, but Crowe didn't care. He knew that by linking illegal drugs to the murder, he could legitimately call on outside assistance in the investigation. If the detectives of the Chicago Police Department were not up to the task, perhaps federal agents from the Bureau of Investigation could find the culprits. As he told a reporter, "We shall, by the process of elimination, try to find some one user of drugs who was sufficiently well acquainted with the habits and movements of the Franks family to have contrived a kidnapping plot – dope will be found at the bottom of it all."

It was ridiculous, but the police had nothing else to go on at that point. They didn't realize yet that the entire case would be broken by one innocuous item -- a pair of eyeglasses.

On Monday, May 26, the Franks family held a funeral service for Bobby at their home on Ellis Avenue. It would have been impossible for the service to have taken place at a public location because the crowds would have been too large. The entire thing would have become a circus. Every day since the kidnapping, hundreds of curiosity-seekers had milled around outside their house, gawking at the locked door and drawn curtains, hoping to catch a glimpse of a mourning family member.

On that morning, a select group of people – members of the family, 20 of Bobby's classmates, and a few close friends – gathered around a white casket in the library for the service. Flowers crowded the room and surrounded the coffin. The Lord's Prayer was offered, followed by a reading of the Twenty-Third Psalm, and other passages from the scriptures. Two hymns were sung and then the mourners moved silently and slowly toward the front door, where black limousines waited to take them to Rosehill Cemetery, on the city's North Side. Eight boys carried the casket to the hearse, while other boys from the Harvard School followed somberly behind.

There was now a crowd of 300 people waiting in the street. The family slipped out of a side door with a police escort to escape the photographers. Chief Collins had sent a large contingent of police to maintain order and there were no disturbances. At Rosehill Cemetery, prayers were offered, and Bobby Franks was laid to rest in the family mausoleum.

But, as we will later see, he would now rest there in peace.

BOBBY'S CASKET, CARRIED BY FRIENDS FROM SCHOOL, LEFT THE FRANKS HOUSE FOR ROSEHILL CEMETERY

The police investigation had come to a halt. Detectives had been unable to connect Bobby to anyone with a gray Winton like the one seen by Irving Hartman. There was no evidence to link any of the teachers from Harvard School to the kidnapping. They had been unable to identify the person who had written the ransom note.

There was only one clue left, which no one had bothered to pursue – those tortoiseshell eyeglasses that Paul Korff had found at the murder scene. It took more than a week, but the police finally realized that the eyeglasses were a valuable clue – and likely the only way to track down the killer. The lenses in the tortoiseshell frames could have only been obtained by prescription; they had not been purchased over the counter. Somewhere, there was an optician who had ground the glasses and that optician had a copy of the prescription in his files.

And if he had the prescription, then he had the name of the person who wore them.

Unfortunately, though, the prescription was a common one. It was given to "persons suffering from simple astigmatism or astigmatic farsightedness." The lenses were of a convex cylindrical type, which was also common. The prescription alone wasn't going to get them anywhere – there were thousands of Chicagoans with such glasses – but the frames turned out to be unusual. Composed of Newport zylonite, an artificial composite, the frames had distinctive rivet hinges and square corners. No firm in Chicago – or anywhere in the Midwest – manufactured Newport zylonite frames. They originated in Brooklyn, and only one optician in Chicago sold such frames: Almer Coe and Company. The owner of the firm recognized the glasses immediately. "We identified them as of a type sold by us and not by any other Chicago dealer. The lenses had markings used by us, and as far as we know, not used by any other optician in Chicago. The lenses are not unusual; such prescriptions are often filled by us, possibly once a week. They are lenses for eye-strain or headache and would not materially improve vision. They might be used only for reading or for what is known as mild astigmatism. Their measurements are average in every way."

This seemed to be disheartening news, until detectives found out just how few of the tortoiseshell frames had been sold in the city. On Thursday, May 29, clerks at Almer Coe began the task of checking to see how many customers had purchased those particular frames, with that particular prescription. The number was shockingly low -- only three pair of glasses with such unusual frames had been sold. One pair belonged to an attorney, who was away in Europe, the other to a woman, and the third pair had been sold to a young man who lived in the Kenwood neighborhood on the South Side.

THE EYEGLASSES FOUND AT THE WOLF LAKE CULVERT, NEAR BOBBY'S BODY. THEY WOULD BE THE CLUE THAT FINALLY LED TO HIS KILLERS.

State's attorney Robert Crowe finally felt they were gaining ground in the investigation.

That afternoon, police officers knocked on the door of Nathan Leopold, Jr., a 19-year-old law student at the University of Chicago. He was taken into custody, but it seemed to be nothing more than for routine questioning. The reporters following the Franks case were only mildly curious. Leopold's father was one of the wealthiest Jewish businessmen in the city and the family was socially prominent with influential connections. Nathan himself was a brilliant student who had recently applied to transfer to the law school at Harvard University.

Nathan Leopold obviously had nothing to do with the murder of Bobby Franks, they thought and returned to chasing other leads.

That afternoon was not the first time that the police had spoken to Nathan in the wake of Bobby's murder. A few days earlier, on Sunday afternoon, he had spent two hours answering routine questions about Wolf Lake and the surrounding area. He had often conducted ornithology classes near the Pennsylvania Railroad tracks and had frequently taken boys from the Harvard School to the lake, as well as boys and girls from University High School.

The police had no reason to suspect him of anything and it quickly became apparent that their questions truly were routine. But Nathan had no time for distractions. He had decided to apply to Harvard University law school and that week, he was taking his entrance exams. He needed to concentrate, so he was particularly annoyed when the police returned to his family home at 4754 Greenwood Avenue with more irritating questions.

A maid answered Detective Frank Johnson's knock at the door and he waited with other officers for several minutes until Nathan came downstairs. As Johnson introduced himself, he noticed Nathan's irritation. He demanded to see the police officers' identification. Johnson bristled at the arrogance in the young man's voice.

After showing Nathan his badge and reciting his credentials again, he told Nathan that he was wanted at the state's attorney's office to answer some more questions. As the boy turned to get his jacket, Detective Johnson asked a quick question in an off-handed way, "By the way, do you wear glasses?"

"Yes."

"Did you lose your glasses?"

"No, they are around here someplace."

But Johnson didn't ask him to produce them. He was in a hurry. Robert Crowe had ordered him to bring Nathan to the Hotel LaSalle – not the state's attorney's office – in the downtown business district. Crowe was being cautious. Even though detectives had discovered that Leopold was one of the only people on the optician's list who owned eyeglasses like those found at the scene that hadn't been checked out, he could not link him otherwise to the murder of Bobby Franks. He had little desire to pull the Leopold family into the investigation without a good reason. If Nathan suddenly appeared at the Criminal Courts Building, reporters were bound to speculate. So, Crowe decided to meet with him in secret and give him a chance to provide an explanation as to how his eyeglasses could have been found near a corpse.

The meeting was short. Nathan said that he did have a pair of glasses like the ones that had been found, but that his were in the pocket of his coat at home. He could prove it if detectives wanted to take him home. When he arrived there, he made a show of searching for the glasses, but he now knew that the state's attorney had one piece of evidence linking him to the murder of Bobby Frank – a murder that he had helped commit.

From that point on, the questioning of Nathan Leopold was no longer casual. The police searched his bedroom and study. They turned up two items. Neither of them connected him to the murder, but both the gun – a Remington .32-caliber automatic – and a letter from Nathan to a second boy, Richard Loeb, were unusual and unexpected. Nathan had no permit for the handgun, which made it illegal, but it was the letter that was the real puzzle.

As Robert Crowe read it over, he could discern that the two boys had quarreled – Nathan accused Richard of treachery and threatened to kill him but then wrote that he wanted to continue their friendship. The letter was alternately pleading, aggressive, and submissive. Nathan was angry with Richard and yet desperate that they remain friends. If Richard broke off their friendship, Nathan concluded, "extreme care must be used. The motif of falling out of cocksuckers would be sure to be popular, which is patently undesirable, and forms an unknown but unavoidable bond between us." There was no clue in the letter to say why Richard and Nathan had argued, but it was evident that the boys were lovers who'd had a fight.

Crowe decided to bring Nathan in to the Criminal Courts Building and now he wanted to talk to Richard Loeb. It was unlikely that the second boy – also the son of a wealthy and prominent Chicago businessman – knew anything about the murder, but Crowe could use Richard to get information about Nathan. Crowe had experience with this kind of blackmail – one hint that he would reveal Richard's homosexual secrets and the boy would be willing to talk.

Crowe began hammering questions at Nathan Leopold in the interrogation room. It went on for hours, but he could not discover anything that he could use to link the young man to the murder. He demanded to know how Nathan's glasses had ended up near Bobby's body. Nathan had a quick answer to that – he had been birdwatching at Wolf Lake on the Sunday before the murder and he must have lost them then. He must have been walking right near the drain pipe where the "real killer" had placed the body.

Nathan told his story in a breezy, confident manner, calmly smoking a cigarette as he spoke. But when Crowe insisted that he place the eyeglasses in the coat pocket that he claimed that he'd been carrying them in, and then bend over to see if they'd fall out, he became flustered. He repeated the motion – which he claimed had caused the glasses to become lost – but they stayed securely in place.

But it didn't matter – he had an alibi for that day: Richard Loeb. They had been together all day and had dinner at the Cocoanut Grove Restaurant around the time of the murder, did some drinking, and then went looking for girls to pick up. After finding a couple of young ladies, they drove down Garfield Avenue, almost to Western Avenue, and then went to Jackson Park. They parked for a while east of the Wooded Island, but when the girls "wouldn't come across," the boys asked them to leave. A little later, they drove home.

As Nathan was presenting this alibi to Crowe, Richard Loeb was in an office in the Criminal Courts Building, telling the same alibi to one of Crowe's assistants. The alibis offered by the two young men corroborated each other exactly. Richard also told the tale of the two girls – he recalled their names as May and Edna – and, like Nathan, recounted how he and his friend made them walk home after the girls refused to have sex with them.

Yet the alibi only made Crowe more suspicious. Crowe had not yet told Nathan that one of his detectives had found the latter that indicated that both boys were homosexuals. Why would they spend an evening trying to have sex with two girls?

The state's attorney spent the entire night and into the next morning questioning Nathan, but the boy had still shown no signs of guilt. Richard Loeb was now in an adjacent room. Crowe decided to keep them both in custody, but everyone needed some sleep. He placed Nathan in a cell in the central police station and took Richard to the 48th Street Station.

While the boys slept in their cells on Friday, May 30, the press began to realize that Robert Crowe might have caught the murderers. Reporters from every newspaper descended on the Kenwood neighborhood to try and speak to the parents of Nathan Leopold and Richard Loeb. Of course, both families dismissed the idea that either boy could be involved with murder – they were certain they'd soon be released. It was all a terrible mistake that would soon be corrected. Both families even pledged to assist the state's attorney in any way that they could, even allowing the boys to be held without charges so that the matter could be completely cleared up.

Robert Crowe couldn't believe his luck and things were looking better for the case all the time. More evidence appeared that further convinced him of the two boys' guilt. Nathan's handwriting matched the writing on the envelope that contained the ransom letter. Not to mention, his eyeglasses had been found next to the body. The boys had concocted an alibi that could not be confirmed and late on Friday afternoon, tests confirmed that type legal notes that belonged to Nathan matched the typed ransom letter.

He was holding both suspects without any interference from their families, but he knew that, sooner or later, one or both families were going to alert their lawyers to the situation. Knowing this, he had to get the boys to confess before their lawyers ordered their silence. Neither boy had yet asked for a lawyer and neither had refused to answer questions – they just weren't the answers that Crowe wanted. How could he get a confession?

In the end, he had some help. Two young reporters from the *Chicago Daily News* – Alvin Goldstein and James Mulroy, both of whom had been on the story from the beginning – had gone to school with Richard and Nathan and knew them both. They were surprised to find them in police custody but decided to try and match the legal notes that Nathan had written to the typewritten ransom letter. They provided the information about the letter to Crowe and suggested looking for the portable Underwood that he'd used for both the letter and the legal notes. They searched his house but didn't find it. However, one of the Leopold's maids, Elizabeth Sattler, admitted that Nathan did have a portable Underwood and that it had been in the house just a few days before the murder of Bobby Franks.

All along, Nathan's father had been telling the police that his son could not have abducted Bobby and driven him out to Wolf Lake because the family's driver, Sven Englund, had spent the day of the kidnapping working on Nathan's car, fixing his brakes. Englund, when questioned by one of Crowe's assistants, admitted this was true, but he added that Nathan was not home at the time. He had been picked up by a second boy who was driving a green car. They had left together and had not returned that afternoon.

Englund's account had smashed the boy's alibi. Crowe had been interrogating Nathan when the news was brought to him. He stopped talking. He now knew that both boys had been lying to him about their movements on the day of the murder. They both claimed they had been driving around in Nathan's car all day and now Crowe knew the car hadn't moved from the garage.

Crowe had no time to lose. The Leopold family had sent Englund to the Criminal Courts Building with the belief that his story would clear their son. Perhaps even now, Nathan's father was contacting a lawyer to get his son released. If Crowe could get the confession he so desperately needed, he'd have an open and shut case.

With all the new information in hand, he started over with his interrogations. He would play the two of them against each other and get them to talk. But Crowe was exhausted. He wasn't sure how much longer he could continue the questions.

As it happened, Richard Loeb broke first.

One of Crowe's assistants, John Sbarbaro, had remained with Richard while Crowe was in his office gathering materials – and his wits. Nearly a half hour passed and then Crowe heard a sudden bustle in the hallways outside. Sbarbaro had left the room and was hurrying – almost running – toward Crowe's office. The assistant state's attorney was almost out of breath when he opened the door. Loeb wanted to talk to the state's attorney, there was no time to lose.

"Quick, quick," he said, "before the boy changes his mind!"

Richard told Crowe everything. He said that the murder was a lark, an experiment in crime to see if the "perfect murder" could be carried out. He then denied being the killer and claimed that he had driven the car while Leopold had beaten and slashed Bobby Franks to death.

When his turn came, Nathan refuted this. It was Richard who killed Bobby.

Finally, the boys were brought together and admitted the truth. Loeb had been the killer, Leopold had driven the car, but both had planned the crime together -- they were both guilty of Bobby Franks' murder.

The people of Chicago, and the rest of the nation, were stunned. It was fully expected that the two would receive a death sentence for the callous and cold-blooded crime.

It was a "perfect crime" that was not so perfect after all.

NATHAN LEOPOLD

Nathan Leopold, or "Babe" as his friends knew him, was born in 1906. His grandfather, Samuel, had emigrated from Germany to the United States in 1846, settling in northern Michigan. He opened several small retail stores, each one close to the copper mines of the region, and business was good. A few years later, he opened more stores and soon his reach extended across the entire Upper Peninsula. But obtaining supplies to sell to miners and laborers had become a struggle – there was no railroad or adequate shipping lines to connect to Chicago, the closest big city.

Samuel bought his first steamship in 1867 and soon added two more to his small fleet. He moved to Chicago with his wife, Babette, and their six children, invested wisely, and gradually built up his shipping business so that when he died from septicemia in 1898, his Lake Michigan and Lake Superior Transportation Company was the largest shipping line on the Great Lakes.

His oldest son, Nathan, was born in 1860 and proved to be the kind of capable businessman that his father was. He inherited the family business, married his childhood sweetheart, Florence Foreman, bought a large home at 3223 Michigan Avenue, and made a second fortune manufacturing aluminum cans and cardboard boxes. Through his marriage – his father-in-law was financier Gerhart Foreman – he became connected to some of Chicago's wealthiest and most prominent bankers. Within a single generation, the Leopolds had become one of the most successful families in Chicago.

In 1915, Nathan and Florence moved their family – three sons: Michael, Samuel, and Nathan, Jr. – from Michigan Avenue to Kenwood, eight miles south of the Loop. Their new home on Greenwood Avenue was a three-story mansion, stepped back from the street, and was considered one of the most unique homes in the area. It had an enormous rectangular living room, built in a modernist style, facing the garden on three sides. Around that, the architect had built a house in a traditional nineteenth century style, complete with gabled roofs.

The youngest son, Nathan, Jr., was happy to move to Kenwood – or at least as happy as he could manage to be. The boy -- with his sallow complexion, gray eyes, thick black hair, and curiously asymmetrical face that gave him a scheming appearance – had always been a lonely and sorrowful child. For two years, he'd attended the local public school, just a few blocks from the family's Michigan Avenue home. It had been a terrible experience. He often came to the attention of bullies and his classmates taunted and teased him relentlessly. He knew he was different. He was shy and studious and had little interest in sports. His parents were wealthy and each afternoon, at the end of the school day, his governess embarrassed him by appearing at the school gate to walk him home. And when his classmates discovered that Nathan had briefly attended an all-girls school at age six, the humiliation was complete.

Nathan felt that he had no one to turn to for help. His father was distant and aloof. His mother was bedridden after contracting some mysterious illness during her pregnancy with Nathan. His brothers were older by several years and they were not close. So, he turned to his governess, Mathilda Wantz, who had been hired in 1911. She was an attractive, strong-willed German woman with a heavy accent and a flirtatious manner. She quickly became a strong presence in the house and a substitute mother for the boys, especially Nathan. Florence loved her children – with special regard for Nathan, a weak, frail boy – but her illness forced her to give up control of the household to the governess.

It wasn't long before the maids were gossiping about Mathilda's scandalous behavior. It became common knowledge that she was having sex with Samuel, 17, and even with Nathan, who was only 12. Nathan was smitten with the governess and welcomed her affections. "I was thoroughly devoted to her," he later said.

Regardless of what was happening at home, Nathan was excelling at his new school. After the family had moved to Kenwood, his father had enrolled him at the Harvard School, located at 47th Street and Ellis Avenue. The building was unremarkable-looking but the teachers were, without exception, conscientious and hardworking, devoted to the students, and determined that each boy should, if he desired, attend an excellent college.

Fewer than 200 boys attended Harvard School. The primary school included eight grades, with approximately 15 boys in each grade. The high school was made up of four classes, ranging from freshmen to seniors. The school emphasized academic excellence and the size of the classes enabled the teachers to give each boy individual attention. Occasionally, a boy might graduate and go directly into his father's business, but more typically, every member of the graduating class went on to college. Most alumni went to the University of Chicago or to an elite private institution like Yale, Cornell, or Dartmouth.

The classes at Harvard School were too small to support sports teams and that was fine with Nathan – he was indifferent to that kind of activity. He loved the classwork. In addition to his assigned course, he took electives in German and classical Greek, and each year, he earned the standing of top in his class. He was still an outsider –his classmates regarded him as an eccentric loner – but by junior year, he had won a few friends who shared his interest in ornithology. He had a passion for collecting birds and kept his collection in a study that adjoined his bedroom. He had over 2,000 specimens. On weekends, he went to the Wolf Lake, southeast of the city near the Indiana state line, to hunt for new species for the collection.

By the spring of 1920, Nathan, 15, was a junior at Harvard School, but had come to the conclusion that he had no more to learn from his teachers. He had accumulated enough credits to skip his senior year and go straight to the University of Chicago. He was excited about the challenge and plans were made for him to enter the university's freshmen class.

But that summer, in June 1920, Nathan made a new acquaintance, an impossibly good-looking young man with brown-blond hair, blue eyes, and a ready smile.

His name was Richard Loeb.

RICHARD LOEB

Like his new friend, Richard also came from a wealthy, well-connected family. His father, Albert, was the vice president of Sears and Roebuck and a close friend of millionaire philanthropist Julius Rosenwald. Richard's mother, Anna, was an important member of the Chicago Women's Club and an associate of Jane Addams, founder of the settlement house movement in the city. His uncle, Jacob, was a lawyer in private practice in 1920 but had once been president of the Chicago Board of Education. He had been responsible – most notoriously – for the "Loeb Rule," which prevented teachers in public schools from going on strike.

Albert Loeb had begun his career as a lawyer. He had been admitted to the Illinois bar in 1889 and worked for the firm of Loeb and Adler for 12 years. In 1901, he had accepted Julius Rosenwald's invitation to work for Sears and Roebuck and, within a decade, became vice president of the company. As the business expanded in the early part of the century, Albert accumulated a personal fortune of more than $10 million. He and Anna had four sons – Allan, who lived in Seattle and managed Sears and Roebuck on the west coast; Ernest, a student at Vanderbilt University; Thomas, who was in the eighth grade at the Harvard School; and Richard, who at 15 had just completed his freshmen year at the University of Chicago.

Richard had always been the smartest member of the family. At an early age, he had been encouraged by his governess, Emily Struthers, to read widely in history and literature. She introduced him to everything from the novels of Charles Dickens to the adventure stories of Ernest Thompson Seton. Historical novels, based loosely on actual events, were all the rage in America in the early 1900s and Richard became caught up in the craze, listing books like *Ben-Hur* and *Quo Vadis* as his favorites. Emily was ambitious for her young charge, imagining that he might grow up to be an ambassador or diplomat. She encouraged the literary classics but also made sure he read serious historical works, as well.

Richard was a dutiful student and always read the books that Emily picked out for him. But he never divulged his true obsession, which was for crime and mystery stories. He had discovered a copy of Frank Packard's thriller *The Beloved Traitor* among his brother's books. Alone in his bedroom, he spent hours reading about a famous criminal who could get out of almost any complex or dangerous situation. He became enthralled by such adventures – the more intricate the story, the better. He read every kind of mystery story that he could find, from Sir Arthur Conan Doyle's stories of Sherlock Holmes to books by Maurice Leblanc, Wyndham Martin, and more.

In October 1917, just three months past his twelfth birthday, Richard entered the freshmen class at University High School, which was adjacent to the University of Chicago. The school had been created by John Dewey as a way to overturn the traditional methods of teaching. There was no rote learning or memorization. It was a new idea that was meant to encourage innovation, initiative, and experimentation. Dewey believed that students should be educated in the way that best prepared them for daily life, so students at University High were expected to solve practical problems creatively and in cooperation with their classmates.

Thanks to this, the first two decades of University High were filled with creative activity both inside and outside the classroom. The University of Chicago took special pride in the high school and offered resources and financial support to make it successful. In 1917, there were 500 boys and girls enrolled at University High. Many of them were sons and daughters of university professors.

Extracurricular activities flourished at the school. There was a jazz band, symphony orchestra, Glee Club, Sketch Club, Discussion Club, and Engineering Club. Each class organized a Literary Society that met for readings, debates, and music recitals. There were three academic honor societies: Kanyaratna (for girls), Triplee (for boys), and Phi Beta Sigma, which was for any pupils with outstanding academic records. Boys from all four classes joined the Boy's Club and the girls organized the Girl's Club as a counterpart. The students organized three publications: *The Midway*, a literary magazine that was published every two weeks; *The Correlator*, the school's yearbook; and *University High School Daily*, a four-page newspaper that appeared every day but Monday during the school term. There were also sports teams – football, soccer, and baseball for the boys and basketball for both boys and girls.

Richard was excited about his entrance to the school. His older brother, Ernest, was a senior and captain of the soccer team and would provide guidance if Richard needed it. But he didn't believe he did. He was outgoing, easy to get along with, and made friends easily. He had no particular talents that set him apart from his classmates – he was not inclined toward sports and played no musical instruments – but he was likable and engaging and soon became popular.

He joined the Discussion Club and the Engineering Club, two groups that recruited members from all four classes. Predictably, the upperclassmen dominated the affairs of both groups and Richard attended the meetings sporadically during his freshmen year and said very little. His reserved his enthusiasm for the meetings of the Freshmen Literary Society and threw himself into it wholeheartedly. There was rarely a meeting that went by without his contributions. He was an excitable presence, always volunteering his thoughts and remarks, and, perhaps for this reason, it was such a cruel disappointment when he narrowly lost the election for Freshmen Literary Club president to Henry Abt.

His election loss was the sole blemish on an otherwise successful year. Everyone liked Richard – he was one of the most popular boys in the class. Teachers liked him because he did so well in his studies and participated in class. In January 1918, at the start of the winter term, he was elected as treasurer of the freshmen class and in February, he helped organize the freshmen-sophomore dance. Like everything else he was involved in, it was a huge success.

Richard was doing very well at his new school, but his governess, Emily Struthers, had greater things in mind for him. Emily was an attractive woman in her early thirties with a strong sense of duty. She had moved to Chicago from her native Canada in 1910 and felt fortunate to have found a generous and considerate employer like Albert Loeb. She was determined to repay his trust in her by raising Richard in the best way that she knew. She was neither harsh nor cruel, but she expected to be obeyed.

Richard grew up knowing that he never questioned Emily's commands. While his friends were off playing or fishing in the Jackson Park lagoon, he was reading and studying. Every evening, she sat beside him at his desk while he completed his homework to her satisfaction. Richard's parents were too busy to interfere and trusted Emily to take care of things as she saw fit. She was a kind but domineering presence in the boy's life – one that he grew to resent. As he got older, Emily's close supervision became unbearable and he chafed at the situation. He began lying to Emily in order to avoid her watchfulness.

Richard entered the sophomore class at University High in September 1918. He was only 13-years-old, but Emily had already decided that he should graduate from high school the following summer, two years ahead of his class. It seemed, to Richard's teachers, a nonsensical decision. It served no purpose and, in fact, might be harmful to the boy to carry such an accelerated workload. Richard was smart, they knew, but he was not as exceptional as his guardian believed him to be.

But Emily would not be dissuaded. She always felt that her lack of education was a disadvantage and she resented her inferior status as a governess. She blamed that on her failure to continue her education after high school. She believed that Richard would be a great lawyer or a professor and that would only happen with great effort. So, during his sophomore year, Richard took all the classes that would enable him to graduate in 1919.

During the fall term, Richard attended meetings of the Sophomore Literary Society, occasionally taking part in the activities and debates, but he soon ran out of steam. He was taking too many courses – and had too much work to do – to have time to participate in extracurricular activities. Emily's demands were insistent. It became a struggle to complete his homework each week.

Emily pushed him all throughout this sophomore year. She sat with him every evening while he did his homework, discussed his progress with his teachers, and made sure that all his assignments were completed. Her persistence paid off. Richard graduated from University High in June 1919 – just a few days after his 14th birthday. He had earned all the necessary credits to enroll at the University of Chicago in the fall.

Emily was exuberant, but Richard simply felt drained. His success had come at a heavy price. He resented Emily's insistence that he take so many courses. He was bitter that his parents paid no attention to his complaints. Most of all, he envied his classmates their freedom. He had missed out on everything that had made his freshmen year at University High so enjoyable.

It quickly became apparent that Richard – high school diploma or not – was ill prepared for college. He was 14-years-old when he first attended classes at the university. Most of his classmates were three, four, even five years older than he was. Richard struggled to keep pace with the demands of the college curriculum. He worked hard during his first year – Emily continued to supervise his work – but Richard was a mediocre student and his grades were disappointing. Even in history, his favorite subject, he performed dismally.

It became an inauspicious start to his college career. And Emily, who had played such an important part in Richard's life, left the Loeb household in the summer of 1920 after his parents decided that Richard, now 15, no longer needed a governess. Emily had made some poor decisions, but she had been a constant source of emotional support in Richard's life. Without her steadying presence, Richard, by his own admission, went off the rails. As he later said, "When she left, I sort of broke loose."

It was the same summer that Emily left that Richard became friends with Nathan Leopold, an awkward, self-conscious, shy boy with no self-confidence who had attended Harvard School. Nathan would also begin at the university that fall. Richard had the advantage of already having spent a year at the University of Chicago and the two young men bonded over Richard's explanation of what his new friend could expect in the coming semester.

RICHARD LOEB AND NATHAN LEOPOLD

They became close, despite the vast differences between them. Richard was outgoing and sociable while Nathan was backward and aloof. Richard impressed people with his easy charm, his sense of humor, and pleasant manner. Nathan, who had an air of disdain and arrogance about him, seemed to be exactly the opposite. Almost immediately, those who met him didn't like him.

They seemed, to all appearances, to have nothing in common. Richard, without Emily, now had no reason to devote all his time to his studies. He had hoped to join a fraternity, but none of the Jewish fraternities on campus had taken his pledge because he was too young. Early in his sophomore year, he joined the Campus Club, a social organization for students who hadn't yet pledged a fraternity. Members of the Campus Club copied the rituals and rites of fraternal groups and sponsored dances and events, but it was a poor imitation of the real thing. For Richard, as it turned out, the Campus Club was a bore. He preferred to spend his evenings drinking and gossiping with friends at one of the speakeasies on the South Side – the Granada Café on 65th Street was popular with college students – or picking up girls at the Trianon Ballroom, a dance hall at 62nd Street and Cottage Grove Avenue.

Richard's friendship with Nathan was a puzzle. No one could understand why they were such close friends. They had no shared interests. Nathan never accompanied Richard when he went out drinking or joined him when he was out picking up girls. Nathan just seemed to want to graduate from the university as quickly as possible. He spent all his free time studying. He made such good grades that the university awarded him advanced standing. He was not the best or the most brilliant in his class, but he was hardworking and determined to make his mark.

It had never been easy for Nathan to make friends and he was delighted to have Richard's companionship. There was so much to admire about him. He was friendly, good-looking, and had a sophistication and worldly knowledge that Nathan envied. As Nathan got to know him better during the winter quarter, he began to realize that Richard led a secret life. Perhaps if he had not been so anxious to obtain and keep Richard's friendship, he might have noticed Richard's purposeless, destructive behavior sooner, but he didn't. By the spring of 1921, though, he had fallen in love with Richard. There was now nothing that he wouldn't do for him. So, when Richard devised a plan to cheat at cards, he readily went along with the scheme. It was not for the money – both boys received generous allowances from their fathers – but for the sheer thrill of the experience. There was great pleasure in doing something wrong and, most importantly, getting away with it.

When Richard started suggesting other adventures, Nathan went along with them, even if he did not fully share his friend's enthusiasm. Some evenings, Richard would have too much to drink and would insist that they find some deserted street close to campus, and while Nathan waited in the car, the engine running, Richard would smash the windshields of parked cars with a brick.

But those adventures only whetted Richard's appetite for something more daring. He discovered that the ignition key of his mother's car, a Milburn electric automobile, would fit any Milburn electric. Once he got his hands on a spare key, he started stealing Milburn electrics that were parked on the street. They had some close calls and narrow escapes. Once, an owner spotted Nathan and Richard sitting in his car and chased after them. On another occasion, the police questioned them about a stolen car, but they were never caught in the act.

Richard loved danger – the more dangerous the better – and he always sought to raise the stakes. It was difficult to explain – even to himself – why he felt he needed the rush, but he only knew that he did. Perhaps it was the knowledge that he was breaking the law that gave him a thrill, or perhaps his ability to evade detection, or even simple boredom, but over time, his need for danger escalated.

Richard's fascination with crime stories and pulp mysteries fueled his imagination. In his mind, he was a master criminal who could not be caught. His narcissism was fulfilled because he had an admiring audience in front of whom he could perform – Nathan Leopold. He became a willing partner in whatever scheme his dominating friend came up with.

The planning that went into his misdeeds thrilled and excited him. During his sophomore year at the university, Richard – always accompanied by Nathan – carefully planned his acts of vandalism in advance. On several occasions, he set fires, none of which, however, resulted in a loss of life. He often left his house in the middle of the night to smash storefront windows in Hyde Park and Kenwood. The preparation for such incidents was almost as pleasurable as the acts themselves.

Nathan was a willing participant in whatever Richard wanted to do. He experienced neither excitement nor regret over the vandalism. In all honesty, he was indifferent to the mayhem they created. But his affection for Richard and his desire to be in Richard's company were now so strong that there was nothing he wouldn't do to hold onto his friendship. It meant everything to him. Richard needed him as an accomplice, and if that was what was needed to keep Richard in his life, Nathan willingly agreed to anything he asked for.

But their friendship almost came to an end. Richard was restless at the University of Chicago. During his freshmen and sophomore years, he had lived at home while studying at the university. Now he was about to become a junior and he was anxious to get away from his family. He had friends at the University of Michigan at Ann Arbor, about 300 miles from Chicago. He had visited there for some football games and it made the University of Chicago seem too quiet, too boring. In 1921, he announced to his parents that he intended to transfer to Michigan to finish his degree.

His parents were disinterested but Nathan was devastated. He was about to lose his closest – perhaps his only – friend. In his desperation, Nathan announced that he would also transfer to Michigan. So, in September 1921, they embarked on their next adventure together.

Everything went wrong for Nathan that fall. He came down with scarlet fever shortly before the start of the semester and arrived on campus after classes had already started. In October, his mother, Florence, died, succumbing to the illness that had kept her bedridden for years. Nathan went home to be with his family and remained until Yom Kippur so that he could attend a memorial service for his mother. When he returned to the university, he was stunned to find that Richard no longer cared to continue their friendship.

On October 17, Richard had become a pledge for the Zeta Beta Tau fraternity. Members of the fraternity had warned him that he was being seen too often in the company of Nathan Leopold, a suspected homosexual. This association was sure to ruin his chances for membership, so if he planned to join Zeta Beta Tau, he needed to cut Nathan out of his life.

Nathan was destroyed by the fact that Richard had abandoned him in favor of the fraternity. He led a solitary existence at school. He ate his meals alone and spent most of his time immersed in his studies. He earned good grades but there was little reason for him to remain in Ann Arbor. So, in the fall of 1922, he transferred back to the University of Chicago.

It was the best move that he could have made, and his life might have turned out much differently if he hadn't later come back under Richard's influence. During his final year in college, he began to seek out friends and to develop extracurricular interests. He joined the Il Circolo Italiano, a society devoted to the study of Italian culture, and became one of the group's most enthusiastic members. He also joined the Undergraduate Classical Club, a literary society that organized meetings, dinners and stage productions. He achieved academic excellence, surpassing all expectations in his courses. He distinguished himself by proving worthy of election to Phi Beta Kappa, one of only 15 students from the university to receive the honor in 1923.

It was also during this time that Nathan developed an even greater love for ornithology. In his spare time and on weekends, he would drive to the marshland around Wolf Lake, near the Indiana state line, in pursuit of new bird species to add to his collection. Ornithology had always been a hobby and yet his studies had become so proficient that during his final year at the University of Chicago, he was able to prepare two scientific papers for publication in *The Auk*, the leading journal for professional ornithologists in the United States.

Nathan felt that he had redeemed himself. His stellar academic record during his final year at Chicago, his election to Phi Beta Kappa, his successful graduation – one year ahead of his class – fulfilled the promise that he had made to his mother before her death. He had promised to distinguish himself at the university – and he had. That spring, shortly before graduation, Nathan decided to become an attorney. He planned to enroll at the University of Chicago law school in the fall.

Richard Loeb also graduated in 1923. He left the University of Michigan after doing very little work but still achieving satisfactory work. When he received his degree, he was a few weeks away from his eighteenth birthday, making him the youngest graduate in the history of the school.

His university career had been lackluster. He had never joined any of the student societies or participated in any extracurricular activities. He never tried out for a sports team or volunteered his services for a student publication or joined the debate society or a discussion club. He had attended lectures when he had to but preferred to spend his time hanging around the fraternity house, playing cards, reading mystery novels, and chatting with his friends. He seemed – even to the fraternity brothers who liked him – to have lost the will to do anything with his life. He drank heavily, and he was drunk so often, even in the early afternoon, that it was sometimes difficult to tell when he was sober. His drinking became so bad – and he was so unfocused and eccentric – that he became an embarrassment to the fraternity. In his senior year, the executive committee of the fraternity formally censured him for his drunkenness and suspended his privileges as an upperclassman.

It was a pathetic conclusion to an inglorious college career. He received his degree but had no plans for the future. But Richard had always enjoyed history and so, in September 1923, he returned to the University of Chicago for graduate work, taking a course in American constitutional history during the fall quarter.

Nathan was also at the University of Chicago that fall. He had received his degree earlier in the year but was taking four law courses that fall.

Tragically, it was inevitable that they met again and returned to their toxic relationship.

Within days, Nathan was once again enthralled with Richard. He fell in love a second time and found Richard willing to indulge Nathan's desires. To his friends, Richard boasted of his sexual conquests – claiming to have many girlfriends among the coeds on the Chicago campus – but in truth, he had little interest in sex. This indifference led to his willingness to succumb to Nathan's devotion.

Richard was not immune to Nathan's attention and flattery. It was true that Nathan was annoyingly egotistical – he could spend hours bragging about his supposed accomplishments – and it quickly became tiresome to listen to his untrue boast that he could speak 15 languages. Nathan also, in Richard's opinion, had a tedious obsession with the philosophy of Friederich Nietzsche and would talk endlessly about the mythical "superman" who stood outside the law, beyond any moral code that constrained the actions of ordinary men. Even murder, Nathan claimed, was acceptable for a superman if the deed gave him pleasure.

It was not that Richard had a moral objection to murder. In fact, he had a great contempt for conventional morality. But Nathan was pretentious, always yammering on about his intellectual superiority, sneering at the boring, ordinary people who obeyed laws that he chose to disregard. Were such speeches merely to impress Richard, who never had much use for the law when he was vandalizing cars and stores and setting buildings on fire? Or did he actually believe it?

It didn't matter to Richard. He was glad to see Nathan finally coming around to his way of thinking. There was no pleasure in committing crimes alone. He needed a companion who could appreciate his careful planning and preparation – Nathan's admiration made it all worthwhile.

Richard had been thinking – ever since his return to Chicago in the fall of 1923 – about how to commit the perfect crime. He had vaguely thought of kidnapping a young child, which would involve, of course, a ransom demand as an essential part of the plot. Richard knew that to obtain the ransom and still avoid capture would present a challenge like none he'd faced before.

He couldn't wait to put his plan into action.

The plan took seven months to develop.

The first step took place in November 1923, when they traveled to Ann Arbor, Michigan, to burglarize Richard's former fraternity house. It was supposed to be a lark, with the added challenge that someone might recognize them from their days on campus. But they arrived on the night of one of the biggest football games of the year. The fraternity house was left unguarded and those who remained in the house were sound asleep, having drank too much during the celebration. They stole penknives, watches, several fountain pens, and about $50 from the pockets of garments hanging in the coatroom. It hardly seemed worth the six-hour drive from Chicago to Ann Arbor, but it had been more for the thrill of it than what kind of loot they'd be taking home.

As they made their way downstairs and walked across the living room toward the front door, Nathan noticed a typewriter on a writing desk on one side of the room. It was one of the latest models, a portable Underwood. He picked it up and took it with them.

It would be useful for typing up his notes from the law lectures.

It was on the long drive home from Ann Arbor that the final elements to the "perfect crime" finally came together. Richard's need to escalate their crimes had become more pressing. They had carried out their robbery without a hitch, but he felt

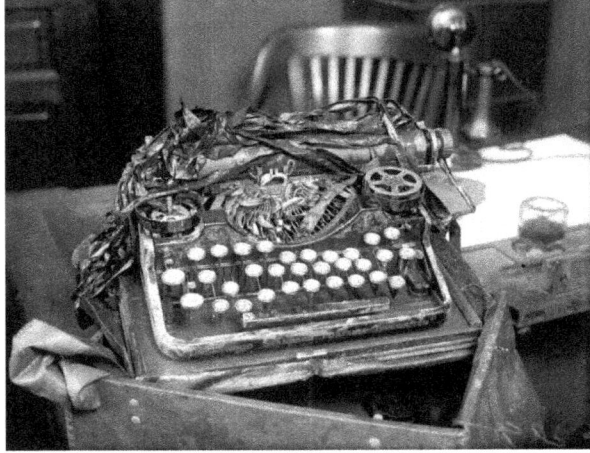

THE UNDERWOOD TYPEWRITER THAT HAD BEEN STOLEN FROM RICHARD'S FRATERNITY HOUSE – AND USED TO WRITE THE RANSOM LETTER. IT WAS LATER RECOVERED FROM A LAGOON IN JACKSON PARK.

unsatisfied. They needed a more complex crime. It should be ambitious – a perfect crime – and one so intricate and complicated that planning and calculating its flawless execution would be a challenge. They would leave behind no clues for the police and no trace of their involvement. It would stand forever as a crime that was impossible to solve.

As Richard outlined his idea for the perfect crime, he grew more excited. They should kidnap a child, he proposed, and to make things more complicated, they would demand a ransom from the child's parents. The money was not important, but it was needed to magnify the seriousness of the crime. They would have to leave directions in order to obtain the ransom, but no clues for the police. They would promise the safe return of the victim, but, of course, that would never happen. They would have to murder the child. It would be foolish to leave open the possibility that their victim might recognize them at a later date.

Would the victim be a boy or a girl? They argued back and forth, going over the benefits of either and then finally decided that they should kidnap a young boy, perhaps one of the students at the Harvard School, someone whose parents were wealthy enough to pay the ransom

It would be a brilliant crime, they mused, one that would shock Chicago with its daring. They would obtain the ransom, dispose of the body, and leave no clues behind. The police would never catch them.

No one would ever know who committed the city's perfect crime.

Christmas and the New Year came and went. After the holidays, the boys picked up their studies again. Nathan resumed his law courses while Richard attended graduate seminars in the history department.

During this time, the details of the kidnapping plan gradually developed. They would lure the boy to their car; render him unconscious, perhaps with chloroform; and drive him to a deserted spot near the Indiana state line. Thanks to his birding expeditions, Nathan knew of a drainage culvert that ran beneath the Pennsylvania Railroad tracks, close to 118th Street and Wolf Lake. It would make the perfect hiding place for the body – no one would find it.

But how to kill the victim so that they could equally share in the death? It would be easy to put a bullet through the boy's head, but in that case, Richard claimed, only the one who pulled the trigger would be the killer. Richard was adamant about the fact that they both had to participate in the murder. If both were guilty, then neither would have the advantage of confessing to the police. They should strangle the victim, each with a hand on one end of the rope.

Both of them needed to be jointly guilty of murder.

In the spring, the details of the plan became clearer. They rehearsed the method by which the ransom would be delivered on April 24. The plan was to telephone the victim's father and send him to a drugstore at 63rd Street and Blackstone Avenue, adjacent to the local train station. He was to wait there for a call, board the train, walk to the rear carriage, and look in the telegraph box for a letter that would instruct him to throw the ransom – securely wrapped in a sealed cigar box – from the train five seconds after passing the distinctive red brick water tower of the Champion Manufacturing Company. They calculated that the package would fall close to 74th Street, where Richard and Nathan would be waiting to grab it and make a quick getaway.

The rehearsal worked perfectly. Nathan, waiting in his car at 74th Street, watched the train travel above him on the elevated tracks. The package landed as expected and Nathan snatched it up and drove away.

It was foolproof! What could possibly go wrong?

The next hurtle to clear was Nathan's car. He drove a very memorable red Willys-Knight sports car, with nickel bumpers and disk wheels. It was much too distinctive to use for the kidnapping. If anyone saw it, they would certainly remember it and the police would have little trouble linking Nathan to the abduction.

They needed to rent a car, but they couldn't do it under their own names. If the rental car was seen, the police would then be able to trace Nathan or Richard through the rental agency records. They would need a false identity to get a car they could use for the crime.

On Wednesday, May 7, Nathan walked into the Hyde Park State Bank and asked a teller about opening a checking account. He didn't live locally, he said, and had no references in the area. He was a traveling salesman from Peoria. Would that be a problem? The teller thought it seemed like an odd request, but he said that it wouldn't and passed him an information card that needed to be filled out. When completed, "Morton D. Ballard" made a $100 cash deposit into his new account.

On that same day, Richard entered the lobby of the Morrison Hotel at Clark and Madison Streets. He carried a suitcase in his hand – which contained four books for the weight – and checked in under the name of "Morton D. Ballard." He was given the key to room 1031 and the bellboy took his bag upstairs to his room for him. An hour later, "Ballard" returned to the desk. He explained that he was a traveling salesman and would only be in Chicago one night but expected to return in a few weeks. There might be mail addressed to him at the hotel – would the desk be able to keep it for him until his return? The clerk was happy to arrange that for him.

Two days later, on May 9, Nathan walked into the office of the Rent-A-Car Company at 1426 Michigan Avenue. He had $400 cash in his pocket, right next to the passbook from the Hyde Park State Bank made out in the name of Morton Ballard.

He explained that he was new to the area – it was the first time that he had covered the Chicago area for his employer – and needed to rent a car. He had a bank account, but since he was a new customer, he was willing to put down a $400 deposit on the rental. He could also provide a reference – the telephone number of his friend, Louis Mason, who would vouch for him.

Two blocks away, Richard entered a lunchroom at 1352 Wabash Avenue, ordered some food, and told the counter clerk that he was expecting a call. The telephone rang a few minutes later – it was a call for Louis Mason. Richard gave a sterling reference for his friend, "Morton Ballard," assuring the Rent-A-Car clerk that he was "absolutely dependable."

The rental agency provided Nathan with the car for the day. He mentioned that he planned to return to Chicago in a couple of weeks and would need a car then. In that case, the clerk replied, the company would mail an identification card to his address – the Morrison Hotel.

They now had a plan for obtaining the ransom without risking capture and had created a false identity with which to obtain a rental car.

They were almost ready.

On Tuesday, May 20 – the day before the kidnapping – they purchased the equipment for the murder. Nathan bought writing paper and envelopes for the ransom note and then went to a drugstore at 4558 Cottage Grove Avenue. He asked the owner, Aaron Adler, for a bottle of hydrochloric acid and a half-pint of ether. The acid, he explained was for experimental work in a science laboratory at the university. He paid 75-cents for the bottle of acid.

Adler handed him the bottle. "Be sure to keep it upright," he cautioned, "because it might leak out and burn your clothes."

That afternoon, Richard completed their purchases, stopping at a hardware store on Cottage Grove Avenue, north of 43rd Street to buy rope and a sharp-edged chisel with a beveled blade and a wooden handle.

The next morning, they met at Nathan's home and wrapped the handle of the chisel with adhesive tape so that it offered a better grip. They also found a blanket and tore some strips of cloth that could be used to wrap up and bind their victim. Nathan placed a pair of wading boots in the car because the boys planned to deposit the body in the swamps near Wolf Lake, located south of the city. He knew the area and feared that they'd need the boots in the swampy spots near the lake.

All they needed to do was to finish writing the ransom note.

There was also one other thing that they'd overlooked – a victim.

So far, they had not agreed on anyone but did feel that their victim should be small, so that he could be easily subdued. They had first considered killing Richard's younger brother, Tommy, but they discarded that idea. It was not because Tommy was a family member but only because it would have been hard for Richard to collect the ransom money without arousing suspicion.

They also considering killing Armand Deutsch, grandson of millionaire philanthropist Julius Rosenwald, but also dismissed this idea because Rosenwald was the president of Sears & Roebuck and Richard's father's immediate boss. They also came close to agreeing to kill their friend, Richard Rubel, who regularly had lunch with them. Rubel was ruled out, not because he was a good friend to them, but because they knew his father was cheap and would never agree to pay the ransom.

They finally made a decision – Johnny Levinson, a 9-year-old boy in the same class at the Harvard School as Richard's brother, Tommy. Johnny's father, Sol Levinson, was one of the wealthiest attorneys in Chicago. He could certainly pay the ransom. Johnny was small enough that he would be easy to handle.

As they traveled to Kenwood, Nathan reminded Richard that directly across the street from the Harvard School, there was an alley that connected Ellis Avenue to a parallel road, Ingleside Avenue. They could park the car on Ingleside, walk along the alley to Ellis, and from the alley, watch the front entrance of the school until Johnny came out.

Nathan waited by the car while Richard walked through the alley to the school. He could see some of the boys were already by the main entrance. Some of the classes had ended already. He continued walking, past the entrance and along the north side of the school, toward the playground in the rear.

Suddenly, Richard saw Johnny, a thin, wiry boy with straight brown hair. He was less than 10 feet from where Richard was standing on the sidewalk. Could he lure him away from his friends? And if so, how could he persuade him to leave the playground and walk with Richard to the car?

Richard started talking to him. The boy had a baseball in his hands. He was waiting on some friends, he explained to Richard, so they could walk over to the lot at 49th Street and Drexel for a pickup game.

THE HARVARD SCHOOL IN KENWOOD, WHERE LEOPOLD AND LOEB FOUND BOBBY FRANKS

Richard left the playground and made his way back over toward the main entrance. His little brother, Tommy, had finished his classes and was standing by the door, talking to another boy.

At that moment, Nathan appeared on the other side of Ellis Avenue, directly across from the main entrance. He whistled for Richard and then waved, urgently trying to draw his attention. There were some children playing on Ingleside Avenue, he told him. Why not take one of them? The street was otherwise deserted. There were no adults around.

No, Richard told him, he had a better plan. Johnny Levinson was on his way to a baseball game. They could go, watch the game, and then snatch him when he left to go home.

But it turned out to be too difficult to watch the game without being seen. They had to be careful. If someone spotted them, and then Johnny was kidnapped, a witness might link them to his disappearance.

While Nathan went home to get his binoculars, Richard stopped at the drugstore at 47th Street and Ellis Avenue. He would find the Levinsons' address in the telephone book. Once they knew the street where Johnny lived, they would know the direction that he would take to get home.

But by the time they arrived back at the lot, Johnny had left the game. They waited to see if he'd return but after a half hour or so, they realized he wasn't coming back.

They spent the rest of the afternoon driving around Kenwood, looking for a victim. Some children were playing near the Leopold house, but that opportunity also disappointed them – the children never left alone but always in small groups.

By now, it was almost 4:30. They had spent two hours in Kenwood, waiting and watching, looking for a child to abduct. Nathan was ready to give up for the day. They could try again tomorrow. But Richard urged him to wait a little longer. They would drive around the neighborhood one more time.

Nathan drove west on 49th Street, turning left onto Drexel Boulevard. Richard sat in the back, behind the front passenger seat. At Hyde Park Boulevard, they turned left again, continuing east for another block. On Ellis Avenue, they turned north, passing the Loeb home. The street seemed deserted. It was almost 5:00 p.m. and the children had undoubtedly made it safely home.

And then they saw Bobby Franks.

He was walking alone on the other side of the street. He was wearing a tan jacket with matching knee trousers, a colored shirt, and a necktie. Richard saw him first and he urgently tapped Nathan on the shoulder. But as Richard looked closer, he realized that he knew the boy. Bobby not only lived directly opposite from Richard on Ellis Avenue, he was also his cousin. Just the day before, he had played tennis with Bobby on the court at the rear of the Franks mansion.

Chosen by chance, he would make the perfect victim for the perfect crime.

Nathan pulled the car up slowly alongside the boy.

"Hey Bob!" Richard called from the rear window.

Richard leaned forward, into the front passenger seat, to open the front door. "Hello, Bob I'll give you a ride."

The boy shook his head – he was almost home. "No, I can walk," he called back.

"Come on in the car. I want to talk to you about the tennis racket you had yesterday. I want to get one for my brother."

Bobby was closer now, standing next to the car. He was so close that Richard could have grabbed him and pulled him inside, but he kept talking, hoping to persuade the boy to get into the front seat on his own.

Finally, Bobby slid into the front seat next to Nathan.

"You know Leopold, don't you?" Richard gestured toward Nathan.

Bobby glanced at him but shook his head. "No," he said.

"You don't mind us taking you around the block?" Nathan asked.

"Certainly not," the boy replied. Bobby turned around in the seat to face Richard and smiled at his cousin with an open, innocent grin. He was happy to see him and was ready to talk about yesterday's tennis game.

The car continued along Ellis Avenue, going the opposite direction from Bobby's house, and Richard reached down to the seat next to him and grabbed hold of the chisel.

At 50th Street, Nathan turned left. As the car made the turn, Bobby looked away from Richard and glanced toward the front of the car.

Richard reached over the seat. He grabbed the boy with his left hand, covering Bobby's mouth so that he couldn't cry out. He brought the sharp-edged chisel down savagely on the back of the boy's skull. He raised his arm and struck again, pounding the chisel with all his strength. But Bobby wouldn't stop fighting. He had now twisted halfway around in his seat, facing Richard, and desperately tried to raise his arms to protect himself from the blows. Richard smashed the chisel down two more times, slamming it into Bobby's forehead, but he struggled for his life.

The fourth blow had opened a large gash in the boy's forehead. Bobby collapsed onto the front seat. Blood from his head wound sprayed everywhere, it showered the seat, splashed onto Nathan's trousers, and spilled onto the floor. Bobby held his hands to his head, curled up in pain on the seat, crying and wailing in pain. His legs were bent under his body, as blood continued to pour out of his head and onto the seat.

When Nathan saw the blood spurting from Bobby's head, he cried out, "Oh God, I didn't know it would be like this!"

Richard ignored him, intent on his horrific task. He reached down and pulled Bobby suddenly upward, up over the front seat into the back of the car. He jammed a rag down the boy's throat, stuffing it as hard as he could, forcing it past Bobby's teeth. He tore off a large strip of tape and slapped it over the boy's mouth. Finally, Bobby's moaning and crying had stopped! Richard relaxed his hold on Bobby and the boy slid off his lap and fell to the floor. A few minutes later, he wrapped him in a heavy blanket.

Bobby continued to bleed for a time and then died on the floorboard of the car.

Nathan kept driving. The car left the city in the direction of Gary, Indiana. A few minutes later, they were in open country. They followed side roads and dirt lanes, aimlessly circling. If they were going to dispose of the body safely, they had to wait until nightfall. There was nothing to do but remain in the car, which was stained with blood.

They both were hungry. They hadn't eaten in hours. They drove the Indiana road, looking for someplace where they could get something to eat. Nathan stopped at the Dew Drop Inn, a roadside convenience store with large billboards on the outside walls offering Cracker Jacks and Coca-Cola. It was ready to close for the night, but Nathan returned to the car with hot dogs and bottles of root beer.

After they ate, Nathan started the car and headed back in the direction of Wolf Lake. By the time they arrived, it would be dark enough to dump Bobby's corpse.

The sun had gone down by the time they reached the culvert near the Pennsylvania Railroad tracks. After pouring acid on Bobby's face and testicles – which did not obliterate his identify as they believed it would and only left a rust-colored stain – they carried the body to the pipe and Nathan tried to shove it inside. He took his coat off to make the work easier. Unknown to the killers, a pair of eyeglasses were in the pocket of Leopold's coat and they fell out into the water when he removed it.

After pushing the body as far into the pipe as he could, Leopold sloshed out of the mud toward the car, where Loeb waited for him. The killers believed that the body would not be found until long after the ransom money had been received. With darkness falling, though, Nathan failed to notice that Bobby's foot was dangling from the end of the culvert.

They drove back to the city and parked the rental car next to a large apartment building. Bobby's blood had soaked through the blanket and had stained the automobile's upholstery. The blanket was hidden in a nearby yard and the boys burned Bobby's clothing at Richard's house. Nathan typed out the Franks' address on the already-prepared ransom note. After this, they hurried back to the car and drove to Indiana, where they buried the shoes that Bobby had worn and everything that he had on him that was made from metal, including his belt buckle and class pin from the prep school.

Finally, their "perfect crime" carried out, they drove back to Nathan's home and spent the rest of the evening drinking and playing cards. Later that night, they made the ransom call to the Franks' house from a public telephone in the Walgreen's drugstore at 47th Street and Woodlawn Avenue.

A woman's voice came on the line and Nathan identified himself as "Mr. Johnson." He told Flora Franks that her son had been kidnapped and that the family could expect a ransom note for his return.

It was finished. There was nothing left for them to do but to play out the rest of the game. They took the bloody blanket to an empty lot, burned it, and then drove to Jackson Park, where Richard tore the keys out of the stolen typewriter. He threw the keys into one lagoon in the park and the typewriter into another.

They placed the second call to the Franks family, instructing Jacob to take the ransom money and go to the drug store near the train tracks. But, of course, Jacob never went. By the time of the second call, Bobby's body had already been discovered in the muddy pipe where they had left it. They were still waiting for the ransom money when the newspapers began putting together their "extra" editions and alerting the public to the tragedy.

The discovery of Bobby's body began one of the largest manhunts in the city's history. The "perfect crime" began to quickly unravel and Nathan and Richard were caught, thanks to a pair of eyeglasses that were dropped at the scene of the crime.

Confronted with evidence of their misdeeds, the two young men of "superior intellect" quickly confessed to the not-so-perfect crime.

In the wake of the confessions, the parents of the two killers turned to Clarence Darrow, America's most famous defense attorney, in hopes that their sons might be saved. For $100,000, Darrow agreed to seek the best possible verdict that he could, which in this case was life in prison. "While the State is trying Loeb and Leopold," Darrow said. "I will try capital punishment."

Darrow would have less trouble with the case than he would with his clients, who constantly clowned around and hammed it up in the courtroom. The newspaper photographers frequently snapped photos of them smirking and laughing in court and the public, already turned against them, became even more hostile toward the "poor little rich boys."

Darrow tried every trick in the book and resorted to shameless tactics during the trial. He declared the boys to be insane. Leopold, he said, was a dangerous schizophrenic. They weren't criminals, he railed, they just couldn't help themselves. After this weighty proclamation, Darrow actually began to weep. The trial became a landmark in criminal law. He offered a detailed description of what would happen to the boys as they were hanged, providing a graphic image of

CLARENCE DARROW (CENTER) WITH HIS INFAMOUS CLIENTS

bodily functions and physical pain. Darrow even turned to the prosecutor and invited him to personally perform the execution.

Darrow's horrifying description had a marked effect on the courtroom and especially on the defendants. Richard was observed to shudder and Nathan got so hysterical that he had to be taken out of the courtroom. Darrow then wept for the defendants, wept for Bobby Franks, and then wept for defendants and victims everywhere. He managed to get the best verdict possible out of the case. The defendants were given life in prison for Bobby Frank's murder and an additional 99 years for his kidnapping.

Ironically, after all of that, Darrow only managed to get $40,000 of his fee from the fathers of the two young men. He got that after a seven-month wait and the threat of a lawsuit.

The verdict was a victory for the defense and a defeat for the state. Guards in the courtroom allowed Nathan and Richard to shake Darrow's hands before escorting them back to their cells. Two dozen reporters crowded around the defense table to hear Darrow's response to the verdict, but he was careful not to sound too pleased. "Well, it's just what we asked for, but it's pretty tough. It's more of a punishment than death would have been." As far as Darrow was concerned, he had defeated capital punishment, which was almost more important to him than saving the lives of the two young killers.

Nathan Leopold, Sr. had already left the courtroom – too overcome to talk to reporters – but Jacob Loeb remained behind to say a few words. "We have been spared the death penalty," he said, "but what have these families to look forward to? Here are two families whose names here stood for everything that was good and reputable in the community. Now what have they to look forward to. Their unfortunate boys, aged 19 years, must spend the rest of their lives in prison. What is there in the future but grief and sorrow, darkness and despair?"

Robert Crowe was furious at the judge's decision, believing that no two defendants deserved the death penalty as much as these two criminals had. It was a bitterly disappointing verdict, and in his statement to the press, Crowe made sure that everyone knew who was to blame: "When the state's attorney arrested the defendants, he solved what was then a mystery. And by the thoroughness of the preparation of the case, the state's attorney forced the defendants to plead guilty, presented a mountain of evidence to the court and made his arguments. The state's attorney's duty was fully performed. He is in no measure responsible for the decision of the court. The responsibility of that decision rests with the judge alone."

The defense had spoken, as had the families of the defendants. The state's attorney had made his excuses for the outcome of the trial, but in all of this, everyone seemed to have forgotten the victim. Had the state found justice for Bobby Franks?

His father spoke to reporters later that day. He was pleased that it was over and happy that there would be no appeal of the verdict. Jacob told reporters, "There can be no hearing in regard to their sanity. There can be no appeal. There can be no more torture by seeing this thing spread over the front pages of the newspapers. It will be easier for Mrs. Franks and for me to be relieved of the terrible strain of all this publicity."

But was it truly over? No -- and not for many years to come.

Neither Richard nor Nathan had ever expressed any remorse for the murder and neither thought to use their final interview with reporters to apologize to Bobby's family – or to anyone else. Nathan, in his cell at the county jail, was his usual arrogant self. He called to Sheriff Peter Hoffman with one final request.

"Go out," he ordered him, "and get us a big meal. Get us two steaks" – he held out his thumb and forefinger --- "that thick."

"Yes, and be sure they are smothered in onions," Richard added. "And bring every side dish you can find. This may be our last good meal."

Nathan still had one more thing, "And bring chocolate eclairs for dessert."

By 8:00 pm, Nathan was fast asleep on his bunk. Richard sat reading on the edge of his bunk, smoking a cigarette, occasionally looking up at the guards patrolling the corridor. Detectives had been stationed in the main lobby of the jail while uniformed police, in addition to the jailers, kept watch on the hallways and corridors. The two convicted killers were set to make a dangerous journey to Joliet Penitentiary the next day.

Feelings about the verdict in their case ran deep in Chicago. People were enraged that two pampered rich boys had gotten away with murder. It seemed every Chicagoan had wanted to see Leopold and Loeb swinging at the end of a rope. It seemed a travesty that Bobby Franks was in his grave while his killers were very much alive, eating chocolate eclairs, and bantering with reporters. The police had been forced to step up security around the jail and to make elaborate preparations for their transportation to the penitentiary.

Fears of an attack proved to be unfounded, though. A three-car convoy – including a Packard limousine, in which Nathan and Richard traveled – made the journey to Joliet. As they approached the high stone walls, they saw a huge crowd outside of the gates. As the cars approached, a roar of recognition went up from the mob. There was no time to waste getting Richard and Nathan into the prison.

The gates clanged shut behind them and the locks turned to shut out the rest of the world. The prison, first opened in 1858, was a forbidding place. Richard stumbled on a paving stone as he stepped out of the car, but quickly caught himself. We'll never know what he was thinking when he looked over the massive walls, metal gates, looming towers, and the prison guards that stared silently down at then with rifles in their arms, but it must have been intimidating.

The warden, John L. Whitman, received their confinement papers from the Cook County sheriff, who turned to leave for the ride back to Chicago. It was 8:30

PRISON PHOTOGRAPHS OF LEOPOLD AND LOEB, TAKEN AFTER THEY
ARRIVED AT JOLIET PENITENTIARY

p.m. and there was no time that night for the customary procedures – photographs, medical history, paperwork – so it all had to wait until morning. Three guards escorted the prisoners across the jail yard and to the isolation block for new prisoners. They had 10 minutes for a shower in the bathhouse and then they received a new set of clothes. Richard discarded his golf sweater and gray flannel trousers and Nathan removed his suit jacket and trousers and they changed into the standard prison uniform of a denim jacket and pants.

They were taken to their cells – Nathan at the east end of the block and Richard, as far away from his as possible, at the other end of the corridor. They were soon fast asleep, and they spent their first night in Joliet peacefully.

It was the first night of many to come.

Time passed, and Nathan and Richard grew accustomed to the daily monotony of prison routine. The guards placed Nathan in a cell in the East Wing of Joliet prison, and mindful that the two murderers be kept as far apart as possible, sent Richard to the other side of the penitentiary. He was locked in a cell in the West Wing.

The prison, after nearly 70 years, was a crumbling wreck. An unhealthy, unpleasant stench permeated the cell blocks, and each individual cell – dank, dark, and claustrophobic – was the worst space that one could imagine. There were no flush toilets and, in the morning, before breakfast, each prisoner carried his waste in a bucket to a large trough in the prison yard. The cells had been designed with windows so narrow that there was little natural light. It was unbearably hot in the summer and freezing in the winter months.

Nathan remained at Joliet prison only until May 1925, when he obtained a transfer to the new prison, Stateville, three miles north of the town of Joliet. The Stateville prion, built in anticipation of the closure of Joliet prison, consisted of four roundhouse buildings, each with an open tower in the center of a large space that was surrounded by a circular arrangement of cells. The guards in the central tower always had a good view of the prisoners in their cells.

Stateville was one of the most modern penitentiaries in the country but there was little discipline within the prison. The Illinois state legislature had provided funds to build the prison but had not provided a decent wage for the guards. As a consequence, corruption was rampant. A convict with money could buy any privilege that he desired, and by the early 1930s, the prison administration was no longer in control of the place. The inmates, as the adage went, truly were running the asylum. A dozen rival gangs competed for control of the prison. Each gang had constructed a motley collection of tar-paper shacks in the prison yard as its headquarters. Within the shacks, the gangs operated whiskey stills, grew marijuana plants, and hired younger and more vulnerable prisoners out as prostitutes.

In March 1931, Richard was also transferred to Stateville. Neither joined one of the many gangs operating behind prison walls, but, thanks to their wealth, they soon gained influence over other prisoners and curried favor with prison officials. They each enjoyed a private cell, books, a desk, a filing cabinet, and even pet birds.

Nathan also managed to ingratiate himself with the prison staff by using his education to the benefit of the clerical office. There were only six people in administrative positions for a prison that held almost 4,000 inmates. Successive wardens recognized his clerical talents as a valuable resource that helped the prison function more efficiently.

Frank Whipp, warden at Stateville in the 1930s, emphasized reform and rehabilitation in the management of the prison. A major purpose of the penitentiary, Whipp believed, was an end to recidivism – meaning that once a prisoner left, he stayed out of prison by not committing more crimes. The sooner that a prisoner demonstrated eligibility for parole, the better. Nathan quickly won his way into Whipp's favor. There was little possibility that Whipp would recommend Nathan's parole, but Nathan adopted the warden's reform ideology and made sure that Whipp knew it. Nathan assisted the prison sociologist in his attempts to determine the suitability of various categories for early release and even published an article – under a pseudonym – on the subject in the *Journal of Criminal Law and Criminology*. Nathan received an appropriate award for these endeavors and, by his own account, soon had the run of the prison.

Richard was less eager to work alongside the prison administration. However, he also won a position of privilege, mostly because of the money at his disposal. Richard kept a permanent deposit of $500 in the prison office. This money, provided by his brothers, was available for his personal use at any time. His parents, unaware that Richard had a private banking arrangement with the prison, sent him an additional $50 each month.

Richard used his money wisely, carefully bribing the prison guards to grant him privileges. He had keys to parts of the prison normally accessible to prisoners at only certain times of the day and on a restricted basis. Richard was one of a small number of prisoners – Nathan was another – allowed to buy whatever he wished from the commissary. He was also allowed to eat in his cell or dine with Nathan in the guard's lounge. It was not even necessary for Richard to wear a prison uniform – he customarily wore a white shirt and flannel trousers.

Richard also used his influence with the guards to pursue sexual favors from other inmates. Convicts who were willing to have sex with Richard might be rewarded with cigarettes, alcohol, a larger cell, or an easier job within the prison. Inmates who fell out of favor with him might find themselves shoveling coal in the yard or laboriously weaving rattan chairs in the furniture shop.

James Day was a 21-year-old serving a one- to ten-year sentence in Stateville for armed robbery when he first met Richard in 1935. Day was a small man – just five feet, six inches and 135 pounds – and had lived an unsettled life. He had never known his father and his mother had died in 1921. He moved to Chicago to live with his aunt and uncle and was constantly in trouble for fighting, theft, and petty crime. He was first arrested as a juvenile in 1928 and sent to the St. Charles School for Boys. He served a second juvenile sentence in the Boy's Reformatory in Pontiac. In 1935, Day graduated to a cell in Stateville.

Richard took an immediate interest in Day's welfare, perhaps seeing someone that he could easily manipulate, as he had done with Nathan. He arranged for guards to move Day to a cell in C House, in the same gallery as his own, and began sending the young man presents of cigarettes and small amounts of money. He also got Day a job in the prison office building and even hinted that he might be able to arrange a parole hearing for him.

It was a calculated scheme on Richard's part to put Day into a dependent position so that he'd agree to have sex with him. Day resisted but Richard was persistent. He reminded Day that he might lose all his privileges if he didn't submit. Wouldn't it be easier, he asked, if he just went along with what Richard wanted?

On the morning of January 28, 1936, George Bliss, a convict in C House, secretly passed a straight razor to James Day. Just after noon, a work detail began its march from the dining hall, the prisoners in a double file line under the supervision of one guard. Day was the last in line, and his column passed through the prison, he slipped away when the guard wasn't looking. Earlier that day, Richard had mentioned that he would be taking a shower at noon, casually suggesting that Day might meet him in the shower room. Richard had a key and could lock the door from the inside, allowing them to meet in private.

Day was in an angry, violent mood. Richard had been harassing him for weeks, demanding sex, and threatening to withdraw his privileges. When he entered the shower room, Richard advanced toward him, probably thinking that his persistence had finally paid off. Instead, Day struck at him with the straight razor, cutting him on the neck and abdomen, inflicting 56 wounds before he ran out of the room, leaving Richard on the floor in a pool of blood.

Of course, again, there's no way to know what ran through his mind – shock, bewilderment, and terror, most likely – but it probably was not all that different than what went through Bobby's mind on that day in the car.

Richard died later that day. The prison doctors worked furiously to save him, but Richard had lost too much blood. Nathan rushed to the prison hospital and watched helplessly as his friend lay dying on the operating table. When it was over, after the surgeons, doctors, and prison guards left the room, Nathan remained behind to wash the body and mourn the loss of the man who was once his closest companion.

James Day went on trial for murder later that year. He claimed self-defense and no one, not even Nathan, contradicted his story. The jury found him not guilty of murder.

Richard's death caused an uproar outside the prison walls. When Clarence Darrow was told of his death, he slowly shook his head. "He is better off dead," the great attorney said, "For him, death is an easier sentence."

But most people were outraged to learn that Richard had corrupted the guards to gain special privileges. The new warden, Joseph Ragen, was deeply embarrassed and, as a consequence, Nathan found himself under sever scrutiny in case he, too, should step out of line. All of Nathan's privileges were revoked.

The years that followed Richard's death were lonely, bitter ones for Nathan, and yet, he survived and even began to contemplate the possibility of parole. To dream that he might get out of prison had once seemed impossible, but he knew that memories would eventually dim and perhaps he could convince the parole board that he was sorry for the terrible crime that he committed. At the time of Richard's death, Nathan had already served 12 years and he would be eligible for parole in 1957. The parole board would require him to proclaim his regret for killing Bobby, but that would not be difficult. He would also need to show that he had been rehabilitated and if released, would never commit another act like the one that sent him to prison in 1924.

It is truly possible that Nathan was indeed sorry for the things that he'd done. Even though it had been his talk of superior intellects that were above the law that had inspired Richard to begin planning a "perfect murder," Nathan, as arrogant as he was, would have never gone through with it on his own. Perhaps neither of them would have. But if we recall the year that Nathan spent separate from Richard – attending the University of Chicago, while Richard was in

Michigan – we get a glimpse of the man that Nathan *could* have been without the horrible co-dependent relationship that he had with Richard Loeb.

Of course, this didn't change the fact that Nathan had committed a heinous murder or that he had a long way to go to redeem himself. Nathan now immersed himself in the management of the school for prisoners that had been set up at Stateville. The school was an ambitious undertaking, offering classes in English, algebra, geometry, bookkeeping, and history. Money for pencils, paper, and other supplies came from the prison's Inmate Amusement Fund. Nathan soon had over 400 prisoners taking classes, but its rapid expansion soon proved to be its downfall. The warden, Joseph Ragen, taking note of the popularity of the classes among the inmates, directed that each student's academic record be reported to the central administration. Ragen intended that each of the prisoner's accomplishments be presented to the parole board as tangible evidence of rehabilitation. But he had not seen the predictable outcome – prisoners with no previous interest in study, and with no desire to learn, began enrolling with the intention of forcing the teacher, by threats, if necessary, to award high marks to present to the school board in order to win early release.

In 1941, Nathan was transferred to a position as an x-ray technician in the prison hospital. Later that year, he wheedled his way into a position as a nurse in the hospital's psychiatric ward. He now had more responsibility – and less supervision – than ever before. The prison doctors relied on the nurses to look after the psychiatric patients, even allowing them to medicate the patients in their care.

In September 1944, scientists working for the federal government came to Stateville looking for volunteers to test a new antimalarial drug. In Europe, World War II was in its final stages, but troops fighting in the Pacific still faced a challenge from the Japanese – and from a wide range of diseases, like malaria. Scientists had already started testing the drugs on patients at the nearby Manteno State Hospital for the Insane but needed more volunteers for the tests to be reliable.

Almost 500 prisoners – including Nathan – volunteered. He was dosed with malaria and on July 2, began showing symptoms. His body shook uncontrollably, his head felt as though it would split, and his fever shot up to 104. The symptoms lasted for five days and would reoccur two weeks later. The doctors administered the new medicine and while it turned out to be effective in preventing the appearance of symptoms, it was too toxic as a cure for malaria. Nathan, who had previously been healthy, now had signs of kidney disease and diabetes.

The "malaria cure" did permanent damage to his body but it also managed to get him some consideration for the length of his sentence. Thanks to his participation, Governor Adlai Stevenson, reduced his kidnapping sentence from 99 to 85 years. The difference might have seemed trivial because either way, he would spend the rest of his days at Stateville. But in terms of early release, he had been eligible for parole in 1957 and now that had been moved up to as early as January 1953.

When Nathan did finally appear before the parole board, there was an air of sadness about him. The cockiness that he had shown at his trial was gone, worn down by the long years of incarceration. In its place was an air of quiet resignation. He'd gained weight, his hair was receding, and there was a sorrowful look in his heavy-lidded eyes. He said all the right things – his life had changed completely, his outlook had changed, he'd never get in trouble again if he was released.

Why did he murder Bobby Franks? How did he explain the killing?

"I couldn't give a motive that makes sense to me," he replied. "It was the act of a child – a simpleton kid. A very bizarre act. I don't know why I did it. I'm a different man now. I was a smart aleck kid. I am not anymore. I can only tell you that what happened in 1924 can't happen again." He repeated that it had been a foolish act by two foolish boys and he was unable to account for the murder. "It seems absurd to me today, as it must to you and all other people. I am in no better position to give you a motive than I was then."

Nathan had tried to make a good impression, but to his listeners across the table, his answers seemed trite and too quick, too rehearsed. There was still something about his manner that betrayed the arrogance of youth. His remarks, it was later reported, seemed almost offhand.

Simply put, he didn't seem sorry for what he had done. His parole was denied.

Five more years passed before the parole board again met to consider Nathan's release. The intervening years had given him time to prepare and to learn from his earlier failure. He hired an attorney, Elmer Gertz, to present his case to the board and he had reached out beyond the prison walls to enlist the support of prominent supporters. Former classmates had secured job offers for Nathan. All agreed that he needed to avoid a return to Chicago and the glare of the city's newspapers. He had job offers from Florida, California, and Hawaii. The Church of the Brethren, which was based in Elgin, Illinois, offered him work in a mission hospital in Puerto Rico. A representative from the church had met Nathan's brother, Sam, several years earlier and now offered to sponsor Nathan's employment as a medical technician at the hospital.

The parole board met in February 5, 1958. Elmer Gertz presented a case for Nathan, highlighting his job offers, his work in the prison hospital, his exemplary record, and the length of time that Nathan had already spent in prison. Gertz blamed the length of his sentence on the publicity that surrounding the case, pointing to other inmates who had done worse things and who had already been released. He also urged the board to look back at the original court documents and see that it was Richard Loeb who had planned the scheme, initiated the kidnapping, and committed the murder. Yes, Nathan had been an accomplice, but the real blame, Gertz insisted, fell on Loeb.

A succession of character witnesses followed: John Bartlow Martin, a writer for the *Saturday Evening Post* who had interviewed Nathan in prison; Martin Sukov, a prison psychiatrist; Eligious Weir, the prison chaplain; and famous poet Carl Sandburg, who even went as far as to offer Nathan a room in his own home. All of them testified that Nathan had earned parole through his outstanding rehabilitation.

Finally, it was Nathan's turn to speak. He had learned his lesson the last time around. He told the board, "It is not easy to live with a murder on your conscience. The fact that you did not do the actual killing does not help. My punishment has not been light. I have spent over one-third of a century in prison. During that time, I have lost most of those who were dear to me. I never had an opportunity to say a prayer on their graves. I forfeited all home and family. I forfeited all the chances of an honorable career. But the worst punishment comes from inside of me. It is the torment of my own conscience. I can say that will be true for the rest of my days. All I want in this life is a chance to prove to you and the people of Illinois, what I know in my heart to be true, that I can and will become a decent, self-respecting, law-abiding citizen, to have a chance to find redemption for myself by service to others. It is for that chance I humbly beg."

The board members listened politely as Nathan spoke. When he finished, board president John Bookwalter asked Nathan about his attorney's assertion that Richard had conceived and planned Bobby's murder. Was it, he questioned, also Nathan's belief that Loeb had a stronger personality and that he was more or less a follower?

Nathan agreed that this was true.

"Through your adoration for him?" Bookwalter pressed.

"That is correct."

"As you sit here today, don't you take an equal share of blame for this?"

"Definitely."

"You're not trying to place it on him?"

"Believe me," Nathan replied, "it is not easy to try and push blame on a man who is dead. I did not want to throw blame on another. It is not an attractive thing to do, but I must answer the question honestly."

But Bookwalter was still not satisfied. Nathan seemed to want it both ways – he wanted to express remorse but still deny that he had a meaningful role in the murder. Bookwalter knew the case. He'd read all the transcripts. He pressed again, "You are taking an equal share of the responsibility?"

"Very definitely."

"I understand there were articles used in this crime purchased by you and stored in your house?"

"My share was equal," Nathan replied cautiously, fearing that his parole was about to be denied yet again.

Bookwalter suddenly changed the subject. He asked Nathan if he knew that if the board granted him parole that this meant he had to avoid all television and radio appearance? Did he understand that he was not to give statements to the newspapers? Every media outlet in the country would want an interview with him.

Nathan hastily replied, "I don't want any part of lecturing, television, or radio, or trading on notoriety. This is the last thing... All I want, if I am so lucky as to ever see freedom again, is to try to become a humble little person."

On February 20, 1958, the board announced that they had agreed to parole Nathan Leopold. He was released three weeks later, on March 13. He walked out of Stateville to confront a mob of newspaper reporters, television crews, and photographers. He looked around nervously as they shouted questions at him. His voice quavered as he spoke into a microphone: "I appeal as solemnly as I know how to you and your editors, to agree that the only piece of news about me is that I have ceased to be news. I beg, I beseech you and your editors and publishers to grant me a gift almost as precious as freedom

LEOPOLD AT THE TIME OF HIS
RELEASE IN 1958

itself – a gift without which freedom ceases to have much value – the gift of privacy. Give me a chance – a fair chance – to start life anew."

It was a meaningless appeal. The crowd pushed forward, shouting again. Elmer Gertz gently pushed Nathan away from the microphone and toward a waiting car. Its engine was running, and the driver was ready to make a quick exit. The reporters immediately reacted, rushing to their own cars so that they would not be left behind.

Nathan was taken towards Chicago, running with scores of other cars in pursuit. Ralph Newman, one of his closest friends, had offered his home in Oak Park, west of the city, as a temporary refuge. But, within minutes of his arrival, Nathan looked out a window to see dozens of reporters on the street. He was given a police escort into Chicago, where he planned to stay at an apartment on Lake Shore Drive with a college friend, Abel Brown.

But it became impossible for him to stay even a few days in the city. He had hoped to visit the graves of his parents, but journalists had discovered his hiding place and camped outside, waiting for him to leave the apartment. He had no choice but to leave immediately. He had accepted the job in Puerto Rico and knew that only after he had left the United States would he find peace.

The tranquility of the town of Castaner, on Puerto Rico, was a welcome change from Chicago. High in the mountains, it was an idyllic spot. Nathan spent his days peacefully, working as a medical assistant in the hospital, enrolling as a graduate student in social work at the University of Puerto Rico, and making new friends.

But the past refused to leave him alone.

Meyer Levin, a contemporary of Nathan and Richard at the University of Chicago, had written a novel called *Compulsion*, based on the murder. The book was overwrought, exaggerated, outlandish, and the character based on Nathan was far from flattering. Now Nathan learned that Twentieth Century Fox was making a film of the novel, starring Orson Welles. Nathan decided that this was an invasion of his privacy and in October 1959, he instructed Elmer Gertz to file suit against Levin and the film production company, Darryl F. Zanuck Productions, for the "appropriation of the name, likeness, and personality of Leopold and conversion of same for their profit and gain."

To most people, the lawsuit seemed insane. One of the most notorious murderers in American history was now complaining that a fictionalized account of the crime appropriating his name? Leopold had filed suit for $1.4 million in court. If he collected, would he not, in fact, profit from his crime? Meyer Levin, who had publicly supported Nathan's parole, was indignant that his generosity was rewarded with such ingratitude.

The case wound its way endlessly through the courts, eventually reaching the Illinois Surpreme Court in 1970. There, it was finally dismissed. Meyer Levin spent tens of thousands of dollars in his defense. In the decade of legal wrangling over the case, no publisher would reissue *Compulsion* after its initial print run for fear of incurring damages if the courts decided in favor of Nathan.

While the lawsuit was taking place in Chicago, Nathan was still living peacefully in Puerto Rico. Not long after his arrival on the island he met Trudi Feldman, 53, a woman from Baltimore who was the widow of a physician. In October 1961, after obtaining permission from the parole board, the two were married in Castaner. They lived comfortably on Nathan's sizable inheritance, which had accumulated interest while he was in prison, and Trudi opened a flower shop in San Juan.

In 1963, Nathan was released from his parole, allowing him to drink alcohol, drive a car, stay out at night, and travel outside of Puerto Rico. Neither Trudi nor Nathan had seen much of the world, so they traveled widely in the 1960s, visiting Europe, South America, Asia, and the Middle East. Nathan returned to Chicago often, to see old friends, visit his old neighborhood, and place flowers on the graves of his parents and two brothers.

The murder of Bobby Franks had passed into legend. It had become a sort of catchphrase – the "Leopold and Loeb case" – and it periodically popped up in books and in newspapers as time moved on.

Nathan wrote his own account of the story in a book called *Life Plus 99 Years* and continued to be hounded by the press for his role in the "perfect murder" that he had committed decades before. He stated that he would be "haunted" by what he had done for the rest of his life. He died of a heart attack on August 29, 1971, bringing his story to an end.

It also brought an end to another story that had been taking place since 1924 – a sadder and much more tragic one than the alleged rehabilitation of Nathan Leopold.

The conviction of Nathan Leopold and Richard Loeb did not, according to many people, bring an end to the terrible case of Bobby Franks. This belief has been supported by the accounts of a restless spirit that continued to walk for many years after the two killers were safely locked behind bars. That spirit, the accounts stated, was Bobby Franks, who took nearly 50 years to find peace.

During those decades, visitors to Rosehill Cemetery on the north side of Chicago often reported seeing the ghost of a young boy standing among the stones and mausoleums in the Jewish section of the graveyard. It is there where the Franks family mausoleum is located, although its location is not listed on any maps of the cemetery and employees are instructed not to point it out to curiosity-seekers. This is a tradition that dates back all the way to the 1920s, when the family so desperately wanted to avoid publicity from daily stories that appeared in every newspaper in the city.

Even so, people found the tomb within the confines of the beautiful burial ground, and starting in the late 1920s, maintenance workers and visitors alike encountered the ghostly boy. It was, they all believed, the spirit of Bobby Franks, unable to rest in the wake of his bloody and violent death – and perhaps restless because he did not feel that justice had been served in his case.

The boy continued to be seen wandering for years. He was always reported from a distance, though. Whenever he was approached, the apparition would vanish. These sightings continued for years, but eventually, they came to an end – in 1971.

Encounters with Bobby's spirit ended at almost exactly the same time that Nathan Leopold died in Puerto Rico. Coincidence? I'd prefer to think that it's not.

I'd like to think that it means that poor Bobby Franks was finally able to find some peace on the other side.

1927:

HELL CAME TO

MICHIGAN

Andrew Kehoe was mad.

Not just angry – he was certifiably insane. The people in the small town of Bath, Michigan, simply regarded Kehoe as a man with a "few quirks." He was always willing to help those who needed it. There was no question that he was skilled with his hands, kept a tidy farm, and was a sure hand when it came to handling dynamite. In fact, he was the man that all the local farmers came to see when they needed advice on how to remove stubborn tree stumps from their fields. Andrew knew what he was talking about and could explain to a man just how much explosives he needed to use and just where to put them.

If you needed to know about dynamite – ask Andrew Kehoe.

And electricity – Kehoe knew about that, too. Houses in town were just starting to get wired up to a central line and Kehoe understood the many details of wires and cables and switches. He tinkered with generators – which was how most people were electrifying their homes – but had a keen understanding of the power lines that were being strung up all over the community, including at the new Bath Consolidated School. Kehoe was on the local school board and spent countless hours working on the building and insuring that everything was operating smoothly.

That would have seemed odd, though, if Kehoe had not been on the board. Most folks in town knew that you should never mention the new school to Andrew. He'd been dead set against the new building – everyone knew that. If you didn't know, then all you had to do was to get in heated conversation with him about it at the local drug store and he'd fill your ears full of such vitriol about the waste of taxpayer's money that your head would spin.

One of the old farmers in town said Andrew "was nutty on the subject of that school." And the farmer was right – he was. But no one knew just how "nutty" Andrew Kehoe actually was.

And they had no idea what he planned to do to prove it.

"He was the nicest man."

That was what one of the survivors of the horror created by Andrew Kehoe said about him in its aftermath. If he was at the school when children arrived in the morning, he always smiled at them and said hello. Another survivor – who encountered Kehoe as he was driving to the school on the morning of May 18, 1927 – tipped his hat to her and waited politely as she crossed the street before he continued his fateful drive. He was a good neighbor, said a local farmer. He was always willing to help those who needed it, said another.

"He was," wrote a reporter in the wake of the destruction," the world's worst demon."

Andrew Kehoe was born in Tecumseh, Michigan, on February 1, 1872. His father, Phillip, was an Irish immigrant who had left home after the potato famine of the 1840s. When he arrived in the United States, Phillip, his six brothers, and their parents settled in Maryland. He grew restless as he grew older, headed west, and settled in Michigan, not far from the Ohio border. He bought some land near Tecumseh and became one of the many farmers in the territory. He became successful raising crops and cattle and his parents and brothers eventually joined him.

Phillip wed Mary Malone – another Irish immigrant – and their first child, a daughter, was born in 1860. A second child arrived in 1862, but Mary died soon after from complications. Phillip soon remarried another Irish Catholic, Mary McGovern, and between 1862 and 1870, they had four daughters. Andrew, the first son, was born two years later. Two more daughters and another son followed shortly.

Andrew grew up in a small farmhouse that was overflowing with children. He began his education at the Culbertson School, not far from home. He learned all the basics in class, but outside of school, he became fascinated with electricity in the same way that other boys become enthralled by sports. His father's farm became Andrew's laboratory and he regularly devised crude gadgets with hopes of improving farm production. He built his devices alone, lost in his thoughts, his

ANDREW KEHOE AND HIS WIFE, NELLIE

own best companion. He lived in isolation simply because he had no need for company.

Phillip Kehoe was just the opposite. He was a community leader, a larger-than-life figure who held minor political offices throughout the region. He was a staunch Democrat but managed to win votes in a largely Republican area. He was also deeply religious and was an important member of the Catholic parish in nearby Clinton. The family was so devoted that one of Andrew's sisters later entered the convent.

Phillip was also active in local organizations that served as venues for social outings. When the groups met, they encouraged everyone to speak their minds about politics, home life, and, of course, farming. Phillip took part in every meeting, using them as a platform to expound on his theories about farming. He engaged in heated discussions with other farmers about ways to oversee every aspect of production, from raising crops to setting prices. He believed that by withholding crops from market, farmers could maintain financial control over their product. It's likely that Andrew attended some of these meetings because Phillip's ideas and philosophies stayed with him and influenced him after he bought his own farm in Bath.

Another topic of conversation was taxes. Again, Phillip made his thoughts clear on this subject to anyone who would listen. He demanded more oversight of public funds. If the people's money was being spent on the local government, utilities, and schools, then the people needed to have a say on how those things were run. This was something else that stuck in young Andrew's head. He'd revisit his father's philosophies many times over in the future.

For now, he was just a boy – a boy who loved his mother. And there was something wrong with Mary. When Andrew was around the age of 10, his mother noticeably changed. She was often sick and wasn't strong enough to keep up with the large and unruly Kehoe clan. She was diagnosed with a "disease of the nervous system," a condition that slowly and painfully took away her physical abilities. Throughout Andrew's adolescent years, Mary was confined to her bed, beginning a decade-long decline. By the time he turned 18, she had been reduced to complete paralysis. Mary finally died on November 5, 1890.

After her death, Phillip – now 60-years-old and in pain from arthritis – married once again. His new wife, Frances Wilder, was a widow with several children – was considerably younger than he was. She was so young that Andrew was three years older than his father's new wife. Phillip was enamored with the young woman and built a new brick home for her near the old wooden farmhouse where the family had been living for years.

Andrew and his new step-mother quickly developed a mutual hatred for each other, which ultimately led to Andrew leaving his father's home.

This period is a blank spot in the murky history of Kehoe's life. It's thought that he enrolled at Michigan State College (later Michigan State University) in East Lansing, where he briefly studied the new science of electrical engineering. At some point, he headed south to St. Louis, where he studied electrical engineering at a school there – or so it's believed. Little is known about his time in St. Louis, except for an incident that was later revealed by one of his sisters-in-law. She claimed that Kehoe suffered a severe head injury in St. Louis in 1904. Kehoe was in a coma for two months. Whether this injury contributed to Kehoe's madness will never be known, but it certainly seems possible. His behavior became more and more erratic after the accident, even after he was physically recovered.

Back on his feet after the accident – which could have been anything from falling off a ladder to getting an electrical shock, no one knows – Kehoe returned to his passions for electricity. He drifted through the Midwest, acquiring knowledge and putting it into practice. He worked as a lineman in Iowa for a time and then returned to Michigan in 1905.

He found Phillip's life to be greatly changed when he arrived home. There was a new Kehoe child, three-year-old Irene, and although his relationship with his father was strained, Andrew moved back into his childhood bedroom and resumed working for Phillip on the farm.

And found another passion – explosives.

Like many farmers of the era, Andrew began clearing his father's fields of tree stumps and rocks with dynamite and pyrotol, an incendiary explosive that was first used during World War I and now could be easily purchased as surplus. They were commonly-used resources of the day and Andrew became an expert with them.

He was happy working the farm but over time, his resentment toward his father's new family turned to hatred. He was the first son, seemingly the one to inherit his father's estate, but now there was a step-mother and a half-sister young enough to be Andrew's own daughter. Phillip's arthritis had crippled the old man, forcing him to use a cane, and he was completely dependent on Francis. Andrew, meanwhile, was doing all the work and getting nothing in return.

The relationship between Phillip and Andrew continued to deteriorate and it took a terrible tragedy to change all that.

On Sunday, September 17, 1911, Frances was in town and hurried home to make the noontime meal for the family. She entered the kitchen – a small room at the back of the house that was dominated by a large stove that was state-of-the-art for the time – and began preparations for cooking. The oil stove had a small flaw in that Frances had to light the pilot every time she wanted to use it. She struck a match and touched it to the pilot light.

In that moment, her world began to burn.

A flame of enormous size whooshed out of the stove, engulfing Francis in a small inferno. Doused in the oil from the stove, her clothing was instantly incinerated, and her skin began to melt. In agony, Frances stumbled through the kitchen, desperately trying to put out the fire that was consuming her flesh. Her screams rang through the house, echoing up the stairs, down the hallways, through the open windows, and out in the yard.

Irene ran into the house – chilled by the horrific sound of her mother's screams –and saw an unrecognizable figure in flames with arms that flailed helplessly at its burning head and body. Phillip Kehoe moved as quickly as he could toward the kitchen, his cane moving him along only inches at a time.

Andrew – some later claimed – stood and watched Frances burn.

When he finally grabbed a pitcher of water, he doused Frances with it, it made things worse. The water spread the oil into a thin layer, causing an even more rapid spread of flames. The fire raced all over Frances's body, rapidly turning what little skin she had left into liquid. Oil fires are best dowsed using a flour or baking soda to smother the flames. Water is the worst thing to use when trying to extinguish a kitchen fire.

Andrew Kehoe was aware of that fact.

Somehow, the fire was finally put out. Andrew and Irene took the moaning and smoking Frances in to the bedroom, where they tried to make her comfortable. Her skin was blackened, her flesh burned down to the bone. The hellish stench of scorched meat permeated the house.

When Phillip eventually reached his injured wife, Andrew and his half-sister went for help. The Kehoe house had no telephone, so they went to the home of their closest neighbors, the Murphys, to call a doctor.

Hettie Murphy was in her kitchen, preparing dinner for the family. She lived with her husband and in-laws and was expecting her first child very soon. Years later, when she recalled that day, Hettie remembered a simple knock at the door – a nonchalant tap – not the frantic sound of someone who desperately needed help. She answered the door to find Andrew on the front porch. He seemed to be "without a care in the world," she recalled.

Andrew asked her to call a doctor and when Hettie asked if someone was sick, he calmly replied, "No, Frannie got burned." He started to turn and leave the porch and then he added, "And you might also want to call a priest."

There was nothing that a doctor could do for Frances Kehoe. The priest delivered the last rites as the blackened, burned woman wept and moaned in tortured pain. Mercifully, she died that same afternoon.

It would be many years later when questions began to be asked about Andrew's possible involvement in Frances's death. Did he cause her horrible death to happen? Having tinkered with gadgets and machinery since his childhood, he conceivably had the knowledge to rig the stove to explode.

But did he? We'll never know. The incident will always remain a small part of the greater mystery that is Andrew Kehoe.

Phillip Kehoe had never expected to outlive his young wife. His health and spirit now broken, he began to rapidly decline.

Andrew was concerned with things other than his step-mother's death and his father's health. Now in his early forties, he renewed an old courtship with Ellen Price – who was always known by her nickname of "Nellie" – whom he'd met years before at Michigan State. Their relationship had ended when Kehoe left for St. Louis, but Andrew now made an effort to see her again.

Nellie had been born to an Irish immigrant family – Patrick and Mary Ann Price – in 1875. Her mother had died when Nellie was just 18. As the oldest daughter in a family of five, Nellie had been tasked with raising the younger children. They lived in Bath, where Patrick Price farmed the land owned by his older brother, Laurence. In 1908, Patrick moved to Lansing, where he and the children could be closer to Laurence, a Civil War veteran and successful businessman. Laurence made his fortune in the fledgling automobile industry, opening a factory that manufactured car parts for Henry Ford. Wealthy and with an interest in public service, he turned to politics. He won several elections for public office and became a well-known and important figure in Lansing social and business circles.

On May 14, 1912 – just seven months after Frances's gruesome death – Andrew and Nellie got married. They moved to Tecumseh, where Kehoe resumed working his father's farm. Phillip, by then confined to a wheelchair, died on January 8, 1915.

Andrew and Nellie largely kept to themselves, although they briefly attended a nearby Catholic church. When the original parish church was torn down, congregants were assessed a fee to pay for a new one. Andrew's share came to about $400. He simply ignored the bill. One of the parish priests called at the Kehoe home to collect the money and found himself ordered off the property. Kehoe never returned to the congregation and he forbade Nellie to attend the new church.

There was another story – many of which surfaced in the wake of the horror at Bath – told about Andrew's belief that he had been cheated by a neighbor in a livestock sale. After buying eight steers, Kehoe penned the animals in a clover field on his property. The field, wet from a recent rainstorm, turned out to be deadly. Two of the cattle bloated badly from the damp feed and quickly died. Kehoe harvested their carcasses, sold the hides in town, then demanded half of his payment back from the seller. It was an unreasonable request that the neighbor refused to honor – but it wasn't unreasonable to Andrew. The two men never spoke again.

But inside, Andrew seethed with hatred.

In 1916, Nellie's uncle was nominated as the Democratic candidate for the U.S. Senate. Although Laurence Price lost to Michigan's Republican incumbent, Charles E. Townsend, he was still a respected man in the Lansing area. When he died on February 12, 1917, he left behind a considerable estate with money going to a variety of charities and family members. His house and land in Bath – Nellie's childhood home – remained in the family.

The 80-acre farm was ideal for Andrew and Nellie. At the center of the property was a three-story house with a spacious front porch and an elegant set of bay windows on the second floor. There was also a large barn on the property, as well as a chicken coop. The land was rich and good for crops. There was a wooded area to the east that was not only beautiful but provided the farm with a curtain of privacy.

Andrew purchased the land from Richard Price – one of Laurence's other brothers – for $12,000. The deal required a $6,000 down payment with the balance and interest held in a mortgage to the Laurence Price estate. On March 27, 1919, the deed was handed over to Kehoe.

The farm in Tecumseh was sold for $8,000 and Andrew and Nellie packed their belongings for the move. Before leaving, Kehoe made one last business transaction. There were 15 cords of wood on his Tecumseh farm, so he approached a neighbor, offering to sell the load at half the original price. It was a great bargain, but the neighbor turned it down. He had all the wood he needed.

But Kehoe refused to take "no" for an answer. He demanded that the neighbor accept the deal. He didn't want to leave the wood for the farm's new owner. The house and farm were sold but the wood still belonged to Kehoe – he'd be damned before he'd leave something on the farm that had not been bought and paid for. The neighbor finally bought the wood, probably for no other reason than to get Andrew Kehoe out of his life for good.

☠

The new folks seemed like good neighbors; everyone thought so. Of course, Nellie wasn't new to the community. A few of the older folks remembered her from when she was a child and it was nice to have her back home again. Her husband was, to say the least, an interesting character. He had a few eccentricities, but all imagined that he would get along with everyone just fine.

While Nellie remained in Lansing with her sisters, Andrew moved their belongings to the farmhouse. A rented truck brought furniture, shipped via the Michigan Central Railroad, from the depot downtown. Kehoe also brought with him three horses and what one farmer recalled as "some very fine thoroughbred hogs." More impressive was his two loads of farm equipment. Unlike most of the locals, Kehoe's machinery was modern and well beyond the means of the average person in Bath.

David Harte – whose farm was across the road from Kehoe's – helped his new neighbor unload his furniture and move it into the house. Although Kehoe tried to call Nellie on the telephone, he could not get in touch with her. When Harte asked where Mrs. Kehoe was, Andrew wouldn't give him a straight answer. He implied that she was at church. Harte shrugged it off – it seemed a reasonable enough answer.

Despite the modern farm equipment in Andrew's barn, he lacked an automobile of his own. Other than a tractor, he owned no machine, neither truck nor car. When groceries or farm supplies were needed, the Kehoes relied on the kindness of their neighbors. Lulu Harte – David's wife – regularly drove Nellie into Lansing to go shopping.

As the new man in town, Andrew exhibited a polite, friendly demeanor. In fact, he was always willing to lend a hand to anyone or chat with anyone. He liked

ANDREW KEHOE'S FARM OUTSIDE OF BATH

to tinker with machinery, especially with electrical gadgets. He seemed happiest when repairing or adjusting the machinery on his farm. New ways of carrying out old chores intrigued him, and he was constantly looking for ways to improve the farm.

Job Sleight – like most of the farmers in the region – still worked his land with the old-fashioned methods of ox and plow. He was fascinated by his neighbor's gas-powered tractor. Sometimes Job just stood along the edge of the road and watched Andrew work. Eventually he introduced himself, explaining his interest in modern machines, and Andrew happily let the older man try out the tractor for himself. Most times, though, Job was content to watch the other man work.

And what a sight that must have been to the veteran farmhand.

Farming was dirty work. Dirt got on clothing, under the fingernails, on the back of the neck, and on the soles of a man's shoes. Equipment maintenance added to the mess. Gas, grease, and oil clung to shirts, pants, and hands. A farmer literally wore his work home with him every night – unless he was Andrew Kehoe.

Overalls – a standard uniform for farmers of the era – were not in Kehoe's wardrobe. He worked his fields like a businessman going to the office. He always wore clean suits, a vest, and shiny shoes to the field. There was never a hair out of place on his head. The clean-cut, nattily-dressed man plowed and planted under the hot sun and if he stained his shirt with sweat or soil, he went into the house for a replacement.

His tools were just as orderly. They were always stacked neatly in his shed and hung in the wall according to a system. There was never a hoe or a rake out of place. Anyone who visited the Kehoe farm found that the barn was cleaner than most of the houses in Bath.

His land was just as neat and orderly. Just as he had been in Tecumseh, Kehoe proved to be a master at removing stumps and boulders from his land with dynamite and pyrotol. Explosions were often heard on his property, although the sound was certainly not out of place on any farmer's land in those days. Dynamite and pyrotol were efficient and fast, even if they were loud and dangerous. Easy to buy and easy to store, they were as common as a plow when it came to breaking up land. There was one thing everyone knew, however – it took an experienced hand to set up and detonate these potentially deadly substances.

In no time, Andrew Kehoe became the go-to man for the proper care and use of dynamite for all the other farmers in Bath.

In a small town largely populated by families with children, the Kehoes were something of an oddity in that they were childless. There were others in town of the same age, but almost all were parents or grandparents. Andrew and Nellie seemed out of place – but no one held it against them. They were a likable couple and good people. Lulu Harte – during her many shopping trips to Lansing – developed a warm though not terribly close friendship with Nellie.

The Kehoes were active in town social events. For instance, they were stalwart members of the Friday Afternoon Club. They particularly enjoyed playing euchre, a regionally popular card game. Euchre pitted four people in two partnerships. Kehoe was adept at the complicated game, although he often annoyed his opponents by pointing out their errors or their violations of the rules. The couple was also good at puzzles and Kehoe created complicated metal devices that others had to untangle. Some club members noticed that – other than his irritating comments during euchre – Andrew seemed to think over every word before speaking and never talked much about his personal life.

Andrew became a regular fixture at the local farm bureau, where farmers met to discuss techniques, economics, and other issues of life and work. He quickly gained a reputation for his intelligence, expertise in modern technology, and growing interest in local affairs. He eagerly volunteered his time and was a popular speaker at bureaus and granges throughout the region.

And yet, there were moments that revealed another side of Andrew Kehoe. David Harte discovered this early on. The Hartes, like many farm families, allowed their dogs to run free on their land. One of the family pets, a terrier, enjoyed scampering in the front yard where the Harte home face the Kehoe house. After a hard day of running and barking, the dog always came home. But in March 1920, nearly a year after the Kehoes moved to Bath, the terrier went missing.

There were several versions of what happened to the dog – Kehoe either shot it because it was barking, shot it because it was digging under his fence, or poisoned it because it annoyed him – but regardless, the dog was dead, and Andrew killed it. There was no argument over the incident. Kehoe and Harte still spoke, acted neighborly, and even helped one another thresh their crops.

Lulu Harte, however, never took Nellie shopping in Lansing again.

The building that would become the target of Andrew Kehoe's wrath was not the first schoolhouse in the region.

There had been many other schools -- all tiny one-room buildings where different grades shared the same classroom and teacher. At one point, there were 10 small schoolhouses that served Bath and the surrounding area. By the 1920s, though, things were starting to change. The rest of the country was setting up schools in single locations that were divided by grade level. It was more organized, and children were receiving a better and more complete education. If it was being done elsewhere, why not in Bath?

The idea was not without opposition. It was a radical change and it had its detractors. The idea of consolidation raised many challenges that many people felt were insurmountable. How could nearly 300 children be transported from home to school? Who would feed them lunch? Where would the teachers come from? Who would oversee this new school?

And most important to some – who was going to pay for it?

A meeting was held on July 22, 1921. A state official was brought in to make the case for consolidation. A vote was held three days later, and the referendum was passed. By mid-August, a school board was up and running and the hunt for a location was underway. A hill near downtown Bath provided an ideal spot. A former school building that had housed grades 1-10 was salvageable and could be moved to the new location. This, it was decided, would be the basis for the new building. Classrooms for the elementary grades would meet on the first floor with high school students taking the second story.

On November 12, 1921, a vote was held on a bond proposal to fund the new school. With the new school came a bond for $43,000. The school board had already raised $8,000 to pay for an athletic field and electrical facilities – the additional $35,000 would come from property taxes.

Out of the 76 bond proposal votes collected, only 20 people opposed the plan. Any guess as to who one of the opposing votes belonged to?

Emory E. Huyck was born on July 3, 1894, on a small farm outside of Butternut, Michigan. He was one of 11 children. After high school, Emory attended the Ferris Institute, a small college in Big Rapids, Michigan. Like so many men of his generation, he volunteered for military service when America entered World War I. He served as a training officer at Camp Custer in Augusta, Michigan, teaching English-language skill to raw recruits. After his discharge from the army, he returned to school for his bachelor's degree. He majored in agricultural studies at Michigan State College, and while still a student, married his wife, Ethel, who became a schoolteacher.

With his agricultural degree and his work as a military educator, Emory was considered ideal for his new job of superintendent of the Bath Consolidated School. He was young, talented, and had great potential. He could also do double-duty as an administrator and teacher. Best of all, since he was barely out of school himself, Emory's initial salary could be set fairly low for a man in his position.

BATH CONSOLIDATED SCHOOL SUPERINTENDENT EMORY HUYCK, THE MAN WHO WOULD BECOME ANDREW KEHOE'S ARCH ENEMY

Teachers were hired next. Arrangements were made for their housing and then the board tackled the transportation problem. While some students could still walk to school – just like in the local, one-room schoolhouse days – six motor-driven vehicles were needed for the rest. Five of them were standard buses, while the sixth was a Model T Ford that was fitted with a detachable body. In fall, winter, and spring, children were transported to school in this machine. In the summer, the body was removed, and the Model T was used for farm work. There was also a seventh bus that was sometimes used. It was a horse-drawn wagon equipped with a potbellied stove, so the passengers could stay warm during cold Michigan winters.

When the school opened in the fall of 1922 with 236 students, it began a new era for the community. Modern education had come to Bath, ushering in a time of great promise for the region.

And then there was the school board.

The new board wanted things to be simple: administration of the school was their responsibility and oversight of the teaching was to be done by Emory Huyck. On the surface, it seemed like a good idea. The majority of the school board members had previous experience running one-room schoolhouse districts. But the consolidated school offered different challenges.

BATH CONSOLIDATED SCHOOL

With a small regional school board, it was inevitable that many members would be friends or relatives of people living in their district. Conflicts of interest – like giving bus contracts to family members and hiring friends of friends – were usually overlooked. The board also held its meetings in private rather than opening the proceedings to the public. Most important, keeping a school in line with modern educational standards required a constant flow of money. Funding came, of course, from local taxes.

For the most part, the money was well spent. Emory Huyck pushed hard to help the school earn accreditation, which would prove that Bath Consolidated School was serious about the future of its students. Essentially, educational accreditation was a quality certification granted by a third party, an assurance that the school has set goals to achieve excellence. In this case, the accrediting agency was the University of Michigan. The criteria were basic: teachers had to have educational backgrounds, classes had to meet state standards, and members of the faculty and administration had to adhere to proper standards of conduct for members of their profession. Huyck proved himself worthy of the task. Accreditation was granted in May 1925, not quite three years after the school opened. With it came financial resources in the form of federal and state Home Economic Aid and other government grants.

In the wake of World War I, the country was suffering from an economic recession, so any government grants were welcome. Local farmers were struggling to make ends meet, particularly with increased property assessments to pay for the consolidated school. There was discontent among many of the locals, leading to considerable discussion about how the Bath School Board was handling its finances.

The loudest voice of complaint came from Andrew Kehoe. He was very vocal about his unhappiness with the new school and complained constantly about the increase in his taxes. It was, he stated, illegal and unfair. And he decided to back up his words with action.

The school board treasurer, Enos Peacock, came up for reelection. Enos was a well-known and well-liked man in the community. His family had lived in Bath for several generations and had built the one-room Peacock School, which had been replaced by the consolidated building. Although Peacock had always been considered an excellent manager of the people's tax money, Kehoe led a vocal coalition that demanded new leadership rather than the "old boy's network" that made up the current board.

The election was held on July 14. Six men – including Kehoe and Peacock – were running for a trustee position on the board. A winner would be decided when one man received the majority of all the votes cast. This was not easy with six men on the ballot and yet Kehoe was the top vote getter of the day. He won a school board position that was due to expire in July 1927.

Andrew was sworn in a week later, as one of two new board members. Perhaps due to his reputation for being tight with a dollar, his fellow trustees named him as treasurer. School board meetings were inevitably long – with continual arguments over educational and administrative issues – but having Kehoe on the board brought a new element to the proceedings.

Although respectful toward the other members on the board, he considered at least one person in attendance at the meetings to be his bitter enemy – superintendent Emory Huyck. The other board members saw Huyck's presence at the meetings as the sign of a responsible administrator – but Kehoe saw it differently. He was convinced that Huyck was manipulating the votes. Kehoe believed Huyck should do his job and let the board handle the rest. He had been elected to serve the people's interests – not Huyck – and he was determined to fulfill that responsibility. Huyck, he was convinced, was influencing the other members of the board to vote for higher taxes and Andrew wanted him to be banned from all board meetings. This was not only against the wishes of the other board members but was also against Michigan law. Kehoe was told that in order to receive state funding, the superintendent was required to attend all of the board's meetings.

Kehoe became obsessed with Emory Huyck. The two men openly loathed one another, and that dislike grew over time. For Kehoe, the superintendent became the symbol of his hatred for the school, the injustice of property taxes, and the destruction of his life. As for Huyck, he paid little attention to the bitter, strange man. He was popular in the community – professionally and socially – and just wanted the best for his students. Putting up with Andrew Kehoe's strange behavior was a small price that he had to pay to insure the success of his school and his students.

But Kehoe refused to leave things alone. He constantly complained about Huyck's salary and in what must have felt like a victory, he managed to harass the other members into cutting the superintendent's vacation to one week per year and to get his annual salary reduced to $100 instead of the customary $200.

After that, Kehoe challenged the patronage system of school business. Bus service was routinely contracted to Ward Kyes – son of board member Melville Kyes. It didn't matter that Ward's bids were higher than other potential contractors – Ward was Mel's son and that's how business was done. Kehoe fought to stop the practice, but his challenge was easily defeated. Cutting the superintendent's pay was one thing, but some things just weren't trifled with.

Despite his cantankerous approach to board politics – when things didn't go his way, he would make a motion for the meeting to be adjourned – Kehoe's obsession with fiscal responsibility did earn him begrudging respect from some and praise from others. As treasurer, his books were always balanced to the penny.

This reputation for meticulous accounting landed him in a position to complete the last year of the township clerk's term when she unexpectedly passed away in April 1925. Kehoe took the part-time position, believing it was a stepping-stone to something bigger. With his place on the school board and now as township clerk, he had the potential to make a personal impact on the community.

His hopes were soon dashed, however. A year later, in the next general election, local Republican Party officials picked another candidate for township clerk. Despite his talent for balancing the books, Kehoe's confrontational reputation on the school board backfired on him. Although it was obvious that his presence was no longer required, Andrew and Nellie sat quietly throughout the nominating process for clerk held at the community hall. He remained stone-faced and silent through the entire proceeding and then walked out.

He made one last attempt at public office. In the spring of 1927, he was nominated for the position of county justice of the peace. Again, he was soundly defeated and again, he and Nellie were present in the town meeting where the voting was held.

Everyone, Andrew Kehoe believed, had turned against him.

At the school board meetings, Emory Huyck wanted investments for the educational future of the school. Kehoe saw them as mounting expenses that were a burden for the taxpayer. Every meeting that Huyck had with the accreditation body meant more spending. Decisions on what were needed were jointly made by representatives from the University of Michigan and the Bath superintendent. Although his fellow board members believed this was efficient, Kehoe only saw an out of control superintendent trying to take over his job. Why didn't the accreditation committee meet with Kehoe instead? Huyck, he believed, was using taxpayer money as though it were a blank check.

In the fall of 1926, Huyck's salary was raised back to its original level – and then raised another $100. Kehoe objected but no one listened. Purchase items grew, and expenses soared. The students needed new books. Encyclopedia sets were needed for the library. The home economics classes for the girls and the shop classes for the boys needed updated resources. Classrooms had to have pictures on the walls to enhance learning. At one point, a fireproof safe was added to the purchase list. There was also a demand for updated playground equipment.

Kehoe smoldered. Huyck remained calm. They were tied together by the Bath Consolidated School. Whenever they were in the same room together, everyone braced for a storm.

Home economics teacher Ruth Babcock inadvertently gave Kehoe ammunition that he tried to use to take Emory Huyck down a notch. The superintendent, a no-nonsense man, had difficulties with the headstrong teacher. Her methods were outdated and didn't mesh with Huyck's modern ideas. There were frequent battles between the two of them and at the end of the school year in 1926, Huyck recommended that Ruth's contract not be renewed. Babcock wrote a letter, complaining about Huyck, and sent it to the school board – and into the eager hands of Andrew Kehoe. He demanded that the issue of Ruth's employment be reconsidered at the next meeting. The board agreed under the condition that Kehoe "investigate" the situation.

At the June meeting, Kehoe presented Ruth to the board. She explained in detail what she felt was necessary for home economics – a vital part of every young woman's education – to succeed at the school. And then she listed all her grievances about Emory Huyck, which was undoubtedly Kehoe's favorite part of her presentation.

Her issues were considered. A vote was taken. Huyck's decision stood and Ruth Babcock had to look for a new job in the fall of 1926.

Kehoe seethed but was not as angry as he was during the school board meeting in July. The entire community turned out and asked that voting rules be suspended so that two pro-Huyck board members be reelected by acclamation. Through a series of procedural confusions, the standard rules were followed, but Huyck's supporters were easily retained. Kehoe's tightfisted ways were clearly no longer in favor with the citizens of Bath.

Kehoe was now looking less like a crusader and more like a crank. Still, he did have some standing in the community as an active participant in school interests. As an expert electrician and mechanic, his assistance was often sought – and freely volunteered – when various problems occurred at the Bath Consolidated School. One of his most lauded contributions was bringing an end to a bee infestation. Over the winter of 1925-26, a nest of bees hibernated under the school. As the furnace warmed up the building during those cold days, it aroused the sleeping bees – which sent them swarming through the halls and classrooms, stinging children and adults alike. The school board authorized

Huyck and his principal, Floyd Huggett, to do anything necessary to stop the bees. They tried twice and failed both times. Finally, Kehoe offered his services.

The bees were quickly annihilated. Just how Kehoe got rid of them was unclear. No one seemed to know what he did beneath the school, but his solution did the trick.

After demonstrating his ability with the bee infestation, Kehoe was asked to do some much-needed work on the school's electrical system. The board also authorized him to oversee other aspects of the school's maintenance program – plumbing, tiling, general repairs – and he agreed. He did all these chores without any assistance. He now had access to the building – day and night – whenever he needed.

This work demanded intimate knowledge of the building, inside and out, upstairs and downstairs. Kehoe learned every corner, every crevice, every bit of unused space.

It was a perspective that would have fatal consequences in the future.

No one knows when Andrew Kehoe conceived the idea of the horror that lay ahead but based on his activity at the school and the purchase of explosives, his plan likely began about a year in advance – soon after taking over the maintenance responsibilities for the building.

A short time later, Kehoe gave a list of repair supplies for the school to his neighbor Job Sleight and asked if he'd mind picking it all up for him. The list included things like bolts, pipes, fittings, and parts for the furnace. Sleight was happy to oblige and helped Andrew unload it all at the school when he returned.

Soon after, he asked Sleight for another favor. Would he mind making another trip for him? This time to Jackson, a round trip of about 100 miles? Sleight agreed, and Kehoe thanked him and told him that he needed to contact his supplier in Jackson so that his order would be ready. When Sleight asked him what he'd be picking up, "pyrotol" was the reply. Kehoe said he wanted to blast some old tree stumps on the west side of his farm.

Sleight did the neighborly thing and picked up 10 boxes of pyrotol for Kehoe – about 500 pounds worth. He also picked up four boxes of blasting caps. When he returned to Bath, they unloaded the boxes into Kehoe's barn, said their goodbyes, and Sleight went on to his next errand, a trip to the local freight house where he needed to pick up a stove. A neighbor named Harry Barnard ran into him there and he mentioned picking up the explosives for Kehoe.

"I wish I had known that," Barnard said. "I would have sent for some."

Sleight mentioned that Kehoe had more than he could possibly use so if he asked., he might sell him some. A little later, Sleight ran into another friend who said his brother needed explosives for stump blasting. Sleight suggested that he contact Kehoe also.

As it turned out, though, Kehoe didn't have any left.

In the summer of 1926, Kehoe stopped needing rides to pick up supplies. Seven years after moving to town, he finally bought his own vehicle – a flatbed Ford truck. It was good transportation for a farmer, although an expensive one for a penny-pincher who didn't seem to be getting rich in the farming business.

Around this same time, Nellie Kehoe, the quiet woman who lived in the shadow of her boisterous husband, developed serious health problems. She was hospitalized for a short time, followed by a series of terrible headaches and a severe cough. She began to lose weight, which sent her back to the doctor. She was in and out of Saint Lawrence Hospital in Lansing throughout the fall and winter. Doctors at first thought it was tuberculosis, then decided it was asthma. When she returned home, she rarely left the house, becoming a recluse to her already small social circle. A young woman was hired to help around the house because Nellie could no longer do much for herself. The doctor visits, medicine costs, and hospital bills piled up – and went unpaid.

Despite Andrew's reputation in town as a man who paid close attention to how public funds were paid out, he lacked any personal sense of financial responsibility. The failure to pay Nellie's medical bills was only the latest problem. He had started piling up massive amounts of debt years before.

Up through March of 1921, he made regular payments on his mortgage to the Lawrence Price estate. And then he just stopped. Spring turned into summer, then fall, and then it became 1922 and no payments had been made. Not one said anything – not the Price family or Joseph Dunnebacke, the attorney who represented the estate. Finally, a letter arrived from Kehoe stating that he was unable to make payments. The estate granted him an extension. Another year passed, then another. Kehoe wrote another letter, asking if he and Nellie would be evicted. No, came the reply. The estate was happy to work with him – he was family after all.

But still no payments.

In August 1925, Lawrence Price's estate released a percentage of its legacy payments to the late man's heirs. Nellie Kehoe's share was $1,200. The Kehoes arrived at the attorney's office, collected the check, and left. Although Dunnebacke was polite to them, he was shocked that no mention was made of their defaulted mortgage.

Things took another strange turn a month later. The judge overseeing Lawrence Price's estate received a letter from Nellie. Enclosed was a card on which she asked the judge to write down the appraised worth of the Kehoe property.

There were still no payments.

In March 1926, Joseph Dunnebacke was bound by the terms of the estate to pay Nellie another $500. This time, the attorney applied the money to payment on the house and sent the Kehoes a note to explain what he had done with the check. Nellie wrote back, thanking the attorney, and asking how much she and her husband still owed on the mortgage. She also mentioned that Andrew was deeply involved with school board activities, but at some point, would like to come to Dunnebacke's office to discuss their debt.

Instead – in the days that followed the mess over Ruth Babcock – Kehoe contacted Kelly Searl, one of the best legal minds in the region. Searl was a former Circuit Court Judge who had left the bench to go into private practice with his son, William. Searl agreed with Kehoe's argument that executor had inappropriately diverted Nellie's inheritance check. Legally, the money had to go to Nellie and the executors of the estate could not make decisions on Nellie's behalf without her consent. Notice was sent to Dunnebacke and Richard Price – who had sold the property to Andrew and Nellie – and a meeting was arranged in the chambers of the probate judge. Kelly Searl agreed to represent the Kehoes.

The probate hearing – held in August 1926 – was supposed to be a simple matter with the dispute being solved between the lawyers. But to everyone's surprise, the Kehoes showed up, too. They had not been notified of the time and place; Andrew found out on his own. Dunnebacke was dismayed. He'd gone out of his way to help the Kehoes, particularly in light of Nellie's health, and felt they should leave the matter to be sorted out by legal authorities.

But that wouldn't work for Andrew.

Dunnebacke thought it was peculiar that the inheritance belonged to Nellie, the property was in her husband's name, and the mortgage was held by the couple together. Legally, Nellie had the final say about how to use her inheritance. The judge's decision was simple – yes, the Price estate had acted inappropriately, but applying the $500 toward the mortgage was in everyone's best interest.

Searl advised his clients to accept the decision. Nellie liked the idea, but Andrew strongly disagreed. Polite but firm, he insisted that the money go to Nellie immediately. She could decide to use it without any legal intrusion. Nellie went along with it and they were issued a check for $500.

Two months passed with no further word from the Kehoes. No payments were made and no agreements or offers were made to fix the problem. Having exhausted all other avenues, Dunnebacke decided to file a motion of foreclosure with the county sheriff. He and his wife drove to the sheriff's office only to find that he was out. Rather than making the trip twice, he mailed his notice to the sheriff a few days later.

That afternoon, he ran into Nellie's sister, Elizabeth, and told her about the foreclosure. He assured her that this legal maneuver was not an attempt to drive the Kehoes off the property; rather an attempt to push them into negotiating a payment plan.

Elizabeth thought this was a terrible idea. No, she told Dunnebacke, he must not file the suit. Nellie's health was fragile, and any added stress could have dire consequences.

Dunnebacke agreed not to move ahead with the plan. He tried to call the sheriff but there was no answer. He continued to call late into the night and finally sent a telegram, instructing him not to serve Kehoe's summons until he received further instructions from the attorney.

The telegram arrived too late, though. A deputy had already gone out to the Kehoe house with a notice of foreclosure. Andrew came to the door and took the papers from him. He looked them over before he spoke: "If it hadn't been for that $300 school tax, I might have paid off the mortgage."

Every part of his life seemed to be waging war with Kehoe – the mortgage, Nellie's health, the hospital bills, and the taxes. His political ambitions had been beaten out of him. There were the constant fights with the school board and the ongoing war with Emory Huyck. Kehoe spent most of his time in a state of rage. His mind took him always in different directions. His behavior – once considered cantankerous and eccentric – became more erratic.

In mid-November 1926, Kehoe drove to Lansing and purchased two boxes of dynamite. He went back a few days later to buy two more boxes, along with blasting caps. In December, he returned to Lansing. This time he bought a Winchester rifle and 100 rounds of ammunition.

On December 31 – as 1926 became 1927 – Bath celebrated the season with a dance at the community hall. Friends gathered for dinners and parties. As midnight struck and kisses and well wishes were exchanged, massive explosions rocked the area – was Bath under attack? A series of bright flashes lit up the overcast sky above the Kehoe farm. Then all was silent.

It was an unsettling way to ring in the new year for the people in the small town. It was something that everyone talked about for days afterward. Job Sleight – Kehoe's neighbor – ran into a friend a few days later and Job was asked if he had heard the explosions on New Year's Eve. Of course, he'd heard them, they happened right next door.

A few days later, Job and his wife paid the Kehoes a visit. The foursome talked for a bit and Job asked Andrew about the holiday blasts. Kehoe told him that he just wanted to "shoot some off." He was testing out a timer device, he explained, he'd set things to go off at midnight.

Job later recalled that Nellie – who had just been released from another of her hospital stays – didn't say a word about her husband's New Year's festivities.

There were still no mortgage payments being made.

In February 1927, a professor at Michigan State College, hoping to purchase a farm for his father, made an offer on the property – the original $12,000 price that Kehoe had paid in 1920. Andrew considered it, but then the offer was withdrawn before he could decide. The potential buyer decided that the taxes on the land were exorbitant.

Kehoe could have told him that – he'd felt that way for years.

Even though the property wasn't officially for sale, there was more interest in the following month. Another possible buyer asked Joseph Dunnebacke about the farm, but the attorney wisely stayed out of the situation. He sent the man to speak to Nellie's sisters. Nothing came of the offer.

On March 31, Kehoe paid an unexpected visit to Dunnebacke's office. He told him that someone was interested in buying the farm. As part of the sale, Kehoe was offered equity in an unnamed property and would have to sign an option agreement. What did Dunnebacke think about that?

The attorney told him that he "wasn't crazy about the deal." It would put Kehoe in a bad negotiating position. He'd have to sign an option, but the buyer would not. With so little information about the second property, he advised against getting involved in it.

Kehoe thanked him. It seemed like good advice, he said.

In mid-April, Dunnebacke and Kehoe ran into each other downtown. The two men shook hands and made small talk. The attorney asked him what he'd done about the deal and Kehoe told him that his advice was good. He had decided not to sign the option.

Dunnebacke would always remember it as a pleasant enough exchange. It seemed that the animosity between them was over. Dunnebacke was relieved. Perhaps Andrew had finally come to his senses – and perhaps he might even start making some mortgage payments.

He didn't. And that was the last time that Dunnebacke saw Andrew Kehoe alive.

In the spring of 1927, Nellie Kehoe's health grew worse. She still had a constant, wracking cough but now they were accompanied by blinding headaches. There seemed to be no end to her misery. She was constantly in and out of Saint Lawrence Hospital. Alone during those times, Andrew usually ate his meals in town. He often drove to Lansing to visit his wife in the hospital.

David Harte sometimes saw Kehoe's truck at night, coming home from what he assumed was a trip to the hospital. He always knew when Kehoe was away; the man never shut his garage door when he left and always closed it up tight when he returned. None of his trips were late. He usually returned each night between eight and nine o'clock.

In mid-April, Harte noticed that Kehoe was away more often than ever. When he returned, he usually had boxes covered with some kind of tarp in the bed of his truck.

Kehoe never said a word about what he was bringing home.

In late April or early May, Kehoe bought a hotshot battery from an automotive and radio supply shop in Lansing. A hotshot battery was commonly used as an alternative to the hand crank when starting at Model T Ford. It was made up of four one-and-a-half-volt dry cell batteries. The combined voltage of the cells was about six volts, enough to fire up a car engine – or any other sort of device that needed a handy electrical spark.

In early May, custodian Frank Smith was making his rounds of the Bath Consolidated School building and went down into the basement. He noticed something funny while he was there. There were a couple of trapdoors down there, each about 18 inches square. One of them was open.

Frank had a thought: this wasn't the first time that he's seen that. He was pretty sure that he'd found both of the trapdoors open two or three times before.

Had he left them open? He couldn't be sure, so he closed the trapdoor and went on about his day.

On Saturday, May 14, a construction crew that was working on a bridge near Bath placed a call to the sheriff's office. They'd had some items go missing overnight. A deputy began a report and asked what was missing.

A large quantity of dynamite, the foreman replied.

On Sunday, May 15, Kehoe was supposed to pick up Nellie from the hospital. But someone from the hospital called Andrew on Sunday morning and asked him to pick her up on Monday instead. It was a rainy day and they feared the weather would aggravate her lung condition.

Kehoe agreed. He picked her up on the afternoon of May 16 instead. They spent the evening with Nellie's sisters in Lansing. Andrew seemed in a fine mood; happy that Nellie was out of the hospital. When the visit was over, they said goodbye to the Price sisters and went home to Bath.

After the Kehoes returned to the farm, the telephone rang. It was a call from Blanche Hart, a fifth-grade teacher. Having heard that Nellie was out of the hospital, she called to see how she was doing.

"She is getting along fine," Kehoe told her. "I have got her home here with me, and she is fussing around."

One of the Price sisters called the house the following day to see how Nellie was doing. There was no answer. They heard from Andrew that evening. "Have you been trying to get us on the telephone?" he asked› Nellie's sister said that she had been, expressing concern about Nellie.

Kehoe explained, "Nellie is over to Jackson. She was lonesome here, and we have some friends by the name of Vost who we used to know at Tecumseh, and it occurred to me to take Nellie over there because I thought it might be a good thing for her."

Before he hung up, he added, "I am to go back for her on Thursday."

Andrew Kehoe had lied.

He looked across the room at the lifeless eyes of his wife. They stared glassily through the blood that was still slowly dripping down her face. He had bashed her head in while her back was turned. He hadn't wanted her to know what was coming. He loved Nellie. She was one of the only people in his life that he had ever truly loved – but he could not let her live. He couldn't bear to have her face the storm that would be coming.

After he had finished with the telephone call, he loaded her body onto a hog cart and pushed it over to the chicken coop. Piled around her on the cart was silverware, jewelry, and a metal cash box that contained the ashes of the farm's mortgage papers. He would cover the body with straw a little later. He wanted it to burn.

Kehoe then began his next grim task. He had placed homemade firebombs in every building on the farm. They were crude devices made from containers filled with gasoline and wired with automobile spark plugs attached to a car battery. If all went according to plan, his property would simultaneously explode and burn to the ground before anyone could stop it. The house, barn, and outbuildings would be destroyed in a matter of minutes.

There would be nothing left for anyone to take when the Price estate finally foreclosed on the farm.

Later that day, David Harte saw something odd taking place across the road. Andrew Kehoe's arms were full of straw as he walked into the henhouse. David recalled that he had seen him doing the same thing yesterday – but Kehoe had no chickens. He'd sold his brood some time ago. Why was he spending so much time filling his chicken coop with straw?

David thought back to the weekend, when his wife, Lulu, called his attention to something even stranger on the Kehoe farm. Andrew had pulled his truck over in front of the barn and was loading it with some very strange cargo – nails, old tools, pieces of farm machinery, and assorted pieces of scrap metal. It wasn't the sort of thing that a farmer would normally pack into a machine.

"You don't suppose he's junking his tools?" Lulu asked her husband.

Around 8:30 that same evening, Fordney Hart, a freshman at Bath Consolidated, was leaving the school. Although well past the end of the school day, the building was busy with adults attending a Parent-Teacher Association meeting where Fordney had performed as part of a small orchestra ensemble.

As he was walking down the sidewalk, Fordney noticed someone standing in front of the building. He wasn't doing anything, just standing, looking at the building. But Fordney thought the man looked familiar – and then he placed him. He was always in and out of the school, the repair guy who got rid of the bees.

Andrew Kehoe. That was the man's name.

Fordney nodded to himself and walked on past. The boy and the man never acknowledged each other. Fordney started walking home. Kehoe remained standing in front of the school, deep in thought.

He was ready.

For months he had been transporting pyrotol and dynamite into the Bath Consolidated School. It was all done in small increments. No one had noticed anything out of the ordinary. He calculated exactly what he needed each day and brought just that amount. He wired the explosives throughout the basement of the school, connecting various charges of explosives beneath the floors and in the basement rafters. He slithered into the sub-floors and crawlspaces beneath the school, hiding large amounts of pyrotol behind pipes and beams.

Thousands of feet of wire were run throughout the building. Under the feet of unsuspecting students and faculty members, Kehoe had placed over 1,000 pounds of dynamite.

He had no remorse for what he was going to do.

On the morning of May 18, the children began arriving at school around 8:00 a.m. To the students, it was a day like any other. They laughed and talked, pushed and shoved in the hallways, and hurried to their classrooms. The children and teachers on the first floor had no way of knowing that – just inches beneath their feet – hundreds of pounds of explosives waited for an electric current that would either end their lives or change their lives forever.

Under the north wing of the building, in a dark, quiet basement nook, a small alarm clock ticked away. When the hands reached 8:45, a wire connected to the clock set off a spark. The spark began that reaction, firing electricity along the lines that had been rigged throughout the basement. At the end of the wires were blasting caps. The current ignited the blasting caps, sending a charge into the bundles of dynamite and pyrotol.

On that bright May morning, a carefully planned trail of electricity unleashed an explosion of cataclysmic proportions beneath the north wing of the Bath Consolidated School.

Outside of town – also at 8:45 – Lulu Harte was in the henhouse, tending to the family's chickens. She heard a loud sound and went outside to see what had happened. She at first thought it was a gunshot coming from the Kehoe property across the road.

She had seen Andrew Kehoe drive off in his truck that morning and now she saw smoke billowing from the roof of Kehoe's corncrib. In moments, the building was engulfed in flames.

Lulu ran to find her husband. She called out that Kehoe's corn crib was on fire and they ran together to see that his barn was now burning, too. Flames ripped through the building while thick smoke began churning from the Kehoe house. Banging sounds could be heard from inside its walls.

The Bath Consolidated School – meant to last through several generations of students – shuddered like a great animal in pain. Dynamite and pyrotol combined in a powerful blast of energy. The walls of the north wing were forced upward about four feet. They fell back down, collapsing outward with a crash of wood, plaster, glass, and metal. The roof of the building slammed down onto the crumbling brick walls.

Throughout the building, walls shook, and floors buckled. Windows of nearby homes were blown out. The blast sounded across the township and it was later said that it could be heard as far as 10 miles away.

The school's roof fell onto the remains of the first-floor classrooms. The outer walls had toppled over on the sides, although a back wall remained steady. It was as if a giant hand had smashed the school's north wing to the ground, leaving the remainder of it untouched except for broken windows. Among the chunks of wood and the broken bricks, small bodies could be seen.

For a moment, there was silence.

And then the air was filled with screams.

Neighbors rushed toward the Kehoe farm. The house and buildings were burning. Job Sleight had heard the initial blast from Kehoe's corn crib but assumed his neighbor was out ripping up tree stumps from his farm. Job looked in the direction of the farm and saw nothing out of the ordinary.

But then a woman appeared on the road. It was another neighbor, Mrs. Miller. "They say the school has been blown up!" she exclaimed breathlessly.

"That can't be possible," Job replied. Again, he looked toward Kehoe's farm. Buildings on the property were now engulfed in flame. Several dull blasts could be heard. Job knew the sound immediately – it was dynamite.

Another neighbor, Monty Ellsworth, was planting melons that morning. Without warning, a loud noise nearly made him jump out of his skin.

His wife, Mabel, was cleaning upstairs in the house when she heard the deafening sound. She ran to a window and looked out. On a clear day, she could see the chimney of the schoolhouse – a couple miles east of their farm – but now all she could see was a cloud of smoke in the direction of Bath Consolidated.

The faint sound of screams was being carried through the air.

Mabel ran out of the house and joined her husband. "My god! The school is blowed up!" she cried.

Monty looked east and saw a black and white fog about 100 feet high coming from the direction of the school. Kehoe's farm would have to burn. He had to get

THE BATH CONSOLIDATED SCHOOL AFTER BEING ROCKED BY THE
EXPLOSION CREATED BY ANDREW KEHOE

to the school – where his son was a second-grade student. He ran to his Ford pickup and drove off toward town.

Nearby, a group of linemen from Consumers Power – who were installing the first electric lines in the area – felt the ground shake from atop the wooden poles they were perched on. In the distance, they could see a cloud of smoke. Just down the road, there was a farm in flames.

Something terrible was happening in Bath.

O.H. Buck, a Consumer Powers foreman, and some of his men crawled through a broken window of the Kehoe farmhouse. They looked around the smoky living room, looking for anyone who might be trapped inside the burning building. Buck and the others called out, hoping they might find someone. There was no answer, so they decided to salvage what furniture they could before the fire spread into the living room. A davenport was shoved out the window, then a table and chairs.

Buck looked around to see what else might be saved and that's when he saw something in the corner of the room – dynamite.

Buck later said, "Without thinking much about what I was doing, I grabbed an armful and handed it to one of the men."

The room was thick with smoke and the men got out. As they tumbled out into the yard, several neighbors were arriving. They could see that Kehoe's barn was beyond saving, but maybe some of the furniture could be pulled out of the house. From the looks of it, some of the Consumers Power linemen had the same idea.

Then one of the linemen burst out of the house. "My god!" he yelled. "There's enough dynamite in there to blow up the county!"

Across the road, they heard a woman – Mabel Ellsworth – scream, "The school is blowed up!"

Buck and his men ran to their machines. They were needed at the school, not at a house that some madman had wired with explosives. As O.H. Buck later told reporters, "I began to feel as if the world was coming to an end."

And for many, it was.

When neighbors Sidney Armstrong and Sidney Howell pulled up to Kehoe's farm, the entire place was engulfed in flames. Hot winds whipped the fire, nearly setting Armstrong's automobile ablaze. Quickly, Howell got out so that his friend could move the machine to a safer distance.

Through the flames and thick smoke, Howell spotted a figure next to one of the buildings. It was a man backing up a truck. The got out of the vehicle, pulled a funnel from the gas tank, and then got back in. The truck pulled forward, disappeared into the smoke, and then emerged again.

Howell finally made out the driver – it was Andrew Kehoe.

Kehoe had a wild gleam in his eyes. He drove quickly in Howell's direction and stopped next to him. "Boys, you are my friends," he said. "You'd better get out of here."

Kehoe rammed the truck into gear and added, "You better go down to the school."

Stunned, Howell ran to the road and caught up with Armstrong. Kehoe had roared past him, heading east – in the direction of the school.

Before the dust from the explosion had been able to settle, townspeople were already digging through the rubble of the school. The explosion drew people from their homes, customers from the barber shop and pharmacy on Main Street, businessmen, housewives, and farmers from the fields around town. The scene was terrifying. It was later estimated that 230 to 275 children were in the school at the time of the blast.

The sound of children screaming, wailing, and moaning could be heard coming from the ruins. Fully half the building, the northwest wing, was gone. The walls were destroyed, and the roof lay on the ground. Bodies of children could be seen protruding from the bricks and stone, little arms and legs only partially visible. Faces, covered with blood and dust, peered through the broken windows and between splintered beams of wood. Frantic mothers ran screaming to the scene for almost every family in town had at least one child enrolled at the school. The sobbing of trapped children could be heard as some of the mothers fought with rescuers to pull their own children from the wreckage. Men worked feverishly in the mountain of rubble, pulling aside bricks and pushing twisted metal, as they searched for the children that were howling in terror.

Superintendent Emory Huyck rushed into the madness, as calm and collected as he could be in the face of catastrophe. High school students, desperate to escape, were perched atop the roof. He ordered someone to go and get some ladders and "help get those scholars off the roof."

Huyck scrambled up there himself, trying his best to make order from chaos. He

AN AUTOMOBILE DESTROYED BY THE EXPLOSION

teetered across the shattered roofline. The high school students – many ready to jump from the precarious height of the damaged building – surrounded him. Fearing they would be injured, he begged the students to hang on for a few more minutes – someone was bringing a ladder.

Many listened, others didn't. There was a small building below and many students jumped onto its roof and then made a second leap to the ground. It didn't seem that dangerous, and it certainly looked safer than staying on the roof. They made the leap, landed, and realized that the small building's roof wasn't big enough to hold everyone making an escape. Teenagers landed all around, thumping hard on impact. To some of the onlookers, it wasn't clear if they were jumping or falling. Many of them broke their legs.

When Huyck came down from the roof, he picked through the

ANOTHER VIEW OF THE BOMBED-OUT SCHOOL – AND THE SHOCKED LOCALS WHO GATHERED AT THE SCENE

rubble. Bodies of dead children were being pulled out. Other children were digging their way out, forcing their way out of the piles of wood and brick. Huyck carefully picked up one boy and carried him across the bricks. The child remained unconscious as he carried him to safety. He took him to the telephone exchange office, laid him on a couch that someone put on the front porch, and went back to the school.

The boy, a fifth-grader named Carlton Hollister, it was later said, was the first injured – but alive – victim pulled from the rubble.

Homes all over town were opened as temporary hospitals. Bedsheets became bandages as wounded children were pulled from the wreckage. Many of the women made coffee and sandwiches, knowing the rescuers would need food to keep up their strength for the heavy work.

It's impossible to accurately describe the scene of heartbreak and destruction at the school. Parents, desperate to find their children, clawed with bare and bloody hands through the wreckage. On the sidewalk in front of the school, a man knelt over the body of his dead son. Wracked with grief, he slammed his hands on the ground over and over again, screaming out prayers. Parents called out names. The lucky ones had frantic reunions, tightly hugging children who were coated with dust.

On the grassy field in front of the school, a morgue slowly began to grow. Blankets covered each body as dead children were laid out in rows. Mothers and fathers, partly in hope of what they wouldn't find but mostly in dread of what was underneath, gingerly lifted the edges of the blankets for a glimpse of the body. Now and then, a howling, anguished cry could be heard above the sound of the chaos as a parent identified their dead child.

Horror reigned.

Monty and Mabel Ellsworth soon arrived in town. They ran across the front lawn of the school, urgently searching for their son. He's safe, someone told them, we've got to help the children still inside.

Monty stared at the rubble. Beneath the heavy roof, he could see children trapped in a grisly pile. He later recalled, "There was a pile of children of about five or six under the roof and some of them had arms sticking out, some had legs, and some just their heads sticking out. They were unrecognizable because they were covered with dust, plaster, and blood."

With no cranes or heavy equipment readily available, work was done with steady hands and strong backs. The heavy roof was the biggest concern. It had to be wrenched free if the men were going to be able to reach the children trapped inside the north wing. Someone suggested that perhaps heavy rope would do the trick, if they could get enough men to pull the beams out of the way.

Monty immediately volunteered. "I have lots of rope in my slaughterhouse," he called out. He ran back to his Ford Pickup and headed back home. As her was driving back to his farm, Ellsworth passed Andrew Kehoe, driving in the opposite direction on the road.

"He grinned and waved his hand," Monty later said. "When he grinned, I could see both rows of his teeth."

Kehoe was now closer to the school.

Albert Detluff, the town's blacksmith, left the scene and ran toward the telephone exchange on Main Street. It was the town's communication center, run by Lenora Babcock. Calls needed to be made to Lansing to inform the authorities about what had happened and to nearby communities to ask for help. With all the confusion, Detluff wanted to be sure that no one had forgotten to make the calls.

But Lenora – just 17-years-old – was furiously working the lines. She had called Lansing, Dewitt, and other nearby towns. "The school has blow up, we need help!" she had repeated dozens of times.

Emory Huyck – still the calm center of the storm – was also at the telephone exchange. Now that the initial rescues were underway, he was also making sure that calls had gone out for help. Huyck told Detluff, "Bert, there is no use calling anybody. I have done all that can be done. I have called the State Department and the State Police, and there is no help that you can get. It is all done."

One of the calls had reached Chief Hugo Delfs, head of the Lansing Fire Department. It took him only moments to assess the situation once he got word of the unfolding disaster and he went into action. He first sent out a chemical firefighting unit under the supervision of his assistant chief Paul Lefke. Next, knowing that communications would be essential, he sent a truck with telegraph and telephone equipment.

The trucks roared toward Bath with their sirens wailing. It took just 12 minutes from the time Delfs got the call for the rescue vehicles to arrive on the scene at the school.

Assistant Chief Lefke couldn't believe what he saw. He'd seen disasters before, but nothing like this. The school looked as though it had been destroyed by bombs during the war. Bodies were on the ground, the wounded, the dying, the dead – all children. Adults were running everywhere, some carrying bleeding children, others providing supplies to the volunteers. Others knelt next to cold, still bodies. The cries of the kneeling were ghastly – they were the sounds of people being ripped apart by grief.

And their wails were mixed with the unearthly sounds coming from the rubble of the school, the terrified voices of children crying for help.

Frank Smith's house, across the street from the school, was turning into a temporary hospital for the wounded. Bleeding children were brought there and then loaded into automobiles for transport to hospitals in Lansing. Rows of hastily built cots filled the living room. Other wounded children were tucked into the Smiths' bed.

Superintendent Huyck – fresh from the telephone exchange – looked over the situation. He asked Leone Smith if she could accommodate more children. She told him yes as she went upstairs to open more rooms for the wounded. Huyck told her goodbye – he was on his way back to the scene to see what else he could do.

Minutes later, as Leone came back downstairs, the house was rocked by another explosion.

Although there were no children in her home, Mrs. Warner's house was a hub of activity. People came for bedding and cots to be used in the triage area. Mrs. Warner – along with several other ladies – were making sandwiches and coffee.

Then, without warning, a second explosion – even louder – stunned Mrs. Warner. Her windows shattered. A lock blew out of one of her doors, sending screws flying across the room.

Don Ewing was pulling children out of the wreckage of the school. He wondered what could have caused such a terrible explosion. Maybe the boiler had exploded? Or maybe something had gone wrong in the chemistry lab? He didn't know – he only knew that he needed to save as many children as he could.

He pulled a few victims from the wreckage and then went looking for more. That was when he also heard the second explosion. Through the trees, he could see a ball of flame rising into the sky.

O.H. Buck – the Consumers Power man – couldn't believe what was happening. First there was the burning house filled with dynamite and now the school was in shambles. When he arrived, he could hear the voices of children crying out from the rubble.

Then there was an explosion behind him, knocking him off his feet. He looked back over his shoulder and saw a terrible black cloud of smoke mushrooming over what looked like a blasted truck.

Andrew Kehoe had returned to the school.

There are several versions of what happened next at the Bath Consolidated School. What can be strung together from the eyewitness and news reports states that Andrew Kehoe arrived on the scene less than 30 minutes after the initial explosion. Of course, no one knew that the vehicle had been loaded with dynamite and metal debris.

When he arrived, Kehoe called Emory Huyck over to his machine. The superintendent hurried over, which was a natural reaction. Kehoe was a school board member and should be informed of the situation. Huyck did not know that Kehoe's farm was already burning.

THE RUINS OF ANDREW KEHOE'S TRUCK AFTER HE SET OFF THE SECOND EXPLOSION, KILLING HIMSELF AND EMORY HUYCK

When he reached the truck, he asked Kehoe for help. His machine could be used to haul rope and poles for the improvised rescue. As Huyck leaned in to speak to him, he placed his foot on the truck's running board.

"All right," Kehoe said, "I'll take you with me."

Suddenly, Huyck was filled with horror. "You know something about this, don't you?" he cried out.

Kehoe then reached over and fired a rifle – or flipped a switch, accounts vary – inside the cab of his truck. Huyck may have tried to stop him. Regardless, the shot was on the mark and the dynamite in the truck exploded.

Another wave of destruction rocked the town. A huge ball of flame shot upwards and shrapnel was sent flying in every direction, ripping apart trees, splintering houses, shattering windows, and cutting down everything in its path. The blast ripped Kehoe's and Huyck's bodies apart. Their limbs were torn off, their heads burst, and body parts flew into the air and then slammed to the ground. They landed far apart, about 60 feet from the scene, a good distance from Kehoe's exploded vehicle.

The truck explosion, like the schoolhouse bomb, was heard through Bath and beyond. People threw themselves on the ground. The screams of children and adults filled the air. Automobiles near the truck bomb caught on fire.

Shrapnel ripped into bodies. A bolt hit eight-year-old Cleo Clayton, who'd just escaped his destroyed classroom without injury. It tore into his stomach, lodging next to his spine. He died a few hours later.

Anna Perrone saw the car explode from nearly a block away but was hit by a scrap of metal that tore into her eye. Another piece of metal blasted a three-cornered hole in her skull. Amazingly, neither her baby, Rose, whom she held in her arms, nor her toddler, Dominic, who was at her side, were injured.

Steven Stivaske, a sixth-grader, lay in the street with both legs broken. A piece of metal ripped into his arm just below the elbow.

F.M. Fritz, a father with three children at the school, was struck by a metal screw in the chest, just above his heart. The metal sliced up to his shoulder, fracturing and ricocheting off bone, then headed down his arm, snagging just above his elbow.

Perry Hart was struck in the heel by a two-inch piece of scrap iron. It lodged in his heel as he fell, bleeding all over the street.

Thelma Medcoff, who was 50 feet from the blast site, was also hit by flying shrapnel. Her legs were sliced open in three places.

The carnage closer to the truck yielded more horrific results. Nelson McFarren was killed instantly by the blast. His body was thrown against a nearby tree. His son-in-law, Glenn Smith, was mortally wounded. His entire left side was in ruins – one leg sheared off at the thigh, hand and arm mangled, and his entire body blackened. A piece of metal was lodged in his right leg, just above his ankle. B.D. Rice, a veterinarian who had been examining farm animals nearby, applied his medical knowledge to the dying man, managing to splint his damaged right leg. Another man used a belt to stem the bleeding from the stump of Smith's left leg. Amazingly, Smith could still speak. "I have been hit," he told his brother, Frank, the school janitor. "It is all up with me." He kept whispering to the men who tried to help him, "I don't want anybody to feel bad if I go."

Someone grabbed hold of Principal Huggett, who was standing in shock nearby. A panicked voice declared that the explosions had been done on purpose. "They got Mr. Huyck! They will get you!"

Huggett sighed and looked around the scene. His school was in ruins. His children were dead, dying, and wounded. Cars were burning. The body of the superintendent and the bodies of his friends were lying in the street. West of town, a farm was burning.

Huggett later said, "I realized there was nothing I could do. I went on helping the youngsters there."

Principal Huggett may have been the calmest person at the scene. Workers and volunteers were panicked and confused. No one understood what had happened, most imagining that they were under some sort of military attack. Rumors swept through the crowd about more explosions to come.

In the distance, Kehoe's farm was still burning, sending a column of black smoke high into the air. Smaller explosions could still be heard from the farm as Kehoe's leftover pyrotol continued to explode. Across the street from the school, trees, houses and parked cars were on fire from the original blast. Pieces of human bodies were strewn on the grass and in the bushes and many family members had fainted or had become hysterical. Over 100 people had been injured and more injuries were being found every minute. At that point, no one had any idea just how many had been killed.

Slowly, though, the collective understanding of Bath changed. It wasn't a faulty boiler that had leveled the school. Kehoe's farm was burning. Kehoe had blown himself up. A ruined chassis and motor were all that remained of his truck. A steaming tangle of intestines were lodged in the steering wheel.

Andrew Kehoe was at the center of the horror.

Minutes after Kehoe's truck exploded, the Lansing Fire and Police departments arrived on the scene. They were followed by the Michigan State Police and the Department of Public Safety, but nothing could have prepared these hardened veterans for what they saw – wrecked and burning cars, downed trees, a collapsed school building that was filled with screaming children, fires everywhere. It was like a battle scene from some distant war.

Sheriff Fox and States Attorney William Searl knew they were getting close to Bath when they saw the cars – automobiles were backed up on the main road into town. Fox drove his official automobile around the traffic jam. He was waved through cordons that were being set up by State Police officers on the scene. He and Searl passed through the barricades, silenced by the terrible scene. It was destruction beyond their comprehension – men, women, children running, howls of pain, cries for help, blaring automobile horns, bricks falling and being tossed. They saw frantic men pulling at debris in the rubble of the school and white sheets – stained with blood – covering small, still forms that were stretched across the lawn. There was the smoking remains of some sort of vehicle and cars nearby, ruined by the fire.

This was hell on earth.

Fox and Searl got out of the car and they heard the whispers. Kehoe was the man behind it all. Kehoe's farm was burning. He blew himself up and he took Superintendent Huyck with him.

A short distance away from Kehoe's destroyed car, on the edge of Frank and Leone Smith's property, a pair of volunteers from Lansing – Alex Urqhart and Dr. Milton Shaw, the Red Cross director – were making bandages for the victims. One of them noticed something on the side of the road. It looked like a reddish clump with tattered cloth attached to it.

Urqhart – a World War I veteran – was unnerved. He'd seen a lot of carnage on the battlefield, but nothing compared to what lay in that ditch. It was a body – or what was left of one. The corpse was completely gutted and ripped apart. The body was a bloody carcass, but the face and head were more or less intact. Gray hair was matted on what remained of the skull. In the mess of clothing, they could see that two documents protruded from what might have been a coat or shirt pocket.

One was a driver's license. The other was part of a bank book from the Lilley State Bank of Tecumseh. Andrew Kehoe's name was on both of them.

A woman, hair wild and dirty face streaked with tears, stopped suddenly near the two men. "What's the name?" she demanded.

Urqhart examined the license. "Andrew Kehoe."

"That's the man!" the woman screamed.

Sherriff Fox walked over, and he was handed the license and bank book. He brought over some of Kehoe's neighbors to view the body. A positive identification was made. They finally understood what Kehoe had said to them as he drove away from his burning farm. He had urged them to go to the school. They could have never imagined what he had planned there.

Hundreds of people climbed through the wreckage that day, trying to find and rescue the children pinned underneath it. Area contractors sent all their men to assist, and volunteers came from everywhere in response to the pleas for help. The injured and dying were transported to Sparrow Hospital and Saint Lawrence Hospital in Lansing. Michigan Governor Fred Green arrived during the afternoon of the disaster and assisted in the relief work, carting bricks away from the scene. The Lawrence Baking Company of Lansing sent a truck filled with pies and sandwiches, which were served to volunteers in the community hall.

And then, under the school, a chilling discovery was made.

Two police officers – Lansing's Captain John O'Brien and William Klock, a sheriff's deputy from nearby Ingham County – were in the basement when some falling debris got their attention. The two men cautiously approached the coal room, where they could see part of the ceiling had fallen and was now scattered on the floor.

But it wasn't the fallen plaster that got their attention – it was what was mixed up in it. As they pulled it away, they found a bundle of dynamite, connected to some kind of wire. O'Brien and Klock didn't search any farther. They quickly got out of the building and spread the news of their terrifying find. All rescue efforts were immediately halted, and fear spread through the rescuers that the rest of the building could explode at any time.

Officials regrouped and put in a call for volunteers to go back into the basement. Five men bravely volunteered – Assistant Fire Chief Paul Lefke, Michigan Department of Public Safety Assistant Chief Lieutenant Lyle Morse, state troopers Ernest "Buck" Haldeman and Donald McNaughton, and Michigan State College engineer F.I. Phippeny. They carefully went back into the basement. The wire on the dynamite was traced to a tin pipe. The pipe, connected by small bolts, ran a considerable distance through the ceiling and into other rooms in the basement. The team could see that this conduit was packed solid with dynamite.

More dynamite was planted in the ceiling, hidden by wire mesh that was covered with plaster. Wire connected the caches of explosives to a blasting cap. The men followed the trail toward the section of the basement that was

SOME OF THE EXPLOSIVES THAT WERE REMOVED FROM BENEATH THE SCHOOL. LUCKILY, THEY HAD NOT DETONATED, ACCORDING TO KEHOE'S PLAN. IF THEY HAD, THE DEATH TOLL WOULD HAVE BEEN MUCH HIGHER.

underneath the main building. More wires were found, stapled to wooden beams. The staples were a little rusty, indicating that they had been in place for some time.

This has not been a plan that Andrew Kehoe had recently devised, they realized, he had been working on it for months.

The wires led to more blasting caps, attached to more explosives – bundles of dynamite and heavy sacks of surplus pyrotol. The wire trail led to a hotshot battery, connected to a clock. Had this other timer gone off as intended, the entire Bath Consolidated School would have been destroyed – not just the one wing – and every student in the building would be dead or seriously injured. By some miracle, only the north wing's explosives had detonated.

Some experts suggested that Kehoe – despite his extensive electrical knowledge – had made a serious error. There simply wasn't enough power in the timing devices to set off the massive amount of explosives he'd concealed under the main building – but that didn't make them any less dangerous to the men who were now tasked with removing them.

Haldeman and McNaughton, working in the dark basement lit only by flashlights, carefully disconnected the blasting caps from the tangle of wires. It was a delicate task. They knew that even a slight mistake could conceivably result in a massive explosion that was even more deadly than the first. Finally, with this stage safely completed, they began to dismantle what remained of Kehoe's mad plan.

But some of the cavities and burrows were too small to accommodate a full-grown man to get at the explosives. They found a volunteer who was willing to help – 14-year-old Chester Sweet, whose younger brother and sister had been in the school when it exploded that morning. He had been working on the family farm at the time. He volunteered for the deadly mission without any hesitation. He was led into the dark passageways of the basement and, showing no fear, squeezed into the tight spaces and gently removed all the explosives he could find.

More explosives were found in a carefully concealed hiding spot. Kehoe had used rain gutters and ran them along the ceiling of the basement. They perfectly blended into the plaster. He lined the inside of the gutters with dynamite and pyrotol by shoving the explosives deep into them with a metal rod or wooden pole. School janitor Frank Smith spent a good deal of time in the basement, yet never once saw the gutters. They were practically invisible in the darkness and unnoticeable to anyone except the madman who had installed them.

In all, officers carried out 504 pounds of explosives from under the school, along with wires and detonating devices. The dynamite filled nine bushel baskets. There were eight 30-pound sacks of pyrotol, 10 blasting caps, and two timing devices. It was estimated that only about 100 pounds of explosives had detonated under the north wing.

If it had all gone off – as Kehoe planned – it's possible that no one would have survived the destruction.

☠

The following day, police and fire officials gathered at the Kehoe farm to investigate the scene. The destruction was nearly perfect. The house, tractor, farm equipment, and outbuildings had all been destroyed by a combination of fire and explosives. An elaborate wiring system snaked throughout the farm grounds. It was sophisticated work that proved once again Kehoe's expertise as an electrician. Only the chicken coop was left standing.

An unexploded bomb in the henhouse ironically demonstrated Kehoe's talent for mechanical invention. The device resembled a standard fountain used to provide drinking water for chickens. It used an upside-down quart bottle filled with gasoline, tucked into a tin can. An automobile spark plug and a coil – intended as an ignition device – were connected to the bottle, which had a yarn wick protruding from it. To make sure that the fire spread, Kehoe had packed his contraption with a heavy layer of straw. Somewhere along the line, his wiring from the timer in the house had failed, just like the botched timers in the basement of the school.

In the ruins of the barn, Kehoe's two horses were burned down to their skeletons. Their feet had been bound with wire to prevent them from escaping.

But that was not the worst discovery that they made. Two state troopers who had been helping with the search of the property stopped to take a well-deserved break for cigarettes near the chicken coop. Nearby, they saw a cart – a sort-of makeshift wheelbarrow made from a hog chute that had been attached to a metal axle and a set of wheels. Men had been passing by the cart all day, but no one had looked closely enough at it until now.

Human remains, charred to the bone, lay on the cart – Nellie Kehoe had been found.

Her left arm lay over the axle, disconnected from the shoulder. The right was bent backwards, bones shattered. It was impossible to tell if they had been broken by violence or fire. Although both feet were burned away, Nellie's left big toe was only scorched; others more or less intact. The body had apparently been dressed because fabric remains were found where the arm was across the axle and corset stays were found on the ground. Her skull had been cracked at the forehead, but because the head was so badly charred, it was impossible to say how she was killed. Regardless, it was assumed by many – legal authorities, newspaper reporters, members of the inquest jury, and Nellie's family and neighbors – that Kehoe had bludgeoned his wife and moved her body to the spot where it was found.

The officers also found the items that Kehoe had left next to Nellie's body. There was silverware next to her head and atop her chest. A metal box was next to her corpse. Inside were items that probably had personal meaning – a lady's gold watch, a brooch and chain, earrings, two rings, a dozen teaspoons with a K on the handle, a pin from the Knights of the Maccabees, a social organization with members across the state. There were also badly scorched papers, including a marriage license and statements and bills from the Saint Lawrence Hospital in Lansing and the Henry Ford Hospital in Detroit. There was also a large roll of what appeared to be uncashed Liberty Bonds left over from World War I – likely enough to pay off all the debts that drove Andrew Kehoe mad.

Did he know about these funds? It was another secret that Andrew – and Nellie – took to their graves.

But one thing that was not a secret was the meaning of the crude wooden sign that Kehoe had wired to a fence on the farm. He'd left it behind as a message that he likely imagined would explain his madness. The message on the sign became Andrew Kehoe's final words:

CRIMINALS ARE MADE, NOT BORN.

All over the world, newspaper headlines announced the shocking tragedy in Bath. The press struggled to find reasons for Kehoe's rampage, but, of course, there were none. The Bath community was devastated, and the loss could not be measured in simply the number of children that had been killed. There was no one in the community that had not been touched by the tragedy. Everyone had lost a relative, friend, classmate, or teacher. In addition to the human toll, Bath faced financial catastrophe. A new school would have to be built by a town that had already sacrificed a great deal to build the first one. The future now looked bleak.

The American Red Cross, which set up operations at the Crum pharmacy, did what it could to provide aid and comfort for the victims. The Lansing Red Cross headquarters stayed open until 11:30 on the night of the disaster to answer telephone calls, update the list of the dead and injured, and provide information. The Red Cross also managed donations that were sent to pay for both the medical expenses of the injured and the burial costs of the dead.

Over the next few days, there was an endless wave of funerals in Bath, with 18 of them being held on Saturday, May 22. The last funeral was held on Sunday, May 23, the same day that Charles Lindbergh completed the first solo transatlantic flight to Paris. This event stole away the newspaper space from the tragedy in Michigan.

Over 100,000 automobiles passed through Bath on the weekend after the bombing. It was a staggering amount of traffic for the small village, but most saw it as a show of sympathy and support from surrounding communities. But was it? To many of those grieving, it was an unwelcome intrusion. To the more cynical, it was nothing more than an endless parade of curiosity-seekers. Many of them wandered the rubble of the school – picking up macabre souvenirs – or went searching for the Kehoe farm. The ghoulish tourists were followed by the headline-seekers, like the Ku Klux Klan, who said that the actions of Kehoe, a Roman Catholic, were the result of his adherence to the stance of the Catholic Church against what they considered "Protestant or godless schools."

A coroner's inquest was held the following week. The coroner had arrived at Bath on the day of the disaster and had sworn in six community leaders to serve as the investigative jury. The Clinton County Prosecutor conducted the examination and dozens of Bath citizens and law enforcement personnel testified before the jury. Although there was never a doubt that Andrew Kehoe had carried out the bombing, the jury was asked to determine if the school board or any of its employees were guilty of criminal negligence.

The testimony lasted for more than a week and in the end, the jury exonerated the school board and its employees. In the verdict, the jury concluded that Kehoe "conducted himself sanely and so concealed his operations that there was no cause to suspect any of his actions; and we further find that the school board, and Frank Smith, janitor of the school building, were not negligent in and about their duties, and were not guilty of any negligence in not discovering Kehoe's plan."

It was also determined that Kehoe had murdered Emory Huyck on the morning of May 18. Their findings also concluded that the school was destroyed as part of a plan that was carried out by Kehoe alone, without the aid of conspirators, and that he had willfully injured 58 people and caused the death of 44 others, including his wife, Nellie. On August 22, some three months after the bombing, fourth-grader Beatrice Gibbs died following hip surgery.

It was the final death attributed to the Bath School Massacre.

The jury returned a judgment of suicide as the cause of Andrew Kehoe's death. His body was eventually claimed by his sister. Without any ceremony, he was buried in an unmarked grave in an initially unnamed cemetery. Later, it was revealed that Kehoe was buried in the pauper's section of Mount Rest Cemetery in St. Johns, Clinton County, Michigan. Nellie Kehoe was buried in Mount Hope Cemetery in Lansing by her family – although her tombstone was marked with her maiden name of Price.

The people of Bath were left with no other choice but to move on.

Governor Fred Green created the Bath Relief Fund and money poured in from the state, local governments across Michigan, and thousands of Michigan residents. More money came in from across the country, which eventually allowed for the demolition of the damaged portion of the school and the construction of a new wing with the donated funds.

School resumed on September 5, 1927, and for the first school year, it was held in the community hall, the township hall, and two retail buildings. Most of the students returned. An architect from Lansing, Warren Holmes, donated plans for a new school and the school board approved contracts for a new building on September 14. On September 15, Michigan's Republican U.S. Senator James Couzens presented a personal check for $75,000 to the Bath construction fund and the school's new wing was named in his honor.

In 1928, artist Carlton W. Angell presented the board with a statue called "Girl with a Cat." The statute currently rests in the Bath School Museum, which is located in the school district's middle school and adjacent to the bombing site. Angell's inscription on the piece stated that it was dedicated to the courage and determination of the people of Bath. The sculpture was funded by donated pennies from students all over Michigan. According to legend, the pennies were melted down and used to cast the statue.

Following World War II, it was decided that the James Couzens School could no longer meet the educational needs of the community. Across the road, a new elementary school was built in 1953 and a second building followed in 1961. The Couzens School – now in poor, worn-out condition – was finally closed in

1975. Now stuck with an empty building, the school board contracted a wrecking crew to tear down the shuttered facility. Razing what was left of the school was not a popular idea with some Bath residents. It was all that was left of the Bath Consolidated building and they insisted that it could still be used as a library or some other use.

But sentiment was overruled. On May 18. 1975, the wrecking ball came for the school. Across the street, the school's principal asked for a few minutes of silence for those killed in the 1927 bombings – timing his announcement to the moment of the first explosion. When the moment ended, the wrecking ball began to swing. Debris crashed to the ground as the first section scheduled for razing – the north wing – was knocked down.

The school was replaced by a small park, dedicated to the victims of the tragedy. At the center of the park is the cupola of the original building – the only part that's been preserved – and at the entrance there is a bronze plaque that lists the names of all who were killed on that terrible day.

The parents of the children who were killed may have survived the massacre, but their lives were never the same. Some of them moved away from Bath in the years that followed, but they never escaped the horrible memory of that day. For those who stayed in town, the bloody history of that day was always present and even after all these years, the community remains a place where death came calling on what should have been a beautiful spring day. Instead, it became a day when the twisted obsessions of a deranged man claimed the lives of dozens of innocent children and forever stained the landscape of rural Michigan.

Stories and rumors persisted for years about the strange things that happened after the bombings – about the children who died that day and yet, somehow, still managed to make it home. The stories claimed that parents experienced the sounds of their children's laughter, their voices, footsteps in the hall, and running up and down the stairs in the weeks and months that followed the bombings – even though their children had died in the initial blast.

One woman swore that she had hurried to the scene of the disaster, desperately looking for her son, and was relieved when she saw him standing at the edge of the rubble waving at her, with a smile on his face. She spent the afternoon bringing water to the volunteers and helping the wounded and then went to collect her son in the evening. She looked everywhere but was unable to find him. She asked everyone she knew – had they seen her son? But no one had. Finally, a neighbor pulled her aside and lifted the sheet off one of the bodies that was lined up on the lawn. The woman immediately recognized her son's bloody face. He'd been dead all along, they told her, he'd died when the first bomb went off.

Were such stories merely wishful thinking on the part of grieving parents who were unable to let go? It's possible, for what parent wouldn't want to have a little bit of their lost child to remain behind as a happy memory? But what if those encounters weren't just imaginations at work? It's possible that those children –

their lives ended so suddenly and prematurely – weren't quite ready to let go either and chose to make their presence known for as long as they could.

And it has not just been the parents who don't want to let the memory of those children die. Even today, stories persist that the small park in Bath where the school once stood is haunted by lingering spirits. There are a lot of people who claim to hear children's voices and laughter on nights when the park is empty and there is no one else around.

Imagination? The need to experience something so badly that we can make ourselves believe in anything? Perhaps – or perhaps not. Even if spirits don't remain here, history does, and perhaps history has left such a violent imprint at this spot that it's not quite finished with it yet.

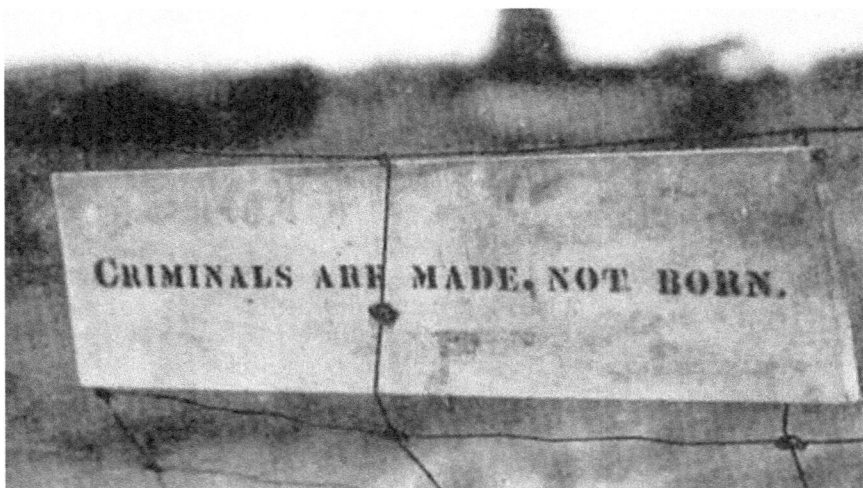

CRIMINALS ARE MADE, NOT BORN.

1928:

"CHANGELING"

The boy used the sharp edge of the nail to dig at the wood around the door frame. He scraped it back and forth, shearing away splinters and digging it into the wood as hard as he could. He had to get the door open. He was the last one left – the three other boys were gone. And they had not been the first to vanish. He knew that if he did not get out of the ramshackle little building, something terrible was going to happen to him.

The wood split and he could see the gap between the door and the frame widen a little more. Was it enough? He pushed the nail into the space and then pushed it upward with his fingers. He could barely see the metal hook that was holding the door closed. It was so dark in the chicken house but there was a light burning in the house beyond. He just needed to use the nail to lift the hook from the latch so that he could get the door open. The nail was stuck. Had he scraped the opening wide enough? He tried to lift it again – and it worked! The nail pushed the hook upwards and it dropped out of the eye latch.

The door was open.

The boy carefully eased the door open. It creaked loudly on its hinges, as he knew it would do. He had been listening to that sound for weeks as his captors brought food into the chicken coop. Or worse, when one of them came to take one of the boys away with them. Sometimes, the boys never came back. The last three boys – two brothers and another boy – had disappeared recently, leaving the last boy alone. He had to leave – right now.

If he didn't, he was certain, then he would be next.

The boy pushed the door open, as quietly as he could, and stepped out into the yard. The ranch was filled with shadows. Only the glow of a single lamp could be seen in the house. If he hurried, he would be safe. No one would see him. He crept along the side of the building, trying to stay in the darkness, and slipped around a corner. His plan was to run into the open fields beyond the ranch and keep running until he found someplace safe. Around the corner, he would be out of sight of the house, even if someone looked out the window...

But there was someone standing in the yard.

The boy froze in his tracks, but it was too late. He'd been spotted. Near the woodpile, he could see a lone figure standing still, motionless in the moonlight. It was the younger one, the boy realized, not the monster that terrified him so much. The younger one would lock him back in his cage, but at least he wouldn't hurt him – he hoped.

But the figure did nothing. He remained standing in the same spot, his eyes locked on those of the boy. He did not speak but his head moved slightly. He nodded just a tiny bit toward the open land beyond the farm. And then he turned his back to the boy, looking out toward the road in the distance, now invisible in the darkness that had fallen on the California countryside.

The boy began to run, and he never looked back.

Eventually, he made it home to his parents, who had reported him missing and imagined that he was dead. When the newspapers began to fill with horror stories about the farm where the boy had been held captive, they remained silent, fearful about getting involved. Years would pass before the boy told his story to the police – a tale of terror, abuse, and murder.

On March 10, 1928, Los Angeles mother Christine Collins was faced with every parent's worst fear – the disappearance of her child. Her son, Walter, had vanished. When Walter disappeared that day, the police initially suspected that he had run away. Christine, however, feared the worst. She refused to believe that her 10-year-old son would simply run off and she came to the terrible conclusion that he had been kidnapped.

The story of the missing boy shocked newspaper readers, who were still reeling from the December 1927 kidnapping and murder of a young girl named Marion Parker by a psychopath named William Hickman. He had taken the girl because he had a grudge against her father, Perry Parker. Hickman had demanded a ransom but had already murdered the girl. He was arrested and convicted just weeks before Walter Collins disappeared (For the story of the kidnapping and brutal murder, see my book "I Want to Come Home Tonight" – author)

Marion had been the daughter of a prominent banker but Christine Collins was a telephone operator with an ex-husband who was locked away at Folsom Prison, so it seemed unlikely that her son was taken for ransom. Without money as a motive, the police decided that revenge was just as likely, so they started for anyone with a grudge against the Collins family.

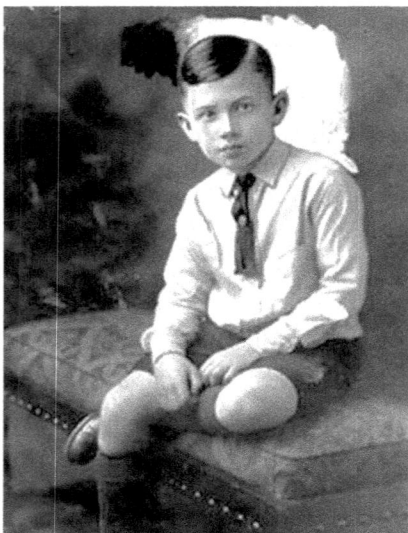

WALTER COLLINS AND HIS MOTHER, CHRISTINE

The investigation into ex-convicts wasn't productive but asking questions along the Collins' street and throughout the Lincoln Heights neighborhood where they lived did turn up a few leads. A neighbor, Mrs. A. Baker, claimed that she saw Walter in an automobile, begging to be released. The car had been driven by two "foreign-looking people."

More neighbors came forward. They said that in the days before Walter's disappearance, an Italian-looking man and woman were asking for the Collins' address. No one could offer a complete description of the couple. Detectives interviewed some of Walter Collins's classmates and one of them, a 12-year-old named Lloyd Tutor, partially identified a mugshot of an ex-convict who had been looking for the Collins home. But that lead didn't work out either.

More than 200 officers began a thorough search of the northeastern section of the city. There was no trace of the boy or his alleged kidnappers. After searching lakes, ponds, and every water source they could find, the case went cold.

Christine was devastated but refused to give up hope. Months passed, and she couldn't afford to stay home from work, so she split her time between her job and assisting in the search for Walter. She worked even harder most days, trying to keep worries about Walter's fate out of her head. She slept little, lost weight, but did not surrender to the idea that her boy was lost forever.

Then, five months after he vanished, Christine received the news that Walter had been found alive in DeKalb, Illinois. The how and why of Walter's trek east

CHRISTINE COLLINS WITH THE FRAUDULENT "WALTER" THAT WAS GIVEN TO HER BY THE LAPD. IT WAS CLEARLY NOT THE SAME BOY, BUT THE POLICE REFUSED TO ACCEPT THE EVIDENCE FOR WEEKS.

was hazy, but it appeared that an ex-con named J.S. Hutchison – who had a record of statutory offenses against young boys – may have taken him. Strangely, though, records showed that Hutchison was supposedly still incarcerated at San Quentin. Unless he could be in two places at once, there was something very strange about the story.

But Christine didn't care about the story – all she wanted was her son.

The boy was put on a train and sent to Los Angeles. The reunion of mother and son was celebrated as a massive success for the police department, which had recently been criticized in the papers for scandals caused by bribery and mistreatment of suspects. There was one problem – as soon as the boy stepped off the train, Christine realized that he was not her son.

"I do not think that is my boy," she said.

Captain J.J. Jones of the Los Angeles Police Department refused to listen to what Christine was claiming. He insisted that the boy had changed because of passing time and because of the traumatic conditions under which he'd been living. Christine rejected his claims – she'd know her own son, no matter the circumstances. But Jones insisted that the LAPD would not have made a mistake. Trying to avoid humiliation, Jones forced Christine to take "Walter" home with her for a while, to see if her memory would clear and she'd realize that he was her boy.

He advised her to take the boy home and "try him out for a couple of weeks."

Under pressure from the police, the press, and the public, Christine agreed to take the boy home with her. Subsequently, the police began to question

"Walter" in hopes of finding his abductor. He was asked how he had escaped, and how he had ended up in Illinois. Detectives and doctors were unable to get straight answers from him. He said little to nothing but insisted that he was "Walter." Christine knew he was not her son, but she agreed to care for him because he had no one else. She still worked to prove that she was right because she didn't want the police to stop looking for her actual son. She took him to her family dentist, where she obtained the real Walter's dental records to show the difference between her son and the boy who was living in her house. The records didn't match, so she took them to Captain Jones.

The dental records proved to be no help. Jones still didn't believe her – or at least he claimed that he didn't. He concluded that Christine was only trying to humiliate the LAPD and he wouldn't stand for slander – especially from a woman. He knew an easy way to shut her up – one that had proven effective before – and had Christine committed to the psychiatric ward of the General Hospital as a Code 12 internment. This was a method used by the police to lock up people they saw as being "difficult."

Christine was treated inhumanely in the hospital. She was drugged and abused so that she would come to her senses and admit that the boy found in Illinois was her son. She spent 10 days locked in the mental ward. She was finally released when "Walter" confessed that his real name was Arthur Hutchins, Jr. His only excuse for the ruse? He saw a picture of Walter in the newspaper, saw a resemblance, and decided to seize the opportunity. He knew that if he pretended to be Walter, he'd have a one-way ticket to Los Angeles, where he might meet some of his favorite stars and have a chance to make it in the movies.

Even though Christine was relieved that the ruse was over, her son was still missing. She returned to work and her daily routine of working, going home, and hoping to learn Walter's fate.

In May 1928, Christine Collins was living a nightmare. She had been going through the motions of living for more than two months as she waited for word about her missing son, Walter. Her job as a telephone operator kept her busy during the day. After work, she tried to keep up with the investigation, while her nights were filled with sleeplessness and worry.

If she was reading the newspapers at the time, she may have seen a story about two boys who had gone missing from Pomona, California. The boys, brothers Nelson and Lewis Winslow, had vanished after a meeting of the Pomona Model Yacht Club.

Nelson was 10-years-old, with light hair, blue eyes, four-feet in height, and dressed in a blue shirt and knickers. Lewis was older at age 12, and three inches taller than his little brother. But he had the same light hair and blue eyes and had been wearing a Boy Scouts uniform. According to their family, the boys had not been in any trouble and there was no reason for them to have run away from home.

Nelson and Lewis had been missing for a couple of weeks before the Winslows received a note from them. It was written on the flyleaf of a book that had been taken from the Pomona Public Library. The note said they'd left Pomona

NELSON AND LEWIS WINSLOW, THE OTHER BOYS REPORTED MISSING AROUND THE TIME THAT WALTER COLLINS VANISHED. THEY WOULD ALSO TURN UP TO BE TWO OF THE VICTIMS IN WINEVILLE.

and were on their way to Mexico to look for gold. Local police sent telegrams to the border authorities, asking them to detain the boys if they were found attempting to cross into Mexico.

There were no sightings of Nelson and Lewis at the border, however, and no further clues to their whereabouts ever surfaced. The Winslows were forced into the same limbo that was being experienced by Christine Collins. They were afraid to hope for good news and feared that the next telephone call would bring the news they never wanted to receive.

Because the Winslow home was 30 miles east of the Collins' Lincoln Heights bungalow, the police didn't make a connection between Walter and the Winslow boys. The authorities also had no reason to connect the disappearance to the discovery of the headless body of a Latino boy that was found on a roadside in La Puente.

But they were connected. Unknown to the police, a horrific series of events was taking place in the small town of Wineville. It would become known as one of the most heinous crimes in the state's history.

The horror began to unravel in September 1928, when a young woman named Jessie Clark decided to check up on her younger brother, Sanford, who had moved to California two years earlier to live with their uncle, Gordon Stewart Northcutt, and his mother, Sarah Louise.

Northcutt had been born in Bladworth, Saskatchewan, Canada, in 1906 and was raised in British Columbia. He moved to Los Angeles with his parents in 1924. He had asked his father to purchase a plot of land in Wineville, where his father helped him build a house and chicken ranch. To help operate the ranch, Northcutt had lured Sanford Clark from Bladworth to the United States.

SANFORD CLARK

Over the course of the next two years, Jessie had become increasingly concerned about Sanford's safety and his situation with Gordon. She decided to travel down from Canada and see what was going on at their chicken ranch. Her worst fears were soon realized. Gordon was a cruel, abusive man and he treated Sanford terribly. It would later be revealed that he both physically and sexually abused the young man. When Jessie spoke up about the boy's treatment, Gordon slapped her. She tried to get Sanford to leave, but the boy was too afraid. Jessie fled the ranch, returned to Canada, and told her mother everything. Mrs. Clark immediately informed the police.

Later, Jessie would come to realize how lucky she was to have escaped.

When local police were told about the possible abuse, they made a visit to the isolated ranch. When Gordon saw police cars approaching, he told Sanford to stall them as long as he could. The boy did as he told. He was terrified of his uncle – and he'd witnessed two long years of reasons why he should be.

Gordon and his mother fled and were not captured until they reached British Columbia. It was Sanford who put the police on their trail. The boy was traumatized by his life on the ranch and he told a blood-curdling story of the unimaginable brutality and sexual depravity that had occurred there. Sanford confessed to being forced into committing murder by Gordon. He had made him an unwilling accomplice in kidnapping and murder. Boys were held captive at the ranch, murdered with an ax, and then buried.

One of those boys, Sanford confessed, had been Walter Collins.

It was Sanford's confession that connected his uncle to Walter Collins, then the Winslow brothers, and finally to the unidentified headless boy who had been found in La Puente.

In shock and disbelief, the police allowed Sanford to lead them back to Wineville, where they began searching for the remains of the dead boys. In the chicken coop where Gordon and Sarah Louise had imprisoned them, they found clothing that belonged to missing boys. They also found the library book from which the paper had been torn to write the note from the Winslow brothers to their parents. They had, obviously, never made it to Mexico.

Sanford took the police to the graves of the Winslow brothers, which were located behind one of the ranch's outbuildings. The bodies were gone – only scraps of clothing and a few stray bones remained. Gordon and Sarah Louise had burned the bodies and scattered the remains in the desert after Jessie Clark had left the ranch without her brother. A search of the

GORDON STEWART NORTHCUTT

ranch by investigators did turn up some human bones, an axe with blood on it, and a blood-soaked mattress, leading them to believe that at least 20 children may have been killed at the ranch. However, the Northcutts could only be charged with the deaths of Nelson and Lewis Winslow and the unidentified Latino boy that Gordon referred to as "Alvin Gothea."

Gordon and Sarah Louise were extradited back to Los Angeles to stand trial. Newspaper reporters flocked around him, writing about his clothing and his appearance, noting that he was "a good-looking youth, and has a disarming manner. His fair hair sweeps back in an easy wave from the parting on the left and there is a ready smile on his lips beneath his well-modeled nose. His eyes alone are peculiar. They are deep blue, but possess a fixed, staring quality, as if their owner is in a thrall."

From his seat on the train – to which he was chained and surrounded by detectives – he told reporters, "There have been a lot of stories circulated about me. They are all untrue. What awful things to say about a man. Some people have been suffering from too much imagination, and a lot of people will be sorry when this case is cleared up." He explained that he was innocent and had only gone on

SARAH NORTHCUTT

the run to shield his "poor little mother." Gordon told a reporter, "I had to protect poor little mother from this. I simply could not tell her of this. I simply could not tell her of what they were accusing me. If poor little mother had known of these charges, it would have killed her. So, I kept it from her, newspapers and everything. I was forced to hide them. I wanted to get her away to a safe place. Then I intended to go back alone and fight this thing."

Keep in mind that this "poor little mother" admitted to using the blunt end of an axe to bash in the skull of Walter Collins.

On December 3, 1928, Gordon Northcutt confessed to the three murders but hinted that there had been at least four more. The authorities still believed they killed at least 20. Sarah Louise Northcutt confessed to the murder of Walter Collins, but his remains were never found.

The pair confessed, but, to no surprise, each quickly recanted their confessions.

At trial, arrogance and stupidity ruled the day when Gordon fired his attorney and chose to represent himself. His inept cross-examination of Sanford Clark was so damaging to his case that the prosecution never once offered any objections. Despite his terrible performance, Gordon was pleased with himself. "I'm not such a bad attorney after all, am I?" he asked reporters.

Sarah Louise, meanwhile, surprised everyone when she suddenly decided to plead guilty to the murder of Walter Collins. She seemed willing to take responsibility for all the atrocities committed at the Wineville ranch, but no one believed she was the sole perpetrator of the crimes – she was clearly attempting to save her son. Sarah was sentenced to life in prison for Walter's murder. She was spared the death penalty because she was a woman. During her sentencing hearing, Sarah Louise continued to claim that her son was innocent and made a variety of bizarre claims about his parentage, including that he was the illegitimate son of an English nobleman, that she was actually Gordon's grandmother, and that he was the result of incest between her husband, Cyrus, and their daughter. She also claimed that, as a child, Gordon had been sexually abused by the entire family. She served her sentence at Tehachapi State Prison and was paroled after less than 12 years. She died in 1944.

Gordon's trial continued, but its outcome seemed inevitable. The jury in Judge George R. Freeman's courtroom heard a grisly tale of kidnapping, molestation, torture, and murder and after 27 days, they returned with a guilty verdict on February 8, 1929. He was sentenced to death.

Gordon was hanged on October 2, 1930 at San Quentin. He was 23-years-old. It was said that he had to be supported during his climb up the steps and then collapsed on the gallows. He was more or less pushed onto the trapdoor, where he strangled to death at the end of the rope.

If this is true, it was no less than what he deserved.

At the time of Northcutt's capture, Christine Collins still believed that her son Walter was missing. Since his remains had not been found, she held out hope that he might still be alive. She traveled to the penitentiary to meet Northcutt and ask if his mother had truly killed her son.

Sanford Clark had already told a grim story about Walter's fate.

A few days after abducting Walter, Gordon had received a telephone call from his mother, Sarah Louise, informing him that she was on her way to see him at the ranch in Wineville and that she was going to stay for a few days. By then, Gordon had already imprisoned and molested Walter for a few days. During his mother's visit, he'd kept the boy in a chicken coop.

Sarah Louise became suspicious of the chicken coop and of Gordon's attempts to keep her away from it. At some time during her visit to the ranch, she discovered Walter in the chicken coop. According to Sanford Clark's testimony, she told her son that Walter could identify him because Gordon had once worked at a grocery store where Walter had shopped for his mother.

Because of this, she'd told her son that Walter knew too much and would have to be silenced permanently. Sanford Clark testified that Louise decided that all three of them should participate in murdering Walter. That way, none of them could implicate the other two without placing themselves at risk. Northcott suggested using a gun, but Louise feared that a gunshot would alert the neighbors. Louise chose the blunt end of an axe to bludgeon Walter in the head as he lay sleeping on a cot in one of the chicken coops. Sarah Louise – according to her own testimony – struck the first few blows and then Gordon and Sanford joined in.

Despite this horrific story – and the fact that he and his mother had both confessed to it – Gordon told Christine that they had not killed Walter. Since Walter's body was never found, there is a very slim chance that Gordon was telling the truth. More likely was that he was merely taking advantage of her and possibly hoping to extend his life with "new information" about the case. But I suppose we will never know for sure – he took the truth to the grave with him.

Christine did sue the LAPD and won a $10,800 lawsuit against Captain Jones for sending her to the psychiatric ward and for his insistence that Hutchins boy was Walter. He never paid her, and he was only given a four-month suspension for what he had done.

Some of the other figures in the case didn't fare much better than Gordon Northcutt. Christine Collins's attorney, Sammy Hanh, committed suicide in 1957 by tying concrete blocks around his neck and jumping into the pool at his cabin in Tick Canyon. In the heyday of his career, he had been one of California's most prominent attorneys, defending the famous evangelist Aimee Semple McPherson when she was under investigation for allegedly staging her own kidnapping, as well as representing Louise Peete, who left a string of suicides, suspicious deaths, and murders in her wake before becoming one of only three women ever executed in the state of California.

Gordon Northcutt's father, George, moved to Parsonsburg, Maryland, where he lobbied for his wife to be paroled. In November 1935, he wrote to prison authorities that there was no evidence that the boys had even been murdered. It's impossible to know if he really believed that his wife and son were innocent or if he was simply going along with the new story that had been cooked up – that Sanford and Jessie had made up the whole crazy story out of jealousy and spite. What was clear was that George still loved the wife who had said terrible things about him on the witness stand. He wrote, "I want her, I need her – no better wife ever lived than Louise Northcott." Even after hearing confessions of murder, even after being accused of raping his own son and impregnating his own daughter, George declared he would always consider his son innocent. Gordon was "simply batty," his mind "warped, unbalanced."

Sarah Louise was released from prison in 1940 and returned to live with her husband. She died four years later.

Sanford Clark was never tried for any of the crimes at the Wineville ranch. If he participated in any of the murders, it was under extreme duress. He was sent to the State Industrial School for Boys in Whittier, California, for two years. During his time there, he impressed the staff with his desire to lead a productive life and was released in 1931. He returned to Canada and settled in Saskatoon, Saskatchewan.

He was married in 1935 and he and his wife, June, later adopted two little boys. During World War II, he served with the 21st Battery, 6th Field Regiment of the Royal Canadian Artillery. He worked for the postal service until suffering a major heart attack in the 1970s. He died in 1991, leaving behind numerous grandchildren and a lifetime of quiet community service. Family and friends who were closest to him say he rarely discussed his experiences on the ranch.

In 1933, a young man appeared in a Los Angeles police station with a remarkable and harrowing story to tell. Five years earlier, he had run away from his parent's home and had been kidnapped by Gordon Northcutt. Held captive on the chicken ranch, he eventually escaped by forcing open the door to a chicken coop and disappearing into the night. He returned home to his parents, but they kept his story secret, fearing that he might be blamed for the murders of the boys who were confined with him – including Walter Collins.

Arthur Hutchens -- the boy who arrived in Los Angeles as the fake "Walter Collins" – led a more stable life after his California excursion. Confined to Iowa's State Training School for Boys until he reached the age of 14, he worked in various carnivals before settling down back in California to train horses and to be a jockey, which had been his lifelong dream. He later married and had a daughter, who grew up idolizing her adventurous father. He died in 1954.

As for Christine Collins, she later remarried but had no more children. She clung to the words that Gordon Northcutt had said to her from his prison cell and never gave up hope that her son might be returned to her alive. She died in 1964, still refusing to believe that he was dead.

Sadly, Walter Collins never returned.

The town of Wineville, California, was so traumatized by its connection to Gordon Northcutt that it officially changed its name to Mira Loma on November 1, 1930, only a month after Northcutt's execution. Over time, the chicken ranch was swallowed by the town and vanished into the neighborhoods. The outbuildings were torn down, the land was developed, and for a time, the horrifying story of what occurred on the land was largely forgotten. Or it would have been –if the house where such terrible things had occurred had not been left standing.

And if that house did not have a reputation for being haunted.

For the most part, the gruesome history of the house remained unknown in Mira Loma until the release of the 2008 film *Changeling*, which was directed by Clint Eastwood and starred Angelina Jolie as Christine Collins. Thanks to media interest in the film – and the true story behind it – locals soon learned of the horrific events that had occurred in their community. The Northcutt farm had been dismantled years before, but the house that Gordon had lived in was still standing on Wineville Road. At the time of the film's release, there was a couple living in the house. When they learned what had taken place there, they moved out of the house and the area. Did they leave because of the stigma attached to

NORTHCUTT'S HOUSE AT THE WINEVILLE RANCH.

the property, or was it – as many who lived in the area believed – because they finally had an explanation for why their house was so haunted?

Past occupants of the house later came forward with their own stories about living in a house where the deviant behind the "Wineville Chicken Coop Murders" had preyed on his victims.

One young woman recalled living in the house when she was about eight-years-old. Neither she, nor her family, had any idea about the house's history. They had moved in because the house was owned by a friend of the family, who allowed them to stay there for free, as long as they looked out for the place.

It seems the friend had trouble keeping tenants.

The young woman noted that she always felt uncomfortable in the house, as though someone was watching her. She mentioned the sensation to her parents, but they dismissed it as the imagination of a child. One night, though, she was on her way to use the bathroom and walked past her parent's room, glancing in to see the shadow of a man on the wall. She assumed at first that it was her father, but then she heard gurgling and choking noises coming from inside the room. It sounded like someone trying to spit something out, she said.

"Who's there?" she called out.

There was no answer, so she pushed the bedroom door open the rest of the way – the room was empty.

Her most frightening memory of the house took place one summer when her aunt, uncle, and cousins came to visit the family. It was late in the evening, around 11:00 p.m., and the children were playing in the yard. They were excited to get to play together after some time apart and all the cousins were too rowdy to go to sleep. And then, out of the darkness, they heard what sounded like young boys screaming and crying. The family owned two large dogs and the animals immediately reacted. Their ears laid back on their heads and the dogs began barking loudly – at nothing.

And then they saw the shadow on the white wall that surrounded the yard.

It appeared to be a man's shadow and he wasn't alone. He was holding a small boy, dangling him in the air. The boy's legs flailed and kicked out at the man, but they were too short to reach him. He grabbed hold of the boy by the hair, she recalled, and then swung something with his other hand, cutting the boy's head from his body. As the man still held the head in his hand the body fell to the ground.

"We stood there with our mouths open but no screams coming out," she said. When they heard a chilling laugh that seemed to come from everywhere in the backyard at the same time, the children ran screaming into the house.

Not surprisingly, neither set of parents believed the wild tale. It was not until the girl's two older sisters admitted that they, too, had also had frightening experiences in the house that the adults decided to listen. The older girls reported seeing shadows walking outside their bedroom window at night and hearing footsteps in the house when no one else was home.

They didn't move out of the house right away and she claimed to continue to experience weird things during the rest of the family's time there. "One time, my younger sister fell on the concrete without tripping over anything and cracked her skull," she remembered. "She felt unseen hands grab her and push her down hard. There were a lot of things that couldn't be explained but my parents insisted there must be an explanation to everything. I think they just wanted us to feel more comfortable in that house since we all knew we were going to stay there a little longer." The family lived in the house for three years before they moved to another part of Mira Loma. She definitely didn't miss the place once they left it behind.

Other families also had uncomfortable times in the house. One man often stayed there with his aunt and uncle when he was a boy. This would have been in the 1950s, when people in the area still had livestock, chickens, and horses. He recalled that one night, the horses in the barn began behaving strangely, banging on the stalls, stomping their hooves, and making a lot of noise. His uncle went outside to see what was wrong and then quickly returned to the house. He hurried inside and bolted the door. His face was white.

He had seen a boy outside near the barn – a boy who had disappeared right in front of his eyes.

After the Northcutt ranch was sold, the land was divided up into lots and new homes were built on the property, surrounding the original house where

Gordon had lived – and had terrorized his young nephew. A couple who lived in one of the homes that was built on the ranch property also came to believe their house was haunted.

They moved into the house in 2007 and a few months later, witnessed something they would never forget. In October, the couple had just returned from a birthday party in Los Angeles. It was late, about 1:00 a.m., and they were sitting at the dining room table talking about the fun they'd had at the party. Their son, who was nine-years-old at the time was already asleep in his room.

Suddenly, both of them looked up and saw a young boy wearing what appeared to be denim overalls over a white shirt step halfway out of their son's room. The mother yelled out their son's name and ran towards the room to see what was going on. The man later recalled, "I knew it was not my son immediately because of the clothing, and I just froze, trying to analyze what was happening."

"Did you see that?" his wife demanded, and he told her that he had.

Now they believed all the things their son had been telling them since they'd moved into the house.

For weeks, he'd been telling his parents that he often saw a little boy sitting in the corner of his room. They'd assumed that it was an "imaginary friend." He was the right age for it and they hadn't noticed anything out of the ordinary in the house until that night.

After the incident, their son began refusing to sleep in his room. He insisted on going to sleep in the guest room and he always wanted a light left on, something he'd never asked for previously. And he was not the only one who had trouble sleeping. When family members came to stay, many of them complained about how some rooms in the house were too cold, or about hearing footsteps, or about doors that opened and closed on their own. After a visit or two, most of them simply refused to come back – or at least to stay in the house after dark.

It would not be until the release of the film based on the Walter Collins case that the couple realized the morbid history of not only Mira Loma, but of their own property. They had a ghost in their house, they realized, and based on what had happened there, they weren't surprised.

1929:

A LAWSON FAMILY

CHRISTMAS

Buck Lawson and his cousin, Sanders, trudged through the six inches of snow that had fallen on the simple streets of Germantown. It was a rare thing to see that kind of snow in North Carolina, but seeing as how it had fallen on Christmas, the boys felt no need to complain. It seemed like the perfect day for it.

In fact, it was pretty much the perfect Christmas, Buck thought to himself. The wiry 16-year-old had enjoyed a breakfast with his family and when he had left on an errand to town, his sister and mother were busy starting on Christmas supper. His sister, Marie – and boy, she could cook – was making a special raisin cake for the family. Buck's mouth watered just thinking about it.

Even Buck's father had been in a bright mood that morning. Buck's father, Charlie, could be a difficult man. He was prone to bad tempers and fits of rage and could be harsh and even violent with his children. Buck knew that he often stepped out of line, and probably deserved some of the spankings that he'd gotten as a child, but he also felt that his father often took things too far. Not long ago, he'd stood up to his father and the two of them had gotten into a real knock down brawl. That had been an ugly day. Buck still remembered the way that his mother had cried, and how scared his younger brothers and sisters had been. That was worse to Buck than his father's anger. But one thing was sure, Charlie hadn't hit Buck again. He hadn't hit Buck's mother or his brothers and sisters again either. That was worth the scrapes and bruises from that terrible day.

Charlie seemed more like himself on Christmas morning. He was affectionate, funny, and had a smile on his face. After breakfast, he had suggested that he, Buck, and Sanders, who had spent the night with the Lawsons, meet up with some of the other local farmers for a shooting competition.

Buck smiled at the memory. They'd had a good time with the neighbors, blasting away at targets, and good-naturedly joshing one another about their bad aims.

It wasn't long, though, before they started running low on bullets and shells. Charlie finally called a halt to the shooting match. He wanted to go rabbit hunting later in the afternoon and didn't want to run out of shotgun shells. In fact, he told Buck, he was pretty low already. Would he mind going into town and buying some more?

Buck agreed and Sanders volunteered to go along with him. It was only a couple of miles into town and even though none of the stores would be open on Christmas Day, most of the owners lived on the premises and could easily be convinced to open just long enough for one sale. Charlie pressed a few dollars into his son's hand and the two boys walked off without a care in the world.

Now, Buck and Sanders were on their way home. A box of shotgun shells rattled in the pocket of Buck's wool coat. The boys laughed and joked with one another, thought of ways to spend their afternoon, and dreamed about the supper that was going to be on the Lawson table that night. They'd worked up an appetite hiking to town and wondered if they could convince Buck's mother to let them sneak a little taste of Christmas ham.

As the boys walked along, they heard the sound of tires crunching in the snow behind them. They had been walking in the middle of the empty street. No one was out driving on Christmas morning, or so they thought. Buck glanced back and pushed his cousin a little bit to edge him toward the side of the road. But then Buck looked back again. He recognized the car that was slowly creeping up behind them. It belonged to Charlie Hampton, the boyfriend of his sister, Marie. Maybe Charlie was on his way out to the Lawson farm and could give them a lift.

Buck turned around with a grin and waved at Charlie Hampton – but Charlie didn't wave back. Strange, Buck thought, he and Charlie were pals. Why did his friend look so serious? The auto came to a stop and Charlie opened his door and stepped out. Buck had never seen his face look so pale. His eyes were haunted and dark.

"Buck," Charlie said, his voice wavering and high. "I need you to get into the car with me."

Buck was no longer thinking about a ride. Something was wrong and he knew it. "Charlie, what's going on?" he asked. Hampton opened his mouth and started to answer, but instead of words, he belched out a harsh, wailing cry. He began to sob. He buried his face in his hands and tried to choke out the words.

That was when Buck knew that something terrible had happened and it was at that moment that he knew that his life would never be the same again.

Buck's father, Charles Davis Lawson, was born on May 10, 1886, in Stokes County, North Carolina. He grew up on a tobacco farm. His father worked the land and as a boy, Charlie, along with his younger brothers, worked it, too. In 1911, Charlie married Fannie Manring and, as was common at the time, they started having children right away. Daughter Marie was born in 1912. She was quickly followed by James Arthur – who would grow into the nickname of "Buck" – in 1913, followed by William in 1914. Another daughter, Carrie, arrived in 1917.

Charlie's brothers, Marion and Elijah, decided to start their own farms and moved a short distance from their father's farm, settling near Germantown. In 1918, Charlie decided to follow them, packed up the family, and moved to Germantown. He found a farm to work as a sharecropper, but his dream was to own his own land. Sharecropping could be a hard way of life. Charlie was essentially a tenant who worked the land and had to pay a share of the crop that he raised to the property owner. He was responsible for the cost of planting, seed, harvesting, and labor. After the crop was sold, the landowner took his share of the profits as rent and the farmer kept the rest. Depending on the season and how well the crop did, a sharecropper could make a little or he could make next to nothing. It was almost impossible to feed a family as a sharecropper, which was why Charlie wanted to own his own land someday. It was his dream and he was determined to succeed.

But the dream – along with his life – was almost cut short in November 1918 when he had a run in with a black worker at a Winston-Salem tobacco warehouse. Charlie was visiting the Piedmont warehouse on Trade Street when Jesse McNeal clipped his leg when he pushed past him with a tobacco cart. Charlie gave McNeal and angry warning about watching where he was going and the next thing anyone knew, the two men were rolling on the floor in a vicious fight.

McNeal produced a knife and stabbed Charlie in the head and the chest. After several onlookers broke up the fight, Charlie had to be rushed to the hospital. According to the *Charlotte Observer*, "his condition is regarded as serious, little hope being entertained for his recovery." McNeal, meanwhile, had run off, later to be arrested and locked up by the police.

Charlie beat the odds and was released from the hospital on December 5. After a short period of rest at home, he returned for McNeal's trial on December 20, and was in the courtroom to see the man found guilty of assault and sentenced to 18 months on the Forsyth County road gang.

Charlie recovered from his wounds, and while he and Fannie sadly lost their son William to pneumonia in November 1920, they continued to add to their

THE LAWSON HOME

family. Maybell was born in May 1922, James in April 1925, and Raymond in February 1927.

After years of scrimping and saving every penny, Charlie bought a house and barn on Brook Cove Road -- and 128 acres that went with it -- just two months after Raymond was born. He borrowed $3,200 from the Wachovia Bank for the purchase, making a deal that set his mortgage payments at $500 a year. The farm was just outside of Germantown and close to the Lawson and Manring families. It was important to Charlie and Fannie to be near their families so that their children could grow up with cousins and other children all around. That sentiment became even more important in 1929 when another daughter, Mary Lou, was born.

The family set about to make the primitive, but sturdy, cabin into a comfortable home and soon Charlie's tobacco crop was doing well enough that he started thinking about replacing the cabin with a modern home. He was well-respected by his neighbors, who all described him as a hard-working, sober, and honest man. He was strict with his wife and children -- often to the point of brutality – because Charlie had a bad temper. He was quick to punish the children with a switch, or even with an open hand or his fists. Fannie was not exempt from his punishments. Neighbors saw it, as did family and friends, but in the 1920s, such behavior was rarely seen as abuse. It was far too common, and it was either ignored, or never talked about. It was no one's business, most believed, what a man did in his own home.

In the summer of 1928, an incident occurred that likely affected the rest of Charlie's life. He was digging a trench to drain water out of his tobacco pack house's basement and using a mattock to do it. A mattock is a wooden-handled digging tool with a large flat blade on one side of the head and a spiked one on the other. Tom Manring, Charlie's brother-in-law, later recalled that Charlie had marked off an area to be dug, which was next to a wire fence. He was concentrating on where he needed to dig and forgot about the wire fence. The mattock stuck on a strand of wire and sprang bac, swinging up and hitting Charlie in the head.

The injury left Charlie with a nasty cut on his scalp and two spectacular black eyes. He didn't seem too severely injured at the time, but several weeks later, started seeing the local doctor for the "misery in his head." He began having blinding headaches and trouble sleeping. Charlie's nephew, Claude Lawson, later said that he thought the mattock had damaged Charlie's brain. Fannie said that he would often be sitting calmly at night and then suddenly jump up and run around the house to be sure his guns were loaded. The Lawsons' family doctor, Chester Helsabeck, later confirmed that Charlie had suffered from "some sort of nervous trouble." The exact definition of what he considered "nervous trouble" will never be known. Local doctors in the small towns of North Carolina in the 1920s were not known for their psychiatric expertise.

We do know that Charlie's friends, neighbors, and relatives all thought he started acting strangely around this same time. He often walked away in the middle of a conversation, wandering about the cabin after dark, or making sure that he stayed in the shade when outside, as if avoiding any bit of direct sunlight. One night, Fannie woke up to find the bed next to her was empty. She went outside and found Charlie kneeling alone in the middle of a harvested cornfield, where he seemed to be alternating between fervent prayer and periods of uncontrollable weeping. It was only after she convinced him to stand up and come back into the house that she realized he had brought his shotgun with him.

Charlie had always had a bad temper, which he took out on his wife and children, but his fits of rage grew worse after his injury. Buck was the only one of the boys old enough to help with the heavy work on the farm, but Charlie often found fault with the job that he did and would beat him with a wooden switch. Buck endured this until May 1929. By then, he was 16-years-old, strong, and an inch taller than his father. Charlie confronted him, told him to stand still for a beating, and Buck refused.

"You'll never be man enough to whip me again," he told his father, took the switch from his hands, and snapped it in two. Charlie just looked at him and backed away.

Buck was now determined that Charlie would never beat him, or any other member of the family, again. He started sleeping in his clothes, ready to defend the rest of the family if Charlie had one of his violent fits in the middle of the night. He was strong enough to control Charlie, who had no choice but to accept the fact this son was bigger and stronger than he was. Buck had become the family's protector, a responsibility that wore on him and haunted his sleep.

The summer of 1929 passed into fall. Aside from Charlie's occasional outbursts of temper – now muted by the watchful eye of Buck – the Lawson family went on with their lives as they always had. They tended the fields, worked the garden, and cared for their livestock. The older children attended school, cared for the little ones, and overall, their lives were happy ones.

Autumn came and went with relative calm. Buck stayed vigilant and Charlie managed to hold his temper. Winter arrived, and the days got colder. The farm chores changed, and the children spent more time indoors. Then, a little less than two weeks before Christmas, Charlie announced that he had a surprise for the family, but he had to take them to town for it.

Any trip to town was exciting for farm children, but with the promise of a surprise, the littlest ones could hardly contain themselves. They piled into the truck and rode into Germantown, where Charlie sent them all on a shopping trip. He told all of them to pick out new sets of Sunday clothes, whatever they wanted, no matter the cost. Many of the children had never had new clothes before. Hand-me-downs were common with so many children in the family, each outgrowing clothing that could be passed on to the next, so this was a special event.

THE LAWSON FAMILY PORTRAIT, TAKEN IN DECEMBER 1929. BACK ROW: ARTHUR (BUCK), 16; MARIE, 17; CHARLIE, 43; FANNIE, 37; MARY LOU, 4 MONTHS. FRONT ROW: JAMES, 4; MAYBELL, 7; RAYMOND, 2; AND CARRIE, 12.

After they had picked out new clothes and changed into them, Charlie revealed the rest of his surprise – they were going to visit the town's photographer for their first family photograph. They excitedly lined up for the portrait and then waited patiently for the photo to be taken and the plates developed.

It must have been a happy occasion and, yet, the existing photograph shows a family that seems haunted by the cares of the world. Buck, a boy of only 16, and yet looking like a powerful young man in his 20's, seems already worn down by the weight of protecting his family. None of the children, save for a slight smile on Carrie's face, seem glad to be posing for the portrait. The eyes of Fannie, who is holding Mary Lou, the baby at just four-months-old, are filled with suspicion, while Marie, a beautiful young woman who had a boyfriend and was likely planning to soon move from her family's home, just seems stunned. If some versions of the Lawson family story are to be believed, Marie may have been hiding a secret from her family – a secret that some say led to her death.

But it's the eyes of Charlie Lawson that are the most captivating in this family portrait. He is looking at something just off to the right of the camera. Was it the photographer, or someone else in the room? We'll never know, of course, but in hindsight, there is one thing that we can say about Charlie Lawson's eyes – they are the eyes of a madman.

As Christmas approached, the children grew more excited. They knew that they couldn't expect many presents, especially since they had already received new clothes, but Christmas Day was always special. There would be lots of food and Christmas was traditionally a time for special dishes that they only enjoyed once a year. Family and friends would spend the day visiting back and forth and Christmas supper would be shared with the Manrings, Fannie's parents and family.

As often happens in much of the country, but not usually in North Carolina, it snowed on Christmas Eve. By Christmas morning, there was a six-inch blanket of snow outside. The day started with a hearty breakfast, shared by Charlie's nephew, Sanders, who had stayed the night.

At the same time, a few miles away, another Lawson family was also having breakfast. It would be one they would never forget. John, one of Charlie's brothers, had a premonition that something terrible was able to happen. He was not a superstitious man, but he just knew that something was wrong. The feeling was so strong that he started to cry and had to leave the table. He tried to convince himself that he was being foolish, but he couldn't shake the dread that had overcame.

He would soon receive news that proved his premonition was correct.

After breakfast at Charlie's farm, Charlie, Buck, and Sanders joined a group of other farmers for a friendly shooting competition. They set up bottles and cans to bang away at, all the while pointing out the fresh rabbit tracks that could be seen in the snow. Several of the men mentioned trying to bag one for the stew pot later in the morning.

Inside the house, Fannie and Marie – listening to the sounds of shots ringing out in the woods – prepared the family's festive evening meal. Marie made a cake for the occasion, coating it with white frosting and dotting the entire surface with raisins as decoration. She placed it in the center of the table – hopefully out of reach of little brothers' probing fingers – and then turned her thoughts to the date she had that evening. She and her boyfriend, Charlie Hampton, were planning to attend the Christmas play at Palmyra Church in Germantown. Marie wanted to look her best. She put out a bowl of water to wash her hair and placed her curlers in front of the fire to warm them up.

Fannie was keeping busy herself, dividing her time between the stove and the needs of little Mary Lou, who was playing in her crib. She darted back and forth, wooden spoon in hand, stirring and preparing.

Outside, Charlie, Buck, and the others continued the shooting match, joshing and teasing each other after every hit or miss. Charlie was in good spirits. Cooking smells began drifting out of the house around 11:30 and that started everyone thinking about lunch. One by one, the men drifted off toward their own farms and the hefty meals that awaited them at home. Soon, only Charlie, Buck, and Sanders remained.

Charlie reminded the two boys about his plans to go rabbit hunting in the afternoon and suggested they walk into Germantown to buy some more shells. It was doubtful that any of the local stores would be open, but Charlie assured them that they could find someone who would open long enough for them to buy a box of shells. He really had a taste for rabbit, he grinned at them, but he needed more shells if he planned to shoot some.

Buck and Sanders readily agreed. It was a nice walk into town, following the railroad tracks, they could go and be back in plenty of time to eat. With a wave, they started toward town.

Charlie watched them go. His shotgun was resting on his shoulder and his hand was buried in the deep pocket of his winter coat. It was loaded with shotgun shells. They rattled together as they moved through his fingers. He had lied to his son. He had plenty of shells – more than enough for what he planned to do next.

About an hour after Buck and Sanders left, Fannie glanced at the clock on the masterpiece and saw that it was almost 1:00 p.m. She had arranged for Carrie and Maybell to visit their Uncle Elijah's family for Christmas lunch, so she called the girls over, buttoned them into their winter coats, and sent them out the door. It was a short walk to Elijah's house. Marie was still busy with her hair. James and Raymond were happily playing on the floor in front of the fireplace and Mary Lou was content in her crib. Fannie finally relaxed for the first time that day. The cooking and dishes were done, and the house was in order. She could rest a bit before she had to get things ready for supper.

Carrie and Maybell's trip to their uncle's house took them along the old stagecoach road that ran the length of the Lawsons' farm. Trudging through the snow, they passed the family's wood pile and the tobacco pack house that Charlie had been draining when he was struck in the skull by the mattock. The girls followed the curve of the road toward the first of Charlie's two barns. The barn stood only a few hundred yards from the house and – like all the farm's other big buildings – it faced directly on the stage road. As they rounded the road's sharp curve, the girls could see the barn looming ahead of them.

They had no idea that their father was waiting for them there.

Charlie was standing out of sight, behind the northwest corner of the barn with a 12-gauge, double-barreled shotgun and a 25-20 rifle. Hearing his daughter's excited laughter as they approached, he pressed himself against the wooden wall of the barn, making sure that he could not be seen. He gripped the shotgun tightly in his hands and waited for the girls to pass by. As soon as they had, he took careful aim at Carrie's back and pulled the trigger. As she started to fall, he fired the second barrel at Maybell. A cloud of red mist spread over the snow as she fell to the ground.

THE BARN WHERE CHARLIE WAITED TO KILL HIS DAUGHTERS, CARRRIE AND MAYBELL

Charlie snatched up the rifle and walked over to the girls. Maybell was perfectly still, but he could see that Carrie was still breathing. He fired a single rifle bullet into her head. Then he took a piece of scrap wood from outside the barn and bludgeoned the two little girls' heads until they were nothing more than bloody, unrecognizable masses. He stood there for a moment, the board dripping gore onto the snow, and looked down at his daughters. Then, he tossed the plank aside and picked up each girl in turn, carried them into the barn, and laid them on the floor side-by-side. He put a stone under each of their heads as a pillow, crossed their arms on their chests, and drew their eyelids closed. He looked lovingly back at the two dead girls as he latched the barn door shut and started walking toward the house.

As he walked, he loaded two more shells into the shotgun.

When he approached the cabin, he saw Fannie outside. She had gone out into the yard to gather some more firewood for the stove. She turned toward Charlie as she started back to the house and he raised the shotgun and fired directly into Fannie's chest. The wood in her arms flew into the air and she fell, dead before she hit the ground. Charlie dragged her to the house and dropped her on the front porch. Her skull knocked hollowly when her head struck the boards.

Inside the house, Marie heard the roar of the shotgun and looked out to see her father dragging her mother toward the house. Fannie was covered in blood. Marie began to scream. The front door banged open and Charlie fired the second barrel. The load slammed into her chest. Pellets pierced her heart and shattered the mantle clock behind her. Both died at the same time.

The two youngest boys -- James, 4, and Raymond, 2 -- had been quietly playing on the floor when Charlie burst through the door. After the door slammed open, thundering blast of the shotgun, and Marie falling to the floor, the boys began to scream. They both ran to hide, but not before Charlie saw them. He went after James first. The little boy ran to his bed and crawled underneath, getting as close to the far wall as he could. But Charlie reached under the bed, pulled James out, and slammed the butt of the shotgun into his head until his skull shattered. While James' screams were filling the house, Raymond had frantically scrambled behind the stove, trying to wedge himself into the corner. Charlie first tried to pry him out with the shotgun, using the barrel to try and lever the stove far enough from the wall to get at the boy. As the left barrel began to bend out of shape, Charlie gave up and began clawing for him, ignoring the heat from the stove, which singed his shirt. He managed to snag Raymond's shirt and he jerked the boy from his hiding place. As Raymond tumbled onto the floor, he slammed the butt of the ruined shotgun into his face, fracturing his skull, just as he had done to James.

Only one child remained alive in the house – baby Mary Lou. She was lying in her crib, screaming at the sounds of terror around her. Thankfully, she was too young to understand what was about to happen to her. Charlie raised the shotgun and crushed her tiny skull with the butt of the weapon. He slammed it down on her head over and over again. She was now reunited with her mother, brothers, and sisters in death.

Frantic and soaked with blood, Charlie went to work preparing the bodies to be found. Family members could start arriving at any time for a Christmas visit. He had no time to spare. He dragged Fannie inside, closed the door, and satisfied himself that his entire family was dead. He laid Fannie out on the floor, and placed Mary Lou in her arms. He then laid Marie, James, and Raymond alongside their mother. He then climbed the narrow staircase to the house's attic room where the children had slept. He collected four pillows, brought them downstairs with him, and gently placed one beneath each of their heads. Just as he had with Carrie and Maybell, he closed their eyes and crossed their arms on their chests in a position of quiet repose.

Charlie sat down for a moment on the bed that he had shared with Fannie in the house's main room and looked at what he had done. He believed in that moment that he had saved the souls of his family. He truly believed that his wife and children – lying on the floor in spreading pools of blood – would rest in peace.

"Almost done," he sighed to himself. "Almost done."

☠

One of Charlie's brothers, Elijah, along with his two sons, Claude and Carroll, had spent their Christmas morning hunting rabbits, south of the Lawson farm. Claude had killed a rabbit, which now hung proudly from his belt. By 2:00 p.m. all their ammunition was gone, and they started for home. Since their route across the railroad tracks would take them close to Charlie and Fannie's house, Elijah suggested that they stop there and wish the family a merry Christmas. When they got within sight of the house, Claude ran excitedly on ahead and bounded onto the porch, ready to greet everyone with great holiday spirit.

He threw open the door with the greeting on his lips, but the words froze before he could speak them. What he saw inside of the house was more than his young mind could comprehend. Years later, he would remember nothing in that room except for one thing – blood. He stepped back from the door with no recollection of leaving it open, or of slamming it, to try and make it all go away.

Either Claude slammed the door, or his father did, because Elijah's view of the carnage came through the front window. He saw the blood and now he noticed the drag marks on the porch. Something was terribly wrong at Charlie's house. It was obvious that everyone was dead, and they had not been dead for long. The blood that was pooled on the floor was still wet and it was dripping between the floorboards.

Elijah's first thought was that an intruder had entered the cabin, and for some unknown reason, had murdered the family. But where was Charlie? Realizing that they had walked into something horrible – and with no ammunition to defend themselves if the killer was still around – Elijah and the boys ran for their lives.

Thrashing through the snow, they made it to the top of the hill overlooking the Miller farm, which was closest to Charlie's house. Elijah yelled down to Mr. Miller, telling him to call the sheriff and alert the neighbors – "someone had killed Charlie's whole family!"

Word spread in person and along the telephone lines and soon, farmers from all around were grabbing their shotguns and converging on the Lawson farm. They wanted to see what had happened and wanted to see what they could do to help. Dr. Helsabeck was summoned from town and he was followed by Sheriff John Taylor.

The first arrivals saw the bloodstained snow outside the house. Someone had obviously been shot there. But it was the bodies they found inside that stunned the men. One newspaper account reported, "The bodies of Marie and James were lying with their heads near the bureau. Raymond's body, in a pool of blood, was to the right, the mother's body at the foot of the cradle. There was a big puddle of blood in front of the fireplace and in this blood were several combs similar to those used by women to hold their hair."

Photographs that were taken of the blood-spattered room tell their own story. Even with the bodies removed from the frame, the house was a horrifying sight. There was a dark semi-circle of blood covering the floorboards around the fireplace like a ragged and torn rug. Marie and James' stained pillows were propped against the bureau. The black-and-white photographs showed a black spray of gore at the head of Mary Lou's crib. There was another grim stain on the bed next to the fireplace, left there when Charlie sat down to contemplate the horror he had unleashed. One eyewitness later recalled, "There was blood all over the place. I mean blood everywhere! I haven't forgotten a bit of it."

As the news of the murders spread throughout the county, more and more people arrived. Worried men left home with instructions for their wives and children to prop chairs under the doorknobs – few people in the area had locks on their doors – and to let no one inside until they returned home. There was, they believed, a deranged killer on the loose.

At this point, Charlie, Buck, Carrie, and Maybell were still missing. Sheriff Taylor began organizing men into a search party to find them. First, though, they had to make sure the killer was not hiding in the attic of the house. It was the one place where no one had looked. Elijah Lawson feared that they had all been killed and their bodies perhaps laid out as carefully upstairs as the bodies that had already been found. Could the killer be hiding up there, too? The only access to the attic was by way of a narrow, enclosed staircase, which would make anyone climbing those stairs an easy victim for a killer waiting above. Deputy Robert Walker and a local doctor named Bynum carefully climbed those stairs with guns in hand, but found nothing in the attic except for a few bloody footprints that Charlie had left behind. Searching the house downstairs, others in the search party discovered Charlie's rifle and both his shotguns were missing. Had the killer taken them?

He had – but at this point, no one realized who the killer of the Lawson family actually was.

A neighbor named Steven Hampton found the bodies of Carrie and Maybell in the barn. He first discovered blood and drag marks in the snow and followed the trail into the building. As the men looked around the barn, they found a trampled spot in the snow where their killer had waited in ambush for the two girls, along with a discarded plank of wood with one end that was soaked in fresh blood. A little blue hat that had belonged to Carrie, now crushed and blood-soaked, was found near her body on the floor of the barn.

Word had finally reached the farm that Buck was in town with his cousin, which meant that only Charlie was missing. Was he another victim? Or was he, as some were beginning to fear, the perpetrator of this terrible crime?

Someone in the search party spotted tracks in the snow leading away from the tobacco barn where Carrie and Maybell had been found. They veered off toward the trees and the creek beyond. The footprints were those of a full-grown man and from the length of his stride, he had apparently been running. Cautiously, the men followed the tracks into the first thicket of trees, across an open field, and into the woods again. It was there, at just after 4:00 p.m., that they found Charlie Lawson's body. He was slumped against a tree, a few hundred yards away from the house and barn.

The scene around him was a strange one. Charlie had evidently been in the woods for some time, walking around and around a single tree. He had circled the tree so many times that the snow had melted in the path he walked. He eventually sat down on the ground at the base of the tree, put his single-barreled shotgun to his chest, and pulled the trigger. He had a gaping wound in his body and the gun had fallen on the ground beside him.

Four men picked up Charlie's body, each taking a limb, and hauled him back to the farm. His suicide confirmed what the lawmen and Charlie's neighbors had started to suspect – that Charlie had finally snapped and murdered his entire family. The coroner's jury convened by Dr. Helsabeck agreed. Sheriff Taylor searched the dead man's pockets and found several bills of sale recently struck with tobacco buyers in the area. Two of them had Charlie's penciled handwriting on the back. One note cryptically read, "Trouble will cause." The other began "Blame no-one but..." Everyone assumed the missing word was "me," but no one could say for sure. He never finished writing it.

A few believed that Charlie had started to explain his actions that day, and then decided against it. Perhaps, in the end, he decided to leave it a mystery. No one will ever know what was going on in Charlie's head when he decided to slaughter his family. He had $58 in his pocket when his body was found, and the tobacco paperwork showed that his business was doing quite well. Whatever problems had led to Charlie's breakdown, poverty was not among them.

Why did Charlie spare Buck from the murder spree, intentionally sending him away that day? Was it because he loved him more? Or did he want his son to suffer, as the only surviving member of the family? This seems to be the most likely scenario – a bit of petty revenge against the boy who stood up to him. He knew that Buck would have to live with his failure to protect his family for the rest of his life. Buck would have died to protect his mother, brothers, and sisters and Charlie knew it. He was the only obstacle in Charlie's twisted plan. He sent Buck off to town and the boy had gone willingly, never realizing that he would never see his family alive again.

Charlie Wade Hampton, Marie's boyfriend, found Buck on the snowy streets of Germantown after he learned of the murders. He had to break the news that his entire family had been dead. Buck was brought straight back to the farm, where his uncles and their families tried to comfort him as best they could. "I don't know why he did it," Buck wept to one of the reporters on the scene. "I guess it's just like they say – he must've suddenly gone crazy."

There were no formal crime scene arrangements in those days and no official police clean-up crews either, so it was left to Charlie's relatives and neighbors to help Sheriff Taylor deal with the aftermath of the massacre. Women from nearby farms brought their own bedsheets to give the bodies a decent covering. Volunteers dug the Lawson grave at Browder's Cemetery, excavating a trench that would hold eight caskets. Mary Lou would be buried in her mother's arms.

The snow of the past few days had made the steep road leading up to the Lawson house impassable for most cars, so all the remains had to be carried down to waiting hearses by hand. Boley Tuttle, the owner of a local hardware store, took Mary Lou's battered little body in his arms and carried her gently down the hill. Years later, he recalled, "It was just awful. I barely made it to the hearse."

The bodies were taken to Madison, about 13 miles to the east, where an embalming firm – run by T. Butler Knight – and Yelton's Funeral Parlor were waiting to care for them. Dr. Helsabeck was waiting there, as well. He worked through the night to complete his formal examination of the corpses. By a remarkable stroke of luck, Sheriff Taylor's brother, a newly-qualified pathologist at John Hopkins Hospital in Baltimore, was visiting his family for Christmas. Dr. James Taylor volunteered to assist Dr. Helsabeck with the autopsies. These, combined with what Dr. Helsabeck had seen at the farm, allowed the two men to determine the causes of death in each case – and to piece together each step of the massacre.

Initially, it was thought that Carrie and Maybell had died while fleeing the carnage in the house, but this was discounted when it was pointed out that they certainly would not have taken the time to bundle up in their winter coats before they ran away. In addition, Charlie wouldn't have had time to kill all five of the others in the house and still overtake the two girls before they reached the nearby barn. Carrie and Maybell, they realized, had been the first victims. The disturbed snow by the barn, the bloodstains, and the discarded wooden plank told the rest of the story. Anyone who heard the first shots – including Charlie's family – would have shrugged them off as more noise from rabbit hunting in the woods.

The bloodstains outside showed that someone had been killed there. The drag marks in the snow and across the porch led to Fannie's body.

Buck testified that the clock on the cabin's mantelpiece had been working perfectly when he'd left the house just before noon that day, but Sheriff Taylor had found it stopped at 1:25 p.m. The only shot fired inside of the cabin was the one that killed Marie, which marked her time of death, and provided the window of time during which all the killings occurred.

Based on the footprints in the attic – and the tracks leading from the barn to the woods, and not from the house – Charlie was likely hiding in the attic when Elijah and his boys approached the house after the murders. Would he have killed his brother and his nephews if they had climbed the stairs? We'll never know, but as soon as they left, Charlie seems to have dashed to the barn for one last look at his slain daughters before running into the woods. He paced around the tree until he worked up the nerve to take his own life. The coroner's jury confirmed that it was that single-gauge shotgun that killed him.

On the morning after the murders, the massacre at the Lawson farm made front-page news in at least 19 different states. Wire services, like the Associated Press, sent the story out from New York to California. Radio broadcasts and local gossip spread the story even further. "There is," as one newspaper editorial correctly stated, "a peculiarly morbid interest in contemplating this terrible affair."

Coverage was naturally the heaviest in Charlie's home state. By December 27, newspapers were illustrating their stories with a copy of the family portrait that Charlie had so thoughtfully provided a few days before things went so terribly wrong. On the same front page, they also carried a crime scene photograph that showed the family's living room painted with blood.

The newspaper and radio coverage brought scores of curiosity-seekers to the scene. Everyone wanted a piece of history. There was so much blood in the house that one of the volunteers who helped clean up the crime scene had to scoop it up with a coal shovel. He dumped it into an old tin wash tub and a neighbor helped him carry it outside. Out of decency, they dug a shallow grave and poured the blood into the ground before covering it over. While they were doing it, he later recalled, a visitor was busy funneling Fannie's blood from the house's porch into a little souvenir jar.

The morbid visitors looted the cabin. Even the tree that Charlie leaned against as he took his own life was stripped bare within a few hours of the discovery of his body. The crowds wanted something to take with them – something to say that they had been at the scene of the tragedy. They took Charlie's guns, the bricks from the house that was later demolished, and even the raisins from the cake that Marie had baked a few hours before her death.

The crowds also turned the funeral into a nightmare.

Charlie had been a member of a fraternal organization called the Junior Order of United American Mechanics and the local chapter helped Buck and his uncles organize the family's funeral. There would be no formal church service. There was to be just a few words from the pastors at Browder's cemetery and burial in the mass grave that had been dug there by neighbors. The ceremony was scheduled to start at noon on December 27.

Six hearses were loaded with bodies at Yelton's in Madison that morning. Since Mary Lou would be laid to rest with her mother, there were seven caskets in all. Yelton's had been hard-pressed to handle so many bodies at once so, despite the fact that the family had wanted white coffins for everyone, a light gray one had to be substituted in Charlie's case. Someone scrounged up a piano stool and a small table to supplement Yelton's five coffin stands for the viewing at the cemetery. Lacking a seventh hearse, they transported little Raymond's casket in a private car.

Rows of men – with only a few women in the crowd – lined the sidewalks to watch the hearses pull away. Hundreds of tourists were waiting at the cemetery to watch them arrive. Automobiles had crowded the highway coming into town and were parked several miles up the road. People walked through mud, water, and wet grass to be close to the show. They soon filled the surrounding woods, too. Reporters circulated through the crowd and found onlookers who had traveled more than 100 miles to view the funeral. The newspapers agreed that at least 5,000 people turned up at Browder's that day. Some watched in silence, some came and went, taking the opportunity to also visit the Lawson house while they were in the area.

The quarter-mile dirt road leading from the highway to the cemetery was too wet for cars and soon the highway was also impassable. It had not been designed for so much traffic and the melting snow soaked the ground. Dozens of cars became stuck and had to be pushed out. The traffic and muddy conditions caused the hearses from Madison to arrive more than an hour late.

The vehicles got as close to the cemetery as they could, and then men from Charlie's fraternal order had to shoulder the caskets the rest of the way. Sheriff Taylor, who had already recruited some men to keep an area next to the grave free of spectators, pushed open a path through the crowd for the pallbearers to use. The seven coffins were laid out in a line, starting with Charlie's full-size casket and tapering down to Raymond's tiny one at the other end of the row. Charlie had been a member of the Primitive Baptist Church; whose elders Watt Tuttle and Boss Brown conducted the service at the graveside. "Why this thing has occurred," Brown said, "I do not know."

The coffins were then opened so that anyone who wished to do so could say one last goodbye. Seeing the battered faces of the family was too much for Buck. He collapsed in grief and had to be helped to recover so the viewing could continue. His distress was made worse by what would haunt him for the rest of his life – if he had not fallen for Charlie's ruse in sending him to Germantown, he might have been able to stop his father before the killing ever started.

As friends consoled the heartbroken boy, a line formed on each side of the coffins and people started to slowly file past. It took more than three hours for everyone present to get a look.

As the afternoon light faded, the coffins were sealed once more and were lowered into their shared grave. For the mourners – and the ghouls – gathered at the graveside, it was time to go home.

Buck, his uncles, cousins, and relatives were not the only ones haunted by the murders – the entire community was confused, angry, saddened, and stunned by the tragedy. The mystery of why Charlie had done it hung over them like a dark, angry cloud. It was a topic of conversation at every dinner table, over coffee at the local diner, and across every neighborhood fence. People wanted to know – they *needed* to know – why he had committed such a horrible act. Rumors spread. Stories were concocted. Everyone had an idea, but no one had any real answers.

Most believed that Charlie's head injury was at the root of the murders – he had been driven insane by the blow to the head. Or perhaps he was in such pain that he believed he was going to die and decided to take his whole family with him. In his delusional state, he would spare them the pain and suffering that would result from his death.

It seems likely, but the evidence says otherwise.

When Charlie was autopsied by Dr. Helsabeck and Dr. Taylor, they were well-aware of Charlie's 1928 accident with the mattock. They had heard the gossip that suggested that the accident was the cause of the killing spree. Eager to investigate this possibility, they concluded their overnight work by removing Charlie's brain to study it. The next morning, Dr. Helsabeck made a sobering announcement – there was no evidence of any damage to Charlie's brain. As painful as the mattock's blow might have been, its impact stopped with Charlie's skull and had not damaged the brain inside.

But there was more. The doctors did find an unusual spot in the middle of Charlie's brain that was caused by disease, not injury. Dr. Taylor was going to take the brain back to Johns Hopkins so that it could be studied further. In January 1930, it was announced that the study was underway and that results were expected in four weeks. And that was the last anyone ever heard about it. No report was ever made; no findings were ever released. If the murders were caused by a tumor or defect in Charlie's brain, we'll never know. But we do know that he didn't kill his family because he was hit in the head. Whatever was going on in his brain remains a mystery.

The injury was just one theory that went around the community. There were plenty of others. Since the murders coincided with the start of the Great Depression, some leapt to the conclusion that Charlie's farm had gone bust – but there's no evidence of that either. According to the papers found on Charlie's body, his farm was doing pretty well in December 1929. Ruined financiers may have been jumping from skyscrapers on Wall Street at the time, but the crash hadn't affected Charlie Lawson. Like his neighbors, he had no stock market investments to lose.

The craziest theories were, of course, the ones that people talked about the most – namely that Charlie hadn't killed anyone, and his suicide was staged to make him look guilty. Some fingered Jesse McNeal as the killer. He was the black worker who had served time for stabbing Charlie back in 1918. However, most people who told that story claimed that the warehouse fight took place no more than a year before the massacre when it actually happened more than a decade before. Even assuming that McNeal was still alive on Christmas Day 1929 – which is by no means certain – it seems hard to believe that he would nurse a grudge for 11 years before taking such extreme and calculated revenge.

Others theorized that Charlie might have witnessed some sort of organized crime activity, perhaps a mob murder. He and is family must have been killed in retaliation, they claimed. But since Stokes County wasn't exactly a hotbed for gangsters, this theory doesn't hold water either.

The discussion about Charlie's motives went on for years. Then, six decades after the massacre, the rumors took an even more sinister turn. Stella Boles, born in 1915, was Marion Lawson's daughter and she'd had a front row seat for everything that went on in the family before and after the murders. She confirmed some dark Stokes County rumors by telling the story of a meeting of Lawson women that took place on December 27, 1929, when she was 14-years-old. Ida and Nina Lawson, who had each married one of Charlie's brothers, were among the group. Years later, Stella questioned her Aunt Nina about what was said that day.

Nina told her that Fannie had discovered that Marie, Charlie's daughter, was pregnant and to make matters worse, Charlie himself was the father of the baby. Charlie had warned his daughter that if she told her mother or anyone else about the baby, "there would be some killing done." Fannie had discovered the incest in her family just before Christmas and had confided in Ida and Nina. She agonized over what she should do. Even years after the fact, Nina insisted that Stella keep the information to herself and so Stella did not reveal the secret until 1990.

A few years later, Stella's story was confirmed by Ella May Johnson, who had been Marie's best friend. Ella May said that Marie had slept over at the Johnsons' house a week or two before Christmas 1929 and confided that she was pregnant by her own father. Soon, others grudgingly admitted that they, too, had heard the rumor.

If Marie was pregnant, she clearly wasn't very far along. The family portrait, which was taken about the same time as the sleepover at Ella May's house, show's Marie's belly quite clearly and she doesn't look pregnant. This might explain why neither of the doctors who conducted the autopsy noted any sign of pregnancy.

It's certainly possible that the shame over such a horrible misdeed could have helped to spark Charlie's killing spree and I'm also sure that a family of that era would have guarded such a secret very closely. Hill Hampton, Charlie's closest friend and neighbor, later admitted that he knew of serious problems going on within the family. He knew the nature of the problem, but it was personal, and it was not his place to reveal it. If the pregnancy was real, Charlie may have felt trapped by his own actions. Maybe he felt the only way out was to destroy all the evidence and the witnesses. His religious beliefs claimed that everything he did in his life was preordained – he had no real choices. God had intended him to wipe out his family before he was even born.

In the end, the only thing that we really know about what was going on in the mind of Charlie Lawson is that we will never know. It was then – and remains – an unsolvable mystery.

With the funeral behind him, Charlie's brother, Marion, started worrying about financial matters. Buck was the next in line to inherit the farm, but that was a mixed blessing since that also put him in line to inherit Charlie's mortgage payments. Buck was only 16, so he could hardly be expected to run the place, so this meant that another source of income needed to be found.

Marion remembered the huge crowds that had come to town to watch the funeral. There were still at least 90 carloads of strangers showing at the Lawson house every single day to look around. There was no indication that interest in the murders was going to fade away anytime soon. Most of the family's property was still in the house, just as they had left it. Many things had already been stolen, even though relatives tried to keep a close watch on the place. They had their own farms to operate, though, and couldn't be on hand all the time. The neighbors weren't much help. Most of them took exception to the "ghouls" and several fights had started when sightseers were run off the property. The most serious involved a man who needed three stitches in his arm after being slashed by a neighbor's knife one night. He had been peering into the window of the Lawson house. Clearly, a long-term solution was needed.

After consulting some friends, Marion came up with a decision. Along with his sons and a few other relatives, they went out one morning and started planting posts in a circle around the house and tobacco barn. They strung heavy chicken wire between the posts, effectively fencing off the murder scene. Some of the neighbors believed that Marion was trying to keep the curiosity-seekers away, but he had a much different idea. With all of the interest in the killings, he decided to charge visitors 25-cents each to take a guided tour of the property. The cash raised would go to Buck to help him make ends meet, make the mortgage payments, and, hopefully, make sure that the farm stayed in the Lawson family. Buck agreed to the scheme, even though Fannie's family was appalled by the idea, as were Charlie's other brothers. They tried to talk Marion out of it, but he refused to listen.

The new "attraction" was opened on January 15, 1930, and the steep admission price failed to deter visitors – sometimes as many as 100 people showed up every day. Marion recruited friends and family to staff the cabin tours. He supplemented the income from admissions by offering refreshments and offering a pack of five souvenir photographs that visitors could buy before they left.

Fannie's family, the Manrings, made one more attempt to get through to Marion about the tastelessness of the tours. They met with him and begged him to stop, but Marion was unmoved. He told them that people were going to come to see the place anyway, so someone should benefit from the attention. The tours continued.

Locals – especially people in Germantown – complained, too. The tours were shameful, they said, and Marion was embarrassing them all. A committee approached him and asked him to stop. Again, Marion refused.

Interest in the murders dropped off a little after the first few months but held steady for a surprisingly long time. By then, several murder ballads had been written that told the story of the Lawson massacre – "The Lawson Tragedy" by Wesley Wall, "The Song of the Lawson Family Murders" by Elbert Puckett, and most popular, "The Murder of the Lawson Family" by Walter "Kid" Smith – and this helped to keep bringing tourists to the door.

The site had become a legitimate attraction to the people who came to see it, like an alligator farm or an amusement park. They paid their admission and could walk right in and see the bloodstains on the floors and walls without having to sneak in after dark. So, they kept coming – for a long time.

After several months, the locals stopped complaining. There hadn't been any real trouble and while they still considered it in bad taste, the tourists who showed up stopped in town to buy gas, eat in the diners, shop in the stores, and stay at the new hotel. Soon, Germantown was thriving during a time when most of America was suffering from the Depression – all thanks to Charlie Lawson.

In time, interest in the Lawson farm started to fall off, but the 1930s saw a rise in popularity in traveling carnivals and sideshows, so the Lawson murders were taken on the road. Parts of the murder scene were sold off to a sideshow promoter and he took the artifacts on tour. Whatever the family wouldn't sell, he simply duplicated and passed them off as the real thing – like Charlie's guns and Marie's raisin cake.

The raisin cake is an interesting side note to the story of the Lawson attraction. When the house first opened for tours, Marie's cake was still sitting on the table. Over time, it hardened and dried out, but it was left in place. Soon, though, family members noticed something unusual about the cake – the raisins were disappearing. As visitors made their way through the house, they occasionally reached out and plucked a raisin from the cake. They wanted a little piece of gruesome history to take home with them. The cake eventually crumbled into pieces and was thrown out.

The Lawson family sideshow toured the country for years, appearing along with Bonnie and Clyde's blood-spattered and bullet-ridden "death car," a mummy that purported to be the "real" John Wilkes Booth, and other morbid attractions. Years passed, and sideshows vanished, along with their attractions. No one knows what happened to the artifacts from the Lawson house – they vanished many years ago.

☠

The Lawson farm attraction closed, and the sideshow disappeared to likely gather dust in a barn somewhere, but stories of the Lawsons lived on. The subject of the tales now turned from murder to ghosts. People were starting to claim that some of the members of the family did not rest in peace.

Rumors spread of eerie happenings that were occurring in the Lawson house after dark, long after the tour guides had gone home, and the doors had been locked behind them. Articles appeared in newspapers that freely stated that the house was haunted. A new batch of curiosity-seekers began parking on the road at night, watching the house, unsure of what they might see. Would it be the mysterious lights that people spoke of, dancing about in the darkness? Or would they hear the reported moans and cries that others had reported echoing in the stillness of the night?

The local chapter of Charlie's old fraternal order – the Junior Order of United American Mechanics – began using their most infamous member as part of their initiation ceremony. After the stories of the haunting began to circulate, new members were told to go out to the Browder cemetery and take a rock from the Lawson grave. After that, he had to go to the abandoned Lawson house and walk around the property with only a lantern to light the way. If the prospective member was brave enough to pass the initiation, then he was considered worthy of becoming a "Junior."

Decades passed, and the house fell into decay. Children and adults wandered the property, exploring and sometimes looking for ghosts. Many who ventured onto Charlie's old farm claimed to leave the place with a feeling of deep sadness. Many inexplicably burst into tears. Photographs taken there were often found to be blank when developed. Batteries failed in the flashlights that were used for nocturnal explorations.

By 1980, the Lawson house was gone. Some of the wood was salvaged for a small bridge that was built a few miles away, but aside from that, it had vanished. The site of the house and tobacco barn was plowed under. There is nothing left to see today.

But, even so, it is said that the ghosts remain.

The land once owned by Charlie's closest neighbor, Hampton Hill, is now home to the Squires Inn Bed and Breakfast, a rustic farmhouse that plays host to scores of travelers each year. They come for the peace and quiet of the secluded farm – not for murder and ghosts.

Sometimes, though, they get more than they bargain for.

Shortly after the owners opened the bed and breakfast, one of them saw a little boy and girl peering in at her through the glass of the front door. She walked over to the door to open it, but the children disappeared. The porch was empty. There were no children anywhere nearby. Over the next few weeks, the children kept coming back. After seeing them several more times, she started investigating and spoke with a local historian – which is how she first heard the Lawson murders on the neighboring farm.

During the discussions, the owner was shown the Lawson family portrait, taken shortly before the family was killed. She immediately recognized her two visitors in the photograph – Maybell and James Lawson. There was no doubt about it, she told the historian. The mystery was solved, but the sightings continued. In fact, they still go on today.

According to local recollection, the Lawson children often crossed the field where the bed and breakfast now stands so that they could play with the neighbor children. They continue to make this journey, even after death. Their lives violently ended, but perhaps they have finally found some peace.

The old Lawson farm was not the only thing haunted by the past.

Buck, the massacre's only survivor, eventually married and started a family of his own. He and his wife, Nina, had a son and three daughters. His son, Arthur, was his namesake and he named two of the girls for his murdered sisters. Buck tried to have a good life and while he had many happy times, he was terribly damaged by the events of Christmas Day 1929. He drank to forget and when things got especially bad – usually around the holidays – he locked himself in a room with a bottle and played one record over and over again. It was a recording of a popular bluegrass group, the Carolina Buddies, performing "The Lawson Family Murders."

Buck escaped death in 1929, but he was not destined to grow old. On May 10, 1945, he and another man were riding in a work truck that became stuck in a deep crevice that had been cut in a road for repairs. Witnesses said that they had not seen the warning signs and had accidentally driven into the construction zone. The passenger in the truck was seriously injured – Buck was killed instantly.

Even in death, he was haunted by his father's actions.

The first three paragraphs of his obituary were a description of the murders in 1929. Buck's life and death were not even mentioned until the fourth paragraph.

Arthur "Buck" Lawson was laid to rest in the Browder cemetery, alongside the family he had lost years before. In his lifetime, Buck never stopped believing that he had failed his mother and his siblings, so we can only hope that he found some comfort on the other side.

1930:

MURDER WITHOUT MOTIVE

Headlights flashed across Denver's Berkley Park as the automobile slid through the gloomy night, rounding a curve that led to the lake. The surface of the water looked black in the pale light of the moon. As the car neared the water, its headlights winked out. If there had been anyone in the park to listen that night, they would have heard the crunch of gravel beneath its tires. They would not have seen much, though. The dark-colored automobile blended with the shadows until suddenly, the red flare of brake lights appeared and then vanished. The dull murmur of the engine fell silent.

A slight figure emerged from the driver's side door. A coat was wrapped tightly around the person on this chilly, October night. A hat was pulled low on the figure's head. They hurried around to the trunk of the car and it popped open with a small squeal of hinges. The figure bent over and stayed that way for a moment. Then, with a sigh of effort, stood up with a bundle in their arms. It was large, nearly as large as that of the figure, and was wrapped in what appeared to be a bed sheet.

The figure stumbled once, twice, and then slowly walked toward the lake. Carefully navigating the large stones around the edge of the water, the figure eased down toward the darkness of the lake. As they started to bend over, the moon emerged from behind the clouds and illuminated the scene. If anyone had been watching, they would have seen the pale face of an attractive woman, struggling to maintain her balance as she picked her way toward the lake. With a grunt, the woman placed the bundle on the ground at her feet. As she did so, the sheet fell away and revealed what it had been wrapped around.

It was a young girl.

A tangle of sandy-colored hair could be seen above a face that had been battered and bruised. Her lip was split. Dried blood was smeared across her cheek. The girl was silent and still – her face frozen in death.

The woman quickly pulled the sheet away and the girl's body rolled over onto the sand. She was dressed in what appeared to be a school uniform – a white blouse and plaid skirt. But there was no time to look. The woman forcefully lifted the girl into her arms again. She walked out to the very edge of the water – the toes of her feet chilled by the icy lake – and then shoved the corpse away from her, lifting her as far as she could. The body splashed into the blackness and sank beneath the surface. A moment later, a pale hand appeared, then some clothing, a white face, and a floating knot of hair.

It was done.

The woman hurried away from the lakeshore toward her car. The rear compartment was closed with a thunk and the door opened and closed. When she started the engine, the lights of the dashboard turned her face into an eerie mask.

It was the face of a killer.

It was also the face of the dead girl's stepmother.

☠

On Wednesday afternoon, October 15, 1930, 10-year-old Leona O'Loughlin was reported missing from her home in Denver, Colorado. On an ordinary morning, Leona walked to school with her friend, Betty Scott, who lived across the street, and then returned home when school had ended. But on this day, she was nowhere to be found and, to make matters worse, her family learned that she had not been in class all day. With most children, it would have simply been assumed that they had skipped school – but not Leona. For one thing, she was an obedient child, did well in school, and was supposedly happy at home. For another, her father was a well-known detective in the Denver police department and had a lot of enemies.

A NEWSPAPER PHOTOGRAPH OF LEONA O'LOUGHLIN AFTER HER BODY WAS DISCOVERED.

Leona, it was initially believed, had been kidnapped.

But the real story was a lot worse. It began nearly two years earlier when Leona's father, Leo O'Loughlin, married Pearl Millican, a divorced woman with a young son named Douglas. Pearl was a vivacious woman, who attracted a lot of attention. She was a tall, slender redhead with big, dark eyes and a brilliant smile.

A reporter later wrote that she was "famous in her Denver neighborhood for her good looks."

She and Douglas moved into the neighborhood when she married Leo in January 1929. He had been sharing the house with his own child from a previous marriage – pretty, blue-eyed Leona – and with his bachelor brother, Frank. Leo's first wife, Maude, had passed away in 1928.

The modest house on Tremont Street soon became a volatile place. Pearl and Leo's marriage was troubled from the start. Within months of the wedding, they were fighting so bitterly that on at least three occasions, Pearl stormed out of the house with Douglas in tow, loudly threatening divorce. She didn't return for several days.

She also had problems with her brother-in-law, Frank. After one terrible argument between them, a mysterious fire broke out in Frank's bedroom closet, destroying most of his clothing. Pearl insisted that she had not started the fire. In fact, she blamed "spontaneous combustion" for the blaze. Frank had had enough of his brother's new wife, however. He refused to have anything else to do with her and stopped eating meals with the rest of the family.

On Tuesday evening, October 14, the house was quiet. The family had enjoyed a peaceful weekend together and it had been a tranquil start to the week. Pearl had even prepared a special supper for the family. There are conflicting accounts of what she prepared. Some say the main dish was lamb chops, others say fish, but all agree that it was accompanied by roasted potatoes and a large bowl of rice, which Pearl was careful to place directly between her husband and her stepdaughter.

Leo, a large, burly man, helped himself to two heaping portions of the rice. At Pearl's urging, Leona also heaped some onto her own plate. But when Douglas – after eating meat and potatoes – held out his plate for some rice, his mother told him that he'd eaten enough and refused to let him have any. Pearl stayed away from the rice altogether.

Soon after dinner, at almost 7:00 p.m., Leo left for central headquarters. He had been assigned to the night shift – but this particular shift would be a short one. He returned home around midnight with what he thought might be a case of food poisoning. His stomach was hurting badly, and his boss had sent him home. He went to bed but slept poorly. He was still having cramps and nausea the next morning but decided to tough it out. He went to work around 7:00 a.m. By mid-morning, though, he was feeling so sick that he had to return home.

He slept through most of the day and when he awoke, Pearl told him that she had some troubling news – Leona was missing. Normally, the little girl arose, ate breakfast, told her stepmother goodbye, and then went off to school in the company of Betty Scott. That morning, Pearl had not seen Leona at all.

Leo was concerned, but not overly alarmed. It was very possible that Leona had simply left the house without telling anyone. It was strange that she was not yet home from school, but it didn't seem to be anything to get too excited about.

Although still feeling sick, he telephoned the Cathedral School and asked if Leona had stayed late. The nun who answered told him to wait while she checked. She was back a few moments later with unsettling information – Leona had not been in class all day.

Leo rang off the line and put in another call to Betty Scott's parents. They told him that Betty had waited as long as she could for Leona that morning but had eventually gone off to school without her. Now a little frightened, the anxious detective telephoned around the neighborhood. No one had seen his daughter.

By then, Leo was seriously worried. He knew that children often ran away from home, but, as far as he knew, Leona was perfectly happy. It wasn't like her to pull such a stunt. She was a good girl. She never caused any trouble. It's true that things around the house had not been great between Pearl and himself, but he tried to make sure that Leona was protected from all that. Besides, Leona liked her stepmother and there had never been any trouble between the two of them.

As sick as he felt, Leo rushed back to headquarters and met his partner, Detective Clarence Jones. He told Clarence what was happening. He wanted to report Leona missing and put out a description. He was sure that she had not run away from home. Clarence suggested taking it up with their captain first. Albert T. Clark, captain of detectives, listened attentively. He didn't believe there was any cause for panic – perhaps, he suggested, the child was just playing hooky – but he did order his dispatchers to spread the word about Leona.

In those days, Denver did not have a two-way radio system. Patrolmen and detectives called in at regular intervals from various patrol boxes and as each one did, the dispatchers gave them Leona's description, adding that she had disappeared either late the night before or early that morning. The dispatchers also stressed the fact that she was the daughter of a fellow officer and that O'Loughlin would appreciate their efforts.

The first call to come back to Captain Clark was from Clarence Jones, Leo's partner, who had gone out looking for Leona after he realized how worried his friend was.

It was a disturbing report.

Going door-to-door in the O'Loughlin's neighborhood, he had come across a neighbor, Amos Johnson, who told him that while lying awake the previous night, he heard a "muffled scream," followed immediately by the "racing hum of an automobile." He was certain that the noises had come from the direction of the O'Loughlin house.

Things now seemed much more serious to Captain Clark. What had seemed to be a routine incident now took on a more sinister aspect. The previous decade had seen more than its share of sensational child abductions and kidnappings and it now seemed as though Leona had been snatched from her home – perhaps by someone with a grudge against her detective father.

Captain Clark acted immediately. He instructed the police telephone operators to spread a general alarm through the state and notify all other law enforcement agencies. Then he called the police identification bureau and requested a list of all the offenders arrested by Leo O'Loughlin within the past few years. He wanted special attention paid to any arrests that he made while a member of the vice squad. Clark feared that the kidnapping might be retaliation by one of the many bootleggers that Leo had locked up since Prohibition had become the law of the land.

The general alarm brought into action an army of officers, including District Attorney Earl Wettengel's investigators, the Colorado Highway Patrol, sheriffs from more than 60 Colorado counties, and several federal agencies.

Then the captain put out a call for Leo and Clarence Jones to report back to headquarters. He also sent out a request that Mrs. O'Loughlin also come to headquarters, too. But there was a problem --- by mid-afternoon, Leo's abdominal pains had become so severe that he had been forced to return home. He collapsed into bed in agony. Now it seemed that Pearl was also ill. Both were suffering from abdominal pains. Captain Clark ordered an ambulance to the O'Loughlin home and he quickly followed.

When he arrived, the police surgeon, Dr. H.B. Culver, told Clark that both the O'Loughlins appeared to be quite sick, possibly from something they had eaten the night before. He suggested that they not be disturbed, but Captain Clark had questions he needed to ask.

"When did you see Leona last?" he asked Leo.

"Yesterday, before I went to work," the detective replied.

"Didn't see her this morning?"

"No," he answered.

Pearl, who also appeared to be in pain, spoke up. "I saw her last about midnight. She'd gone to bed early. I left about seven and went over to a friend of mine, a hairdresser. I stayed there several hours but I came back once, after ten, to get a heating pad I had promised her. I didn't disturb the child then. Later I picked up Leo at headquarters after he got through with work. When I got home I looked in Leona's room. I am sure she was asleep in bed. However, a bureau partly obscured my view."

Captain Clark returned to headquarters, where he explained the case to Robert F. Reed, chief of police. "The child's gone," he told him. "The O'Loughlins are very ill – the thing looks mighty peculiar."

"Give it the works," said Reed. "I'll help you all I can."

The disappearance of Detective O'Loughlin's daughter – along with the mysterious illness plaguing the husband and wife – made front-page news the next day. The deluge of imaginary sightings, false reports, and wild stories began. They came in from all over the state. Crime reporter Ray Humphreys wrote, "Leona was seen in this mountain town and that; she was a captive of a gypsy band in southern Colorado; she had been spirited away by killers of the Leopold-Loeb type; she was 'spotted' in Kansas, New Mexico, Nebraska, and Utah. But each 'tip,' run to earth by investigators, proved a dud."

Psychics, fortune tellers, and the usual assortment of crackpots kept the police switchboard humming with a variety of bizarre "solutions."

Only one presumably reliable sighting came in – a National Guard official named C.I. Mosier swore that he'd seen the bound and gagged little girl in the back of a gray Ford near Golden, Colorado. The car, he reported, had Arizona plates and was driven by a man who was "about 23-years-old, six feet tall, weighing about 135 pounds, with dark hair and a swarthy complexion." State troopers managed to track down the suspect's vehicle, only to discover that the supposedly tied-up child in the backseat was actually a small pile of suitcases with a sweater tossed on top of it."

Captain Clark and most of the other detectives couldn't get past the idea that Leona had been kidnapped by some crook who had a grudge against her father. It seemed the most likely cause of her disappearance. Detective O'Loughlin had been very active in police work and it seemed reasonable to believe that some criminal might use his daughter to get revenge. But who could this criminal be? No one had any solid ideas – so the search for Leona continued to go nowhere.

Meanwhile, Leo's health continued to decline. By Friday morning, he was so sick that he was rushed by ambulance to St. Joseph's Hospital. He was more closely examined by Police Surgeon Culver and by physicians at the hospital and suspicions about his condition began to grow. Captain Clark wanted answers. What was wrong with his detective? What had he eaten that had made him so sick? And, strangest of all, why wasn't Pearl as sick as her husband was?

Leo was still in the hospital when his missing daughter was found.

A call came into police headquarters from a grocer named William McLeod. He owned a store near Berkeley Park on the northwest side of Denver and was out for an afternoon walk by the lake when he saw a small body, wearing a girl's school uniform, floating facedown in the water. He immediately notified the police. Within minutes, a small fleet of official vehicles, including a car driven by Coroner George Bostwick, was on its way to the scene. The body was quickly identified as Leona O'Loughlin.

THE "WICKED STEPMOTHER"
PEARL O'LOUGHLIN

Coroner Bostwick's preliminary examination indicated that the girl had not drowned. She had apparently been beaten on the head with some sort of blunt instrument, then suffocated to death before she was dumped in the lake. She had been dead, he believed, for two days – not long before she had been reported missing.

Officers searched the scene but found nothing useful – no footprints along the shore, no clear tire marks, no weapons, nothing. There was no way to tell where the body had been thrown into the lake. It could have drifted to the spot where William McLeod had spotted it from anywhere.

Leo was in such poor condition that the doctors thought it best to withhold the news from him. Pearl was the first to be informed. Captain Clark sent two of his detectives to escort her down to headquarters. They told her nothing. Captain Clark delivered the news. "We've found Leona," he said.

"Oh! Is she dead?" was Pearl's response.

Clark was surprised by her reaction. "Yes – she's dead," he replied. "Dead – out in Berkeley Park Lake."

"Poor little dear," said Pearl and her eyes filled with tears. But that was all.

Despite her strange reaction, suspicion did not immediately fall on Pearl. Captain Clark again asked her when she had last seen Leona and her answer was the same – in bed, asleep, after midnight, she assumed it was her, it looked like her, even though the bureau had blocked her view. But Clark still believed that the child had been killed by Leo's gangland enemies – at least for a little while longer.

The public demand for a solution to the crime had been loud before and now it was worse. While the whole city of Denver had been wild about Leona's disappearance, the whole state of Colorado, it seemed, now that her body had been found, was clamoring for her killers to be caught and punished. The police were again deluged by false leads, tips, anonymous letters, and telephone calls.

Coroner Bostwick and Dr. B.B. Jaffa, Manager of Health, reported that Leona had apparently been alive when she was thrown into the lake. The blows to her head may have stunned her but they wouldn't have killed her, they said. The autopsy stated that she had died from drowning.

But this didn't answer the most desperate question: Who killed Leona? And why?

It was suggested that the authorities try and drain the lake to search it for clues, but this was impossible. The lake was fed by a natural spring. No matter how quickly the water was pumped out, the level didn't change. That plan was abandoned in favor of thoroughly dragging the lake, but no weapons or clues were found.

And then came the additional report from the coroner, which contained the analysis of the contents of Leona's stomach – it had been laced with ground-up glass. Dr. Frances McConnell, a toxicologist at Denver General Hospital, determined that she had eaten the glass with her evening meal and had died a short time later. Based on the condition of the food in the child's stomach, Dr. McConnell believed that Leona had been dead about 48 hours when her body was found. She was found on Friday afternoon, so she must have been killed on Tuesday night – she had been fed ground glass, beaten, and then thrown in the lake to drown.

When this report made it to Captain Clark's desk, he realized that he had been looking in the wrong place for Leona's killer. And that realization was driven home by another startling report. This one came from the hospital where Leona's father – Clark's detective – was alive and suffering. In an effort to figure out the cause of Leo's illness, his stomach had been pumped. It, too, was found to contain a quantity of ground glass.

When Leo was questioned, he recalled that, at dinner on Tuesday evening, he and his daughter had been the only ones to eat the rice that had been served. Very quickly, Clark's murder investigation shifted from a hypothetical gangster looking for revenge against the detective to the person who'd prepared the meal – Pearl.

Under orders from the district attorney a squad of detectives was sent to the O'Loughlin house. From his hospital bed, Leo told them to "Tear the house down, if necessary." It wasn't necessary. In the kitchen – mostly on the sink board and on the floor – they found particles of crushed glass. In the basement, from the bottom of the washing machine, they took a quantity of fine sand. It would later be matched to the same sand found at Berkeley Lake. Leo recalled that he had seen Pearl washing clothing on the morning after Leona disappeared. He had wondered – in the middle of the chaos surrounding the missing child – why his wife would be worried about laundry. In his illness, he had forgotten to ask or to mention this to anyone.

But those were not the only things detectives found. In the trunk of the O'Loughlin's car, they found a tire iron stained with what appeared to be dried blood. A few strands of blond hair – a match for Leona's in length and color – were stuck to the spot.

Detectives picked up Pearl and brought her into headquarters for questioning. But she stuck to her story, which really wasn't much of a story at all.

She had last seen Leona the night before going to visit her hairdresser friend. Leona had been in bed. She thought she had seen her still there after she returned with her husband after he had left work. That was all – there wasn't anything else to tell, she insisted.

She knew nothing about any ground glass.

The bloody tire iron? She had never seen it.

She told Captain Clark, "I don't believe any ground glass was found in my home. Nor in Leona's stomach. Nor in Leo's."

She was not defiant, angry, or defensive. She played the part of the falsely accused and did so very well. Her attitude of innocence was so convincing that even some of the most hardened reporters began to believe her. A few detectives began to think they had the wrong woman. Pearl's relatives rallied around her.

Soon, only Captain Clark and District Attorney Wettengel believed in her guilt. They ordered her held in custody. The newspapers were shocked. There were still plenty of people who believed her guilty, but the majority of the public, fed a daily dose of smiling photos of a pretty woman, insisted that the police were wasting their time with Mrs. O'Loughlin while the real killer had an opportunity to escape.

"I can't understand all this!" Pearl sobbed to reporters from her jail cell and the public cried along with her. The tire iron and the crushed glass had been planted, many suggested. Pearl was obviously being framed.

Even Captain Clark was beginning to have doubts until a quiet, older gentleman from Fort Collins, Colorado, showed up at the station. His name was David O'Loughlin and he was Leo's father and the dead girl's grandfather. He had a terrible story to tell.

Six weeks earlier, he told Captain Clark, Leo, Pearl, and the kids came to his home in Fort Collins for Sunday dinner. After they left, David, who liked to satisfy his sweet tooth with a few spoonfuls of sugar, took some from his bowl. As soon as he put it into his mouth, he knew something was wrong. "I thought someone put some sand in my sugar," he said.

Curious, he took another spoonful and stirred it into a cup of warm water. "Some of it didn't dissolve," he explained. "When I looked at this closely I saw it was glass – pounded up, ground glass, maybe – and not sand."

Hoping to get to the bottom of this, he had not disposed of the sugar in the bowl. Detectives retrieved it from his home and turned it over to a chemist, who confirmed that the substance was a mixture of sugar and crushed glass.

And there was more. When news that crushed glass was found in two different O'Loughlin homes, Pearl's own sister, Marybelle, came forward to testify that on the night of October 10, Pearl had stopped by her home with some food scraps for Marybelle's pets – a cat and a dog. Later that night, the cat went into convulsions and died. The dog also became sick and died two days later. Curious, the family's veterinarian autopsied the dog and found crushed glass in its intestines.

Pearl continued to protest her innocence, but she was soon taken into custody and held without bail. District Attorney Wettengel questioned her many times, looking for a motive in the murder and attempted murders. "You knew the elder O'Loughlin had a comfortable fortune that would go to his sons, Leo and Frank, if he died. And Leo owned his home. And if Leo died, the grandfather's money and Leo's would go to Leona. And if she died..."

"Why, Mr. Wettengel, that's utterly ridiculous!" Pearl interrupted. "It's really silly!"

But it wasn't silly. It was a bit convoluted, though. The theory was that Pearl was after Leo's insurance money -- $3,200. It wasn't a fortune, even by the standards of the time. Leo said that he'd changed the beneficiary of his policy from his wife to his daughter the week before Leona died. So, with Leona out of the way, Pearl could next kill Leo and get the insurance cash. However, the district attorney also believed she wanted David's money. His estate was the real plum, said to be worth about $35,000. But if it was her father-in-law's money Pearl wanted, she needed to kill him first, so Leo would inherit, then kill Leo. Apparently, she gave up on murdering Dennis after the glass in his sugar bowl didn't kill him but decided to try the method to kill Leona and Leo. Or that was the theory anyway.

It was theorized that Pearl laced the family's dinner with glass, causing everyone except her own son, Douglas, to become ill. When Leona didn't die soon after eating the rice containing the glass, Pearl took the girl to the lake, hit her on the head a couple of times, and threw her in, leaving her to drown. Or maybe she suffocated her first, hit her on the head for good measure, and threw her into the lake. Either way, the police were convinced that Pearl had murdered Leona.

All the evidence against her was circumstantial, though. What they really needed was a confession and the authorities resorted to several different tactics to try and get it. Shortly after her arrest, for example, she was brought to the city morgue and interrogated next to Leona's corpse – a method that managed to draw a few melodramatic tears from her, but no confession. Police also planted a female informant in her cell but had no luck. Aside from a few tantalizing hints – at one point, Pearl said, "I could tell you things, but I won't" – she was tight-lipped about the murder.

From the beginning, Pearl had let it be known that she knew all about police tactics. She hadn't been the wife of a city detective for two years for nothing. She knew about trick questions and the way that words were twisted around by interrogators. Further, her friends stated, she was an enthusiastic reader of detective magazines and it showed. She'd often demand that detectives "Go get the read murderer" instead of pestering her. "I'm innocent!" she declared.

Finally, by the night of October 22, Captain Clark – his patience at an end – subjected Pearl to a brutal six-hour grilling and when it ended, he announced, "she cracked. She admitted responsibility." In truth, her exhausted "confession" consisted of little more than a few vague remarks. "I'll take the blame. I'm the one that has to suffer," Pearl mumbled. Her lawyer intervened before police got her to sign a confession, but she was charged with first-degree murder. Two days later, Pearl insisted she was innocent and claimed the confession was made under duress. She told Captain Clark she had only "made the statements to get away from you and get some sleep."

Public opinion remained bitterly divided about her guilt. While one newspaper painted a picture of a monster, another portrayed her as a hapless housewife who was wrongly accused. Some even attacked Leona. One family friend said that the girl had not been murdered at all. Leona was, they claimed, "impulsive," "quick-tempered," and "queerly morbid," who resented the uniform she was forced to wear to school. Leona, the anonymous witness said, had committed suicide. Of course, this theory doesn't explain her head wounds, cause of death, or the fact that 10-year-old girls don't often kill themselves because they don't like their clothing.

Pearl's trial began on November 28. An enormous crowd of curiosity-seekers turned up at the courthouse for a glimpse of Pearl who basked in the attention. While in jail, she had been more concerned about her appearance than her upcoming trial. She had once told Captain Clark. "I want the pink dress that goes with the pink coat I wore when I came down here. I want some silk nightgowns because I could never get used to the one furnished by the city. Above all, I want my vanity case with powder, rouge, mascara, and lipstick. You'll find it in the upper drawer of the dresser in my room at home."

As she was escorted into the courthouse, she flashed a dazzling smile at the cameramen who pushed and shoved near the entrance. "Go ahead boys, take my picture if you want to." Pearl called out. Seated at the defense table, she made sure to keep her skirt hiked above her knees, giving the men on the jury a good look at her shapely, silk stocking-clad legs.

During the week-long trial, the prosecution built a strong circumstantial case against her, exhibiting, among other damning pieces of evidence, the bloodstained tire iron from the trunk of the O'Loughlin's car and the crushed glass that had been removed from Leona's stomach.

Pearl was ably defended by prominent Denver attorney, John Keating, who persuaded the judge to keep out any testimony about her confession because it had been made under duress. Pearl, Keating argued, had absolutely no motive for the crime. It was her traditionally reviled place in the O'Loughlin home that had led to her persecution. "Everyone is prejudiced against a stepmother," he told the jury. "There had been a mad rush to convict Pearl O'Loughlin. Everyone said 'The stepmother did it. Get that stepmother,' and the police and everyone else went after the stepmother."

Despite his skill, though, Keating could not repair the most damaging part of Pearl's story – where she had been on the evening of October 14 – when, according to expert witnesses, Leona had been murdered and dumped in the lake. She claimed that she had gone to her hairdresser's house for a permanent wave, left briefly and went back again, spending most of the evening there. However, the hairdresser testified that Pearl only came to her house once that night around 10:30 p.m., not wearing stockings and generally looking disheveled. At trial, Pearl also claimed that she had taken a friend to the doctor that evening, but the friend said it was a different night they had visited the doctor. In fact, Pearl's friend insisted that she hadn't seen Pearl anytime during the three weeks before Leona's death.

It took the jury less than two hours to convict her.

Leo, who recovered from his brush with death, testified against his wife at trial. He filed for divorce the day after Pearl was convicted. The handsome, newly single detective received scores of letters from female admirers. But, he told one reporter, "Since my last experience, I am no longer matrimonially inclined."

Leo did marry again, however, although it also ended in divorce. He died in 1956 at the age of 68. His father, Dennis, had passed away in 1936, so if it had been his money that Pearl was after, she would have gotten it if she had just been a little more patient.

Pearl had been sentenced to life in prison at hard labor but after two decades behind bars, she was paroled from the Colorado State Penitentiary on June 30, 1951. During her time behind bars, she worked as a prison trustee and as the housekeeper of Warden Roy Best and nanny for his children.

Pearl – narcissistic and possibly psychopathic to the end – never testified at her trial but she did tell "her side of the story" to the *Rocky Mountain News* in 1950. She said Leona came downstairs "acting silly" on the night she died and told Pearl she had mistakenly taken some sedative tablets belonging to Leo that were on the bedside table. Pearl put the girl in the car to get help, but Leona died before they could get to a doctor, so she panicked and put the body in the lake. "I thought I had to get rid of her," Pearl said.

Of course, this story does not explain Leona's head injuries, the bloody tire iron, or the crushed glass that was found in the little girl's stomach. I think we can dismiss it as just another of Pearl's "stories."

After her release from prison, she moved to California and continued to work as a housekeeper, just as she had done while in prison. She died in San Diego in 1987 at the age of 88, bringing her strange story of murder to an end.

But it does not end without questions.

Why did Pearl O'Loughlin do the things that she did? Why did she choose crushed glass as a murder weapon? It had killed two family pets, so had she assumed she could kill a person in the same way? Perhaps – and it had almost worked. Leo was sent to the hospital after consuming the glass and perhaps Leona might have become just as sick. Or perhaps she did. Perhaps this is why Pearl took her out to an isolated spot, beat her, and then left her to drown in the lake. Perhaps Leona was so sick that Pearl feared Leo would realize what had happened and so she made the girl "disappear" so that vengeful gangsters could be blamed for her death.

But the bigger question is why she did any of it at all? She had an unhappy marriage, but this is not a reasonable excuse for murder – at least for a sane person. Had she decided to kill her husband and stepdaughter to escape from her life? If so, why try to kill her father-in-law, too? Was it all really, as the prosecutor claimed, about money?

We'll never know and perhaps that's what makes this story so scary. Pearl O'Loughlin seemed to be a happy, well-adjusted housewife with an ordinary life. But, obviously, she wasn't. It's often said that we can never know what goes on behind the closed doors of our next-door neighbors. But as this case has proven, we may not know what's going on inside the mind of the person who is sleeping next to us.

That's something that just might keep you awake tonight.

1934:

THE "BABES IN THE WOODS"

The weather had turned chilly near Harrisburg, Pennsylvania. It was November 24, 1934, just two days after Thanksgiving and there was a bite in the wet morning air. John Clark and his friend, Clark Jardine, were walking through the woods, gathering a load of firewood. Clark was the caretaker for Kings Gap Estate, a summer property that was owned by steel magnate James McCormick Cameron. He was responsible for watching over the 2,000 acres of land on the slope of South Mountain, as well as the family's stone mansion, which had been closed for the season for several weeks now.

Clark was a contented man. He had a good job, especially at a time when good jobs were hard to find, and enjoyed working for Mr. Cameron, who entrusted him with the estate. The late fall and winter months were quiet. His most important responsibilities at this time of year were to chase off poachers and to make sure that he kept up maintenance on the house and the outbuildings. He worked hard most of the year and learned to love the quiet of fall and winter.

But that quiet was just about to be shattered.

As Clark and Jardine strolled along the trail, gathering what dry wood they could find after a Thanksgiving rainstorm, the two men chatted about their afternoon plans, which consisted largely of cracking the top of a few bottles of beer and eating whatever leftovers Mrs. Clark decided to get creative with. They weren't paying much attention to the path ahead.

Then Jardine looked up. "What's that?" he asked his friend.

They were near the outskirts of the estate, only a few dozen yards from Pennsylvania Route 223. The woods thinned out and there was a shoulder of dry November grass that reached for the highway. Just at the edge of the trees, there was a stained green blanket lying on the ground. There were several unidentifiable shapes beneath it.

"Poachers, you think?" Jardine asked.

Clark's brow wrinkled as he peered at the blanket. Poachers were an ongoing problem on the estate. He understood it. People needed to eat. But the deer belonged to his boss if they were on his land. It was his job to make sure the hunters steered clear. Maybe he'd missed one. Maybe someone had shot a deer and left the stripped carcass behind. But why'd he cover it with a blanket?

"Don't know," Clark shrugged and walked over to the blanket. The cloth was a drab green color. It was stained with grime and was still damp from the recent rain. Clark lifted the cover – and both men froze.

Neither spoke. They were too stunned. Too scared to say a word. They were too utterly horrified by what they saw that they would never forget it, not for the rest of their lives.

When John Clark lifted the blanket, the two men saw that it was covering a second blanket, which had been folded neatly on the ground beneath. Lying in a row on that second blanket were three little girls.

Three dead little girls.

Within an hour, the woods at the edge of Route 223 were swarming with police officials, coroner's men, and more than a hundred curiosity-seekers, all hoping for a glimpse of the three dead girls. Word had spread. Some of the onlookers hoped to satisfy their morbid curiosity, while others prayed that their own children were not lying beneath that tattered green blanket.

Police Chief Harvey Kunhs from nearby Carlisle, Pennsylvania, was among the first law enforcement officers to arrive. With County Coroner Dr. Edward Haegele, he examined the three girls. They seemed to be huddled together, lying side by side on the blanket. If they had been alive, he thought, they would have looked as though they were trying to stay warm. The youngest of the three was snuggled into the arms of the oldest girl. Taking into account the matching gray eyes of the girls, the dusting of freckles on their faces, and their light brown hair, Chief Kunhs announced that he believed they were sisters.

Dr. Haegele agreed. As he looked over the bodies, he noted that they were dressed in adequate clothing, but looked thin, as if they had not eaten in some time before their deaths. There was nothing on the girls that provided any kind of identification. They were clean and, except for a few marks on one of the girls, appeared uninjured. They seemed to be asleep, not dead. With no immediate

THE "BABES OF THE WOODS" AS THEY WERE DISCOVERED.
PHOTOGRAPHS OF THE GIRLS WERE PRINTED IN NEWSPAPERS IN
HOPES THAT THEY WOULD BE IDENTIFIED

cause of death apparent, he ordered the bodies to be taken to Carlisle for autopsies. Perhaps then, they would find some answers.

The postmortem examination was conducted by Dr. W. Baird Stuart. He estimated the ages of the three girls to be between 7 and 16. Though there had been some suggestion by detectives that the girls had died from carbon monoxide poisoning – and then dumped in the woods – Dr. Stuart came to a different, even darker, conclusion. He reported that all three girls had been "Suffocated to death, either by strangulation, or suffocated by external means." In other words, they had been choked to death. Only one of them had the strength to fight back. The middle girl had some marks on her that seemed to be defensive wounds. No details about them were included in the report. The girls were emaciated, and Stuart determined that they had not eaten for at least 18 hours before their deaths, probably even longer than that. They had been murdered, he believed, three days earlier, on November 21.

On Sunday, November 25, the Pennsylvania State Police called for volunteers. They were concerned that the bodies of the girls' parents might be somewhere in the area. A massive search took place, scouring South Mountain and including the Cameron estate. No additional bodies were found. Where were the parents?

And, of course, that was far from the only mystery. Detectives were baffled by the condition and positioning of the bodies. The girls had been murdered; it could not have been an accident. However, their bodies had been treated gently and with great care, covered from the elements. It seemed that whoever killed them had also loved them. This was not normally what investigators found at crime scenes.

Detectives knew that the first step to discover the identity of the killers was to first learn the identities of the victims. They needed to know who the girls were, which would lead them to the person who had done them harm. Photographs from the scene – of the three girls lying next to one another on the blanket – were released to the press and could soon be found in newspapers from coast-to-coast.

Meanwhile, people flocked to Carlisle, hoping to see the bodies. They came for many reasons – some to gawk like ghouls, but others to try and help. A farmer believed that the girls might be his nieces, who were supposed to be with his sister-in-law who was estranged from his brother. They weren't. Those sisters were alive and well. A woman who operated an orphanage in Baltimore came to see if the girls were three of the five children who had gone missing while under her care. They were not. Another woman was sure that they were her sister's daughters, but they weren't. The police were so desperate to identify the dead girls that they allowed the public to view the remains at the funeral home. It was too great a temptation for people to resist. More than 10,000 onlookers filed past the three plain caskets, staring at the three cold, frozen faces, but no one came forward to identify them.

The first clues were discovered. A man named John Naugle was hiking near Pine Grove Furnace, about three miles from where the bodies were found, and nearly tripped over a black suitcase that had been tossed into the woods near the road. The case contained 15 girls' dresses in three different sizes, and a school book with the name "Norma" written inside in a child's script. The suitcase also had some adult clothing in it – a woman's and a man's – as well as a washcloth and some threadbare towels. Naugle knew he was not far from where the bodies of the three dead girls had been found and he immediately took the case to the police. Detectives believed it was their first solid lead. The suitcase, they were convinced, had belonged to the dead girls, and possibly their parents.

The clothing was carefully unpacked. There were no forensic laboratories in 1934, but what examination could be done was carried out. They looked for fingerprints, for clues, and any trace of the suitcase's owner, but it refused to offer much information. The clothing inside was put on display and photographed for the newspapers. No one had recognized the faces of the three girls, but perhaps they would recognize their clothes. No one did. The newspaper photographs were another dead end, but investigators were sure that the "Norma" who owned the school book was now lying in a Carlisle funeral home.

Another week passed and still the girls remained unidentified. The newspapers had dubbed them the "Babes in the Woods." Finally, it was decided that the three lost girls should be buried. The people of the area had embraced the girls as their own. The local American Legion post organized a funeral for them, largely paid for by donations from the people of Carlisle. Several of the clergymen in town worked together to perform the burial rites. Thousands of people crowded into the Westminster Cemetery for the services. Boy and Girl Scouts from area troops served as pallbearers for the three white coffins and the girls were laid to rest side by side, just as they had been found on that day in the woods.

The girls were quietly buried and while they would not be forgotten, hopes had started to fade about whether they would ever be identified – and whether their killer would ever be found.

☠

But Pennsylvania was not finished with mysteries in November 1934.

Just over 100 miles away from Carlisle, and on the same day that the bodies of the three girls were discovered along that wooded highway, the bodies of a man and a woman were also found.

They were discovered at the abandoned Spring Meadow flag station of the Hollidaysburg branch of the Pennsylvania Railroad, just outside of Altoona. The woman had been shot twice – in the chest and the head – while the man had a single gunshot to the head. An old .22-caliber rifle was found on the ground between them. Police officers immediately suspected that it had been a murder-suicide. There was no identification on either body, but investigators had a few clues to work with.

An abandoned car had been found near McVeytown, not far from Altoona. There was nothing in it that could identify the owner – and the serial numbers had been filed off – but the license plates were still on it. The plates were traced to a man named Elmo Noakes, a former U.S. Marine, whose fingerprints were on file with the military. A check of the unidentified man's prints against those on file with the Navy proved that the dead man was Noakes.

Detectives learned that Noakes had registered the car just a few weeks earlier in Roseville, California. When the authorities in Roseville were contacted, they tracked down some of Noakes' relatives and discovered that he had left town earlier in November, heading east. With him were his 18-year-old niece, Winifred Pearce, and his daughters, Norma, 12, Dewilla, 10, and Cordelia, 8.

The "Babes in the Woods" had finally been identified.

It took some time, but by talking to family members, friends and acquaintances, and to the people who came forward with their encounters with

ELMO NOAKES AND HIS NIECE – AND POSSIBLY LOVER – WINIFRED
PEARCE. THEY HAD KILLED THE THREE GIRLS BECAUSE THEY COULD
NO LONGER CARE FOR THEM. SOON AFTER, THEY COMMITTED SUICIDE

the family after photographs of Noakes and Winifred Pearce were published in newspapers, investigators were able to piece together the story of the Noakes family. It was not a pretty one. But they found out where they had been, what happened to them, and why the dead girls had been found on the edge of a Pennsylvania highway, while their father's body was found alongside some railroad tracks more than 100 miles away.

The story of Elmo Noakes was not all that unusual, but the choices that he made toward the end of his life certainly were. After serving in the Marines, Elmo had married Mary Isabella Hayford in Salt Lake City, Utah, in 1923. Mary had a daughter, Norma Sedgwick, from her first marriage, which had ended in divorce. Together, Elmo and Mary had two more daughters – Dewilla in 1924 and Cordelia in 1926. By all accounts, they were a happy family, but there must have been something dark lurking beneath the surface of their perfect life. In 1932, Mary died from hemolytic septicemia, which was blood poisoning, caused by a self-induced abortion.

When Mary's ex-husband, Norma's father, learned how Mary had died, he petitioned the courts for custody of his daughter, but Elmo packed up the three girls and moved to California before he could be served with papers.

He settled in Roseville, near his family, and started looking for work. He soon found that he needed help raising three young girls. His three sisters and a brother all lived in Roseville, so he hired his niece, Winifred, the daughter of his oldest sister, to be his housekeeper and to watch the girls while he worked at the Pacific Fruit Express Company.

For a while, things seemed to be going well. Elmo worked hard and was liked and respected by his friends and co-workers. He had a good job at a time when a lot of the country was still suffering from the Depression. He had a nice house and there was always food on the table. When Winifred turned 18, she moved into the Noakes home to work for Elmo full-time. This was over the strong objections of her family, who had started to grow uncomfortable about Elmo's relationship with his niece.

Soon after, Elmo became a little... well, strange. He became quiet, and not just around his brother and sisters, but at work, too. At the end of October 1934, he purchased a bright blue, 1928 Pontiac Essex for $46. Then, on November 11, Noakes packed up the three girls, and Winifred, and left town in the middle of the night. No one knew if Winifred went along simply to help care for the girls, or if she was Elmo's lover, as some suspected. But they all left together. Elmo disappeared without collecting $50 that was owned to him for two weeks of work, which surprised everyone as much as his leaving town did. It was unheard of to walk away from a nice house and a steady job – as well as two weeks' pay – in the middle of the Depression.

During the investigation that followed the discovery of the bodies, there was a lot of speculation about why Elmo left Roseville. His sisters bickered, argued, and fought constantly, to the point that the police sometimes had to be called. Elmo and his brother were frequently pulled into their disputes, which both men hated. It became so bad that Robert eventually left town. Perhaps this was why Elmo did also, Robert suggested.

Elmo's sisters had other ideas. Elmo had said that since his older sister and husband, Winifred's parents, did not get along, Elmo had hired the girl as his housekeeper so that she could have a peaceful home. But other family members did not believe that things were so innocent. They suspected that he had left town so that he and Winifred could be together, something they could not openly do in Roseville.

No one knows what really happened. It seems just as likely that the quiet, restrained man was simply losing his mind.

The route that Elmo and the girls traveled east is unknown. It is as much of a mystery as the reason that they went all the way to Pennsylvania. None of them had ties to anyone in the region. They just seemed to have ended up there. They spent the night in a tourist home in Gettysburg, registering under false names, and then left the next morning.

They were in Philadelphia on Sunday, November 18. A woman named Anna Lafauvre told the police of encountering the family in a diner where she was eating with her son. Elmo, Winifred, and the three girls were at the table next to them and she overheard Elmo tell the girls that they only had enough money for one meal, and the five of them would have to share it. Mrs. Lafauvre took pity on them and invited Cordelia – the youngest child – to come and eat with her and her son. Cordelia told the woman, "Daddy is looking for work. I'm kind of tired and this food tasted awfully good."

Lewis Ellis, the owner of the restaurant, also remembered the family. Before they left, Elmo asked him if he knew of any jobs that were available. He would do any kind of work. But there was nothing to be had, and the family left.

Elmo spent the day looking for work in Philadelphia and then spent the night in a camper park in Langhorne, a nearby suburb. They spent the next two nights, November 19 and 20, in another camper park in town. Everywhere they slept, they registered under false names, although no one was looking for them. Each night they slept in the car.

Where the family went next is unknown, but they likely had little or nothing to eat. The police speculated that Elmo found no work, had run out of money, and was becoming desperate. His friends and neighbors in California described him as a kind, loving father, utterly devoted to all three girls. Detectives believed that his desperation became depression, and then panic. He must have decided that he could not watch his daughters starve to death. It was better if they died quickly rather than suffer.

Why was this Elmo's best solution? Why didn't he wire home to Roseville and ask for help from family or friends? Or ask his boss to send him the money that he was owed from work? Or why did he not place the girls in an orphanage? There were thousands of children with one or both parents living who sent them to a place where they could be cared for in those terrible years. Why didn't Elmo Noakes do the same?

In the end, we will never know. We will also never know if Winifred was an active and willing accomplice in the murders, or if she begged him to reconsider his deranged plan. She had to have helped him in some way, even if it was just by keeping the girls distracted as he killed them one at a time.

He suffocated them all. Only Dewilla managed to fight back, but not for long. The girls were too tired, too weak from hunger, and likely too heartbroken to be able to resist their father's cold efforts.

The three dead girls were left on the side of the highway, at the edge of the woods, covered with the only two blankets that the family owned. Elmo and Winifred left them on the cold ground and drove away, probably already planning their own deaths.

They drove east from that lonely spot, running out of gas 75 miles later near McVeytown. They left the Pontiac on the side of the road and started hitching rides. A truck driver took them as far as Altoona. Once there, the couple found a rooming house and checked in under false names one last time.

They woke on a cold morning with nothing to eat. They had no money left. Elmo tried to sell his eyeglasses but could find no one to buy them. They walked to a secondhand store, where Winifred was able to sell her coat for $2.85. Elmo used the money to buy and old, worn-out .22-caliber rifle and a handful of bullets. When they left the store, they walked down the railroad tracks until they arrived at the abandoned flag stop. They were weak with hunger and shivered in the icy morning air. The next day was Thanksgiving, but there would be no family gathering, no wonderful meal, only more pain and sorrow for the couple. They'd never live to see the next day.

Elmo and Winifred went into the station. Once inside, he fired two bullets from the gun – one into Winifred's chest and the second into her skull. Then, he turned the gun on himself. Their strange odyssey of death was over.

Elmo Noakes had served his country as a U.S. Marine. His military record became public soon after he had been identified. Regardless of what he had done, the members of the Carlisle American Legion decided to bury Elmo and Winifred in the cemetery where his daughters had also been laid to rest. Elmo was buried with full military honors and just as Winifred had been next to him when he died, she was placed next to him in the cold, hard ground. The family – who had never been to Pennsylvania before – would remain there for eternity.

No one will ever know why Elmo Noakes took his family away and drove them – quite literally – to their deaths. I have always believed that he simply snapped one day. His mind was broken and could not be fixed. Perhaps imagining some threat to his family, he fled California, traveling as far away from the west coast as he could possibly go. Maybe he killed his girls to protect them from that threat. Or perhaps he simply couldn't go on and knew that they would die without him. He had killed them to protect them, you see. Or perhaps that's what he believed.

We will never know. Elmo's actions will never be explained, and our questions will never be answered.

It's not hard to imagine that a story such as this can leave a haunting behind. The spirits of Elmo Noakes and Winifred Pearce certainly have reasons for lingering behind in this world, perhaps fearing what they might have to face on the other side. They have three very poignant reasons for refusing to leave this world and according to the stories, their fears have kept them chained to the old railroad bed outside of Altoona.

Many who have walked along that rocky, weed-stricken bit of trail say that you just might encounter the shades of a man and a woman there, dressed in old-fashioned clothing and holding onto one another's hands. Their faces are ashen, their bodies are gaunt, and they give off an air of deep depression, trauma, and longing, searching the faces of those who walked along the trail as if looking for someone they recognize. Do they look for the three young girls they murdered and abandoned, perhaps looking for some sort of forgiveness so that they can move on from this world to the next?

Once again, there is no answer to that question. Sightings of the two eerie phantoms peaked many years ago and have faded over time. They were stuck there for decades but have not been reported for some time. It may be that they don't return as often as they once did, or it may be that few venture into that lonely spot anymore to witness their suffering.

And these are not the only spirits to linger from this crime. However, it's difficult to say just who it is that haunts the woods at the edge of Kings Gap State Park – the former Cameron estate – next to Route 233. Witnesses say that sometimes, when conditions are right, the sound of quiet weeping can be heard among the trees. The sobbing seems to come from everywhere. When heard, it is said that the air grows heavy and thick and it becomes difficult to breathe. Those who hear the heartbreaking sounds are overwhelmed with sadness, a feeling that stays with them long after the crying has faded away.

This patch of woods has been haunted for decades. Boy Scouts who camp in the woods have used the place as a test of courage, daring one another to sit there, alone in the dark and wait for the sounds to echo among the trees. Nearby is a road sign, erected by highway workers in 1968, that reminds visitors of the three dead girls that were discovered – the "Babes in the Woods." Is it any wonder that the area is permeated by despair?

But specter cries in the darkness? Is it Elmo Noakes, weeping over the murder of his daughters? Is it Winifred, traumatized by the role she played in their deaths? Could it be Norma, saddened because she was unable to protect her younger sisters? Or is it Dewilla or Cordelia, unable to understand what has happened to them? The misery of the place leaves visitors with a traumatic sense of loss.

And it leaves more questions that will never be answered.

1937:

THE "BABES OF INGLEWOOD" MURDERS

It was Saturday afternoon in the suburban town of Inglewood, just a few miles from Los Angeles. Three little girls – Jeanette Stephens, 8, Melba Everett, 9, and Madeline Everett, 7 – left home with sandwiches to have a picnic in the park, just as thousands of other ordinary children were likely doing in thousands of other ordinary towns across the country.

But this Saturday would turn out to be anything but ordinary.

Hours passed, and the afternoon began to turn to evening, but the girls had not come home. Their mothers grew uneasy. Mrs. Stephens sent her son, Garth, 7, to the park to look for them but the park was empty. The girls were gone. An hour later, the parents called the police. By midnight, a community-wide search was on and the disappearance of the three lost girls was broadcast on the Los Angeles police network. By the next morning, the alarm was out all over the state.

On Monday afternoon, six Boy Scouts who were part of a volunteer army that was scouring the countryside for the girls, stumbled into a deep gully about two miles from the road in Baldwin Hills. Deep in the weeds, lying facedown in the dirt, were the half-naked bodies of the three missing girls. They had been raped and strangled.

As the horrible news of the murders spread through the Los Angeles area, the police began rounding up suspected sex criminals and piecing together possible clues. Little did they know that the killer they were seeking was standing just a few feet away.

Wearing a WPA badge and serving as a volunteer policeman at the scene of the discovery of the bodies was a slim, 32-year-old man who had known the three little girls from his work as a crossing guard in front of their elementary school.

At the discovery of the bodies, he asked the men in the crowd not to smoke "out of respect for the dead."

When he went home that night, his 24-year-old wife, Isabel, helped him to add the day's newspaper clippings about the tragedy to a scrapbook that he had started when the girls were first reported missing. He'd known them after all. He saw them every day at school. He told Isabel that he couldn't get their little faces out of his mind.

By week's end, angry crowds were protesting in front of the Inglewood City Hall, threatening to lynch suspect after suspect that the police were bringing in for questioning. Isabel's husband was right there with them, raising his voice louder than all the rest.

Until he was the suspect to which the police turned. He begged them to take him to Los Angeles, where he could give his confession. The people in Inglewood will "tear me to pieces," he said.

When Isabel heard the news that her husband had confessed to the terrible murders, she wept. He "couldn't have done this terrible thing," she sobbed, "We both loved children. We lost two babies of our own."

But he had done that "terrible thing." He had lured the girls into the woods, murdered them, and then raped them one by one. Then, in a fit of remorse, he had prayed over their broken bodies and asked God to forgive him.

And perhaps God did, but the people of California did not. And neither did those three little girls. According to the killer himself, their spirits literally haunted him into the grave.

On Saturday, June 26, 1937, there were plenty of people enjoying the day at Inglewood's Centinela Park. The park was then described as a "sixty-acre beauty spot" where "city dwellers can dip in a pool, picnic, play tennis, and horseshoes." It was the perfect spot for three neighborhood girls to have a picnic on a sunny afternoon. The Everett sisters – Melba and Madeline – were there with their best friend and next-door neighbor, Jeanette Stephens. They arrived around 10:00 a.m. with a blanket, some toys, sandwiches, and a bottle of milk. They spent about two hours playing with their friends, eating their lunch, and, at some point, speaking to a man someone later described as dark-haired, unshaven, and in his late twenties. He was about five-feet, nine-inches, weighed around 140 pounds, and was "wearing a tan work shirt and dungaree trousers."

Around noon, Mrs. A. Crafcroft – who newspapers called the "matron of the pool" but she was really just a park attendant who had been roped into lifeguard duty – saw the girls running from the wading pool toward the picnic area. She

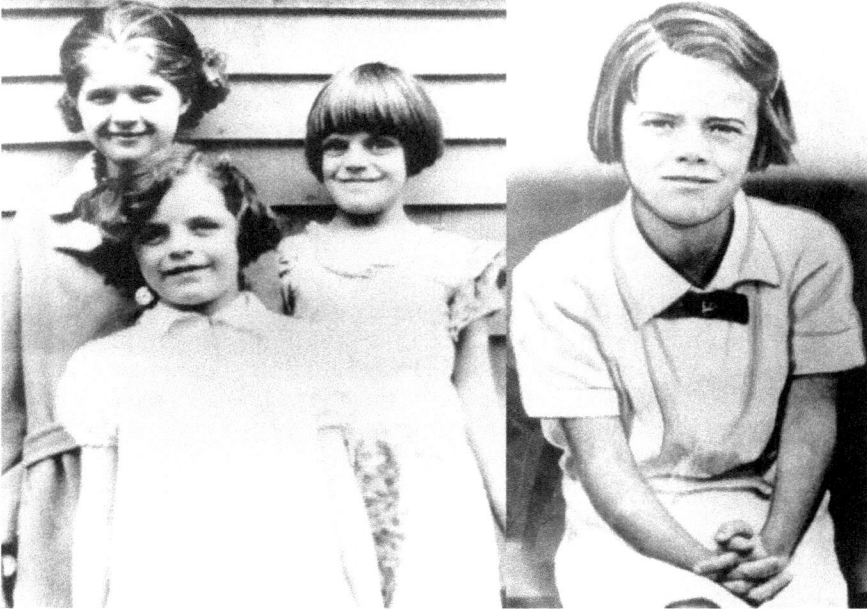

SNAPSHOTS OF THE EVERETT SISTERS (LEFT TO RIGHT) OLIVE, MADELINE, AND MELBA MARIE, AND A NEWSPAPER COMPOSITE OF NEIGHBOR JEANETTE STEPHENS.

asked them where they were going. Jeanette shouted back, "Rabbit hunting!" She sped past with her two friends.

"Don't go too far!" Mrs. Crafcroft called back and gave them a wave.

Except for their killer, she was the last person to see the three girls alive.

When the girls failed to return home that night, their parents first sent Garth Stephens to see if he could find his sister and her friends. When he came back without them, they frantically made their own search of the park. Finding no sign of their daughters, they contacted Chief Oscar E. Campbell of the Inglewood Police. A description of the missing girls was sent out to every police station in the Los Angeles area, noting their ages, weights, hair color, and the clothing they had been wearing when they left for the park.

Inglewood's entire police department – as well as the fire department – began the search. They were joined by officers and deputy sheriffs from all over Los Angeles and the surrounding areas, more than 50 members of the Santa Monica Mounted Police, hundreds of American Legion volunteers, scores of private citizens, and nearly 200 Boy Scouts. They were in automobiles, on horseback, and on foot, and they spent all day Sunday combing the countryside,

239 | SUFFER THE CHILDREN

including the ravines and gulches along the banks of Centinela Wash, a rugged section of the park.

Although newspaper headlines suggested that the girls had been kidnapped for ransom, Chief Campbell was skeptical of this theory. For one thing, the families were not well-off. Merle Everett, the father of Madeline and Melba, was a department store clerk. Jeanette's father, Floyd, clerked at a grocery store. Also, by Sunday evening, neither family had received a demand for money.

"It is definitely not a ransom kidnapping," Chief Campbell finally announced to reporters late on Sunday afternoon. When asked if he thought the girls might be in the hands of a "degenerate," he gave a grim reply: "I'm beginning to fear the results of the search. I'm afraid to say whether we'll find them alive."

Even after night had fallen, volunteers continued the search using torches and flashlights, roaming the Baldwin and Palos Verdes Hills, their voices echoing in the trees as they called the names of the three little girls over and over again. Local women served coffee and sandwiches to the men who walked the woods throughout the long night.

By Monday, the searchers – now more than 500 men – were joined by a pair of airplanes that flew over the rough, rolling hills to see into places that the volunteers on the ground couldn't reach.

Newspapers called it the "most intensive manhunt in Southern California in more than a decade." The reporters were referring to a case from 12 years before, when two sisters – Many and Nina Martin – vanished mysteriously while walking just a few blocks to their grandmother's house. The skeletal remains of the two girls were discovered five months later in a nearby ravine. An autopsy determined that they had been slain by a "sex-mad killer."

It would not take nearly as long to find the bodies of Jeanette, Madeline, and Melba but that discovery – as feared by Chief Campbell – would be just as terrible.

It was a Boy Scout named Frank Portuna who found them. It would be a long time before the 16-year-old would sleep well again. Around 2:00 p.m. on Monday afternoon, June 28, Frank and five fellow members of Inglewood Troop 20-30 were carefully making their way down the rough slope of a hidden gully in the Baldwin Hills. Just as Frank reached the bottom, he looked up and choked at the ghastly sight.

Lying face down in the dirt were the bodies of three little girls. They were each half-naked, with their skirts pushed up around their waists. Each of them had a piece of clothesline twisted tightly around her neck. Strangely, all three were barefoot. Their shoes had been removed and then carefully placed up in a precise line not far from the bodies.

Leaving his companions to watch over the scene, Frank raced back to town and informed the police about what they'd found. One reporter wrote: "The town was filled with horror. Business came to a virtual standstill. Huge crowds formed in front of the police station. Slowly but surely, the mob spirit rose. The mothers of the little victims collapsed, while their husbands tried to stand up to the news."

The news that the bodies of the missing girls had been discovered spread rapidly in newspapers and on the radio. The people of Southern California were horrified by the reports and the newspapers further sensationalized the case by calling the murdered girls the "Babes of Inglewood," a heartbreaking moniker that sold even more papers than before.

In Sacramento, Governor Frank F. Merriam called on police officers throughout the

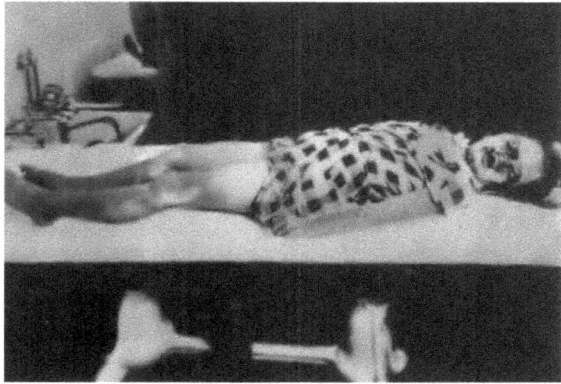

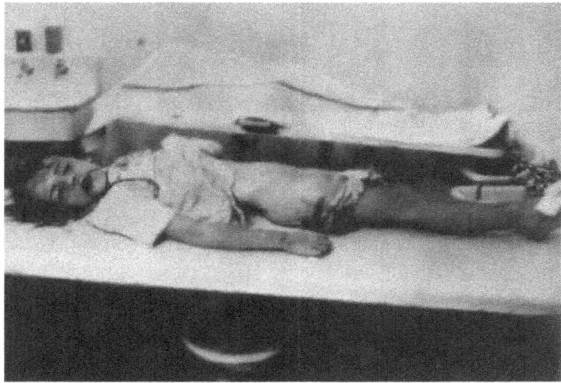

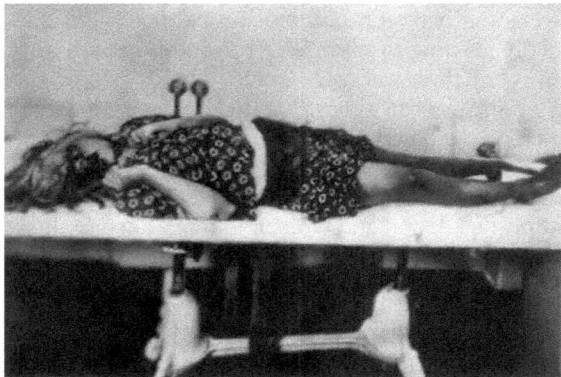

THE THREE "BABES OF INGLEWOOD VICTIMS: MADELINE, JEANETTE, AND MELBA

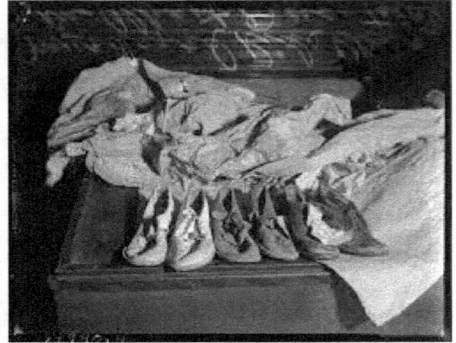

DETECTIVES PUT THE CLOTHING THE THREE "BABES OF INGLEWOOD" HAD BEEN WEARING ON DISPLAY IN HOPES OF FINDING MORE WITNESSES WHO HAD SEEN THEM ON THEIR FINAL DAY

state to devote themselves to capturing the killer, perpetrator of "the most fiendish crime in the whole criminal annals of Los Angeles County." While this was a bit of an overstatement, it authorized hundreds of lawmen to join in the investigation.

During interviews with other children who often played at Centinela Park – including Olive Everett, the 11-year-old sister of Madeline and Melba – detectives learned of a possible suspect. He was known as "Eddie the Sailor" and he had approached several little girls in the park, entertained them with "rope tricks," and offered to take them to his car and "show them rabbits." He was described as a Mexican-looking man in his late twenties, about five-feet, nine-inches tall, weighing between 150 and 165 pounds, with dark brown hair and mustache, badly needing to shave, a tattoo on his lower right arm, and wearing a tan work shirt and dungarees.

This was an almost identical description of the man last seen talking to the girls on the day they vanished.

Over the next several days, dozens of men who roughly matched the description were hauled into the Inglewood police station for questioning. Mobs of outraged men and women loitered outside the station, trying to get a look at the men who were being brought inside. Among the likeliest suspects were Othel Strong, 22, who had already been arrested four times on morals charges; Robert Rasmussen, a convicted rapist who had been reported bragging of having "killed three people"; Fred Godsey, 34, a reportedly "oversexed" ex-convict; and Luther Dow, 33, a tattooed transient who had been identified by two Inglewood women as the man seen playing with the three girls before their disappearance. All four of the men had solid alibis, however. They were questioned and released.

Another suspect was Albert Dyer, 32, a crossing guard at the victims' elementary school who – according to witness Mike Huerta – "knew Madeline, Melba, and Jeanette" and was "always acting queer around little girls." However, Dyer had volunteered to help in the search and had recently been seen in the crowd outside of the police station. He'd been told to pipe down after he'd shouted out threats to several of the men who were brought inside for questioning. He seemed like an unlikely killer, but the detectives were thorough. When they went to his house to speak to him, Dyer's wife told investigators that her husband was at home with her on the afternoon of the murders, working in the yard and gardening. They scratched him off their list.

As with any sensational case, the investigation became bogged down with telephone calls, false reports, and dead-end leads.

In Bel-Air, a butler reported that, several hours after the girls were strangling, a man wearing blood-stained clothing and resembling the killer's description had appeared at the back door of the home where he worked and desperately tried to sell his car. The man begged him to take it, saying that he desperately needed to get rid of it. He offered to sell it for $10 but was turned away.

A shadowy figure dubbed "Otto" was briefly sought by the police after Carol Sims, 20, reported that the stranger had followed her from a San Pedro café, forced her into his car, and drove her to a cabin in the Palos Verdes Hills. He kept her captive there and repeatedly raped her before she could escape.

On June 30, the search turned toward Glendale and northbound highways when a motorist named Andy Stankiewitz telephoned police to say that he had seen a young man fitting the description of the killer – even down to the tattoo on his right arm – pick up two young boys at North Figueroa Street and San Fernando Road.

And there were many more – each of them leading nowhere. By July 1, after pursuing scores of leads, checking out pointless tips, and questioning more than 100 men, the police were no closer to finding the killer of the three girls.

After chasing leads and interviewing suspects for days, investigators went in a different direction and contacted Dr. Joseph Paul De River, the sole police psychiatrist for the Los Angeles Police Department. While Dr. De River's greatest achievements were still a decade in the future -- when he became intimately involved in the infamous "Black Dahlia" case – he'd already earned a reputation for himself with the LAPD, screening the nuts, crackpots, and other deluded individuals who stepped forward with a confession or claim relating to a murder. He was also able to offer insight into both crimes and criminals, which the Inglewood detectives badly needed.

Dr. De River visited the crime scene and viewed the bodies in the morgue. He noted that the girls had been laid facedown, their dresses pulled up, and their shoes placed side by side in a row. After considering all the evidence, he described the type of person the police should be seeking: a sadistic pedophile in his twenties who was meticulous in his appearance, religious, and remorseful. He

DR. JOSEPH DE RIVER

might have a past record of annoying children or loitering where they played. The crime had been planned and the killer had known how to approach the girls without scaring them. They had trusted him, and he'd used that to his advantage.

As it turned out, Dr. De River's description of the killer was eerily accurate. Even though he was in his early thirties and had not been previously arrested for bothering children, the profile was almost a perfect match for the perpetrator when he was finally arrested. Dr. De River's profile of the killer in the Inglewood case was only the second case in history of a criminal profile being used to try and catch a killer. The first was the landmark profile of serial killer "Jack the Ripper," which was drawn up by two London physicians in the 1880s. Their profile had failed – Dr. Dr Rivers's had not.

Although perhaps it's not fair to say that the police "caught" the killer of the three murdered girls. It might be more accurate to say that he caught himself.

☠

On the evening of July 2, District Attorney Buron Fitts, Captain William Penprase of the sheriff's homicide detail, Chief Investigator Eugene Williams, and a dozen or so other officers and detectives were conferring in the second-floor police headquarters at Inglewood's City Hall when a black-haired man with darting eyes and a frantic look on his face burst in the room. The detectives knew him but had never seen him look so harried.

It was Albert Dyer, the school crossing guard who had briefly been considered a suspect in the murders. His wife had provided him with an alibi and detectives moved on to other leads. Dyer had been a slightly irritating fixture in the investigation. He'd volunteered during the initial search and had made an effort to shake the hands of every officer he encountered, thanking them for the efforts being made to solve the crime. He had been in the crowd outside with the other irate citizens, yelling "Lynch the S.O.B.!" when he'd seen suspects being brought into the station for questioning. He'd even been photographed among the men carrying the small bodies of the victims into the morgue.

Most of the officers in the room probably had one thought go through their mind: "What did he want now?"

But this was different. "What do you fellows want with me?" he shouted at them. "Why do you suspect me?"

The group fell silent. Detective Williams finally spoke, "Why don't you take a seat over there? We'll be with you shortly."

Albert stalked across the room and sat down hard in a chair. He fussed and shifted back and forth, getting more agitated as Detective Williams allowed nearly 20 minutes to pass.

Finally, the detective walked slowly over to where Albert was fidgeting in the chair. "Now, what's this all about?" he asked.

Albert cried out, "I want to know why you suspect me! I haven't done anything! I can prove where I was! Ask my wife!" By this time, Dyer knew that investigators had been to his home and had spoken to his wife. What he didn't know was that his wife's statement had cleared him of suspicion – until now.

Williams was a veteran detective and he knew that something was seriously wrong with this situation. He knew how guilty men behaved and no matter what Dyer's wife had told officers, her husband was acting very strangely. But with a suspect as highly-strung as this one, he knew the best way to handle him.

"Why, we're not looking for you," Williams assured him. "You're getting all worked up over nothing. Why don't you go home and get a good night's sleep?"

Although still visibly upset, Albert nodded and tried to give the detective a relieved smile. It faltered on his face and then disappeared. He got up from the chair and headed for the door.

Detective Williams patted him on the back. "Just remember," he said soothingly, "you're okay as far as we're concerned."

The moment Albert left the room, Williams turned to a pair of officers – Detectives R.O. Williams and G.E. Chandler, members of the LAPD burglary detail who had been assigned to help with the Babes of Inglewood investigation – and ordered them to follow the distraught crossing guard.

"Don't let him out of your sight," he ordered them as they hurried out after Albert Dyer.

They followed him all day on Saturday, July 3, and reported back that Dyer had "acted peculiarly all day." Something was definitely going on with him – and it gave the two veteran detectives "an edgy feeling." Williams listened to their report and instructed him to go out and get Dyer early the next morning, even if he was in bed. "Take him to the crime scene," he told them, "and see how he behaves."

They returned to the station around 2:00 p.m. the following day, more convinced than ever that Albert Dyer was their man. They just couldn't prove it yet. They told Williams that when they got him to the crime scene in the Baldwin Hills ravine, he started trembling and crying. He didn't say anything, but he was clearly upset. When Detective Chandler outright accused him of involvement in

ALBERT DYER – UNDER ARREST

the slayings, Dyer denied it. He admitted that he knew the three little girls, though, and added that he had developed a "keen liking for them." The school faculty warned him twice about his behavior with the children. Albert admitted also that he called himself "Eddie the Sailor" because he liked to entertain kids at the park with fancy knot-tying and other rope tricks.

Detective Williams had heard enough. "Arrest him," he told the other officers.

Later that same afternoon, Albert was picked up at his home and taken to the Inglewood station, which was soon surrounded by as many as 1,000 enraged men and women. He begged to be taken somewhere else. The mob would kill him, he said – and he'd done nothing wrong! The police smuggled the suspect to the district attorney's office in the Los Angeles Hall of Justice building. At the same time, his wife, Isabel, was also picked up and brought to the city for questioning.

For the next two hours, Albert continued to protest his innocence. "I liked them very much," he said of the three slain girls. "On that Saturday, I met them in the park about 10:30 and showed them some rope tricks. About 12:30, I left them and went home and spent all afternoon hoeing in the garden."

And then he added once again, "You can ask my wife."

In a separate room, detectives were doing just that. At first, Isabel stuck to her original story. Finally, about 7:30 that evening, she cracked. She had been lying, she wept. Her husband had left home at 10:00 a.m. and returned for lunch around noon. He left immediately afterwards and didn't return until after dark. He told her that he was very tired and went straight to bed.

When he was informed of his wife's statement, Albert broke down. Oh, God," he cried out, "I did it. I killed all three of them. I'm so sorry!"

"Why? Why did you do it?" one of the detectives asked.

"Sex. No other reason," he shook his head. "Just sex."

It took two lengthy interrogations by District Attorney Fitts, Detective Williams, and other officers – along with a team of psychiatrists brought in to evaluate his sanity – to get to the bottom of Albert Dyer's perversity and the atrocity that it drove him to commit.

Although he had enjoyed a seemingly satisfactory sex life with his wife of two years, Albert had become obsessed with the idea of sex with little girls. He became a crossing guard so that he could look at them. Even the smell of young girls drove him close to madness. But Albert knew he would never have the chance to have sex with them unless he killed them. "Being dead," he explained, "they would not be able to resist him."

About a month before the murders – the urge for a child had become irresistible – he scouted out the ravine in the hills. A few weeks passed while he made his selection, finally choosing Janetta, Madeline, and Melba as his victims. On that fateful Saturday morning, he spotted the three of them at the park. They were sitting in the grass near the baseball diamond and he approached them to show off his rope tricks. The girls were delighted. They knew Albert from school and believed they had nothing to fear from him. When he asked them if they wanted to go rabbit hunting, they leapt at the chance.

Staying a short distance ahead of them – so that if anyone saw him they would not know he was with the children – Albert led the girls to the isolated ravine. After telling them that he could only take one of them at a time to see the rabbits, he first led Madeline off into the bushes. The other two girls waited a short distance away. As soon as he had Madeline out of sight, Albert grabbed her and strangled her with one of the pieces of rope that he carried in his pocket. He returned to the other girls and explained that he'd left Madeline at a spot where she "could catch the rabbits if they ran down the hill."

Melba was next. She was the only one who struggled, Albert told the investigators. "Please don't!" she cried as he tightened the rope around her neck. But Albert paid no attention to her pleas. He killed her and then went back for Jeanette.

Albert admitted that he became more excited with each murder. At last, once they were dead, he pulled off their underclothing and "fulfilled his sexual desires on each child."

When the horror was over, Albert had to face what he had done. He was a monster – but he would learn to live with it. According to his statement, he arranged the shoes neatly in a row because he wanted whoever found them to think the children had been orderly to the end. He knelt beside the girls and he prayed for God to save the souls of the children and "save my soul and forgive me for what I have done."

Albert claimed that he felt satisfied and fulfilled when he left the bodies behind in the ravine and that he had a good night's sleep, but Dr. De River would have disputed this if he was still consulting on the case. Albert had left the bodies of the girls face down in the sand so that he would not have to look upon their faces. That way, they could not see his shame. Only a man under tremendous guilt would have come into the police station the way that he did and demand to know why the police suspected him. He brought the attention to himself. He wanted the police to obtain his confession. He was a monster – he tried to live with it, but he could not.

There was nothing, he knew, that could save his soul.

After his confession, Albert was taken to the Los Angeles County Jail. He was booked, given a shower, outfitted in regulation prison denim, and escorted to a solitary cell. As he walked down the corridor, he was yelled at and threatened by other inmates. There was no sympathy, even among rapists and murderers, for a child killer.

Meanwhile, detectives were searching Albert's home and uncovered physical evidence linking him to the crime, including three lengths of bloodstained rope and the bone-handled pocketknife that he had used to cut the lengths of line that he strangled each girl with. They also found the scrapbook that Albert had been making. It started on the day the girls disappeared and was filled with newspaper clippings about the search and the discovery of the bodies. He had been obsessed with the case – for reasons that now seemed evident. Detectives came to believe that his behavior outside the station – as a ringleader of the disorder whenever a new suspect was brought in for questioning – was to divert suspicion from himself.

But it's also possible that he just couldn't help himself. By continually calling attention to himself, he wanted someone to notice him – someone who would ask questions and discover the horrific crime that he'd committed.

Albert was arraigned on Tuesday, July 6. As the indictments were read, he fainted in the courtroom. Deputies carried him unconscious back to his cell. Examined by psychiatrists for both the prosecution and the defense, he was found to be a "sadistic degenerate" but legally sane. As he awaited trial, he paced his cell, read the Bible, and smoked an endless number of cigarettes.

And he spoke to the dead.

According to Dyer – and witnesses among the guards and the other inmates – the ghosts of the three dead girls visited him in his cell. They spoke to him endlessly at night, he claimed, and refused to let him sleep.

Was this just an attempt to resurrect an insanity defense? Was Albert Dyer truly insane? Or was he really being harassed by spirits? Of course, we will never know for sure, but Albert continued to claim that the ghosts of Jeanette,

Madeline, and Melba haunted him, even after he was on Death Row and had no legal recourse that would save him from the hangman.

Albert's three-week trial began on Friday, August 6. Over 500 would-be spectators – mostly women – came hoping for seats in a courtroom that would not hold more than 150. A special contingent of deputies was assigned to maintain order.

After a lengthy jury selection, the prosecution began its case on Friday, August 13. The state summoned several dozen witnesses who identified Dyer as the man they had seen talking to the three girls on the day they disappeared. They also saw him leading them out of the park toward the Baldwin Hills. Albert's entire 48-page confession was read into the record and gruesome morgue photographs of the slain children were shown to the jury.

The jury began their deliberations on Tuesday, August 24. Two days later, seven men and five women found Albert Dyer guilty on all three counts of first-degree murder – a verdict that carried a mandatory sentence of death.

On his way out of the courtroom to be transported to San Quentin for his execution, Albert turned to his wife and spoke, "Well, I guess I'll see you in heaven," he said.

Isabel must have thought that this seemed unlikely.

Albert spent his days on Death Row just as he had spent his days awaiting trial – smoking cigarettes, reading the Bible, and pacing his cell. He had little interest in prolonging his life. He didn't wait for word from the governor that his sentence had been commuted. Instead, his spent his days remembering what he had done, and he spent his nights trying to sleep. He tossed and turned but the ghosts refused to let him close his eyes. They were angry, he told his jailers, and they hated him for what he had done.

God might forgive him for his sins, but his victims would not.

They would literally haunt him to the very last moments of his life.

On the morning of September 16, 1938 – after a last meal of ham, eggs, pancakes, and coffee – Albert Dyer was hanged. He was the second-to-last person to be executed on the gallows in California before the state began using the gas chamber.

It was a fitting end for a killer who strangled three little girls with a rope.

If only he could have been hanged two more times.

1945:

THE MISSING CHILDREN

The shrill sound of a telephone ringing woke Jeannie Sodder from her sleep.

As she stirred in her bed, she was confused at first about the sound and where it was coming from. Her husband, George, slept soundly beside her. Across the room, in a small bed, her youngest child, Sylvia, snored peacefully. Jeannie's head cleared, and she realized it was the telephone in her husband's office at the other end of the house. Not wanting the clanging sound to awaken everyone in the house, Jeannie quickly got out of bed and hurried to the office. Her knee bumped hard into the desk as she reached for the receiver.

"Hello?" she spoke into the handset.

From the earpiece, Jeannie could hear music and several voices, as if someone was calling from a party. There was a rustling on the other end of the line, as if the caller was having trouble holding onto the receiver.

Then a woman's voice spoke, asking for a man that Jeannie didn't know.

"I'm sorry," Jeannie replied. "There is no one here by that name. I'm afraid that you have the wrong number."

The woman on the other end of the line laughed. Jeannie later said that her tone was very "strange." It was a laugh that would haunt her for many years to come. The line went dead, and Jeannie hung up the telephone.

Jeannie closed the office door behind her and walked back toward her bedroom. As she was crossing the living room, she saw her 17-year-old daughter, Marian, was asleep on the couch. The family had celebrated Christmas a little early with presents that Marian had brought home from work and the living room was left in a chaotic state. The window shades had not been drawn and the front door had been left unlocked when everyone had gone to bed. Jeannie quietly turned the lock on the door, pulled down the shades, and pulled Marian's blanket up to her chin. It was chilly in the house at night.

Minutes later, Jeannie was back in bed and soon, had dozed off, the unusual telephone call largely forgotten. Later, she would have no idea about how long she had been asleep when she was awakened again. Her sleep was broken by a loud thump followed by what sounded like a ball rolling across the roof and off the side of the house.

Years later, the driver of a passing bus reported that he had "seen balls of fire being tossed on the roof of the Sodder house" that morning.

Jeannie thought about waking George but decided to go back to sleep. But she awoke once again a short time later. It wasn't a sound that awakened her this time, though, it was the smell of smoke.

She sprang out of bed and ran into the hallway to try and get to the office telephone, but she saw flames were already burning in that part of the house. The path to the telephone was blocked. She screamed for her husband and ran to wake Marian, who was still sleeping on the couch. She told her to get Sylvia from the bedroom and go out the front door and wait. Jeannie pushed past her and shouted up the stairs for the rest of the children.

By now, George was awake and struggling to get into his clothes. He ran outside to the water barrel that stood near the house.

John and George, Jr., the two oldest Sodder boys at home appeared at the top of the stairs and ran down them. The fire was roaring along the wall and both of them received minor burns as they fled from the flames. John had shouted for his younger siblings – or he had gone into the bedrooms to awaken them, according to one of his statements to the police – and thought he heard them respond. The boys fled outside, where Marian, Sylvia, George, and Jeannie were shivering in the cold.

Realizing that the rest of the children were still inside, George tried desperately to get them out of the house, but the front of the house and the staircase were now engulfed in flames. The water barrel had been frozen solid, so George used it as a step to try and climb up the side of the house. He quickly fell. So, he smashed a window, badly slicing his hand and arm, but the fire was too hot, preventing him from getting inside.

George called frantically toward the upper floor of the house, pleading with his children to come to the window. He then remembered the ladder that he kept at the side of the house and ran to where it should have been – it was gone.

Panicked, he came up with another idea. He would drive one of his trucks up to the house and then climb on top of the cab so that he could reach the upper windows. He ran to the nearest truck, climbed into the cab, and cranked the engine. It wouldn't start. He jumped down and ran to his other truck. He tried to start this one, too, but the motor wouldn't turn over. Both trucks had worked perfectly the day before.

While George was struggling with the trucks, Marian had handed Sylvia to their mother and had run to a neighbor's house to call the fire department. She pounded on the door until a light appeared in the window. She quickly explained what was happening and begged to use the telephone. Marian clicked the receiver, but no operator answered to put the call through. It was a shared party line, and no one was on duty during the early morning hours of Christmas Day.

Around 1:00 a.m., another neighbor spotted the fire and ran to a local tavern to call for help. He was also unable to get an operator on the line, so he drove two miles into Fayetteville, West Virginia, to wake up the fire chief, F.J. Morris.

And then came the next delay. Morris had to find firefighters to help with the blaze because he was unable to drive the fire truck.

At the Sodder home, the fire continued to burn unchecked, while the family and a scattering of friends and neighbors crowded around. Later, everyone who was there that morning agreed that they never saw a child's face in an upstairs window and never heard a cry for help.

The house burned. The onlookers saw the lights in the house go out and saw the Christmas lights in the window flicker and then go dark. It took only 30 minutes for the Sodder house to be turned into a pile of smoldering brick and wood.

One of the most haunting mysteries to ever occur in West Virginia – and perhaps even in America – began during the predawn hours of December 25, 1945. The fire that occurred at the Sodder home that night was the key to the mystery, but whether it was a vanishing, a kidnapping, or a mass murder has never been determined. What is known is that five children of George and Jeannie Sodder were apparently lost in a mysterious fire that destroyed their home. But how were they lost? Their bodies were never found in the ruins and the children were later spotted in various places, creating a puzzling, complex, real-life mystery that is more baffling than anything that can be found in fiction.

What happened to the Sodder children? Did they die in the fire, or were they kidnapped for unknown reasons? And if they were, why has no trace of them ever been found?

It was the holiday season in the West Virginia countryside near Fayetteville. A light snow was on the ground and all seemed right with the world. George Sodder, Sr., and his wife, Jeannie, were the proud parents of 10 children and lived in a new home outside of town. George, a 50-year-old Italian immigrant had recently started the Dempsey Transfer Company, a new coal-trucking firm that he ran from an office in his home. It was already prospering. He owned two trucks and two of his sons were working for him. Another Sodder son, Joe, was in the army, but because World War II had ended several months earlier, he was out of danger. The rest of the children were at home with their parents, celebrating the season with gifts, food, and family.

Life was good for the Sodders and the new year promised to be even better.

The Sodder children opened their presents on Christmas Eve, including toys that had been purchased by Marian from her job at the dime store in Fayetteville. George went to bed early that night and so did the older boys, John, 23, and George, Jr., 16, who worked for their father in the coal-hauling business. The other children -- Maurice, 14; Martha, 12; Louis, 10; Jennie, 8; and Betty, 6 -- all said they were too excited to sleep, but finally went to bed around 10:00 p.m. The upper floor of the Sodder house was divided into two large rooms with one for the boys and the other for the girls.

Jeannie went to bed soon after the children did, taking two-year-old Sylvia into the bedroom she shared with her husband. She was looking forward to a good night's sleep before the holiday festivities of the next day.

But Jeannie didn't get a good night's sleep – not that night, or for any night for the rest of her life.

Jeannie was roused from her sleep three times that night – by the ringing telephone, the unusual sound on the roof, and finally by the fire. In the confusion, half of the family made it out of the house, but five of the children sleeping upstairs never came out.

George tried to get into the burning house, but the stairs were engulfed in flames. He searched for the ladder to reach the upper floor, but it had vanished. The Sodders later found it 75 feet from the house and thrown down an embankment. The coal trucks -- each of which had run perfectly on Christmas Eve – refused to start.

Attempts to call the fire department failed but, eventually, Fayetteville Fire Chief F.J. Morris was reached. But even after that, the fire department did not arrive until 8:00 a.m. – seven hours after the blaze began. The lapse was explained by the department's lack of manpower during the war and by the chief's inability to drive Fayetteville's fire truck. Morris had to wait until he could track down a qualified driver and Fayetteville didn't have a fire alarm in 1945, so they had to rely on a "phone tree." An operator would call one firefighter, then another and another. But with no operators seemingly on duty, the calls took hours to complete. By the time the firefighters arrived, the Sodder home had been reduced to a crumble of ruins over a smoking, ash-filled basement.

There was little the firefighters could do, other than hose down the few smoldering embers that remained in the debris of the house. A brief search of the ruins ended at 10:00 a.m. on Christmas Day, with Chief Morris telling the Sodders that no trace of the children could be found. He suggested that the fire was hot enough to completely cremate their remains and he suggested that they keep some of the ashes to create a memorial for the lost children. The fire department and the police authorities left, saying that they would return for a more thorough investigation of the site.

Jeannie, Marian, and Sylvia – who had been staying with Jeannie's sister – returned home and the family set up a make-shift apartment in an outbuilding on

THE SODDER CHILDREN WHO WERE BELIEVED TO HAVE DIED IN THE
HOUSE FIRE – BUT EVIDENCE SOON EMERGED THAT THEY MAY HAVE
BEEN TAKEN INSTEAD

the farm. The Red Cross and members of the local Board of Education visited them, offering food and any assistance the Sodders needed.

Meanwhile, the official investigation was continuing. A quick coroner's inquest was held, and the six-man jury took little time to decide that the fire was caused by faulty wiring. A report from the State Police agreed. How Trooper F.E. Springer, who wrote the report, came to this conclusion is unknown. He also stated that it was his belief that the fall of the house's two chimneys would have had enough heat and weight to destroy any corpses inside – the first of many explanations of why no human remains were found after the fire. There would also be rumors spread that George had stored significant quantities of oil and gasoline in the basement, something that George would always deny.

Even if he had, it would not explain the missing bodies. What we know today – that was not known in 1945 – is that the fire, which leveled the Sodder home in about half an hour, never reached the temperature required for the total cremation of human remains. That would have taken two to three hours and would have required a temperature of 1,400 to 1,800 degrees. In fact, various household appliances found in the burned-out basement were still recognizable.

But George and Jeannie didn't have that information. They were heartbroken, believing the jury's verdict that their five children had died in the fire. George could not stand to look out the window of the outbuilding where they were living and see the hole where his house used to be – and where he believed the ashes of his children remained. On December 29, he obtained a bulldozer and covered the basement with five feet of dirt, explaining that he planned to plant flowers and preserve the site as a memorial to the children.

On December 30, death certificates were issued for the five children. As far as the authorities were concerned, the case was now officially closed.

But was it really?

That's the real question here. Because there were strange things happening to the Sodder family – before and after the fire they make even the most skeptical among us take notice. There was something very unusual at work in their lives but what it may have been, no one can – or is willing – to say.

The weird events began in late 1945. Jeannie and some of the children had noticed a strange man parked on the road near the house each day, around the time that the children returned home from school. He did not get out of his car or approach the children in any way. He simply sat and watched the younger children walking home. Jeannie grew concerned but before she could confront him, he was gone and didn't return.

Another day, a man approached George in the yard asking about possible work around the farm or with George's trucking company. George didn't have anything to offer the man but as the stranger was turning to leave he pointed out a new exterior fuse box that had been recently upgraded for an electric oven the family had installed. He warned George that the new fuse box could "cause a fire someday."

In October 1945, George turned down an insurance policy that had been offered to him by a local salesman. The man flew into a rage and warned him that his house would "go up in smoke" and his children would be destroyed over "dirty remarks" that George had made about Benito Mussolini, Italy's fascist dictator, who had been lynched in April 1945. Interestingly, the same insurance salesman was a member of the coroner's jury that decided that the fire at the Sodder house was accidental.

A newspaper report also stated that, just before the holiday season, a woman and three men had shown up at the Sodder house and asked Jeannie if they could "see their babies." The newspaper didn't make a note of Jeannie's reaction, but I'm willing to guess that she closed the door in their face.

Then, on the night of the fire – while the house was still burning – a man was spotted breaking into the Sodders' garage and stealing an auto block and tackle. The man, identified in the newspaper as "Johnson," was later tracked down and arrested. Strangely, he was never investigated as to any involvement with the fire itself.

When a telephone repairman came to the Sodder home site to install service to the outbuilding where the family was living, he told them that the telephone line that had been running to the house had not been burned through, but rather had been cut 14 feet off the ground and two feet from the nearest utility pole. This meant that it had been cut between the time of the laughing lady's call on Christmas Eve and the fire itself. Later, Johnson, the block and tackle thief admitted to cutting the telephone wire, allegedly mistaking it for the power line. He would have needed a ladder to get to where the line was cut, which might explain why the Sodders' ladder was not found in its usual spot next to the house.

But why would he cut the electrical line into the house so that he could steal tools from the garage? It's possible that he had other reasons for wanting the house to be without lights. What Johnson was really doing that night was just another of the unanswered questions in the case.

There turned out to be a lot more.

The inquest verdict that the fire had started because of a blown electrical box made George and Jeannie question the things they had seen on Christmas morning. Based on the jury's findings, the electricity in the house should have gone out immediately. But the Sodders – as well as their neighbors – remembered the lights being on while the house was burning. They had seen the Christmas lights in the window go out long after the blaze started.

They were doubting the official version of events but before they could go to the authorities, they decided to do some investigating on their own. Jeannie put chicken and pig bones in a metal container and set them on fire. After burning for a few minutes, the fire went out, leaving scorched but intact bones behind. She also read a newspaper article about a nearby house fire. The house had also burned completely to the ground. Seven people had been trapped inside and after the fire, all seven bodies were easily identifiable.

The Sodders also learned about the late-night bus driver who reported seeing unknown persons throwing "balls of fire" onto the roof of their house. In March 1946, Sylvia Sodder found a green, hard-rubber object near the ruins, which some believed was some sort of firebomb. The Sodders later claimed that the house had burned from the roof downward, rather than from the ground floor up, but no evidence remained to prove their story. However, the idea of firebombs being thrown onto the roof might explain the strange noise that Jeannie heard when she was awakened a short time before the fire started.

George and Jeannie had now started to believe that the children had somehow been removed from their house before the fire. But how? If the children had seen a stranger, surely, they would have called out. How could kidnappers have not disturbed John and George, Jr., who shared a room with two of the missing children? And how could strangers have gotten the children out of the house without anyone noticing?

Despite these questions, they took their suspicions to the authorities – who had no interest in reopening the case. The Sodders were told that they needed to accept the jury findings of death by accident. It was a tragedy, they were told, but their children were dead, and they needed to find a way to move on.

But George and Jeannie refused to go along with the official conclusions. They hired two private detectives, C.C. Tinsley and George Swain, and began using their own money to pursue an investigation. The two men went to work, not only trying to run down information about the children, but also looking to see who might have hard feelings against the Sodders and if any possible enemies might have had something to do with the fire or with kidnapping the children. Things would soon become even more confusing and convoluted.

And then the sightings began.

First, the manager of a motel that was located halfway between Fayetteville and Charleston, West Virginia, claimed that he saw the five Sodder children there on Christmas Day. A resident of Charleston later said that he saw four of the children – Martha, Louis, Jennie, and Betty – with four unknown adults, about one week after the fire. The adults spoke Italian and were never identified.

And there would be more to come.

In 1947, a church minister from Fayetteville named James F. Frame told the Sodders a strange story. While Fire Chief Morris had stated that no remains were found at the fire scene in 1945, he privately claimed to have found "a heart" in the ashes, which he placed in an empty dynamite box and buried at the scene without reporting the discovery. The clergyman said that Morris did it in secret because he didn't want to make the Sodder family more upset. He said that he'd hoped they would find the organ in the ruins of the house and call off their private investigation. George and Jeannie eventually persuaded Chief Morris to show them where he had buried the box. They dug up the box, took it straight to a funeral home, and asked the director to open the box and examine it. When he opened the box, he found what looked like a decayed beef liver. It was untouched by the fire, meaning that it had been placed there after the blaze.

A few days later, C.C. Tinsley went to the funeral home to retrieve the liver and get an official statement about the mystery organ, but it had disappeared from the mortuary. The mortician said that since they did not have cold storage equipment on the premises, he had left the liver just sitting on his back porch until Tinsley could get there to claim it. Maybe it had been thrown out with the trash, he suggested.

What was the behind the buried liver? Morris's actions make no sense. If he had wanted the Sodders to find the liver to "put their minds at rest," as he explained, how did he think they would find it, locked in a box and buried under several feet of dirt? And wouldn't the fact that it was in a box indicate that someone had purposely placed it there? Even the fire marshal stated there was no clear reason for Morris's "peculiar actions." This led the newspaper that covered the story to say that it was obvious the case had not been investigated thoroughly enough and that more should be done.

But the authorities were not interested. They again urged the Sodders to move on with their lives.

But George and Jeannie refused to give up. They sent letters to the FBI, trying to get them involved with the investigation. The bureau declined, saying they considered "the matter related appears to be of local character and does not come within the investigative jurisdiction of the bureau." The FBI did eventually investigate the case as a possible kidnapping but found no new leads.

In August 1949, the Sodders managed to convince Washington, D.C. pathologist Oscar B. Hunter to do a thorough search through the dirt and ashes left at the site. The local fire marshal rejected the idea of a further search of the spot where the house had stood. He believed that the initial search had been good enough and there were no new clues to find. But the dig went ahead – and added more confusion to the case.

In the middle of the search, four spinal vertebrae bones were found. State authorities refused to examine the bones, so Tinsley sent them to the Smithsonian Institution and experts there determined that the bones belonged to a male between the ages of 19 and 22 – an age range that did not match any of the missing children. Published reports stated that Tinsley later traced the bones to a cemetery in Mount Hope, West Virginia, but no explanation was available concerning their theft from an unidentified grave or how they managed to end up at the Sodder fire scene. That's just one of the many lingering mysteries in this story.

Despite the evidence that the vertebrae did not belong to any of the missing children, private investigator George Swain formally left the case. He issued a statement that said he considered the case to be closed and his agency would not be "taking part in pursuing this matter further."

The Sodders quickly replaced him with Troy C. Simmons of the West Virginia Merchant Police. He brought a new enthusiasm to the investigation, saying that he believed the children were killed in a "grudge murder," hinting at organized crime. He also believed that the five missing children never left the county. He and his men planned to search abandoned wells and coal mines in the area. He also added that he felt confident that arrests would be made in the "next few days."

But no arrests were ever made.

While Simmons was going to work searching the coal mines in the region, the Sodders used the Smithsonian report to interest the FBI in their case. In 1950, the bureau opened a file on the Sodder children as a possible interstate kidnapping, but they only pursued it for two years with no results. Around that same time, the West Virginia State Police also looked into the case, but with the same amount of success – or lack of it.

Nothing happened but the family clung to hope. They ran newspapers ads and promised rewards and then in 1952, they erected a billboard near Ansted, West Virginia, that displayed photographs of the missing children with a $5,000 reward for information leading to their whereabouts.

The test of the billboard read:

On Christmas Eve, 1945, our home was set afire and five of our children (ages five through fourteen) kidnapped. The officials blamed defective wiring, although lights were still burning after the fire started.

THE SODDER CHILDREN BILLBOARD, WHICH ASKED FOR HELP FROM
THE PUBLIC UNTIL THE 1980S

The official report stated that the children had died in the fire. However, no bones were found in the residue and there was no smell of burning flesh during or after the fire.

What was the motive of the law officers involved? What did they have to gain by making us suffer all these years of injustice? Why did they lie and force us to accept those lies?

The billboard was a visible manifestation of the lingering hopes of the Sodder family that their missing children would someday come home. Sadly, it brought no useful tips. It did, however, generate a lot of speculation. Rumors were constantly spread and included lurid stories of Italian fascists, mafia gunmen, and orphanages who snatched children and sold them to childless couples.

George and Jeannie continued to be frustrated by the authorities, who refused to reopen the investigation. But as the years passed, they still refused to give up. They sent photographs of the five children to every possible resource, which continued to generate rumors, vague stories, and alleged sightings from all over the country.

A woman in Charleston reported seeing all the children once and Louis a year later, both times in the company of unknown adults. An anonymous letter writer claimed the children were living in Florida. The Sodders traveled there to find out but school records and birth certificates proved that none of the children in

Florida were the missing children. Another letter claimed that Martha was living in a convent in St. Louis. Someone in Texas claimed to have overheard men talking about a fire that happened in West Virginia on Christmas Eve. A letter sent to a local sheriff in Santa Cruz County in California claimed the missing children were living in the town of Davenport. They weren't.

Once, George saw a newspaper photo of young students at a New York Children's Aid Society ballet school and insisted that one of the girls in the photo was his daughter, Betty. He drove to Manhattan in search of the child, but her parents refused to let him see her. Unable to come up with a plan to get another look at her, he drove home disappointed.

THE MYSTERIOUS PHOTO THAT WAS SENT TO THE SODDERS IN THE MAIL FROM KENTUCKY. GEORGE AND JEANNIE BELIEVED THAT IT WAS THEIR SON, LOUIS

In 1966, a woman in Texas contacted the Sodders to say that she had overheard a conversation between two men, one of whom identified himself as Maurice Sodder. George traveled to Texas but by the time he got there, the man was long gone.

The most promising lead in nearly two decades came in 1967, when Jeannie received an anonymous envelope through the mail. It was postmarked in Central City, Kentucky, and contained a photograph of a young man about the age her son Louis would have been. Written on the back was a cryptic message:

Louis Sodder

I love brother Frankie ilil Boys

A90132 or 35

While George and Jeannie were convinced that the photo was an older-looking likeness of their missing son, they could not interpret the cryptic message on the back or trace the sender of the photograph.

They rushed the photo and envelope to the West Virginia Attorney General's office – convinced this would reopen the investigation – but officials there were not convinced of the photo's authenticity. Frustrated but not defeated, they hired a new private detective to go to Central City and find out what he could. He took their money and was never heard from again.

Heartbroken once again, George and Jeannie had the photograph enlarged and framed and placed it on their fireplace mantel with photographs of their other children. They were sure that it was Louis. They even had the new photograph added to the billboard with new text: *Picture No. 6, received in 1967, Louis (one and the same) now in another state.*

George Sodder died in 1969, still hoping for a break in the case. Jeannie fenced in their property and rarely left it. George's obituary stated that he was survived by his wife and five remaining children. No mention was made of Maurice, Martha, Louis, Jennie, or Betty.

The story remained alive, even though no new leads materialized. In 1984, Jeannie asked her son John to paint over the text on the billboard promising a reward, as she no longer had the money to pay if someone should eventually claim it when the children returned home. She died five years later, still convinced that her children were out there. Somewhere. The billboard in Ansted remained in place until her death, when it was finally taken down.

Today, the youngest surviving family member, Sylvia Sodder Paxton, keeps the family's haunting story alive with help from her daughter, pursuing leads on the internet or wherever information might come from.

Law enforcement officials still continue to refuse to reopen the case.

1946:

"WAITE FOR WORD"

January in Chicago was always brutal. The winter of 1946 was no different. Freida Meyer lived on the first floor of an apartment building on North Winthrop Avenue in the Edgewater neighborhood. She'd lived there for years – she'd forgotten how long – moving in not long after her husband had died. It wasn't fancy, but it was just fine for her simple tastes. It was a nice neighborhood and she had a few friends – mostly widows like she was – who went to the movies, played cards, and went shopping together on Saturday mornings.

If there was anything about her life that she would change, Frieda would wish away her arthritis. The pain wasn't usually too bad. It wasn't often that an aspirin or two didn't do the trick. But winter was especially tough. The temperatures had been frigid, and Frieda's knees had been acting up. She'd even had to postpone her regular shopping trip with a friend that morning. And now, here it was, practically the middle of the night and Freida was still awake. She'd warmed up a heating pad for her knees, but it wasn't doing much good. She just wanted to sleep, but her arthritis wasn't cooperating. Perhaps she'd put the kettle on and have a cup of tea with some milk. That might just do the trick.

Freida gingerly got up from her chair, where she had been listening to the radio, and walked toward the kitchen. She glanced at the clock. Oh my – it was 3:40 a.m. My goodness, she thought, I'm going to be tired tomorrow. Or rather today, she shook her head.

Freida had just entered the kitchen when she heard a loud bang from downstairs. That's odd – the only thing below her apartment was the laundry room. What would someone be doing down there at this hour? Her curiosity got the better of her and she went to the window and peered out of a narrow gap in the curtains.

The noise she'd heard had been the outside door to the laundry room being pushed open. She saw a man go inside. The light from the laundry room spilled out into the space between her building and the one next door. A pale yellow glow splashed against the brick wall, and then was gone. The door was closed again.

Freida shrugged. It seemed an odd time to be doing laundry, but it was none of her business. She put the tea kettle on the stove and opened a bottle of aspirin while she waited for the water to boil.

In the time that it took her to make tea, the man downstairs apparently finished his business. She heard some rustling about and, still curious, she looked out the window again. She couldn't see him very well, but he was wearing a gray hat and a tan overcoat. He was probably in his 30's or 40's. She didn't recognize him.

Freida settled down into her chair and a few minutes later, heard a sound downstairs. The man – whoever he was – had returned. The basement door creaked open and she could hear someone moving around. She pulled herself up from her chair again and pulled back the curtain. The same man in the gray hat and tan coat was hurrying away down the alley.

What in the world? She thought to herself. She was still at the window when he returned a third time, only a few minutes later. This time, he only stayed for a moment – she wasn't even sure he went inside – and then he was gone. This time, he didn't come back.

With the evening's excitement finally over, Frieda's eyelids began to droop. The tea and aspirin had served their purpose. She switched off the radio, turned off the light, and went down the hallway to bed. A few minutes later, she was asleep.

Freida was still sleeping the next morning when it was discovered that a little girl named Suzanne Degnan – who lived just a block or so away – had disappeared during the night.

Suzanne was never seen alive again.

She had been murdered and butchered, her body scattered in pieces throughout the neighborhood. The news sent a tremor of terror throughout Edgewater and residents closely watched the newspapers as the police investigation announced the discovery of the girl's missing pieces.

Then, just steps away from where her head was found, the police uncovered what the newspapers would dub the killer's "murder room." It was the basement laundry room on North Winthrop Avenue – right below Freida Meyers' apartment.

Who killed the girl? That remains a matter of some debate, even after all these years. Even though a young man was tried, convicted, and died in prison for the murder – along with two others – there are many who believe that Suzanne's murder was never actually solved.

And that may be the reason that Suzanne's spirit has never rested in peace.

On the hot summer day of June 5, 1945, the body of 43-year-old Josephine Ross was found in her apartment at 4108 North Kenmore Avenue, a building that overlooked Chicago's Graceland Cemetery. Her body lay in bed, as though it had been posed. Investigators found that she had been repeatedly stabbed – and her throat had been cut – but her body had been washed. Her killer had then tried to put her flesh back together with adhesive tape. Her head was then wrapped in a skirt, perhaps to shield her eyes from the face of the man who took her life.

The murder had been reported by Josephine's daughter, who had to pass a lie detector test to convince detectives that she had not staged the unusual crime scene. The investigators had never seen anything like it. It would soon become obvious that they were completely out of their element.

Although Josephine's body had been washed, investigators still found dark hairs clutched in her hand, presumably from the killer. Several of her former boyfriends and an ex-husband were questioned but leads quickly fizzled out. The case turned cold.

Six months later, on December 10, the body of 32-year-old Frances Brown was found slumped over her bathtub in her home at 3941 North Pine Grove, which was only five blocks from the Ross apartment. Her apartment door was open, and a cleaning woman heard her radio playing loudly and went inside. She quickly called the police.

Frances had been shot in the head and a butcher's knife had been driven into her throat with such force that it came out the other side of her neck. Her body had been stripped naked and – just like Josephine Ross – she had been washed clean of blood. Her head was wrapped in towels.

Again, just as was the case with Josephine Ross, police assumed that she had surprised an intruder, but nothing had been taken from the apartment. Instead, this time a note was left behind. It had been written on the living room wall with Frances's lipstick:

For heaven's sake catch me before I kill more. I cannot control myself

This note earned the murderer the name "Lipstick Killer."

Fortunately, the killer left behind a bloody fingerprint smudge on the door jamb into the apartment – along with a witness to his escape. George Weinberg reported hearing gunshots around 4:00 a.m., and John Derick, the apartment building's night clerk, reported seeing a nervous man – age 35-40 and approximately 140 pounds – get off the elevator and walk to the door to the street before leaving on foot.

And yet four days after the murder, Chicago Police announced they had reason to believe the killer was actually a woman.

Newspaper reporters had flocked to the scene, anxious for a story about a multiple killer. Headlines suggested that a new "Jack the Ripper" was stalking the city and promoted the name of the "Lipstick Killer." The police investigation went in circles. Detectives began rounding up sex offenders, deviants, and mental cases, but made no progress. The bloody fingerprint smudge was examined. It didn't match anyone on file and the case quickly died. It looked as though the only chance the authorities might have to catch the killer was if he committed another murder – and made a mistake.

A month later, the "Lipstick Killer" was replaced in the headlines by a missing child case. A little girl named Suzanne Degnan, age 6, had vanished from her family's home at 5943 North Kenmore Avenue. Her first-floor bedroom window was open, and a ladder was placed beneath it, outside the apartment. Police also located a scrawled ransom note on the property. It read:

Get $20,000 Reddy & wAITe foR WoRd.
Do NoT NoTify FBI oR Police. Bills IN 5's & 10's.

On the reverse of the note was written:

BuRN This FoR heR SAfTY

On the morning after it was discovered Suzanne was missing, a man telephoned the Degnan apartment several times, demanding the ransom, but he always hung up before any details could be arranged.

Shortly thereafter, the mayor of Chicago, Edward Kelly, also received a note:

This is to tell you how sorry I am not to get ole Degnan instead of his girl. Roosevelt and the OPA made their own laws. Why shouldn't I and a lot more?

This note changed the course of the investigation – at least for a short time – and sent the police in search of a meat packer. There was a nationwide strike by meat packers taking place and workers were angry with the OPA (Office of Price Administration), which at the time was considering extending wartime rationing and price and wage freezes. Suzanne's father, James, was a Midwest official of the OPA and had recently moved his family to Chicago. Another executive of the OPA had just been assigned armed guards after receiving threats against his children. Also, recently, a man involved in black market meat sales had been decapitated and killed.

The meat packers meant business.

SUZANNE DEGNAN (LEFT) WITH HER
MOTHER AND SISTER

However, that part of the investigation led nowhere. Was the note sent to Mayor Kelly merely a threat by a disgruntled worker, or was it sent by a legitimate suspect in the kidnapping? We'll never know. The police never got anywhere with the lead.

Meanwhile, neighbors of the Degnan family were questioned, but most had nothing useful to report. That is until police received an anonymous telephone call, suggesting that the police look in the sewers near the Degnan home. Officers and volunteers scoured the neighborhood and just after dark that evening, a policeman made a gruesome discovery. Behind a building on the west side of Kenmore – about a block from the Degnan home – he saw a storm drain sewer that appeared to have been tampered with. When he lifted the lid and peered inside with his flashlight, he found Suzanne's severed head floating in the water. A blue ribbon was still tied in her blond hair.

Soon, more body parts began to turn up. Suzanne's right leg was found in a catch basin in the same alley and her left leg in an alley east of Kenmore. Her torso was discovered in a storm drain at the northwest corner of Kenmore and Ardmore. Each piece had been found a little further away from the family home.

It took investigators an additional month to find her arms, which were in a sewer drain on the other side of the Howard elevated train line – more than three blocks from the Degnan home. All the drains had been capped with circular cast iron manhole covers, weighing more than 100 pounds, yet no one heard them being lifted or even slid back into place.

The newspaper luridly reported each new development in the startling case. The public was outraged and called for vengeance. The Chicago Police

Commissioner and State's Attorney both personally appeared at the Degnan home and vowed to capture whoever had carried out such a horrific crime and bring them to justice.

The search of an apartment building at 5901 North Winthrop Avenue – near the spot where Suzanne's head was found – uncovered a

THE LAUNDRY AREA IN THE NEARBY APARTMENT BUILDING THAT THE PRESS BEGAN CALLING THE "MURDER ROOM."

basement laundry room, with four tubs containing evidence that she had been dismembered there. The floor had been mopped but blood was found in the drains of all four tubs. The press began referring to this as the "murder room." It was easy to see why. It was dark, dingy, and grim, and the photographs of the dented laundry tubs was enough to send a chill up the spine of any newspaper reader. The unpleasant moniker was likely inaccurate, however. An autopsy would show that Suzanne was likely alive when she was taken from her home, was murdered at a secondary location, and then taken to the laundry room.

Dr. Kearns from the coroner's office reported that a very sharp instrument had been used to dismember the body. He noted that it was carried out by "either a man who worked in a profession that required the study of anatomy or one with a background in dissection. Not even the average doctor could be as skillful; it had to be a meat cutter." Another doctor agreed, stating that it was a "very clean job with absolutely no signs of hacking."

As excitement about the crime continued to build, more witnesses came forward. The police gave over 170 polygraph tests, trying to root out the truth from the stories and eyewitness accounts.

Ethel Hargrove, the tenant who lived in the apartment above the Degnan family, reported hearing loud male voices downstairs and dogs barking when she arrived home at 12:50 a.m. Another tenant corroborated her story.

Freida Meyer also came forward to tell the police about the man who entered the laundry room during the early morning hours. She provided a time for the man's visits and her story was corroborated by Marion Klein and Jake DeRosa, who had looked out their window around the same time and saw a man in a gray hat and tan overcoat. They said that they saw him start to go into the laundry room – this was the third visit reported by Freida – but he ran away, as if something had disturbed him.

Another neighbor, George Subgrunski, went to the police shortly after the murder and reported seeing a man walking to the Degnan home around 1:00 a.m. He described the man as being about five-feet, nine-inches tall, approximately 170 pounds, and 35 years old. He added that the man was carrying a bag and wearing a light-colored hat and a dark coat.

The most puzzling testimony came from Robert Reisner, a cab driver, who saw a woman behind the Degnan home at 1:30 a.m. She had a bundle under each arm and got into a car that was driven by a gray-haired man. Missy Crawford, who lived across the street, said that she saw a car with a man and woman driving up and down the street at 2:30 a.m. Were they the same man and woman that Reisner saw?

After sifting through the testimony, the police had a description of the killer. He was likely male, between 35-40 years of age, weighing between 140 to 170 pounds. He was under six-feet tall, and strong – strong enough to lift heavy manhole covers that weighed more than 100 pounds. He would have a background in anatomy or dissection since the dismemberment of Suzanne was done with skill and precision. He was likely an angry meat packer, with reason to be upset with the OPA. He might even have a female accomplice.

The first man the police arrested was 65-year-old Hector Verbaugh, a janitor in the building where the Degnan family lived. They theorized that his job might get him access to the laundry room and the state of the ransom note suggested that it had been written by a dirty hand – just like a janitor would have. The problem was that the Belgian immigrant didn't remotely fit the profile that the police had already put together. Tenants in the building called him a kindly old man. He had no surgical knowledge nor skill as a butcher. He was hauled away to the Summerdale District police station anyway, where investigators spent 48 hours trying to beat a confession out of him. They even pressured Verbaugh's wife to implicate her husband in the murder, but she refused.

Verbaugh was badly beaten during his ordeal. He later said, "Oh they hanged me up, they blindfolded me... I can't put up my arms, they are sore. They had handcuffs on me for hours and hours. They threw me in a cell and blindfolded me. They handcuffed my hands behind my back and pulled me up on the bars until my toes touched the floor. I no eat, I go to the hospital. Oh, I am so sick. Any more and I would have confessed to anything."

Verbaugh refused to admit that he had anything to do with the crime. On January 10, lawyers from the Janitor's Union managed to free Verbaugh and it was later determined that he could not write English well enough to have penned the ransom note. He ended up spending 10 days in the hospital after he was released. He sued the police for brutality and was eventually awarded $20,000.

Following another potential lead, investigators looked at Sidney Sherman, a recently discharged Marine who had served overseas during the war. Police reported finding blonde hairs in the back of the Degnan apartment building, near a wire that they suspected could have been used as a garrote to strangle Suzanne. Nearby was a handkerchief with a laundry mark name – S. Sherman.

Detective searched military records and found that a Sidney Sherman lived at the Hyde Park YMCA. When they went to question him, they found that he had left his room without checking out and had even quit his job without collecting his final paycheck.

Sherman was found four days later, in Toledo, Ohio. He explained that he had eloped with his girlfriend and denied that the handkerchief was his. He was given a polygraph test and passed.

The police did eventually find the owner of the handkerchief. It belonged to Airman Seymour Sherman, of New York City – but he had an airtight alibi. He was out of the country when Suzanne was murdered. He had no idea how his handkerchief ended up in Chicago.

In February, another discovery in the case was made – Suzanne's arms were found by sewer workers. Her body had already been buried by this time.

Weeks passed with more dead ends and false clues and the case grew colder. Investigators followed up on the ransom calls that had been made to the Degnan house on the morning after Suzanne had vanished. The investigation led them to a neighborhood hoodlum named Theodore Campbell, who, under questioning claimed to know who had killed Suzanne. He told officers that the killer was Vincent Costello, another neighborhood punk who lived only four blocks away from the Degnans. According to Campbell, Costello told him on January 7 that he had kidnapped Suzanne, killed her, and disposed of her body. He pressured Campbell into calling the Degnans to try and get ransom money from them.

The police knew about the strange calls that had been made to the family that morning, so they had no reason not to believe the story. Detectives were also aware of Vincent Costello. He had attended a local high school until he was convicted of armed robbery at 16 and sent away to reform school. Now, he was out and in trouble again.

News spread, and the *Chicago Tribune* announced that the case had been solved – it hadn't.

Costello was arrested and interrogated overnight. By morning, the story had fallen apart. Both boys were given polygraph tests, and it soon became clear that they knew nothing about the murder. Eventually, they admitted they had overheard police officers talking about the case on the morning after the abduction and thought that maybe they could make some easy money off the Degnans by pretending to be kidnappers.

Neither of them would ever be accused of being smart.

The mystery of the telephone calls had been solved, but investigators were no closer to finding the killer. By April, more than 370 suspects had been questioned and cleared. The press was becoming increasingly impatient, criticizing the police's inability to catch the monster that killed Suzanne.

In June, another suspect emerged. His name was Richard Russell Thomas and he was a nurse, living in Phoenix, Arizona. He had been in Chicago at the time of Suzanne's murder and a handwriting expert for the Phoenix Police Department informed Chicago officials of "great similarities" between Thomas's handwriting and the writing on the Degnan ransom note. He had been accused of writing an extortion note and many of the phrases that he used in it were similar to the ransom note. In addition, he had medical training as a nurse, which matched the profile suggested by the police.

While in Chicago, Thomas had lived on the South Side, but he had frequented a car yard across the street from where Suzanne's arms had been discovered. When questioned by police, he openly admitted to the murder – they were again sure they had their man.

But all that changed when a new suspect came along – a college student who was caught fleeing the scene of a burglary. When Thomas suddenly recanted his confession, the police let him go.

They were convinced that they finally had their killer – and they'd do anything to prove it.

On the afternoon of June 26, 1946, William Heirens, 17, was on his way to the post office to cash $1,000 in savings bonds, purchased with stolen money from a series of small-time burglaries. He had a date with his girlfriend later and needed cash. Heirens stuck a revolver in his pocket before he left home, nervous because he would be carrying such a large amount of cash. When he arrived at the post office, it was closed, but he still needed money – so he decided to steal some.

He went to a building in Edgewater – where he had stolen things before – and slipped into an unlocked apartment on the third floor. Heirens was unlucky on this day. A tenant spotted him in the hall and confronted him. He fled, out and then up the back stairs of another building, but a resident spotted him and called the police. He tried to escape down a staircase and was cornered by two police officers. He pulled out his gun.

According to Heirens, he turned and attempted to run, which resulted in a struggle and an off-duty police officer – Albert Cunningham – dropping three clay flower pots on Heirens's head from the top of the stairs, knocking him unconscious.

The police officers told a different story. In their version of events, Heirens charged both of them with his gun, firing twice, but the gun misfired both times. After that, he tossed the gun away and fought with them until the flower pots were smashed on his head.

William Heirens was taken to the police hospital at Cook County Jail, where he was stitched up, bandaged, and strapped to a bed. He drifted out of consciousness but heard someone say that he was a suspect in the Degnan case and felt his fingerprints being taken.

How did a small-time burglar end up being linked to not only the sensational murder of Suzanne Degnan, but also to the two murders committed by the "Lipstick Killer?"

That is a confusing, complicated, and very ugly story.

William Heirens was born in 1928 and was raised and attended school all over Chicago's North Side. His parents grew flowers in a greenhouse on Chase Avenue, just east of Western, until the Depression put them out of business. His father, George, tried his luck at a small flower shop downtown and when it failed, went to work as a security guard. William attended several Catholic elementary schools as a child, including St-Mary-of-the-Lake Catholic School at 4200 North Kenmore – a half-block away from where "Lipstick" victim Josephine Ross was murdered.

ACCUSED KIDNAPPER AND KILLER, WILLIAM HEIRENS

When William was a teenager, the Heirens' neighbors began noticing that women's undergarments had started disappearing from clothes lines and, later, from dresser drawers. Apparently, William was hiding them away to enjoy later. He outgrew his fascination with women's undergarments but did not outgrow his need to commit burglaries. He began breaking into houses, stealing cash, jewelry, guns, and any kind of valuables he could get his hands on. By the time of his first arrest, he had a collection of about $3,500 in stolen items. He was examined by a psychiatrist for the Juvenile Court and he determined that William had a compulsion for theft. He called it "neurotic stealing."

Many of the burglaries that William committed forced him into death-defying acts, jumping from one building to another, several stories above the street. He climbed into apartment windows on high floors without fear and had a talent for scaling walls that seemed impassable at first glance. During some robberies, he started fires or defecated on the floor, unable to control the strange urges that seized him.

William was arrested for the first time in June 1942. The police had been staking out a building on Sheridan Road that had been burglarized several times and caught him in the act. William was only 13-years-old and in eighth grade. He confessed to 10 other burglaries – only a fraction of the real number that he'd committed – and the newspapers called him a "one-boy crime wave."

Instead of being sent to a reformatory, William was allowed to attend Gibault, a privately-run Catholic school in Indiana. He stayed there for the next year. He was a model student and was sent home in June 1943. His family moved to 1020 West Loyola Avenue – six blocks from where Suzanne Degnan was later kidnapped and murdered.

The Catholic reform school had little effect on William. On August 8, 1943, he was caught inside of a nearby apartment building. According to police, eight or nine apartments had been robbed before William was discovered. The young boy was arrested again.

William's mother, Margaret, pleaded with the judge in the case and convinced him to send William to the St. Bede School, about 80 miles southwest of Chicago. Even though the school did not normally admit students with a criminal record, they made an exception, believing that they could help him. William was there until 1945 and was, again, a model student. After his court supervision was ended, he returned to Chicago.

After his second arrest, William's parents decided that a more rural neighborhood – with fewer houses to rob – would benefit the young man. They rented a farmhouse at Touhy and Keeler Avenues and George Heirens helped his son get a summer job as a laborer for the Illinois Central Railroad in downtown Chicago. He traveled to work each day by catching a bus at Keeler and taking it to the train station in Rogers Park. From there, he took the train downtown.

On June 5, 1945, William left home but never made it to work. The next morning, the newspaper reported the mysterious murder of Josephine Ross – whose apartment was very close to the train line that William took to work.

In the fall, it was time for William to return to school. Although the court didn't require it, Margaret Heirens wanted William to return to St. Bede to finish high school. William was adamant about staying home, however. He heard about a special program at the University of Chicago that allowed selected students to enter college early by taking a special exam. He scored well and in September 1945, entered college as a 16-year-old freshman. His grades were above average during the first semester, when he was also committing burglaries for spending money.

But burglary may not have been all William had on his mind. On October 5, 1945, an Army WAC named Evelyn Peterson was assaulted in an off-campus apartment on Drexel Avenue by an attacker who broke in through a skylight. The attack was interrupted when her sister knocked at the apartment door and the burglar fled. The sister later told police that she had seen a suspicious stranger in the building earlier that day. In July 1946, she picked William Heirens out of a police lineup.

A little over two months later, on December 10, Frances Brown was found murdered in her apartment at 3941 North Pine Grove. The killer – unable to control himself, or so he said – wrote a message asking for help on the wall with Frances's lipstick.

After William was arrested on June 26 – for attempted burglary and assault on the policemen – officers searched his University of Chicago dorm room. They found loot from an estimated 25-50 burglaries, including cameras, jewelry, thousands of dollars in bonds – and a scrapbook that was filled with photographs of prominent Nazi officials. The scrapbook turned out to be a war memento that was brought home from Germany by a former soldier named Harry Gold. It had been stolen from his apartment at 5959 North Kenmore Avenue during a burglary that had occurred on January 5, 1946. This placed William Heirens on the same block where Suzanne Degnan had been kidnapped just 24 hours before she was taken.

It was the first nail in William Heirens' coffin.

Of course, none of the officers who searched William's dorm room had any idea about that. They were simply carrying out a warrant on a burglary charge. They inventoried everything they found and estimated its value. The scrapbook, they believed, was worth about $1.

Soon after those items were taken to the precinct, a whole series of events was set into motion. When the Degnan ransom note had been found in January, the Chicago crime lab had been unable to lift any fingerprints from it, but the FBI, using more advanced techniques, managed to lift one print that was clear. Before William's arrest, fingerprint expert Sergeant Thomas Laffey had compared it to 700 other prints with no luck – but that changed on June 28. It was announced that they had a match – the fingerprint on the ransom note belonged to William Heirens. His prints also matched those found in the off-campus apartment of Evelyn Peterson.

And there was more.

Sergeant Laffey was initially unable to match William to the bloody fingerprint found in the apartment of "Lipstick" victim Frances Brown, but when a more complete sent of prints was taken – which included the joints of his right forefinger – a match was made. The FBI confirmed the match on July 13.

The police also revealed some circumstantial links between William and his victims after detectives began investigating his background. They learned that William had lived near the Degnan home, as well as the Ross and Brown apartments. Although Francis Brown and the Degnan family lived nearly three miles apart, William had burglarized homes on both of their blocks. To the detectives, it seemed impossible that this was a coincidence. State's Attorney William Tuohy believed that they finally had the infamous "Lipstick Killer," as well as the killer of little Suzanne Degnan.

Now they just had to get William to admit it.

As soon as the police informed William that he was being investigated for the three murders, he denied everything. He was interrogated around the clock for six days. He was beaten by the police and refused food and water. He was not allowed to see his parents for four of those days and was refused a lawyer for six. William was subjected to interrogation for three hours under the influence of sodium pentothal, popularly known as "truth serum." The drug was administered without his parents' consent – and without a warrant – by two psychiatrists, Haines and Roy Grinker. While under the influence of the drug, William spoke of an alternate personality named "George" who had actually committed the murders.

After the truth serum wore off, William spoke with Captain Michael Ahern and State's Attorney Tuohy with a stenographer in the room. He again told them that his alter ego, "George," might have committed the crimes. He also said that "George" – his father's first name and William's middle name – had given him the loot to hide in his dorm room. Ahern and Tuohy pressed for "George's" last name but William said he couldn't remember. He said it was a "murmuring name." The police translated this to "Murman" and the newspapers took it, twisted it around, and said it was "Murder Man."

Investigators questioned William's family and friends about this "George" but learned nothing. None of them had ever heard of his alter ego. What William actually said during this interrogation is in dispute and can't be confirmed because the original transcript has disappeared.

The problem with the interrogation is that most scientists believed subjects under the influence of sodium pentothal can be easily influenced, causing statements that are not entirely the truth to come out. By the 1950s, most scientists had declared truth serums to be invalid, and most courts ruled that any testimony gained through their use was inadmissible. Unfortunately for William Heirens, these scientific and legal opinions about truth serums were still a few years away – as were the revelations about the interrogation that eventually surfaced. In 1952 – after William had been convicted – William Tuohy admitted under oath that he not only knew about the sodium pentothal procedure, he had authorized it and paid the Grinkers $1,000 to do it. That same year, the Grinkers admitted that William never implicated himself in any of the killings.

On his fifth day in custody, William was given a lumbar puncture without anesthesia, and then driven to police headquarters for a polygraph test. They tried to administer the test right away, but ultimately had to reschedule it for several days later because William was in too much pain to cooperate. There has never been an explanation for why he was given a lumbar puncture. Typically, the procedure – a spinal tap – is conducted to diagnose diseases and is performed under local anesthesia.

When the polygraph was finally administered, the results were inconclusive. Oddly, though, John E. Reid and Fred E. Inbau published the findings of the polygraph test in their 1953 textbook, *Lie Detection and Criminal Interrogation*, and stated:

> *Murderer William Heirens was questioned about the killing and dismemberment of six-year-old Suzanne Degnan. On the basis of the conventional testing theory his response on the card test clearly establishes as an innocent person.*

There was no such statement made about the "Lipstick Murders."

George and Margaret Heirens didn't have much money, but they managed to hire a team of well-connected attorneys, the Coghlan brothers, to defend their son. They began taking a look at the evidence that had been collected against their young client.

Handwriting analysis could not link William's handwriting to the "Lipstick" message or the ransom note. However, the police claimed his fingerprints matched the bloody smudge on the doorjamb of France Brown's apartment. More troublesome, though, was the claim that his left little finger matched the print on the ransom note – but with only 9 points of comparison. According to the FBI handbook, regarding fingerprint identification, there must be 12 points of comparison to indicate a positive identification. In this case, all of William's points of comparison were all loops, which could be easily matched to 65-percent of the population.

The Degnan murder might have been in question, but William's attorneys were convinced that he was guilty of the "Lipstick Murders." They decided to make it their goal to keep the young man from dying in the electric chair. State's Attorney Tuohy, unsure that he could get a conviction, sought out cooperation from the defense counsel. Tuohy offered William a plea bargain. The agreement stated that in exchange for confessing to the murders of Josephine Ross, Frances Brown, and Suzanne Degnan, William would serve a single life sentence. The Coghlans urged him to accept the agreement. With good behavior, they told him, he would likely only spend about 25 years in prison and be out by the 1970s.

With help from his attorneys, William began to write his confession. He used the *Chicago Tribune* as a guide saying, "As it turned out, the *Tribune* article was very helpful, as it provided me with a lot of details I didn't know. My attorneys rarely changed anything outright, but I could tell by their faces when I had made a mistake. Or they would say, 'Now, Bill, is that really the way it happened?' Then

WILLIAM HEIRENS IN FRONT OF THE JUDGE, WHERE HE WAS SUPPOSED
TO CONFESS TO THE THREE MURDERS. HE BECAME CONFUSED AND HE
WAS FORCED INTO ACCEPTING A NEW PLEA AGREEMENT

I would change my story because, obviously, it went against what was known in the *Tribune*."

William and his parents signed the confession and a date was set for William to make an official statement. On July 30, William and his attorneys went to Tuohy's office, where several reporters were assembled to ask questions. This turned out to be a lot different than using a newspaper as a guideline to tell a story – William tried to cooperate, but he got confused and gave the reporters noncommittal answers. He suddenly claimed that he couldn't remember anything and then got angry. As William later said, "I asked him if he really wanted the truth. He assured me that he did. Tuohy had made a big deal about hearing the truth. Now, when I was forced to lie to save myself. It made me angry... so I told them the truth, and everyone got very upset.

Tuohy withdrew the previously agreed sentence of one life term and made a few minor changes. It stated that it would now be three life terms to run consecutively. William could escape execution, but he would never get out of prison. He told William that if the case went to trial, Tuohy would seek the death penalty.

On the advice of his lawyers, William accepted the new plea agreement. A public forum was once again held in Tuohy's office and this time William spoke and answered questions. He even went so far as to reenact parts of the murders that he had confessed to. He later stated, "I confessed to save my life."

But was he innocent of all the murders? Captain William Ahern – a man who had known William for many years and had even gotten him out of deeper trouble after his early arrests – later said that he never believed that William was the "Lipstick" killer – until he saw how familiar he was with Frances Brown's apartment. Ahern could never get past that.

On September 4, with Chief Justice Harold G. Ward presiding, William admitted his guilt on the burglary and murder charges. That night, he tried to hang himself in his cell – timed to coincide with a shift change by the guards – but he was discovered before he died. The following day, Judge Ward formally sentenced him to three life terms in prison. As he waited to be transferred to Stateville Prison in Joliet, Cook County Sheriff Michael Mulcahy asked William if Suzanne Degnan had suffered when she was killed.

"I can't tell you if she suffered, Sheriff Mulcahy," William answered. "I didn't kill her. Tell Mr. Degnan to look after his other daughter, because whoever killed Suzanne is still out there."

William Heirens continued to proclaim his innocence for the next 65 years.

There is no denying that there were many problems with William's arrest, treatment, and confession. He was beaten, prevented from seeing a lawyer, and subjected to what amounts to torture by the police. He also managed to pass a lie detector test, but that was not enough to get him off the hook. All the evidence against him was circumstantial, including the fingerprint evidence, which didn't hold up to the standards set by the FBI. It's believed by many historians that William was nothing more than a convenient scapegoat, easily framed by the police, who were harassed by the public and the press to find a killer. Many legal experts don't believe that William would have been convicted today. I find it hard to believe that he would have been convicted in 1946, but we'll never know – he was pressured into confessing by his attorneys.

But just because the investigation was poorly carried out does not mean that William Heirens wasn't guilty of something. It's very likely that William was the so-called "Lipstick" killer. Those two murders were obviously the work of one man – an experienced burglar who committed murder when he found the apartment that he was robbing was occupied. Neither of the women were raped but both were found naked. It might be recalled that William's first burglaries involved the stealing of women's underwear. If he had masturbated at the "Lipstick" scenes, this might explain why the bodies had been washed. He had previously left behind evidence of his compulsions when he defecated at burglary scenes. Did he wash away evidence of another compulsion?

It's very possible that William killed twice and may have been overwhelmed with guilt after the murder of Frances Brown, which caused him to leave the lipstick message on the wall. He probably would have killed again – in the case of Evelyn Peterson – if his attack had not been interrupted by her sister's arrival. His guilt may have been the reason that he actually confessed to the murders that sent him to prison.

But did William Heirens kill Suzanne Degnan?

The abduction, murder, and dismemberment of a little girl is a completely different method of murder than that used by the "Lipstick Killer." If all three crimes had not been blamed on William, no one would have ever believed they were related. I think it's very possible that William was initially framed for Suzanne's murder – which the police were under great pressure to solve – and detectives accidentally realized they had captured the "Lipstick" killer instead. But, with no other suspects at hand, why not send him to prison for all three? Suzanne's murder, by that time, seemed unsolvable.

It wasn't hard to pin it on William. He had been in the neighborhood around the time the little girl was kidnapped, as evidenced by the burglary at the nearby apartment. However, this was probably a coincidence. William didn't live far away, and Edgewater was essentially his favorite neighborhood for break-ins.

There was little to link him to the crime – other than the smudged fingerprint that should have never been accepted by the FBI laboratory and a very questionable eyewitness. The man who later claimed to see William near the Degnan home was a 25-year-old soldier on furlough named George E. Subgrunski. On the day after the kidnapping, he had been the one who told the police that he'd seen a man – described as 170 pounds, about 35-years-old, carrying a shopping bag, and wearing a light-colored hat and a dark overcoat – walking away from the house. It was dark, so he could not make out the man's facial features. When he was shown a photograph of William Heirens on July 11, the *Chicago Daily News* said that he was unable to identify the man as Heirens. Five days later, though, at a criminal hearing, Subgrunski pointed a finger at William and said, "That's the man I saw!" The police, anxious to find someone who could put William at the scene of the crime, decided to ignore the fact that Subgrunski was initially unable to identify William – they went with the new identification instead.

William was never the main suspect in Suzanne's murder – that was 42-year-old drifter Richard Russell Thomas, who was passing through town at the time of the murder. Just before William's arrest, Chicago police were interrogating Thomas in Arizona. Police handwriting expert Charles B. Arnold, head of the forgery detail of the Phoenix police, noted similarities between the handwritten Degnan ransom note and Thomas's handwriting. He had been the one who suggested that Chicago detectives investigate Thomas.

I believe that it's very likely Thomas was Suzanne's killer.

Not only did he confess to the crime, but he had previously been convicted of attempted extortion, using a ransom note that threatened the kidnapping of a young girl. Many of the phrases in the extortion note were similar to those in the ransom letter. When he confessed to Suzanne's murder, he was in jail awaiting sentencing for molesting his 13-year-old daughter. He also had a history of violence and had been arrested for beating his wife and molesting two of his three children.

He was a nurse who was known to pose as a surgeon and often bragged about how he stole surgical supplies from a hospital – all of which matched the profile the police had created. This was a man who certainly had the knowledge to dismember a body. He also spent a lot of time at the car agency in Edgewater that was right across the street from where parts of Suzanne's body were found in a sewer.

But, when William was arrested, investigating officers were called off the Thomas case, treating his confession as the ravings of a madman. Thomas served time in Arizona, then faded into obscurity, eventually dying in Tennessee in 1974. His prison record – along with most of the evidence of his interrogation regarding the Degnan murder – has been either lost or destroyed over time.

But even if William did not kill Suzanne, he still deserved to go to prison for the other crimes he committed and to which he confessed. There were no additional "Lipstick Murders" after William went to prison, which makes him the likely suspect in those cases – no matter what he might have claimed later on.

In 1954, the Illinois Supreme Court stated that the authorities violated William's rights while conducting the investigation, but the court also said that he chose to plead guilty to avoid a possible death sentence when he could have challenged the violations. It was decided that his conviction and sentence would stand.

William Heirens never saw freedom, even though his sentence allowed for the possibility of parole. But in spite of being a model prisoner and the first in Illinois to earn a college degree behind bars, his parole was turned down more than two dozen times. In 1998, he was transferred to a minimum security prison in Dixon, Illinois, and moved onto the hospital ward. He was suffering from diabetes, which had limited his eyesight and forced him into a wheelchair. In 2002, a petition was filed on Heirens' behalf seeking clemency. It not only cited doubts about his guilt, but also his model behavior while in prison. The appeal was eventually denied.

In 2007, his parole was denied again. A member of the Illinois Prisoner Review Board, Thomas Johnson, made sure that William knew he would never be released from prison. "God will forgive you," he said, "but the state won't."

William Heirens died in prison on March 5, 2013. He was the longest-serving prisoner in the history of the state of Illinois.

As far as Suzanne Degnan's remaining family members were concerned, the death of William Heirens brought an end to a tragedy that had been haunting them for decades. They had always believed the police and had no reason to doubt the fact that William had killed the little girl. Jim Degnan, born 10 months after his sister had been killed, attended William's parole hearings for 29 years – determined that he would never get out of prison.

Jim said that his parents never spoke about Suzanne when he was a boy. He didn't learn about how she had died until a classmate told him about the murder when he was in fifth or sixth grade, prompting him to ask his parents about it.

Once he knew what had happened, things that he had seen throughout his life suddenly made sense. His mother had installed bars on his bedroom window when they moved into a new apartment several years after the killing. She had also never allowed him to buy black pants – she had always associated them with William Heirens because had had worn them everyday in court. Jim said that he began researching the case when he was in his 20's, after William began claiming that he was innocent. After examining some of the evidence and speaking with the authorities and a retired judge, he was satisfied that Heirens was guilty. He said that William's supporters had decades to prove his innocence, but never could.

Suzanne's older sister, Betty, recalled riding to school in a police car for a time after the murder because of the attention that surrounded the case and fear of a killer at large. She never forgot her sister – or her murder – but always believed that William was guilty, no matter what he claimed. She wanted him in prison, although not for retribution. She helped to keep him locked up by attending his parole hearings out of fear that he might get out and hurt someone else. That was something that she just couldn't live with.

Were those who believed William Heirens killed Suzanne correct, or was there more to the story than anyone knew? There is no question that many problems exist when it comes to linking William to Suzanne's murder – not the least of which a much more believable suspect in Richard Russell Thomas. Did Thomas get away with murder? Has the killing of Suzanne Degnan remained unofficially unsolved after all these years?

Perhaps, because if the stories from those who claim to have encountered her ghost are true, the tragic little girl may not rest in peace.

I first wrote about Suzanne Degnan in 2009 when I was working on a series of books about Chicago crime and murder. The publisher of the series arranged several book signings for me around the city and I met a lot of interesting people, many of whom had stories to tell about incidents or people that were featured in the books. These books weren't about ghosts – but yet sometimes the stories people came to tell me were about ghosts anyway.

And that's how I first heard about Suzanne's ghost.

I was doing a signing at a bookstore in the Uptown neighborhood when a lady came in and purchased a book. She knew that most of my writings were about ghosts and hauntings and she told me that she had a ghost story about one of the cases that was in one of the crime titles. She explained that she had once lived in an apartment at 5901 North Winthrop Avenue, where the infamous "Murder Room" had been located. It was the place where the police believed Suzanne had been dismembered after her death.

When she had lived there, it was no longer a laundry room. The four, blood-stained basins had vanished long ago, but she did live on the basement floor, just down a hallway from the room. And months before she found out what had occurred there, she came to believe that the room was haunted.

It had started with the sounds. She said that on many nights when she came home from work – she was then a bartender in Uptown – she would hear banging noises coming from down the dark corridor that led from her apartment to the former laundry room. Sometimes, she said, they sounded like footsteps. She didn't see anyone, though, and when she turned on the light in the hall, they usually stopped. She was willing to dismiss the whole thing to an overactive, late-night imagination – until she saw the little girl.

One night, she came home and was getting ready to open her door when she saw a movement down the corridor. The light was dim, but she could see a young girl standing there, looking at her. The girl had blond hair, a pale face with slightly chubby cheeks, and was wearing a pale, knee-length dress. She didn't move, she didn't say anything – she just stood there, staring.

The witness called out to her. She told me that she certainly didn't think she was seeing a ghost. She assumed it was a neighbor's child, but one that was wandering the apartment building halls long after she should have been in bed. With her keys dangling in the lock, the young woman started to walk toward the little girl.

And then the little girl vanished.

Startled, the witness said that she let out a small scream and pushed through the door into her apartment, too terrified to look out into the hallway again. "I don't know why I was so scared," she told me. "It just upset me very much."

The witness told me that she never saw the little girl again, but her terror over the sighting turned to curiosity. That's how she found out what made her building – and the laundry room down the hall – so notorious in 1946. She was convinced by photographs that she found that the little girl in the hallway was Suzanne Degnan.

She only lived in the apartment building for another few months after that – her lease was up, she assured me, not because she was afraid – and she did sometimes hear the noises and the footsteps, but she learned to tune them out.

She never saw the ghost that she believed was Suzanne again, but she'd heard that others had. Her curiosity – and fascination – with the story of Suzanne's murder never really went away and she spoke with others who had lived in the basement of the apartment building.

They were sure it was haunted because they had also seen the ghost of a little blonde-haired girl in the basement hallway. I wonder who she is, they sometimes asked the witness and she always replied with a tragic story of a little girl who died long, long before her time.

1975:

THE "EASTER SUNDAY MASSACRE"

That fateful Easter Sunday in 1975 was like any other in Hamilton, Ohio, a middle-class community about 30 miles outside Cincinnati. Children hunted for colored eggs, mothers made last minute preparations for afternoon dinners, and entire families dressed in new clothes to attend morning church services.

But 41-year-old James Ruppert was hungover and still in bed when his brother, sister-in-law, and their eight children arrived at the cramped house that he shared with his mother, Charity. James and his brother were polar opposites – James was an unemployed loner and his older brother, Leonard, had a career and a large, happy family.

When the children came in for lunch – laughing, talking, and aggravating the pounding headache that James was nursing after drinking too much the night before – he finally dragged himself out of bed. Seemingly unaware of the holiday festivities, James told his brother that he was going to do a little target shooting and brought out three handguns and a rifle.

James Ruppert's vehicle at the time was an old Volkswagen and he had recently been having problems with its engine. While most everyone who knew James was aware that the car was falling apart because he failed to keep up with maintenance on the old vehicle, James believed that his older brother had been secretly sabotaging it when he wasn't around. He couldn't prove it – and he'd never actually seen Leonard messing with his car – but he was certain this was the case. James blamed Leonard for most of the problems that he had in his life, so car problems was just another to add to the list.

So, when James came downstairs and walked into the kitchen, where Leonard and his family were gathered, and Leonard asked him about his car, something in James simply snapped.

"How's your Volkswagen, Jimmie?" Leonard asked him.

James didn't speak. He answered by shooting his brother, setting off a spiral of violence and rage that ended as the deadliest shooting spree to ever occur in a private home in America's bloody history.

And it left a grim and troubling haunting behind.

James Urban Ruppert was born on March 29, 1934. His early life was sad and abusive. His mother, Charity, often called him a "mistake," because she had wanted a daughter. When James was a young boy, the Rupperts lived in a long, barn-like structure with no indoor plumbing or running water. His father, Leonard, raised chickens in the rear of the house. James developed a case of asthma – caused by an allergy to dust and feathers – which made him sickly and limited his physical activities for the rest of his childhood.

Unable to run and play like other children his age, he was regarded as a "sissy" by other kids in the neighborhood. He walked hunched over from his illness, too frail to take gym class at school or play sports. He was a shy, introverted child who, from his earliest years in school, was routinely teased by other children and had few, if any, friends. He avoided all extracurricular activities, rarely attending sporting events or dances, and never dated girls.

As if the abuse suffered at school wasn't enough, problems at home continued. His father was a frustrated, unsuccessful man who took out his anger on his family. He was violent, had a quick temper, and had little time or affection for his sons. He died of complications from tuberculosis in 1947, when James was 12 and his brother, Leonard, Jr., was 14. He wasn't missed.

After his father's death, things at home grew worse. His mother often beat and taunted James and encouraged Leonard to do the same. The boy was easy to pick on. James did poorly in school, had few friends, and was always smaller than his brother. As an adult, he was only five-foot-six-inches and weighed 135 pounds. At 16, James was so unhappy at home that he attempted suicide by hanging himself with a sheet.

He failed in his attempt and resigned himself to an unremarkable life.

Ruppert's mother continued to shower love on her older son, who became a constant reminder to James of his own inadequacies. As he got older, his resentment for his bother grew. Leonard was, at least in his younger brother's mind, a vicious sadist and torturer - he was the enemy. Going back to early childhood, James remembered his brother locking him in closets, tying him with rope, beating him with a hose, and sitting on his head until he screamed out loud.

James's math and science teachers always compared him to his older brother, whose grades in the same class had been superior. Leonard graduated from night

LEONARD RUPPERT, JR., HIS WIFE, ALMA, AND THEIR EIGHT CHILDREN.
JAMES'S BROTHER HAD EVERYTHING IN LIFE THAT JAMES COULD
NEVER HAVE

school with a degree in electrical engineering, while James flunked out of college after two years. To make matters worse, Leonard married one of the few girlfriends that James had ever had, with whom he had eight children. Leonard had a great job with General Electric while James was unemployed and living with this mother. Leonard was not only more successful than his brother, but James came to believe that Leonard was plotting against him, conspiring to keep him from leading a better life.

His paranoia escalated in 1965 when a woman who worked at the local public library called the police and reported an obscene, threatening telephone call that she'd received. She recognized the voice as a frequent library patron – James Ruppert. When the police questioned him, he admitted that he'd made the call.

But that wasn't all that he had to say.

He told detectives that his mother and brother were attempting to discredit him by informing everyone he knew about the call and had contacted the FBI to tell them that James was a communist and a homosexual. He now believed that the FBI was tapping his telephone, not only at home but also at the bars and restaurants that he visited. He would later tell psychiatrists that he believed he was being followed by the Ohio Highway Patrol, the local sheriff's department, private detectives, and the Hamilton Police Department.

The police already knew of James Ruppert. He had a collection of guns and he was often down at the local river, firing them off. He hadn't hurt anyone, and he hadn't broken any laws – yet. They suggested that he seek psychiatric help and declined to prosecute him. To the police, James appeared paranoid but not terribly dangerous. They had more important things to deal with than prank phone calls. Ruppert was referred to a mental health professional, who concluded that he was not a threat. He wasn't hospitalized, and he wasn't medicated. He was eccentric, but he didn't seem to be dangerous.

James Ruppert had them all fooled.

By the spring of 1975, Charity Ruppert had reached her limits with her youngest son. She had been charging him rent to live with her and he had fallen behind in his payments. She had also loaned him money, and so had his brother. James had borrowed large sums from both of them after losing what little he had in the stock market crash of 1973-74. Charity was frustrated with his inability to keep a job and his constant drinking. She told him that she was going to kick him out of the house unless he got caught up on the rent.

It was this threat that seems to have finally pushed James closer toward the edge.

Though James had endured a miserable childhood and had access to guns, what happened to cause the murders to take place was a series of triggering events. In general, triggering events might occur over a period of weeks or even months before a murder, or they might occur immediately prior to it. Family killers – as James would turn out to be – are often seen as "gentle" or "passive" individuals. They carefully suppress their hostility toward family members so long as they receive some kind of psychological or monetary reward in return. But when such rewards are withdrawn – like being kicked out of the house or deprived of money – an explosion of anger is likely to occur. Family killers are frequently "loners" who depend almost exclusively on the family to satisfy their emotional needs. The threat of separation by family members is a particularly painful and threatening event.

And, far too often, it ends in blood.

James had no way to come up with the money that his mother was demanding. He went to a local gun dealer and asked about buying a silencer. The man told him that they were illegal, and James would have to go somewhere else to find one. The implication of this visit to the gun shop is clear: James was

CHARITY RUPPERT'S HOUSE, WHICH SHE SHARED WITH JAMES. IT WAS HERE WHERE THE FAMILY GATHERED ON THAT FATEFUL EASTER SUNDAY

planning to kill someone in his family. The exact time of death was yet to be decided – it would all depend on what happened next.

On March 29 – James' birthday – witnesses later reported seeing him shooting at cans with a .357 Magnum along the banks of the Great Miami River in Hamilton. He went out drinking later that night and ended up at the 19th Hole Cocktail Lounge, complaining about his life to anyone who would listen. One of those listeners – because she was paid to do so – was bartender Wanda Bishop. She later recalled that James seemed deeply depressed. He talked about his mother's demands on him and her threat of eviction. He left the bar around 11:00 p.m., telling Bishop that he "needed to solve a problem."

He came back a little while later and stayed there until the bar closed at 2:30 a.m. Wanda asked him if he had solved his problem. "No, not yet," he replied.

The next day, he murdered his entire family.

On Easter Sunday, March 30, Leonard and his wife, Alma, brought their eight children (ranging in age from 4 to 17) to see their grandmother at the house on Minor Avenue. James stayed upstairs, sleeping off his night of drinking, while the children enjoyed an Easter egg hunt in the front yard. Afterwards, they came inside and while Charity, Alma, and Leonard finished lunch preparations, the children played in the living room.

Around 4:00 PM, James woke up, loaded his .357 Magnum, two .22 caliber handguns, and a rifle, and went downstairs. He entered the kitchen, where he shot and killed Leonard, Alma, and Charity. His nephew, David, and his nieces, Teresa and Carol, were also in the kitchen. He killed them, too. James then rushed into the living room, where he killed his niece, Ann, and his four remaining nephews, Leonard III, Michael, Thomas, and John. He killed each of his victims by first taking a disabling shot and then finishing them off with a shot to the head or heart.

The massacre took less than five minutes to complete.

James sat in the house for three hours before he called the police and calmly told the dispatcher, "There's been a shooting." When officers arrived, he was waiting for them just inside the front door. The police chief, prosecutor, and coroner all surveyed a scene that they described as a "slaughterhouse." There was so much blood that one investigator later said that he had to be careful not to let it drip on him as he walked through the basement – the blood was seeping through the floorboards.

The murders shocked the community and made headlines across the country. Those who knew James never believed that he was capable of such violence. He was a quiet, unassuming man and the perfect neighbor.

James was charged with 11 counts of aggravated homicide. Although he had called the police and made no effort to run, James refused to answer any questions and was very uncooperative. His defense attorneys claimed that he was insane, but prosecutors had a different theory. They believed that he had planned the murders and then turned himself in so that he could claim insanity. Since the entire family was dead, James stood to inherit from the estates of his mother, his brother, and even the nieces and nephews that he'd killed. Under Ohio law, he could inherit all that and $300,000 from life insurances policies if he was found to be not guilty by reason of insanity. All Ruppert's financial problems would finally be solved if he could pull it off. This was the theory that the prosecution presented at trial – his motives were financial, plain and simple.

Going to trial, James had the choice of facing a jury or a panel of three judges. While a jury had to rule unanimously, it would only take two of the three judges to reach a verdict. His attorneys decided that the judges seemed the safer risk for a case that would be so emotionally charged. After all, he had killed eight children, one of whom was only four-years-old. Three Butler County Common Pleas judges heard the evidence and arguments regarding the massacre. The trial ended on July 3, 1975, when two of the three judges ruled that he was guilty on all 11 counts of murder and sentenced him to 11 consecutive life terms in prison.

Ruppert immediately appealed his conviction. His attorneys argued that the trial court had misled James and his trial counsel. They claimed they were told that the panel of judges would only be able to convict Ruppert with a unanimous verdict, the same way that a jury

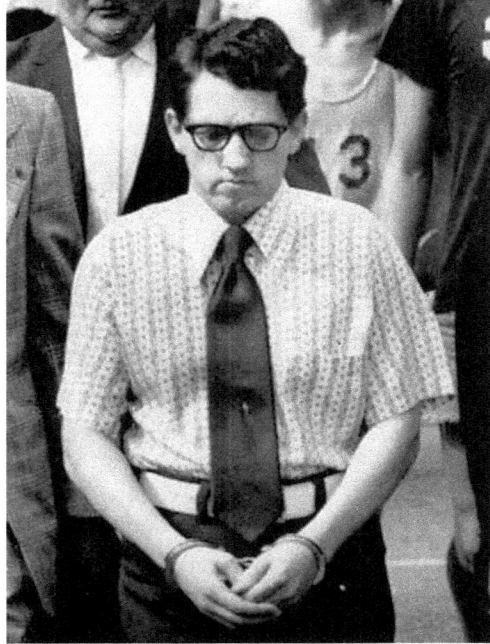

JAMES RUPPERT AFTER HIS ARREST

of twelve would have worked. Ruppert said that if he had known they could convict him with a split vote, he would have asked for a jury trial. The Ohio Surpreme Court said that if this was true – and there is reason to believe that it was not – and he'd been misled, Ruppert was entitled to a new trial. The prosecutors appealed this ruling to the U.S. Surpreme Court, which declined to overturn the state court. This meant that James Ruppert was getting another trial.

While appealing his conviction, Ruppert had been held at the State Hospital for the Criminally Insane in Limo, Ohio. In 1978, his attorney told reporters, shortly after the Supreme Court had refused to rule on the case – which was, for his purposes, the same as winning – that he didn't believe that James was competent to stand trial. He told reporters, "His paranoid condition has worsened. Generally, his entire mental processes are breaking down."

A second trial was ordered in 1982, and the venue was changed to Findlay, Ohio. It seemed unlikely that an unbiased jury could be found in Hamilton. Defense attorney Hugh D. Holbrock, convinced his client was insane, personally funded the hiring of expert psychiatrists from all over the country. His plan failed, at least partially. James was deemed competent to stand trial and on July 23, he was again found guilty of murder. This time, he was found guilty on just two counts – for the murder of his mother and brother – but found not guilty by reason of insanity for the other nine killings. Many people took this verdict to mean that Ruppert knew what he was doing when he killed his brother and mother but then continued killing in some sort of blind rage. He received one life sentence for each guilty count, to be served consecutively. Between 1972 and 1976, the death penalty had been suspended in the United States because of a pending U.S. Supreme Court decision, so James could not be sentenced to death for his crimes.

James Ruppert remains incarcerated today in the Allen Oakwood Correctional Institution in Lima, Ohio. He was granted his first parole board hearing in 1995, but his release was denied, as was his latest attempt at parole in April 2015.

Most likely, he will die behind bars.

☠

In the days that followed the massacre, the 11 victims of James Ruppert's rage were buried in the Arlington Memorial Gardens in Cincinnati. A year later, the house on Minor Avenue was opened to the public so that the contents could be sold at auction. The small, cramped house was cleaned up and carpets were placed over the bloodstains that could not be washed away. The new owners listed the house as a rental and the first tenants were a family that was new to the area and had no idea about the horrifying events that occurred there.

They quickly moved out.

After leaving the house, they claimed that during their brief occupancy, they had been plagued by supernatural happenings. They said they heard voices and strange noises that they couldn't explain. Lights turned on and off, doors slammed, and thudding footsteps were often heard coming down the stairs.

Worst of all, they said, were the voices of the children crying and begging for someone to "stop."

They would not be the last family to move into the house and quickly leave. There were others – quite a few of them over the next decade or so – and none of them stayed very long. All of them reported sounds and voices that could not be explained, objects that vanished without explanation and turned up in other parts of the house, and items that literally flew across rooms.

The place was haunted, they said, there was no doubt about it.

Whether it was the rumors of ghosts or simply the house's tainted past, it was abandoned for several years and left empty and silent. The next family that moved in reported northing out of the ordinary. Whatever eerie haunting that had bothered the previous tenants was over at last. Perhaps the echo of the terrible events of Easter Sunday 1975 – which seemed to leave an indelible mark on the house – had finally faded away.

And perhaps, after nearly 50 years, the spirits of the Ruppert family can finally rest in peace.

1977:

GIRL SCOUT CAMP

MASSACRE

We opened this book with a story of children who lost their lives in the woods, so perhaps it's fitting that we close with one, as well. In both stories, the children were perfectly comfortable, in places they believed were safe. These are not fairy tales of wicked witches or conniving wolves that lurked in the forest and tried to lure the children to their doom. These were picnic areas and, in this case, a Girl Scout camp – places where bad things were not supposed to happen.

And yet they did.

You see, outside of fairy tales, sometimes the monsters are real.

☠

On June 13, 1977, Camp Scott, a Girl Scout camp that was located in the wooded hills near Locust Grove, Oklahoma, opened for its 49th season – the season that would turn out to be its last. At some point in the dark of the night, three young campers were brutally murdered in their tent. The bodies were discovered by a counselor the next morning. It became a summer of horror and tragedy and it left behind a mystery that has never been solved.

As well as an abandoned camp about which stories of ghosts and hauntings are told.

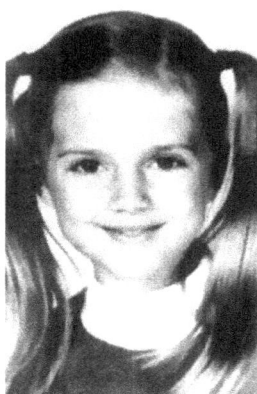

THE CAMP SCOTT VICTIMS: DENISE MILNER, LORI LEE FARMER, AND MICHELE GUSE

But Camp Scott did not start off to be a grim and eerie place. Before that terrible night in 1977, it was a magical place for girls who came there for summer retreats. It had offered hiking, crafting, swimming, and much more for Brownies and Girl Scouts since 1928. Its 410 acres accommodated 140 campers and 20 staff members in picturesque log cabins and tents. The Cookie Trail Road led to 10 camping sites that were scattered throughout the woods. The girls were all assigned "camp buddies" to share tents with. The camp sites were bases made from wood and covered with a 14x12-foot canvas tent. Inside were two bunk beds with mattresses. There were no other amenities, including lights. Aside from the campers' flashlights, the only source of light at night was a kerosene lantern that hung above the nearby latrines.

The tent that was furthest from the counselor's unit was "Kiowa" tent. In June 1977, it was a temporary home to three young girls: Lori Lee Farmer, 8; Michele Guse, 9; and Doris Denise Milner, 10. On the previous day, the three girls had boarded a bus in Tulsa for the 40-mile trip east to Camp Scott for a two-week stay.

When they had kissed their parents goodbye that morning, no one could have known that they would never see them again.

Denise, the oldest of the girls, was a straight-A student who had never been to camp before. This year, however, she had sold enough Girl Scout cookies during the annual drive to finally be able to attend. At first, Denise had been very excited because all her friends also planned to attend. Unfortunately, at the last minute, they had all backed out, leaving Denise hesitant about attending alone. Her mother finally convinced her to go, assuring her that she would make new friends at camp.

Both Lori and Michele had attended camp before. The youngest girl, Lori, had recently been considering attending a YMCA-sponsored camp instead of Camp Scott. She couldn't make a decision, so her mother decided for her – Lori would go to Camp Scott. She'd heard wonderful things about the place. Needless to say, it was an innocent decision that she'd regret.

Michele had been to Camp Scott the previous year and had a great time. She couldn't wait to go back. Her mother, Georgeann, later recalled, "She was very excited, and she came downstairs and she sat on my lap and told me she was going to miss me."

When the girls arrived at Camp Scott, they found themselves assigned to be "camp buddies." None of them had ever met before, but they soon became friends. They were assigned to "Kiowa" tent, which was technically number 7 on the roster, but was always referred to as number 8 when the counselor's tent was included in the count. Kiowa tent included a fourth bunk and it's been said that a fourth girl was preparing to move to the tent that night but because of bad weather, her move was postponed until the next day.

The thunderstorm undoubtedly saved the fourth girl's life.

It also put a damper on evening activities at the camp. The girls had eaten dinner in the Great Hall at 6:00 p.m. Afterward, they sang songs on the porch until 7:00 p.m. but were sent to their tents early when the storm moved in.

At some point that evening, an emotional and upset Denise wrote a letter to her mother to tell her how much she disliked the camp, how homesick she was, and that she wanted to come home. The letter – so heartbreaking in hindsight – read:

Dear Mom,

I don't like camp. It's awful. The first day it rained. I have three new friends named Glenda, Lori and Michele. Michele and Lori are my roommates.

Mom, I don't want to stay at camp for two weeks. I want to come home and see Kassie and everybody.

Your loving child, Denise Milner
,

Aside from Denise, most of the girls were rowdy with excitement on that first night. There was a lot of giggling, talking, and loud laughter. Things didn't settle down until almost 1:30 a.m. when one of the tired counselors finally got everyone to quiet down.

Kiowa tent was already silent. The three girls staying there had fallen asleep hours before. It was a remote campsite, far from the laughter and noise of the other tents. It's generally believed that this tent was specifically targeted by the killer for no other reason than its secluded and dark location.

At some point after the camp grew quiet, counselor Carla Willhite was awakened by some sort of strange sound in the darkness. "It was a cross between a frog and a bullhorn or something," she later said. "It was low and kind of guttural. It wasn't a language. It didn't seem like a language. It didn't seem human. It didn't sound like any animal I've heard."

Carla awoke another counselor in her tent, Dee Elder, and asked if she'd heard the strange sound. She hadn't. Carla tried to go back to sleep, but she couldn't. Finally, she grabbed a flashlight and went outside to survey the nearby woods. She looked around but saw nothing. She paused, listening for the weird sound to return, but all was quiet. She took a quick walk toward the closest tents, but nothing seemed amiss, so she returned to her bunk.

It was later reported that some of the campers also heard the guttural sounds in the darkness. Others reported a strange light that moved through the trees. Tent 6 was flooded with light and then it disappeared.

One camper also said that she heard a girl crying for her mother in the night.

And there was more. Apparently, two counselors had been frightened by two men at the camp on the night before the murders. Several campers said they saw a man in army boots behind a tent. Another man was reportedly seen by a latrine on the night of the murders. Were these just stories told in the frightening days after the murders occurred, or were they warning signs that were missed?

A warning sign like the letter that was found two months before the camp opened for the season? A few months prior to opening day, when counselors were assembled for a training session, someone ransacked a counselor's cabin and left behind a handwritten note in an empty donut box that warned that "four girls would be murdered." If parents had been aware of this threat, it seems likely that many of the girls would not have been sent to camp that year. However, camp officials reported that they believed the note to be a prank and not a genuine threat.

It's easy to understand why they wouldn't take it seriously. The camp had been operating for decades without any problems. It was believed to be a safe place. And as Camp Ranger Ben Woodward said after seeing the bodies of the murder victims, "This is the reason why we moved to the country – to get away from crazy people."

No one could have predicted the events of that terrible night.

☠

The next morning, around 6:00 a.m. counselor Carla Willhite was on her way to the showers and described seeing what she thought was "luggage" under some

THE KIOWA TENT WHERE THE THREE GIRLS WERE KILLED

trees near Kiowa tent. When she got closer, though, she realized that it wasn't luggage – it was bloody sleeping bags. Inside of the sleeping bags were the three girls from Kiowa tent, Denise, Michele, and Lori. They had been pulled from their tent, beaten, strangled, sexually assaulted, and left for dead. Two of them were stuff inside of their sleeping bags. The third was left, partially clothed, on the trail nearby. All three of them were naked from the waist down and had been cruelly bound by two-inch wide electrical tape. The tape had also been placed over their mouths, muffling any cries for help or pleas for mercy. A cord had been tied tightly around each of their necks.

The subsequent autopsy confirmed that Denise had died from strangulation. Michele and Lori had both been bludgeoned to death. All three of them had been sexually assaulted.

Inside of the tent were two blood-soaked mattresses – and there was so much blood that it had seeped through the mattresses and onto the wooden floor. Michele and Lori had been beaten to death inside of the tent. The killer had then pulled them outside while still inside of their sleeping bags. Even more disturbingly, he had taken Denise outside to where her two dead friends lay and then strangled her to death.

The girls had been killed during an act of senseless, inhuman violence – and no one else in the camp heard a thing.

There were several large footprints on the wooden platform leading away from the tent, much too large to be those of any of the girls. The blood on the tent floor had been smeared. The killer had

THE BLOOD-SOAKED SLEEPING BAGS THAT WERE FOUND OUTSIDE OF THE TENT

apparently used mattress covers and towels to try and clean things up, making prints difficult to read. A red six-volt flashlight and a roll of the same electrical tape that was used to bind the girls was discovered at the crime scene. A piece of tape had been used to wrap newspaper over the front of the flashlight, reducing the beam to a narrow shaft of light so that it wouldn't be seen from other parts of the camp. The police speculated that the flashlight had been left behind because the killer remained at Camp Scott until nearly dawn, when he could easily see to escape.

The wooden platform, tent, flashlight, and tape were sent to the State Crime Bureau Headquarters for further analysis, but as Mayes County District Attorney Sid Wise stated, "Logic leads us to conclude that the murderer is a man – a stealthy, physically agile man."

After the bodies of the girls were discovered, the camp directors, Barbara and Richard Day, alerted the highway patrol. Law enforcement officers flocked to the scene. Many of the hardened men, fathers themselves, were moved to tears. One officer later recalled that the scene was like "being in church. People were talking in low whispers. They were quiet. I don't even recall birds singing." The police personnel at Kiowa tent spoke in a whisper and they silently collected evidence from the scene.

Camp counselors woke the rest of the Girl Scouts and told them to pack – they were going home. None of them were told what had happened, but all knew something was wrong. They were put on buses that morning and sent back to Tulsa, not knowing why they were being sent away. The news of the murders slowly filtered out, but the names of the victims were not released, so parents had no idea if their daughters would be stepping off the bus or not.

When authorities came to the Guse home to speak with Dick and Georgeann, they said that Michele had been in an accident. It was only later, while watching television, that they learned how she had met her death.

The entire region was stunned. Anyone who hadn't been locking their doors at night quickly decided to do so. There was a Boy Scout camp, Camp Garland, operating just three miles from Camp Scott. They quickly added a number of security measures to keep the campers safe.

But the authorities assured the public there was no reason to panic. District Attorney Wise released a statement just days after the murders" "I want to impress on you that we fully expect to break this case and bring the killer to justice."

Sadly, this expectation turned out to be untrue.

The grisly search of the crime scene led to an extensive manhunt in the rough terrain of the area. The small town of Locust Grove – the closest community to the camp – was in the heart of the Cookson Hills, the southernmost extension of the Boston Mountains and part of the Ozark Plateau. The entire region was covered in thick timber and the inhabitants -- who came after the Cherokee Indians -- eked out a meager living through farming for generations. Thanks to the rugged mountains and forests of the area, it became a hideout for Oklahoma outlaws and bank robbers in the 1920s and 1930s, including Charles Arthur "Pretty Boy" Floyd.

It was a place in which it was easy for a man to disappear. But law enforcement officials were not giving up. They brought in specially trained dogs from Philadelphia to try and pick up a scent and trace the killer. Within a week, the dogs led investigators to a small cave that was about a mile from Camp Scott. Inside, they found several empty food tins, tape, eyeglasses, and a piece of newspaper that was from the same edition as the piece discovered with the flashlight left next to the girls' bodies.

They also discovered an old photograph of two women that had been taken at a wedding. In the hope that someone could identify the women in the photo, it was restored by lab technicians and published in newspapers across the state. The subjects in the photograph were eventually identified as guests from a 1969 wedding of a prison employee's daughter. An inmate had worked as a darkroom assistant at the time of the wedding and the authorities believed that he'd printed the image. The inmate was a 33-year-old Cherokee man who had been serving a 10-year sentence for the kidnapping and rape of a pregnant woman. After his release, he was arrested again for burglary, but he'd escaped from jail in 1973.

Since then, there had been no trace of Gene Leroy Hart.

But that didn't stop the district attorney from immediately filing charges against him for murder. Even though there was no direct evidence against him, the public was demanding results, so an arrest warrant was issued. Now, all they had to do was find him.

A search party made up of more than 60 officers – including an FBI tactical squad and three special state squads – began combing the dense countryside. Bounty hunters traveled from across the state to join in the search, along with hundreds of volunteers, like Michele Guse's father.

There were few roads and trails in the Cookson Hills, which was the perfect hideout for someone like Hart, who, they discovered, was skilled in wilderness survival. There was plenty of fish and wild game in the region, so Hart wouldn't go hungry. He definitely had the upper hand, but the officers and volunteers were driven and began scouring the forest. Motivated by revenge? Perhaps – but anger also played a part in the seriousness of the task. This was especially true after searchers discovered a derisive message that was scrawled on a cave near Camp Scott.

"The killer was here. Bye bye fools," it read.

As the public learned that it was Gene Hart that the authorities were looking for, many of them came out in support of the well-known former Pryor High School football star. They believed he was innocent of the murders and protested on his behalf. Cookouts and fund drives were held to raise money for his defense. It was widely believed that Hart was innocent and that the murders had been blamed on him because the authorities had been embarrassed by his 1973 escape and because they had been unable to solve the Camp Scott murders.

A member of AIM – the American Indian Movement organization – spoke to newspaper reporters and stated that Hart told him that he didn't kill the girls but was afraid of what would happen to him if he surrendered. He was convinced that he would be killed.

But not everyone believed in Hart's claims of innocence. To many in the community, the fact that the ex-convict refused to turn himself in made him look guilty. Others, though, were simply terrified of the fact that there was still a monster out there – whoever he was – who had brutalized and murdered three little girls.

Doors were double-locked, and no children were allowed to play outside after dark.

Hart managed to avoid the police in the Cookson Hills for 10 months before being captured in April 1978. He was hiding out in an isolated cabin with a man named Sam Pigeon, Jr., and when the authorities showed up at the door, he surrendered without a fight. He had been tracked down after the police received

GENE LEROY HART

a tip that "there was someone living with an old man who lived by himself in a rural area who cut wood and received some type of check." The checks turned out to be Social Security checks and were traced to Pigeon. Hart had been living with him in the cabin since November 1977. No one had ever come around to look.

Hart was arrested and, ironically, was locked up in the same jail he'd once escaped from while he awaited trial. On April 11, 1978, hundreds of spectators crammed into the courthouse as Hart made his appearance in court. With his attorney, Garvin A. Isaacs, next to him, he entered a plea of "not guilty."

A preliminary hearing was held on June 7. During the first week, an array of witnesses took the stand, including camp counselors Carla Willhite and Dee Elder, both of whom detailed the first night at camp and the discovery of the bodies the following morning.

Louis Lindsey, the records clerk at the Oklahoma State Reformatory, who took the wedding photographs found in the cave, took the stand on the third day and explained how Hart was granted permission to work in the darkroom, developing photographs. His opinion of Hart was that he was a trustworthy man and a hard worker.

Hubert Earl Maxey, a chemist and physicist, took the stand on the seventh day. He compared hair samples taken from Hart with the hair samples found at the crime scene. The prosecution tried to state that they were the same, but Maxey disagreed. He stated, "The only opinion I could form was that they looked similar. That's about as far as it goes. There's nothing that would show that it would belong to any particular individual." I'll remind the reader that DNA evidence and testing did not yet exist in the late 1970s, so there was no way to say if the hair matched for sure. Crime scene technicians were also unable to test the semen samples that had been found inside two of the girls, so they could be matched to anyone definitively. It's hard to say what would have been discovered if this could have been done. Hart had had a vasectomy – would the samples have matched or not?

The preliminary trial was the longest in Oklahoma history. In the end, Judge Jess Claton ordered Hart to be tried on first-degree murder charges. The defense would have nearly eight months to build their case.

And they would have the support of Hart's family members and many of the people of the community, who continued to believe that he was innocent. Money had been raised for his defense and there was a vocal outpouring of support. But there was still the fact that Hart was a rapist, a kidnapper, and was known for being violent. The evidence found in the cave seemed to link him to the camp – even though nothing at the murder scene could be directly tied to him.

The trial was held in Pryor, Oklahoma – Hart's hometown – and began on March 5, 1978. The attorneys for the state announced that they would be seeking the death penalty. It took 11 days to seat a jury of six men and six women, who would not be shown the most graphic photographs of the three dead girls that had been taken at the crime scene. The judge ruled them to be too prejudicial to the defense. Some of them – including images of the bound and beaten at the camp and on the autopsy table – still made it into the trial, much to the dismay of Garvin Isaacs, Hart's attorney. Hart's mother, Ella May Buckskin, was in court during every day of the trial – as was Sharon Farmer, Lori's mother. Mrs. Farmer made it a point to tell reporters that she assumed Hart to be guilty. "Someone has hurt our family," she said. "Someone has taken our daughter from us."

One of the more perplexing pieces of evidence presented at the trial was the discovery of a small hand mirror and a corncob pipe. Karen Mitchell, a counselor at Camp Scott, identified the items as ones that went missing from a trunk that she had brought with her to camp. Karen hadn't noticed they had vanished until the trunk was returned to her by the police a few weeks after they had confiscated it for examination. According to investigators, they had been seized from the cabin that Hart had been hiding out in. However, they did admit that they had not been found until after his preliminary hearing. Defense attorney Isaacs argued that they just as easily could have been planted by the police.

And then things got weirder.

Mayes County jailer Allen R. Little took the stand to talk about the wedding photograph that had been discovered in the cave. He made a shocking statement: he had seen the exact photograph on Mayes County Sheriff Pete Weaver's desk more than three years before the murders. So how did the photograph end up in the cave if it had not been in Gene Hart's possession in the first place?

Garvin Isaacs also managed to produce statements that clearly showed that the footprint that was found outside the girls' tent didn't match Hart's, and neither did a thumbprint that had been found on the flashlight. "You can't change your fingerprints or shrink your feet," Isaacs said.

The defense also produced another suspect in the murders – one that had never been investigated by the police. His name was William Stevens and he was a convicted rapist from Kansas. One of the Girl Scouts who had been at the camp that night, Kimberly Lewis, 11, took the stand and identified Stevens as the man she had seen outside her tent with a flashlight. "That looks like the man," she said. "He had on a blue jacket. We heard a noise and one of the girls lifted the tent flap and shined her flashlight in his face."

Joyce Paine, the wife of a friend of William Stevens, also testified. She said that Stevens had borrowed a flashlight identical to the one found at the crime scene from her, claiming that he was going fishing. She noted that the flashlight found at the camp had the same distinctive scratches around the lens as the one that she had loaned to Stevens. "Sure, that's my flashlight," she said when she was shown the flashlight that had been submitted into evidence. "It was given to me by my son."

There were probably thousands of flashlights just like that one sold in Oklahoma at the time, so her identification could have easily been mistaken – however, the testimony that followed from her son was chilling.

Larry Short, Joyce's son, also identified the flashlight and then went on to describe a visit that Stevens had made to his home in Okmulgee on the day after the bodies of the girls were found. He recalled that Stevens had "claw marks on his arms and neck," as well as "red stains on his boots."

The jury acquitted Hart after just one hour of deliberation.

Once the trial was over, the jurors were very critical of the investigation. As one said to a reporter, "In several places, it seemed their investigation was so slipshod, I mean, a layman could have done better." Another noted that, "It tore a lot of confidence I had in the judicial system."

But one juror made sure that the reason for the acquittal was clear. The prosecution had simply not made a case that Hart was guilty beyond a reasonable doubt. The decision was not made to clear Hart – they felt the heinous crime must have been committed by more than one person. "I'm not saying that he's not guilty," the juror said, "but I'm saying that the evidence showed that not one person did it by themselves. We all twelve agreed on that."

When the verdict was announced, Gene Hart placed his head in his hands and began to sob while his family and friends applauded. Their celebration was short-lived, however. Hart was immediately transported back to prison to finish out his previous sentence, as well as additional time for his escape.

Two months later, he died from a sudden heart attack while exercising in the prison yard.

A considerable number of Oklahomans felt that the real killer had successfully eluded capture because the police had been so focused on capturing Gene Hart and pinning the murders on him. Were they right? Or had Hart somehow fooled the jury? Or worse, had Hart been involved in the murders with someone else?

Someone who was still out there?

After Hart's acquittal, the families of Lori Farmer and Doris Milner attempted to sue the owners of Camp Scott for negligence but were unsuccessful, leading to more disappointment and heartbreak. Over the years, as technology has changed, the evidence in the Camp Scott murders has been tested – and tested again. Unfortunately, all the tests have proven inconclusive and it's likely that it will never point to any one suspect.

Sadly, the murders will probably never be solved.

No Girl Scouts ever again walked the trails or slept in the tents at Camp Scott. It never reopened after the murders. It was essentially abandoned as it stood and remains out in the woods, serving as an eerie reminder of a terrible tragedy – and the stolen lives of three little girls.

It also serves as a reminder about the ongoing mystery of the killer who was never caught and of the other mysteries that are still whispered about when it comes to this case. That the ruins of Camp Scott are rumored to be haunted should come as no surprise to the reader. This is a place of horror and tragedy and there are many who believed that the terrible events of June 1977 are still echoing at the camp. It's not so much a lingering spirit, it's believed, but rather a sinister recording of the murders, replaying itself over time.

There have been reports of a shadowy figure and disembodied footsteps that are heard when no living person is around, but more common are the accounts of screams, cries, and the soul-wrenching sound of a girl weeping in the shadows. Those who have dared to venture out to the abandoned remains of the camp never linger there for long.

And there are other stories that are still told about the murders – stories much stranger than ghosts.

Almost from the time of his arrest, rumors swirled about Gene Hart. Despite the support of his family, friends, and some of the people from his hometown, many people still believed that he was somehow involved in the murders. He was acquitted, they said, only because the prosecution did not prove its case – not because the jury felt he was innocent. There are still many who believe that Hart killed the three girls – and that he did not act alone. And then things get a little stranger after that.

The rumors claimed that Hart was a member of an old Cherokee Society called the *Keetowah*, a group dedicated to keeping old tribal customs and rituals alive in the modern day. Hart apparently considered himself part of this group, although there is some question about his acceptance by valid members of the society.

Regardless, there are some who believe that Hart tried to gain acceptance into this society to learn traditional Cherokee spirituality, tribal rituals, and what we would consider "magic." In one of the last newspaper interviews that he gave before his death, he referred to his beliefs as a blend of Christianity and "our ancient and traditional Cherokee religion." Does this mean that he was some sort of "shaman"? Not necessarily, but it's possible that Hart believed that he was.

And so did a lot of other people.

During the investigation, detectives reported that many strange events occurred. It was discovered that Hart had been under the counsel of a Cherokee medicine man during his time in hiding. He already possessed the nickname of "The Sandman," for his allegedly shape-shifting skills. In the religion and cultural lore of many Native American tribes, there are legends of shapeshifters – or "skinwalkers" – people who have the ability to change their physical appearance at will. This was how, some believed, that Hart was able to commit crimes and stay hidden from the authorities for as long as he did.

While Oklahoma State Bureau of Investigation Agent Harvey Pratt was working undercover on the Camp Scott case, he heard from various people – including deputies at the Mayes County Jail – that Hart had the ability to change his form and to shape shift into an animal. One jailer told Pratt that Hart often taunted and laughed at him, telling him that he was able to "slip through the bars of his cell and escape."

And in fact, Hart did escape, twice, from the Mayes County Jail in Pryor. The first time, he cut through the bars of his cell with a hacksaw blade, but with the second escape? Well, the details have never been made clear.

Stranger still, detectives reported that while they were investigating the scene at Camp Scott, they often saw a black dog in the woods that would follow them to various places in the camp – and then mysteriously disappear. There were some who believed that this dog was Hart, watching the investigation while in a different form.

Sounds ridiculous? Perhaps – but a lot of people believed it then, and some still do.

Several people who have visited the abandoned property in recent years still report seeing a black dog wandering around the camp. Could it be, as some have suggested, the spirit of Gene Hart still haunting the grounds after all these years? Perhaps trapped in a place where he took part in one of Oklahoma's most heinous crimes?

Camp Scott was sold off by the Girl Scouts in the 1980s and is now located on private property. Many of the old buildings still stand today, dilapidated and overtaken by nature. This is a haunted place, by both the spirits and the events of the past. Visitors are not welcome at what used to be Camp Scott, but some people trespass there anyway. If you are among them, remember that this is a place where a horror was visited on three little girls and stunned an entire generation of children. Treat this place – and their memories – with respect.

And if you see a black dog walking around, consider that a warning to leave.

BIBLIOGRAPHY AND RECOMMENDED READING

Albright, Evan J., *Cape Cod Confidential*, On Cape Publications, Massachusetts, 2004

Alt, Betty L. and Sandra K. Wells, *Mountain Murders: Homicide in the Rockies*, Dog Ear Publishing, Indiana, 2009

Baatz, Simon, *For the Thrill of It: Leopold, Loeb, and the Murder that Shocked Jazz Age Chicago*, Harper Collins, New York, 2008

Bellamy, John Stark, *The Corpse in the Cellar*, Gray & Company, Cleveland, 1999

Belvidere Daily Republican

Bernstein, Arnie, *Bath Massacre: America's First School Bombing*, University of Michigan Press, Ann Arbor, 2009

Burt, Olive Woolley, *American Murder Ballads*, Oxford University Press, New York, 1958

Casey, Lee (editor), *Denver Murders*, Duell, Sloan and Pearce, New York, 1946

Chicago Daily Journal
Chicago Inter Ocean
Chicago Tribune

Daley, Christopher, *Murder and Mayhem in Boston*, History Press, Charleston, South Carolina, 2015

Eatwell, Piu, *Black Dahlia, Red Rose*, Liveright Publishing, New York, 2017

Ellsworth, M.J., *The Bath School Disaster*, Bath, Michigan, 1927

Erickson, Gladys, *Warden Ragen of Joliet*, Dutton, New York, 1957

Fass Paula S., *Kidnapped: Child Abduction in America*, Harvard University Press, Massachusetts, 1997

Flacco, Anthony with Jerry Clark, *The Road Out of Hell*, Union Square Press, New York, 2009

Freeman, Lucy, *"Before I Kill More..."*, Award Books, New York, 1955

Higdon, Hal, *The Crime of the Century: The Leopold and Loeb Case*, Putnam, New York, 1975

Kelly, C.S., *The Camp Scott Murders: The 1977 Oklahoma Girl Scout Murders*, Amazon Direct Publishing, 2014

Lehto, Steve, *American Murder House*, Berkley Books, New York, 2015

Leopold, Nathan, Jr., *Life Plus 99 Years*, Doubleday, New York, 1958

Logan, John, *Never the Sinner: The Leopold and Loeb Story*, Overlook, New York, 1999

MacGowan, Douglas, *The Sodder Family Tragedy*, Quarrier Press, West Virginia, 2016

Miles, Dorothy, *The Missing Sodder Children*, Kentucky, 2018

Nash, Jay Robert, *Murder, America*, Simon and Schuster, New York, 1980

Paul, James Jeffrey, *Nothing is Strange With You*, Xlibris Corporation, 2008

Renner, Joan, *Deranged L.A. Crimes*, 2012-Present

Rosewood, Jack and Dwayne Walker, *The Lipstick Killer*, Wiq Media, 2015

Roth, Randolph, *American Homicide*, Harvard University Press, Massachusetts, 2009

Schechter, Harold, *Panic*, Amazon Original Stories, Seattle, 2018

------------------------- *Psycho U.S. A.*, Ballantine Books, New York, 2012

Slade, Paul, *Unprepared to Die: America's Greatest Murder Ballads and the True Crime Stores that Inspired Them*, Soundcheck Books, Great Britain, 2015

Smith, James R. and W. Lane Rogers, *The California Snatch Racket*, Craven Street Books, San Francisco, 2010

Taylor, Troy, *"I Want to Come Home Tonight,"* American Hauntings Ink, Illinois, 2017

-------------- and Rene Kruse, *Fear the Reaper*, American Hauntings Ink, Illinois, 2014

Thompson, Emily G., *Unsolved Child Murders: Eighteen American Cases, 1956–1998*, Exposit Books, 2017

Tomlinson, Gerald, *Seven Jersey Murders*, Xlibris Corporation, 2003

Wilhelm, Robert, *The Bloody Century: True Tales of Murder in 19th Century America*, Lexington, Kentucky, 2014

Wolf, Marvin J. and Katherine Mader, *Fallen Angels: Chronicles of L.A. Crime and Mystery*, Facts on File Publications, New York, 1986

SPECIAL THANKS TO:

April Slaughter: Cover Design and Artwork
Lois Taylor: Editing and Proofreading
Lisa Taylor Horton and Lux
Orrin Taylor
Rene Kruse
Rachael Horath
Elyse and Thomas Reihner
Bethany Horath
John Winterbauer
Kaylan Schardan
Maggie Walsh
Cody Beck and Leah Hentrich
Becky Ray
Susan Kelly and Amy Bouyear

www.ingramcontent.com/pod-product-compliance
Lightning Source LLC
Chambersburg PA
CBHW062044080426

42734CB00012B/2555